"Parting ways with queer theory's prefe
Forms feels the touch and re-touch of shapeshifting forms as it sets queer
studies in new and dynamic relation to its objects in the world. In one
of his signal claims, Fawaz uses the materiality of form to rethink the
pervasive and privileged association of queerness with formlessness and
fluidity. Thus, he argues that feminist and queer ideas become meaningful as they take material shape within the realm of popular cultural
production, where they change audiences in ways that neither a pedantic
politics nor a moralizing theory can."
—Matt Brim, author of *Poor Queer Studies: Confronting Elitism in
the University*

"An inspirational history of queer and feminist cultural politics forged
in the 1970s and extending to the 1990s. Ramzi Fawaz brilliantly maps
the forms of relationality that feminist, lesbian, and gay communities
invented to visualize themselves and their futures. In an argument that
is both crystalline and capacious, he has discerned patterns across a
wide range of popular cultural texts, objects, and images, and he demonstrates how radical change has been—and can be—imagined and enacted. *Queer Forms* is generously both history and manifesto. It calls on
us to ask with each other how we want to see our future take shape."
—David J. Getsy, author of *Abstract Bodies: Sixties Sculpture in the
Expanded Field of Gender*

"Fawaz serves up a cornucopia of critical delights: fresh new readings of
Tales of the City and *Angels in America*, of the films *The Boys in the Band,
Zardoz, Thelma & Louise,* and *Moonlight*, as well as of the art of Joe
Brainard and David Wojnarowicz. The book floods us with vivid cultural works richly rendered in their historical contexts and formal experimentation, and breathes life into sclerotic, forgotten genealogies.
Indeed, the flood that leaves fertile soil in its wake is the method of
Queer Forms—with so much to think with and through, we can't help
reaching the conclusion Fawaz argues for: that messy multiplicity and
raucously productive pluralism were foundational to an array of late-
twentieth-century left politics we often dismiss as limited and myopic,
including second-wave feminism. The implications are instructive for
unknotting our stymied political present."
—Darieck Scott, author of *Keeping It Unreal: Black Queer Fantasy and
Superhero Comics*

Frontis: Edie Fake, "Orgy," in *Gaylord Phoenix* #6 (2012)

Queer Forms

Ramzi Fawaz

NEW YORK UNIVERSITY PRESS

New York

NEW YORK UNIVERSITY PRESS
New York
www.nyupress.org

References to Internet websites (URLs) were accurate at the time of writing. Neither the author nor New York University Press is responsible for URLs that may have expired or changed since the manuscript was prepared.

Library of Congress Cataloging-in-Publication Data
Names: Fawaz, Ramzi, author.
Title: Queer forms / Ramzi Fawaz.
Description: New York : New York University Press, [2022] |
    Includes bibliographical references and index.
Identifiers: LCCN 2021057757 | ISBN 9781479829828 (hardback) |
    ISBN 9781479820733 (paperback) | ISBN 9781479816903 (ebook) |
    ISBN 9781479893782 (ebook other)
Subjects: LCSH: Sexual minorities in mass media. | Sexual minorities in popular culture. |
    Mass media—Social aspects—United States. | Popular culture—United States—
    20th century.
Classification: LCC P96.S58 F39 2022 | DDC 306.76—dc23/eng/20220303
LC record available at https://lccn.loc.gov/2021057757

New York University Press books are printed on acid-free paper, and their binding materials are chosen for strength and durability. We strive to use environmentally responsible suppliers and materials to the greatest extent possible in publishing our books.

Manufactured in the United States of America

10 9 8 7 6 5 4 3 2 1

Also available as an ebook

For Cindy, Jared, Leslie, and Tony,
queer forms I live by.

In the early days of [the second] wave of the women's movement, I sat in a weekly consciousness-raising group with my friend A. We compared notes recently: What did you think was happening? How did you think our own lives were going to change? A. said she had felt, "Now I can be a woman; it's no longer so humiliating. I can stop fantasizing that secretly I am a man." . . . Her answer amazed me. Sitting in the same meetings during those years, my thoughts were roughly the reverse: Now I don't have to be a woman anymore. . . . Now the very idea "woman" is up for grabs. . . . [F]eminism will give me freedom to seek some other identity altogether. . . . Feminism is inevitably a mixed form, requiring in its very nature such inconsistencies.
—Ann Snitow, "A Gender Diary," in *The Feminism of Uncertainty* (2015 [1989])

We are a revolutionary group of men and women . . . creating new social forms and relations, that is, relations based upon brotherhood, cooperation, human love, and uninhibited sexuality.
—New York Gay Liberation Front statement of purpose (1969)

[The brown woman] reinterprets history and, using new symbols, she shapes new myths. She adopts new perspectives toward the darkskinned, women and queers. She strengthens her tolerance (and intolerance) for ambiguity. She is willing to share, to make herself vulnerable to foreign ways of seeing and thinking. She surrenders all notions of safety, of the familiar. . . . She becomes a *nabual*, able to transform herself into a tree, a coyote, into another person. . . . A constant changing of forms.
—Gloria Anzaldúa, *Borderlands/La Frontera: The New Mestiza* (1987)

CONTENTS

Color illustrations appear as an insert following page 212.

Introduction

Queer Forms

> What we need is not institutions but *forms*. It so happens . . .
> that life, whether biological, singular or collective, is pre-
> cisely a continual creation of forms. It suffices to perceive
> them, to accept allowing them to arise, to make a place for
> them and accompany their metamorphosis. A habit is a
> form. A thought is a form. A friendship is a form. A profes-
> sion is a form. Everything that lives is only forms and inter-
> actions of forms.
> —The Invisible Committee, *NOW* (2017)

> The gathering impulse to break loose from our existing gen-
> der arrangements, to free ourselves from the fixed symbiotic
> patterns that have so far prevailed between women and men,
> is part of the central thrust of our species' life toward more
> viable forms.
> —Dorothy Dinnerstein, *The Mermaid and the Minotaur:*
> *Sexual Arrangement and Human Malaise* (1976)

The first queer form I ever witnessed was the image of two women clasping hands in solidarity before driving off a cliff. In one of cinema's most iconic scenes, best friends turned outlaws Thelma Dickinson and Louise Sawyer (incandescently played by Geena Davis and Susan Saran-don) find themselves surrounded by a swarm of armed police officers on the edge of the Grand Canyon (figure I.1/plate 1).[1] Despite the duo's grave circumstances, as they stare out at this natural wonder from the front seat of Louise's Ford Thunderbird convertible, Thelma looks to her friend with a glimmer of hope and says: "Let's not get caught. Let's keep *going*." With these words, the two make a fateful judgment: not to

Figure 1.1. Thelma and Louise "keep going." *Thelma & Louise*, dir. Ridley Scott (Metro-Goldwyn-Mayer, 1991).

surrender to the law, explain themselves to a patriarchal justice system, or die violently in a hail of bullets, *but to fly*. I was eleven years old when I first saw Thelma and Louise take to the sky, too young to grasp what was at stake for two women whose humdrum lives as a neglected housewife and unhappy waitress are obliterated in a flash when one of them murders an attempted rapist. But I recall with complete clarity the thought that entered my mind as my eyes widened in surprise and wonder at Thelma and Louise's wild gambit: *this is about freedom*.

Academy Award–winning screenwriter Callie Khouri and director Ridley Scott's *Thelma & Louise* (1991) remains among Hollywood's most radical statements on feminist and queer freedom.[2] The plot begins straightforwardly: on their way to a weekend vacation in the Arkansas mountains, Thelma and Louise stop for drinks and dancing at a bustling bar. In a shocking turn of events, Thelma is sexually assaulted in the parking lot by a violent local Casanova, whom Louise ends up shooting to death in a fit of rage. Instantly, the two become fugitives, fleeing the scene and driving across country in the hopes of getting to Mexico, where they fantasize taking up new identities and "sipping margaritas by the sea, Mamasita!" Throughout, Louise is guilt-ridden over her hasty actions but recognizes that rape law rarely grants women justice or leniency for violence against their perpetrators; and though Thelma is initially reluctant to abandon the security of her domestic life, she quickly realizes her loveless marriage doesn't hold a candle to the emotional rewards of her friendship with Louise. Both discover their freedom can be claimed only by choosing one another and hitting the road. Along the way, they have sex with beautiful men; expertly rob a convenience store out of necessity; discard worn-out romances, lipstick, and hair curlers; talk about their future plans; drive across a majestic Western landscape; shoot up the oil rig of a sexist truck driver; and take a flight into the unknown.

Thelma & Louise is a story about women's capacity to change. It projects women into new social, psychic, and geographical contexts, reimagining what they can be or become. Two women seemingly trapped in their roles as housewife and waitress become outlaws. Two women seemingly defined by experiences of sexual violence reject the labels of "victim" or "survivor," and become "good friends" and "good drivers," boldly taking the wheel of a Thunderbird as much as steering their own lives. Two women seemingly driving the plot of a screwball comedy become the leads in a Western buddy road movie. At key moments in the film, different characters express disappointment in their personal choices, which have led to constrained or unhappy lives. Each time, Louise shrewdly replies: "You get what you settle for." As Thelma and Louise retrace the transcontinental route of US westward expansion, they refuse to settle for anything less than total freedom. And yet what might be considered the film's commitment to fluidity, its depiction of the pair's continual forward motion and evolution into new versions of themselves, is always given concrete form. The recurrent silhouettes of two women in the front seat of a car outlines a bond of female friendship that rejects the traditional construct of the heterosexual couple form. Louise's dazzling Ford Thunderbird gives shape to feminist freedom as a literal and symbolic vehicle for the women's bold movement through space. And the inspiring image of two friends' hands clasped condenses the affective force of entrustment between women into that most intimate expression of human interdependence, the offered hand taken. Together, these figures compose a visual lexicon of uniquely feminist and queer forms, apprehensible shapes that are articulated to diverse expressions of gender and sexual rebellion. *Thelma & Louise* thus encourages viewers to conceptualize feminist and queer freedom in the mind's eye as a practice of shapeshifting, whereby the women skillfully inhabit countless new molds, tear up the social contract, and make commitments based on a mutual promise to grant one another the space to transform, perhaps into something thrillingly unrecognizable.

The feminist and queer forms of *Thelma & Louise* collided with my psyche at the cusp of adolescence, just as I was poised to come out of the closet and increasingly aware of a nascent feminist consciousness. I intuitively understood the film's closing scenes as being about the concept of freedom because I too was preparing to exceed the limits of imposed gender and sexual norms in ways I had not yet fully conceived but could *viscerally feel.* One year later, my mother and I came out to one another in an emotional scene of mutual declaration. In that moment, I imagined our spontaneous disclosure of shared queerness as a performance of Thelma and Louise's act of entrustment, our way of clasping hands and saying: "Let's keep going." We even shared margaritas to mark the occasion (virgin for me), partly fulfilling the duo's unrequited fantasy of "sipping margaritas by the sea, Mamasita!" (In my case, *Mamasita* was my actual lesbian mama.) Sitting on a couch across from my brave, vulnerable, and newly out mother, I began to understand that freedom meant something like the capacity to act in concert with others and "found new forms of political association"[3] that might transform the conditions of one's existence. In holding hands and granting one another permission to "go ahead," my mother and I forged a new association that allowed us to bring our mutual, yet distinct, experiences of gayness out into a shared space, just at the edge of the public realm, but inching closer to a wider world of unpredictable relations with countless other queers. Long before I had the feminist and queer political language to describe my fierce desire to break free of the gender and sexual regulations of my childhood, *Thelma & Louise* provided me a formal vocabulary of images through which I could make sense of myself as a queer outlaw in the making.

Years later, as an undergraduate student at UC Berkeley, I encountered the exhilarating world of feminist history and theory, which helped me better understand what I had witnessed as a wide-eyed eleven-year-old. As I devoured the political writings of 1970s feminists, the kinship between Thelma and Louise suddenly looked like what the Radicalesbians famously called "woman-identification," the willful reorientation of women's political and interpersonal energies toward one another as a basis for their collective liberation.[4] The friends' radical flight from the institutions of marriage, domesticity, and the law paralleled the anarchist project of lesbian separatists, who had argued for the necessity of complete divestment from male dominated society. And Louise's canny explanation of the ways the criminal justice system dismisses women's legitimate claims of sexual violation modeled a classic feminist structural critique of patriarchy ("The law is some tricky shit," Thelma responds). The film magnetizes the political energies and ideas of the radical feminist and queer 1970s without ever explicitly invoking any of its ideologies or orthodoxies. I realized I had encountered some part of the spirit of women's and gay liberation movements through the forms that *Thelma & Louise* gifted me at a critical juncture in my young life. I simply had to receive them, press the gas, and drive.

My experience watching *Thelma & Louise* across time and in distinct personal and intellectual contexts coalesces three ideas central to this book: first, the necessity of feminist and queer cultural forms as vehicles for the expansion of our political imagination; second, the foundational and enduring link between gender and sexual freedom as mutually constitutive political and cultural projects; and third, the importance of understanding the affective or emotional force of queer forms, their capacity to alter, retune, or enlarge the sensorium by allowing us to feel and experience gender and sexual nonconformity in new and surprising ways. To form something is to give it shape and hence make it accessible to perception, but also available for meaning-making and reinvention from different perspectives. Queer cultural forms are those aesthetic or creative figures that concretize aspects of gender- and sexual-nonconforming life so they become conceivable in the mind's eye. These forms become objects of collective attention by providing opportunities to continually interpret and *re*interpret the meaning of gender and sexuality across countless contexts. Not every form is a distinctly queer one, but it could be, with the right imagination.

In *Queer Forms*, I ask: what happens when we attempt to formally represent the experience of being a gender and sexual outlaw? Twenty-first-century feminist and queer theory and politics are consistently marked by an impasse when it comes to formally representing nonnormative genders and sexualities. This impasse results from a tension between two competing aspirations shared by theorists and activists alike: on the one hand, a desire for the social and legal recognition of those who do not fit into prescribed gender and sexual norms, which requires the ability to clearly name and define specific kinds of dissident identities or groups (like gay and lesbian, transgender, or intersex). On the other, the wish to maintain a view of gender and sexuality as fluid and open-ended categories that can never be pinned down *as any kind* of form. In feminist and queer theory, this commitment to formlessness appears in a long-held critical suspicion of ordering principles like sequences, lines, schedules, or historical teleology as well as a rejection of bounded, fixed, or essential conceptions of identity and selfhood. In the work of theorists like Sara Ahmed, Lee Edelman, Jack Halberstam, and José Esteban Muñoz, these organizing structures and categories are cast as disciplinary forces that contain feminist and queer deviations from gender and sexual regulations.[5] In activist circles, the resistance to form is often conveyed in the disdain for binary gender and sexual presentations, the celebration of "fluid" subjectivities, and the radical elasticization of concepts like intersectionality and universal inclusion, which are imagined to accommodate an infinite range of possible identities, rather than specifying the cumulative effects of distinct identities. Against such theorizations and practices, *Queer Forms* refuses the assumption that formlessness or fluidity is the most radical quality of divergent genders and sexualities. I argue for the queer potential of cultural forms, which I theorize as the range of aesthetic figures or structures that can give concrete shape to abstract identities, desires, and experiences. At stake in my project is the capacity to materialize and transmit the specificity of any given queer, feminist, or trans* experience to others, not only in representations of

actual women, queers, and gender outlaws but through formal constructs that can figuratively convey or translate the most heterogeneous
aspects of gender and sexual nonconformity without remaining beyond
comprehension. If contemporary feminist and queer theory and politics
has tended to stress the question of how we can better escape, elude, or
resist the so-called prison house of regulatory forms, I reformulate this
query to discover *what forms gender and sexual rebellion takes.*

Toward this end, I locate the most powerful uses of feminist and
queer forms in the rich cultural experiments that emerged out of 1970s
women's and gay liberation movements. Starting in the late 1960s, these
movements sought to develop concepts for describing and doing justice
to alternative expressions of gender and sexuality, while also fomenting a
cultural revolution to disseminate more open-ended understandings of
these same categories. These dual goals prompted a variety of attempts to
aesthetically represent what gender and sexuality could be. I intentionally turn back to social movements commonly seen as anachronistic,
or else critiqued for their essentialism or failure to account for multiple
axes of identity, because they represented the most sustained attempt to
expand the feminist and queer formal possibilities of US popular culture
in the late twentieth century. Perhaps counterintuitively, such creative
projects to represent queer genders and sexualities often appeared in a
range of traditional, or seemingly generic, popular mediums including
the sequential format of comic strip serials, the stock figures or character types of speculative literatures, the visual conventions of film melodrama, and the serialized rhythm of installment fiction, among others.[6]

To illuminate how these artistic experiments aided in the work of producing new possibilities for gender and sexuality, I assemble a heterogeneous collection of aesthetic forms, which came to be imaginatively
linked to key concepts of women's and gay liberation. The six chapters
respectively explore: the figure of the female replicant in speculative literature as an allegory for the problem of women's *equality.* The bounded
or enclosed utopian commune in science fiction cinema as the architectural model for *lesbian separatism.* The shape of a circle as the diagram
for feminist and gay *consciousness-raising.* The serial rhythm of installment fiction as a narrative description of the process of *coming out of the
closet.* The unfolding sequential format of the comic strip medium as a
structural analogy for successive expressions of queer erotic desire, or

sexual pluralism. And finally, the manifold physiological forms of the gut or digestive tract as metaphors for queer feelings of *political disgust* toward homophobia and sexism. The sheer variety of queer forms I identify and illuminate—among them figures, models, structures, shapes, creative mediums, even bodily organs—continually discloses the equally multiplicious dimensions, meanings, and uses of newly invented political concepts for actualizing gender- and sexual-nonconforming ways of life. Consequently, in each chapter, I show how, far from normalizing or delimiting gender and sexual variety, queer forms gave specificity to, and diversified the range of, possible genders and sexualities that can be conceived.

The chapters that follow represent a feminist and queer cultural archive that is intentionally wide-ranging and eclectic. I study both transparently mass cultural products like Ira Levin's bestselling horror story *The Stepford Wives* (1972) and Armistead Maupin's gay serial fiction *Tales of the City* (1976–1977), as well as experimental visual art and writing that innovated in popular genres like Joanna Russ's lesbian science fiction novel *The Female Man* (1975). I explore acclaimed texts that explicitly state their commitment to gender and sexual politics, like Tony Kushner's epic drama *Angels in America* (1990–1992), and those that implicitly articulate feminist and queer values through fantastical plays on language and narration like Maxine Hong Kingston's *The Woman Warrior* (1975). Though these texts encompass diverse artistic styles, narrative voices, mediums, and creators, all formally register the presence of feminist and queer ideals or principles as catalysts of creative invention across an extraordinarily broad cultural terrain. Hence, in referring to the variety of cultural products in this book as comprising an archive of feminist and queer "popular" forms, I am at once indicating how some circulate squarely in the realm of US mass culture, while others, like the more avant-garde or high art objects I discuss, appropriate, experiment with, and reinvent popular culture icons, genres, and mediums like science fiction and comics. Ultimately, I narrate the cultural prehistory of the contemporary renaissance in feminist and LGBTQ social movement politics by developing a genealogy of late twentieth-century artifacts that proliferated images of gender and sexual dissidence, which came to infuse the US popular imagination in the 1970s and after.

Among other things, then, *Queer Forms* represents my attempt to re-vivify the cultural work of women's and gay liberation for a new genera-tion of gender and sexual "warriors," and to provide us all a usable past that might productively inform, and help refine, our collective political vision in the present. A fantasized ideal of ceaseless gender and sexual fluidity, alongside an equally utopian attempt to produce politics and theory that can account for all identities and experiences simultane-ously, will simply not do in a world where human beings necessarily take shape and inhabit specific forms. I use the term *formlessness* to describe a foundational logic that underwrites the contemporary concept of *fluid identities*, which is a dominant lens through which much queer, femi-nist, and trans* theorizing and social justice politics perceive progres-sive gender and sexual selfhood. The logic of gender and sexual fluidity tactically assumes we should all share (a) an aspirational ideal of effort-lessly inhabiting or modifying any and all gender and sexual identities, desires, or affiliations at will, along with (b) an expectation that others can and must seamlessly recognize, mirror back, and celebrate one's mu-table and ever-changing sense of self (often as a moral imperative). The preferred metaphor for notions of fluid subjectivity is, of course, liquid-ity, a state of flow that suggests the ceaseless transformative movement of gender and sexual identities and embodiments.

In theory, the concept of gender and sexual fluidity is intended to recognize and validate the basic fact that people are and can be many things, including taking on countless gendered and sexual identities, styles, or attributes, sometimes all at once, sometimes in ever-changing succession. This is a noble goal. In practice, however, fluidity frequently shifts from being a description of the commonly shared existential re-ality of mutability and change to a demand that one's personal expres-sion of gender and sexual multiplicity be recognized as the fundamental inner truth of the self. Here, a contemporary value of fluid selfhood whose stated purpose is to resist forms of essential or fixed character paradoxically inverts into its own type of *identitarianism*. This is not as one might presume a traditional "identity politics," which Rostom Mesli reminds us, is about valuing the "multiplication of political identity stand-points";[7] rather it is the transformation of one metaphor or de-scription of gender and sexual variety into an unyielding personal prin-ciple and a universal standard of collective freedom. When gender and sexual fluidity itself becomes a rigid orthodoxy, rather than one perspective among many, it both denies the actual heterogeneous forms that gender and sexual variety take and sets up an impossible expectation that we must be anything and everything at once to properly do justice to gender and sexual outlaws' experience of oppression.[8] Throughout this book, then, I show how the twin constructions of *formlessness/fluidity* and *rigidity/identitarianism* that queer, feminist, and trans* theorists and activists often conceive of as radically opposed are often merely two sides of the same coin.

At the same time, the logic of fluidity, as both an aspirational ideal and commonplace metaphor, tends to shore up the assumption that whenever queerness or gender nonconformity do cohere into something concrete, like a cultural representation or aesthetic figure, they necessarily become imprisoned by constraining identities, normative logics, or essentialist truths. This leads to a widespread suspicion that queer cultural forms are always limiting and inadequate to describe the infinite complexity of fluid genders and sexualities. This double bind traps those of us committed to feminist and queer freedom in an endless loop of disappointment: resentful toward past social movements for a long list of political pitfalls, exclusions, and oversights, and frustrated with contemporary cultural forms for their perceived failure to sufficiently account for the diversity and nuance of feminist, queer, and trans* existence. What would it mean to get beyond this impasse, to reclaim a positive conception of queer forms as *enabling structures*, "to perceive them, to accept allowing them to arise, to make a place for them and accompany their metamorphosis,"[9] rather than reducing every form to a logic of failed or successful representation whose measure of achievement lies in its ability to perfectly recognize "us"?

Moving beyond the frustrating dialectic of formlessness/fluidity and rigidity/identitarianism requires a constructive understanding of form (or forming) as the practice of continually coming into concrete being. Queer form can underwrite an apprehension of gendered and sexual selfhood neither as an infinitely fluid substance nor an adamantine identity, but as a type of *shapeshifting*. This more accurately describes how individuals meaningfully mold and remold their sense of self over time, and the ways that feminist and queer forms evolve, appear anew, or disclose more aspects as they are taken up and interpreted by different audiences. The feminist and queer artists, writers, and filmmakers inspired by women's and gay liberation responded to the constraints of gender and sexual normativity not by putting forward an ideal of amorphous fluidity, but by continuously giving shape to gender and sexual multiplicity. This included placing women, queers, and gender outlaws of all stripes into awe-inspiring and bewildering new environments—from the streets of an increasingly gay San Francisco to a postapocalyptic commune, from a posh, upper–East Side New York City apartment to an all-female version of Earth—and finding new ways to formally render queer genders and sexualities by articulating them to figures, outlines, or icons that could be perceived and inhabited by diverse publics.

Consequently, in *Queer Forms*, I argue that the movements for women's and gay liberation understood two interrelated realities: that gender and sexuality are many things and constantly change; *and* that to significantly respond to this fact, ordinary people habituated to seeing these categories as fixed or immutable must encounter surprising yet apprehensible forms of gender and sexual nonconformity to enlarge their imaginative horizon. Throughout, I use the contemporary terms "queer" and "queerness" in relation to both movements, to describe their expanded range of desires for different kinds of gender and sexual expressions that thwarted dominant definitions of so-called normal, natural, or traditional gender and sexual embodiment. I join the term "feminist" to queer form whenever I study an aesthetic figure or construct that is specifically articulated to women's lives, bodies, political interests, or activist practices. Feminist forms are *also* queer ones because they give shape to women's collective revolt against heteropatriarchy, which includes their turning to one another for social, political, and erotic companionship.

Ultimately, *Queer Forms* reframes movements for women's and gay liberation not only as activist struggles but as formal projects that cohered countless expressions of queer existence in the hopes of radically altering and broadening what people can think and feel about gender and sexuality. At stake in my enterprise is nothing less than the question of how culture facilitates affective transformation, how it steadily and surprisingly works on people's hearts and minds to provoke new ways of perceiving and responding to a heterogeneous world that might otherwise have remained dormant or unimaginable. This book has taken shape from my belief that people can and do change even their most staunchly held ideas and fantasies about what gender, sexuality, intimacy, and desire are or can be; that cultural production is one potent vector for facilitating that change; and that the capacity for transformation is only ever made possible through the endless proliferation of forms.

Women's and Gay Liberation as "Zones of Invention": Toward a History of Feminist and Queer Imagination

The revival of feminism in the United States was a zone of invention. When we started, the books we needed to read . . . had yet to be written. . . . Any historical record of women's past resistance to prejudice, insult, and invisibility was absent from public memory. . . . One had to discover confidence without supporting evidence. Congress was virtually an all-male space [and] leaders were almost always . . . male, including those in radical movements. The first job was to denaturalize this enveloping reality, to bring it back into history—and into struggle.

—Ann Snitow, *The Feminism of Uncertainty* (2015)

Reflecting on her participation in the women's liberation movement, activist and scholar Ann Snitow enchantingly describes the efflorescence of feminist political energies in the 1970s as a "zone of invention."[10] Snitow's phrase invites us to think about the broader struggle for gender and sexual freedom as an open-ended terrain or geography of the imagination, rather than a series of discrete political projects, competing social movements, or coherent ideologies. After all, as Snitow reminds us, movements for gender and sexual freedom like women's and gay liberation had to be *invented*: generated in writing and speech by a variety of political actors, realized in public collective acts as much as interpersonal choices, and creatively envisioned over and over in one's head. This included the cultivation of new social relations among once isolated women and queers. The creation of novel forms of art, literature, film, and expressive culture attuned to feminist and queer lives. The formation of previously nonexistent political collectives. The conceiving of original activist slogans, from the feminist adage "the personal is political" to the lesbian separatist proclamation "the future is female." And the development of ingenious political strategies to publicize and combat shared experiences of gender and sexual oppression, like feminist consciousness-raising (CR) or coming out of the closet. We can thus extend to both movements Victoria Hesford's claim that 1970s women's liberation represented a "surprising eruption of action and thought that coalesced into a feminism [and gay politics] that was generative of new meanings and practices—of feminism [and gayness] but also of femininity, sexuality, race and so on."[11]

The movements for women's and gay liberation that "erupted" onto the US-American political landscape in the early 1970s ideologically overlapped in their shared analysis of gender and sexual oppression. Inspired by the Civil Rights Movement's emphatic assertion of the humanity of African American people, and Black leaders' moral indictment of the system of white supremacy, an emergent generation of straight and lesbian feminists of all races identified patriarchy as a type of structural domination that arbitrarily enforces hierarchies of gender and sexual normativity to render women and queers inferior subjects. Gay liberationists were heavily influenced by the feminist understanding of patriarchy, which they adapted into a critique of the interlocking relationship between gender role enforcement and sexual policing. They argued that far beyond a simple phobic reaction to same-sex erotic desire, societal homophobia was as much, if not more, rooted in the perception that gays and lesbians are people who fail to perform proper masculinity and femininity. Simultaneously, feminists were inspired by (though also at times resistant to) the lesbian critique of heterosexual privilege and familial norms, which uncovered the tight interconnection between patriarchal domination and "compulsory heterosexuality." This mutually evolving analysis of systemic oppression on the basis of gender and sexuality was a foundational building block in a much more expansive world-making project to wholly reimagine what women and queers could be or become when the categories that traditionally constricted them—from proper daughter, wife, and mother to sexual deviant or "pervert"—were questioned or defiantly refused.[12]

In this sense, participants in women's and gay liberation of every race, age, sexuality, or ability had to reinvent themselves in response to their newfound awareness of gendered and sexual oppression and the existence of countless other gender and sexual outlaws. Writing about his psychic and social evolution after joining gay liberation, activist Allen Young explained in 1972: "As I develop a gay identity . . . I am swept up in a process of change which allows me to define myself in terms other than some masculine ideal. I have a growing awareness of myself and my relationships to other people which is exhilarating. . . . I am finding out how to love my brothers and sisters, how this love is the vital revolutionary force we all need."[13] Similarly, in 1978 the Black lesbian feminists of the Combahee River Collective—a Boston-based political action group—expressed how coming into feminist consciousness facilitated the blossoming of self-love and love for other Black women in the face of a society that devalued their existence: "Above all else, our politics initially sprang from the shared belief that Black women are inherently valuable, that our liberation is a necessity not as an adjunct to somebody else's but because of our need as human persons for autonomy. . . . Our politics evolve from a healthy love for ourselves, our sisters and our community which allows us to continue our struggle and work."[14] In their various contexts, Snitow, Allen, and the Combahee River Collective express how feminist and queer political consciousness helped facilitate unexpected interpersonal relationships and affective possibilities (like inter- and intra-group love, self-confidence, and exhilaration), inspire original concepts and bodies of thought, even open up entirely new registers of experience.

These brief accounts of women's and gay liberation as "zones of invention" resonate with recent feminist and queer theorizing that underscores the imaginative and inaugural character of movements for gender and sexual freedom. In her groundbreaking monograph *Feeling Women's Liberation*, Hesford explores the "creativity of [radical feminism's] rhetorical enactment—the newness of its beginnings," including the "rhetorical forms, metaphors, and phrases [that] were deployed and accrued meaning as part of women's liberation's political revolt against . . . sexism."[15] Among these was the emergence of the "feminist-as-lesbian," a popular figure that both promulgated a stereotype of feminist activists as "angry dykes," but also coalesced women's collective dissent against patriarchy around an icon of galvanizing political rage. Similarly, in *Feminism and the Abyss of Freedom*, political theorist Linda Zerilli recovers feminism's "world-making" capacities, namely its ability to found new forms of political association between women. This necessarily involves creatively projecting the category of "woman" into numerous unaccustomed contexts, like the spheres of political organizing or street activism, that subvert received understandings of women's appropriate social roles, and consequently bolster their "right to be a participant in public affairs."[16] José Esteban Muñoz's *Cruising Utopia* identifies distinctly queer world-making practices in 1960s and early 1970s gay and lesbian cultural production, including ebullient, sex-positive, and playful visual art, literature, and performance that undermined the traditional association of gay desire with tragedy and trauma. Muñoz interprets the cultural prehistory of gay liberation as evidencing a wellspring of new exuberant affects, or "utopian longings," that came to attach to queerness as a site of hope for a "not yet here" anti-homophobic world.[17] Finally, Robert McRuer documents concrete expressions of queer utopian impulses in a variety of 1970s "gay gatherings": from the formation of the first gay male living collective in New York City to the queer and multiracial coalition that helped elect Harvey Milk to public office in 1977 to the ecstatic disco dance floor shared by queers, women, and Black and Latinx participants alike. In each of these sites, "coming-out . . . was fundamentally a collective experience: one came out of the closet, certainly, but even more important, one came out to a community or movement . . . involved in the process of reimagining and reshaping the world."[18] Across diverse archives and disciplines, these thinkers offer four interrelated understandings of women's and gay liberation movements as "surprising eruptions of action and thought" that were characterized by the creation of rhetorical, aesthetic, or performative figures of gender and sexual rebellion. These cultural constructs publicized different fantasies, ideas, or conceptions of what a sexually liberated world might look like, while providing portable, imaginative icons around which emergent feminist and queer collectivities could organize and define themselves.

In *Queer Forms* I am concerned with two sites of feminist and queer imagination in the 1970s: (1) the invention of new political concepts for describing and meaningfully responding to gender and sexual variety, which encouraged the proliferation of multiple, divergent visions of collective freedom for women and queers (including both traditional notions of self-determination and unrestricted self-expression, as well as the right of gender and sexual dissidents to free association and participation in public life); and (2) the crafting of aesthetic forms that translated these concepts into a vast array of creative contexts, thus allowing them to circulate within, and adapt to the needs of, countless constituencies. This interconnected set of practices constituted a "gay cultural politics," a term I use to describe any attempt to render, publicize, and circulate cultural or aesthetic forms that model, give shape to, or materialize diverse expressions of gender and sexual nonconformity. Queer forms, then, are the heterogeneous creative products of a gay cultural politics' radical imagination.

Following Zerilli, I understand *imagination* as a cognitive faculty that enables people to project existing categories, concepts, identities, or worldviews into unfamiliar arenas of experience, thereby enabling the generation of new figures for thought. Citing the work of philosopher Cornelius Castoriados, Zerilli argues, "The task of radical movements is to transform . . . society by putting instituted representations into question [which involves] 'the positing of the new forms or figures of the thinkable, which are created by radical imagination'. . . . *Whatever doubts we may raise about an 'established truth' such as gender, in other words, always begin with a productive or creative moment of figuration.*"[19] For example, as I discuss in chapter 1, in the mid-1970s, feminist science fiction writer Joanna Russ put forward the figure of "the female man" in her eponymously titled novel, a phrase she innovates to describe a woman who suddenly imagines herself as a fully realized or legitimate member of "mankind."[20] "The female man" perfectly represents a "creative moment of figuration," because it invents a concept for thought, a distinctly feminine universal, which undermines the "established truth" that women's equality rests on their achievement of a preexisting male standard. Rather, the female man posits the idea that any individual woman already inherently represents "man" (the species) as a whole, *if only she would claim her birthright.*

The movements for women's and gay liberation were fundamentally imaginative projects aimed at radically altering commonly received understandings of gender and sexuality as innate or natural essences bound up in an immutable biological body. In turn, they facilitated the emergence of a distinctly gay cultural politics, which "interrupted and altered the system of representation" used to judge our reality of gender and sexuality by ingeniously inserting manifold expressions of queer genders, erotic desires, intimacies, and kinship formations into countless new lived and fictional scenes. This included disco dance floors, consciousness-raising sessions, street activism, feminist reading groups, lesbian communes, even outer space, alternate dimensions, and the far future. Gay cultural politics aimed at nothing less than transforming categories like woman, gay and lesbian, transsexual, woman of color, or Third World woman from seemingly transparent identities into expansive and flexible ways of life or worldly orientations attuned toward the plurality of gender and sexual expression. As historian Allison Hobson explains, "Queer studies has tended to assume that gay and lesbian politics of the 1970s . . . rested on static and essentialist conceptions of sexual identity. . . . [Yet] many who mark themselves as gay or lesbian in the past conceived of sexuality, sexual identities, and sexual politics in dynamic . . . terms and understood sexuality as intersecting with gender, race, class, and nation."[21]

Hobson's scholarship represents one example of an extraordinary renaissance in contemporary feminist and queer historiography informed by the insights of queer theory, critical race studies, transgender studies, and theories of affect and emotion. Contributors to this intellectual project have recuperated the multiracial, cross-gender, coalitional character of women's and gay liberation, while illuminating the complex political, social, and cultural dimensions of each: from the anti-racist politics of the feminist bookstore movement to the activist role of left-wing queer-of-color performance art; from social histories of Black and Latinx feminist organizing to the varieties of transgender activism.[22] *Queer Forms* is indebted to and informed by this work, but my focus is unique both because I consider women's and gay liberation as mutually influencing imaginative projects rather than as separate or competitive social movements, and because I centralize popular culture forms rather than political documents, social histories of activism, or traditional ideological formations as a primary repository of feminist and queer thought.

Against Narratives of Feminist Supersession and Queer Eventfulness: Bridging Women's and LGBTQ Historiography

Despite the arrival of increasingly multidimensional accounts of women's and gay liberation, both movements' inaugural quality, including the inventive nature of their creative cultural endeavors, has been frequently downplayed or eclipsed by two dominant stories of feminist and queer historiography. The first story, commonly called a "feminist supersessionary narrative," figures 1970s feminism as comprising a series of successive waves, with "white feminism . . . seen as first on the block [and] Black [and] Chicana feminism coming later to add the factor of race/ethnicity to the feminist project."[23] This well-worn narrative has undergone intense scrutiny, most notably by Hesford, Clare Hemmings, Benita Roth, and Robyn Wiegman, who expose how it "obscures the mutual influence that feminist activists had on one another across racial ethnic lines"[24] by "positing a . . . singular origin of the movement [in] the experience of young, white, middle-class women in postwar America."[25] The second account, which I label a "narrative of queer eventfulness," is less often explicitly named or critiqued, but is equally limiting. This story reduces gay liberation's wealth of political concepts, activist practices, and cultural production to a series of historical flashpoints or charismatic leaders whose activism comes to stand in for the broader political and cultural effects of the movement.

Any study of women's and gay liberation that aims to illuminate new dimensions of these movements must reckon with the power of the prevailing "supersessionary" and "eventful" narratives of feminist and queer historiography to circumscribe our understanding of their imaginative traditions. Toward this end, I briefly renarrate each story in broad brushstrokes to emphasize how easily they come to substitute for a range of more nuanced contemporary frameworks for studying feminist and queer social movements.[26] The feminist story goes something like this:

> First, in the early to mid-1960s, mostly white, middle-class professional women organized around the idea of political and legal equality for women, understood as a subordinated class seeking parity with men. This struggle birthed "liberal feminism," a rights-based political project that defined "equality" as being treated the same as men. Liberal feminists downplayed

women's differences, from men and one another, in the interest of presenting themselves collectively, as a unified front, and individually, as similar
enough to their male counterparts to deserve equal treatment under the
law. Next, in the early 1970s, radical feminists, also mostly white middle-class
women, but of a younger generation who emerged out of civil rights activism, critiqued this liberal, moderate demand for equality. They attacked
the cultural foundations of normative gender—grounded in the system of
"patriarchy"—which produced and maintained the notion of women as a
naturally inferior category of persons. Thus, they aimed to dismantle the
assumed male universal standard against which all women are measured.
Yet, like liberal feminists before them, they naïvely assumed women comprised a unified group based on their shared oppression, similarly failing to
deal with differences of race, class, and sexuality among women. Finally, in
response to the missteps of white liberal and radical feminists, women-of-
color and Third World feminists sought to analyze the interlocking nature
of racial, gendered, class, and sexual oppression, what would later be called
"intersectionality." These women jettisoned theoretical and activist ties to
a dominant white feminist tradition; organized their own working groups;
conducted local activism focused on the immediate needs of communities
of color; and pursued coalitional politics to connect Third World struggles
with the internal colonization of Indigenous and racialized peoples in the
US. Intersectionality remains the most nuanced and sophisticated analytical
concept of modern feminist thought.[27]

If the anecdotal history of feminism is frequently a teleological one
documenting successive ideological waves associated with distinct
groups of women divided by race and class, the history of gay liberation
is often an *eventful* one chronicling a series of landmark moments and
the political figures who represent them. The gay story goes something
like this:

The explosive collective rebellion against police harassment on June 28, 1969,
at the Stonewall Inn, a New York City gay bar, fueled the rise of gay liberation. This flashpoint functioned as a near-mythical origin for modern LGBTQ
history, which would be marked by a series of triumphs and losses including
political milestones, the rise and fall of iconic activist leaders, and watershed
media events. Consequently, gay history is: the election of Harvey Milk to

the San Francisco Board of Supervisors, followed by his tragic assassination in 1978. The defeat of the California Briggs initiative that same year, which aimed to repeal employment protection for gay and lesbian civil servants. The June 3, 1981, publication of a *New York Times* article titled "Rare Cancer Seen in 41 Homosexuals," the first public acknowledgement of what would later be named acquired immunodeficiency syndrome (AIDS). The AIDS epidemic and the rise of radical AIDS activism. The Supreme Court's homophobic decision to uphold anti-sodomy laws in *Bowers v. Hardwick* (1986). The Clinton administration's unconstitutional "Don't Ask, Don't Tell" military policy toward homosexuality (1993). Ellen DeGeneres's coming out on national television in "The Puppy Episode" (1997). And the Supreme Court's 2015 ruling to uphold the rights of same-sex couples to be married. Both early and contemporary developments in LGBTQ historiography texture and expand this story: we learn that gay liberation was preceded by a long history of homophile activism. As a result, the formation of the gay male–led Mattachine Society in 1950 becomes the more accurate touchstone for the origin of US gay activism. We learn that transsexual activists long sidelined by both the radical and mainstream gay movements were central to every period of queer activism. Consequently, the August 1966 Compton's Cafeteria Riot in the Tenderloin District of San Francisco, a spontaneous uprising by transsexual patrons of a local diner in response to violent police harassment, becomes the more accurate flashpoint for the origin of queer radicalism in the pre–gay liberation era. The story of the Stonewall Riots is also retold with new heroic actors, namely queer-of-color trans activists like Marsha P. Johnson and Sylvia Rivera. We learn about the Upstairs Lounge fire of 1973, an act of arson in New Orleans that killed thirty-two mostly queer patrons of a secret gay bar, which now becomes the more accurate turning point for public violence against gays and lesbians years before the assassination of Harvey Milk . . . and the list goes on.[28]

By placing these stories side by side we can immediately notice that each excludes the other. The feminist supersessionary narrative leaves almost no room for gay liberationist politics, ideas, or events to be understood as an integral part of the evolution of women's movement history. Lesbian feminism, which was partly born out of the unique contexts of gay liberation, becomes folded into the monolith called "white radical feminism," while the lesbian-inflected thought of Black feminism is subordinated to its analytical focus on race or else wholly eclipsed. In parallel form, the narrative of queer eventfulness bypasses the women's movement altogether, becoming about a series of gains or losses for a distinct political constituency, gays and lesbians. Thus, while nearly every work of feminist and queer history or theory briefly acknowledges the profound impact that second-wave feminism had on gay liberation, or gestures toward the importance of lesbian feminism theorized by women of all races to the women's movement as a whole, no monograph has yet explored the coevolution of these movements in a sustained way. This erasure, or more accurately willful forgetting, of mutual influence between women's and gay liberation is redoubled in the intellectual stance assumed by each of the dominant accounts of feminist and queer political progress, which respectively promote *teleological* approaches to feminist history or *revisionist* approaches to the queer past as a remedy to the whitewashing of both.

As a number of scholars have shown, the feminist supersessionary narrative lends itself to a progressive arc, where seemingly more advanced or ideologically mature waves of feminist thought—almost always associated with women of color—supplant earlier, presumably less sophisticated versions of radical feminism—almost always associated with white women—deemed inattentive to race and class. In Roth's foundational study of white, Black, and Chicana feminisms, she demonstrates how this model obscures the multiracial and multigenerational character of women's liberation and diminishes the genuine radicalness of feminist ideas like equal pay, reproductive justice, and sexual freedom that traveled between different groups of women across race, class, age, and sexuality. In the name of celebrating the political contributions of Black, brown, Asian, and Indigenous feminists, the supersessionary framework also places women of color at the end of a historical process imagined to be initiated by white women, ironically reproducing the very hierarchical sequence it aims to dismantle. Equally troubling, Rachel Lee reminds us that this account freezes the category "woman of color" into a unified experience of dispossession and exclusion from feminism proper, rather than seeing it as "a transformative political subjectivity" firmly grounded within feminist thought, which can catalyze productive disagreement and debate among feminists of all stripes about the meaning and purpose of their political endeavor (as well as pushing them to refine their distinct interpretations of what a feminist of color is or can be). For example, while the foundational feminist concept of women's equality has frequently been associated with middle-class, "liberal" white women assumed to be fighting for legal and political "sameness" with men, it was in fact a broadly shared radical value pursued and theorized by Black and white working-class women, Asian American feminists, Chicano queer activists, and Third World gay liberationists. Each of these groups defined their own version of "equality" in ways that included but also exceeded ideas of legal or political parity with a dominant class (like heterosexual men). Hence, a commonly shared desire for gender and sexual equality generated a dynamic debate across and within various feminist and queer activisms about what equality might mean or look like for numerous kinds of gender and sexual outlaws, thereby expanding feminism's reach to new constituencies and domains of experience.

Alternatively, the narrative of queer eventfulness lends itself to intellectual practices of recovery and revision. In this framework, the political value of LGBTQ history is increasingly located in the discovery of previously ignored political events and actors, so that an archival impulse to look backward and "fill in" the missing details of the queer past becomes the sine qua non of social progress. This is an absolutely necessary project, because it provides us a multidimensional understanding of LGBTQ history by recuperating the contributions of those gay liberationists whose voices have long been absent from the historical record, including transgender people, queers of color, and bisexuals. Yet because the narrative of queer eventfulness places so much value on historical recovery, it can inadvertently promote competition between distinct groups of queers—white gay men, gay men of color, trans* people of all stripes, butch lesbians, Black dykes, etc.—to lay claim to different events and political actors as uniquely their own in the name of social uplift. Consider that in the scramble to "own" the meaning of Stonewall, the event gets perpetually rehashed in popular debates as either a sanitized white gay male affair or a radical riot lead by transgender women of color. This reductive storytelling overlooks the fact that the riots included all these groups in uneven but overlapping ways, and was in fact catalyzed by the rebellious actions of a biracial butch lesbian, Stormé DeLarverie, who was neither gay male nor trans but political kin to both.[29] A revisionist impulse that focuses on ameliorating exclusion, then, sometimes has the effect of facilitating an affective resentment toward historical whitewashing that, while completely understandable and legitimate, can reproduce strict historical boundaries between perceived mainstream (i.e., white gay and lesbian) and more marginalized queer cultures. For instance, this approach has led some to suggest that a gay liberationist concept like "coming out of the closet," the political strategy of publicly disclosing queer sexuality, is inherently "white." This is not only because coming out was espoused by white gay male political leaders like Harvey Milk, but also because it presumably fails to acknowledge the distinct dangers of disclosure for Black, brown, and trans* folks of color, including the potential loss of familial ties and ethno-racial community belonging. Setting aside the problematic assumption that coming out to one's family is necessarily easier for white gay people, it has been well documented that the declaration of queerness was (and is) a meaningful act of performative self- and community-making for Black, brown, Asian American, and Indigenous queers who came out to themselves, their friends and lovers, and their political allies even if and when they chose not to do so to their families.

As these examples attest, both the supersessionary and eventful character of feminist and queer anecdotal histories makes conceptual or interpersonal cross-identification between the various ideological camps or distinct members of women's and gay liberation seem unimaginable. And precisely because of the rigidity of these stories, contemporary concepts of gender and sexual fluidity frequently come to be understood as the only progressive solution to these movements' apparent ideological inflexibility, their failure to break out of the norms they aimed to demolish, or their tacit aggrandizement of white and cis political actors to the diminishment of Black, brown, and trans* leaders. The capacity to inhabit a presumptively progressive, fluid or mutable identity is then annexed to those same overlooked Black, brown, and trans* subjects, forever freezing white and cis women and queers, and their perceived concepts or ideas, into an unyielding monument of regressive, "single-issue" politics.[30]

To be clear, my point is not to say that we *shouldn't* study women's and gay liberation as distinct movements that contained diverse and sometimes antagonistic ideologies and social constituencies, nor that we should abandon the project of recovering critically understudied events, activist groups, or political actors. Rather, I question an over-emphasis on these approaches, which tends to elide the shared history of ideas that exploded outward from movements for gender and sexual freedom, inciting their heterogeneous participants of many races, ages, and class backgrounds as well as a broader public to wholly reimagine gender and sexuality. Certainly these two movements were not identical and regularly clashed in their competing visions of freedom: while feminists often criticized the hypersexualization of women, gay men in the gay liberation movement demanded greater sexual autonomy to pursue multiple erotic connections free of social stigma. And while many straight women hoped to reform men by encouraging them to develop a feminist consciousness, some lesbian feminists argued that women's freedom necessarily required their total divestment from male-dominated society. Despite the many well-documented differences between women's and gay liberation, these movements ultimately shared a utopian investment in opening up the possibilities of what women and queer people could desire from their genders, sex lives, emotional bonds, and the larger society. By conceiving of women's and gay liberation as mutually constitutive histories of feminist and queer imagination, we can better account for the fact that the emergence of revolutionary women and queers in the 1970s was dependent on their continual exchange of innovative political concepts, strategies, and frameworks, as well as the collective production of novel forms of art and culture as a creative terrain for testing out and honing their boldest ideas for gender and sexual freedom.

This reciprocal exchange and collective vision can be registered in four overlapping aspirations inherent to both movements: first, both women's and gay liberation shared a commitment to the *valuation* of women and queers, which involved the social, political, and affective uplifting of commonly denigrated gender and sexual dissidents. In the revival of political slogans like "Gay is Good," or CR's commitment to taking women's feelings seriously as evidence of patriarchal oppression, women and queers performatively declared that gender and sexual outlaws of all stripes mattered, that their diverse ways of life had meaning and positive value. Second, both movements engaged in a sustained project of *expansion*, seeking to enlarge existing categories of gender and sexuality so that terms like "woman," "man," "gay," "lesbian," "Third World woman," "woman of color," and others could accommodate or speak to more kinds of people, experiences, and perspectives. Third, both movements facilitated a *proliferation* of novel or unexpected meanings that might accrue to gender, sexuality, desire, and intimacy, including their politicization and their suffusion with thrilling affective intensities like wonder, enchantment, joy, and rage. When the Radicalesbians declared that a "lesbian is the rage of all women brought to the point of explosion," they expanded the category of "lesbian" beyond a sexual identity to describe a viscerally felt rebellion against patriarchy potentially shared by gay, bisexual, and straight women alike.[31] Finally, both movements celebrated the power of *transformation*, the capacity of all human beings to meaningfully change their genders and sexualities, but also potentially their existing perceptions, beliefs, or fantasies about any and all identities.[32] The shared feminist and queer investment in the valuation, expansion, proliferation, and transformation of gender and sexual diversity would be most potently enacted in the profusion of queer and feminist cultural forms in the era's popular and visual media. It was there, in the aesthetic experiments of creative producers who sought to richly describe and outline countless expressions of gender and sexual nonconformity, that a modern gay cultural politics was born, wedding feminist and queer political values to a renaissance in artistic expression.

Gay Cultural Politics

In the early 1970s, gay liberation reinvented the meaning of the term "gay"—traditionally defined as a denigrated social identity based on same-sex erotic desire—into an ecstatic and joyful way of life associated with openness to sexual and gender diversity and a commitment to pursue intimacies that thwart the direction of heteropatriarchal norms. This was accomplished through explicit political statements that redescribed gayness as a distinct outlook or transformational "process," but equally through the proliferation of new images of queer rebellion in the era's art and popular culture. In 1972, the writers of the Gay Party Revolution Manifesto declared: "Gay is a process of attaining mutual and equal social and sensual relationships among all human beings. . . .

Gay revolution will produce a world in which all social and sensual relationships will be gay and in which homo- and heterosexuality will be incomprehensible terms."[33] In this same period, the phrase "Gay is Good"—which drew upon the etymological roots of the word "gay" to mean "keenly alive and exuberant" or "brilliant in color"—was appropriated from its origins in 1950s homophile activism and relocated in the context of gay liberation, where it indicated an ebullient expression of revolutionary "self-love and love for our gay sisters and brothers."[34] "Gay is Good" soon became an aesthetic feature of buttons, posters, banners, and magazine covers, offering an adaptable rhetorical structure and visual icon for expressing the value of gay lifeways among a wide variety of politicized queers, from the Street Transvestite Action Revolutionaries for *Gay* Power to the San Francisco *Gay* Latino Alliance (my italics).[35] Gayness functioned around 1972 similarly to how we understand the terms "queer" or "trans*" in activism and theory today, as a flexible name for gender and sexual transformation, rather than a prescribed identity. This project resonated with, and ran parallel to, feminism's radical reinvention of what women could be, what new roles they might play in social, political, and cultural life, and how categories like "woman" or "lesbian" might be modified and expanded when different subjects claimed them as their own.

These stunning acts of resignification were part of what I call a *gay cultural politics*. This was a wide-reaching creative project to proliferate queer cultural forms, including works of art, literature, film, performance, and music, that gave conceptual heft to, and publicized, the alternative desires, sensual and erotic intimacies, social bonds, and modes of existence that movements for women's and gay liberation inaugurated and celebrated. I intentionally use the term "gay" in relation to both movements (as I do with the term "queer") to indicate the original term's association with more adaptive understandings of gender and sexuality, and underscore how the cultural experiments of women's and gay liberation were also affectively laden, imbuing categories like "woman" and "gay" with effervescence, joy, humor, or ecstasy in the face of unrelenting sexism and homophobia.

Rather than approaching culture as a site of ideological conflict, where competing dominant and counterhegemonic political ideals vie for audiences' attention, I understand it as a highly unpredictable space of ungrounded fantasy, play, and experimentation. Regardless of the specific political or ideological messages that works of art and popular culture may contain, they are also repositories of countless aesthetic shapes and constructs—including character types, formal techniques, spatial architectures, and physical objects—that can inspire or influence viewers in infinitely varied ways. The field of cultural production, then, always has the potential to leverage open people's sensorial and emotional landscape and viscerally challenge their most firmly held ideas, values, and identities, including potentially galvanizing them to reconsider what they define as "the political." In this sense, I join Ernst van Alphen in conceiving of cultural products as *forms of thought*, which allows us to "consider the intellectual and performative power of art to reinterpret, indeed to rewrite, powerful historical habits," including "naturalized sociocultural gender [and sexual] constructions."[36] Moreover, as social movement scholar T. V. Reed explains, "one crucial role of [art] is to critique and transcend ideology [by] remind[ing] activists . . . that the full lived complexity of cultural life cannot be reduced to any ideological system."[37] My conception of a gay cultural politics allows us to see the broader imaginative and affective impact women's and gay liberation had far beyond the limits of any activist group, by highlighting how new ideas about gender and sexual diversity, autonomy, pleasure, and intimacy were forged and tested out in creative fictional worlds that refused to adhere to strict "ideological systems" or immediate political goals. As a variety of queer forms circulated throughout the 1970s, they collided with the desires, aspirations, and attachments of individual readers and viewers. These encounters sparked countless flights of imagination and fantasizing that could catalyze transformations in how people felt and behaved toward gender and sexuality, perhaps even all categories of difference.

The efflorescence of feminist and queer cultural production in the late 1960s and 1970s overlapped with similar artistic renaissances in a broad cross-section of contemporaneous race- and class-based social movements. This included the expressive oratorical and musical cultures of civil rights protest; the literature, art, and theater of Black, Chicano, and Asian American cultural nationalisms (most notably the Black Arts Movement); and the graphic print cultures of Third World, antiwar, and student movements. Gender and sexual freedom movements frequently shared with these projects a stated (if not always practiced) investment in the collective liberation of all oppressed groups, the political and social valuation or uplift of marginalized identities, and the belief that a distinctly *cultural* politics was necessary for changing popular perceptions about social inequality and stigmatized identities. Yet feminist and queer cultural politics were ultimately distinguished both by their focus on issues previously considered exclusive to the realm of private or personal life—like sexual freedom, gender expression, reproductive rights, and alternative kinship formation—and their desire to fundamentally denature traditional gender and sexual identities. This included aspirations to destroy the gender binary and overthrow the primacy of the heterosexual nuclear family for everyone, not simply self-identified women and sexual minorities.

Just as feminist and queer freedom movements fought against the stigmatization of gender and sexual variance, race-based social liberation projects like Black Power and the Asian American Movement actively deconstructed negative or stereotyped versions of Black and Asian peoples promulgated by white racist scorn. Yet these latter movements' aim was to ultimately reconstitute "Black" and "Asian" identities as coherent, positive, even essentially shared categories of belonging imbued with group pride and solidarity (hence the famed slogan "Black is Beautiful," which inspired homophile leader Frank Kameny to invent the phrase "Gay is Good"). For Black nationalists, including the artists who participated in the Afrocentric aesthetic revival of the Black Arts Movement, the goal of positively resignifying Blackness was not to implode or dissolve the category from within or else draft putatively white or non-Black people to the cause; rather, it was to make Blackness newly available to African Americans as a potential avenue of identification with a global Black and African cultural heritage. Alternatively, notwithstanding the presence and allure of feminist essentialisms, 1970s gay cultural politics sought to validate the existence of gender- and sexual-nonconforming lives within any and all demographics, while potentially recruiting feminist and queer outlaws in the making. An ever-expanding horizon of gender and sexual rebels would thus help constitute many distinct feminist and queer cultural traditions while continually redefining who might count as a woman, as a feminist, as gay, lesbian, or transsexual.

Take, for example, the original promotional poster for Paul Mazursky's acclaimed 1978 film *An Unmarried Woman*, which follows a year

Figure 1.2. Original promotional poster for director Paul Mazursky's 1978 film *An Unmarried Woman*.

in the life of art gallerist Erica Benton (played by Jill Clayburgh) after her husband leaves her for a younger woman (figure 1.2). The film title is printed in bold lowercase letters across the center of the poster. Clayburgh appears casually seated cross-legged atop the letter "m" in the word "Unmarried." Dressed in a timeworn white T-shirt, as though prepared for bed, she stares wistfully beyond the border of the page with a bemused look on her face. At the top of the frame the film's run-on tagline reads: "She laughs, she cries, she feels angry, she feels lonely, she feels guilty, she makes breakfast, she makes love, she makes do, she is strong, she is weak, she is brave, she is scared, she is . . . an unmarried woman." The poster posits the "unmarried woman" as an imaginative category that describes a complex state of being rather than a fixed marital status or sexual identity. An unmarried woman, we are told, is someone with a rich interior life, who feels many things, is capable of many things, and is internally multiplicious. She is less a rigid "type" defined by her external gender expression or sexual behaviors, and more like the figural representation of a liberated mood, frame of mind, or attitude. Here, the broader category "woman" itself becomes imbued with productive "uncertainty, instability, and ambivalence."[38] By rejecting the stigmatized labels of divorcée and spinster, "the unmarried woman" is a "figure of the newly thinkable" that can be inhabited by a variety of subjects, including single and partnered women of any sexuality who remain unmarried. Finally, Clayburgh's contemplative daydreaming associates the experience of being an unmarried woman with playful vulnerability, an emotional openness to possibilities beyond marriage and domesticity.

While the film is a representational feat for women, centralizing female characters and friendships in a major Hollywood production, it is the formal "elaboration" of the multiplex emotional terrain of an unmarried woman's life that animates the film. As cinema scholar Ryan Powell has shown, independent and avant-garde gay male filmmaking during this period similarly circulated new conceptions of same-sex eroticism, desire, and intimacy between "unmarried" gay men: "Twentieth-century gay life might involve expressions of joy . . . representations of bachelorhood . . . a sexual orientation, a cultural and or aesthetic sensibility, [or] a philosophy for living. . . . The filmic elaboration of a multitude of fictional scenarios organized around male-male desire became a way to ask audiences 'what if?'"[39] Beyond the archive of queer and feminist forms I coalesce, then, my broader aim is to develop and model a more capacious method for studying what Powell has called the formal "elaboration" of (feminist and) gay lives, one that can account for their mutual influence and shared cultural destinies. Toward this end, my analyses of various expressions of gay cultural politics in the chapters that follow are informed by four guiding principles.

First, as I have already suggested, I conceive of women's and gay liberation not only as social movements with distinct organizational and political histories but as shared cultural sensibilities, or "structures of feeling," about gender and sexual freedom that circulated widely beyond the realms of activism and traditional political writing. This approach encourages greater awareness of how specific social movement debates about political strategies like feminist consciousness-raising or coming out of the closet were also being creatively developed and adapted within many fictional worlds, across diverse narrative genres, and through numerous modes of address. Moreover, these creative adaptations and reworkings of feminist and queer ideals were often undertaken by writers, artists, and filmmakers who never claimed explicit allegiance to movement activism but were imaginatively inspired by the explosive growth of new conceptions of gender and sexuality emerging from women's and gay liberation. As I discuss in chapter 1, while Maxine Hong Kingston's renowned 1975 memoir *The Woman Warrior* makes no direct reference to feminist equality debates, its proliferation of stories about the mothers, daughters, and aunts in a single Chinese American family demands that readers engage in the difficult imaginative labor of equating or finding common ground between women who are radically different from one another, even within the same lineage. The text recasts equality as a creative practice, rather than a singular political goal, that can be cultivated through the continual comparison of unlike subjects who, despite their differences, are still conceived of as equivalently valuable. In this way, I widen the scope of the kinds of cultural texts that can be considered as participating in the shared aspirational vision of women's and gay liberation, including works of literature, art, film, or visual culture that do not make (or do not *only* make) transparent political statements, but formally capture the spirit of gender and sexual liberation. One outcome is that my chapters frequently draw together unexpected constellations of texts that reveal the remarkable cross-pollination of ideas and shared investments between feminist and queer freedom projects, or else challenge established interpretations of canonical feminist political tracts whose arguments were taken up and modified by artists of many identities, aesthetic styles, and worldviews.

For instance, readers of this book may be surprised to discover that many gay, and some straight, *men* were among the most sustained creative interlocutors for feminist ideas in the 1970s and after. This included Ira Levin, whose bestselling novella *The Stepford Wives* offered a searing critique of second-wave feminist essentialism from a distinctly male feminist perspective, and playwright Mart Crowley, whose acclaimed Off-Broadway play, and subsequent film, *The Boys in the Band* depicted a gay male friendship circle's emotional conflicts in the model of feminist CR circle.

Second, in each chapter, I return to key feminist and queer political concepts, values, or strategies that have been relegated to the "dustbin of history," like women's equality discourse or lesbian separatism, to better understand how they worked practically in their moment and to reinvigorate their conceptual power in the present. I track how these ideas were translated into cultural forms—made legible or redescribed to readers and viewers through imaginative analogies, metaphors, figures, or icons—rather than only explicitly named or pedantically "taught" to audiences. Simultaneously, I model or perform 1970s feminist and queer political values in the way I interpret works of art and popular culture. When I study the consciousness-raising circle in *The Boys in the Band*, I enact the feminist call to take one's emotional responses to patriarchy seriously by analyzing my own visceral reactions to the film's depiction of gay male love, rage, sarcasm, and fierce loyalty. And when I analyze the gay serial fiction *Tales of the City*, I draw upon the coming-out stories of its original readers to show how the text provided ingenious terms like the "logical" or chosen queer family that followers used to disclose their evolving sexual and gender identities to others. By deploying varied types of evidence—including my own feeling states, interviews, the material histories of particular art objects, artist statements, and published accounts of feminist and queer activists—I provide a multidimensional view of the conceptual history of a given queer and feminist political idea or practice, thereby revivifying the contemporary purchase of concepts seen as long past their political or historical expiry date.

Third, at various times I explicitly suspend, thoughtfully question, or else try to carefully parse the traditional labels or names given for distinct strands of feminist and queer thought and activism. I do so to put pressure on the ease with which we tend confine so-called "liberal," "radical," and "women-of-color" feminisms to competing or antagonistic camps, or else self-righteously distinguish between perceived liberal and more radical gay politics. While I do use all of these terms for the sake of clarity, I also want to muddy the waters, to make visible how tenuous all of these distinctions become when we look at, for instance, the ways that actual feminists and gay liberationists interacted interpersonally (after all, Black, gay, trans*, straight, Latinx, lesbian, white, and Asian American feminists and queers were often friends, lovers, and "sisters in the struggle" as much as conflicted fellow travelers); the impact and circulation of activists' political values far beyond any single group or camp; and the unorthodox blending of feminist and queer ideologies, orientations, sensibilities, and desires in popular culture, which has always been a space of conceptual experimentation and play.

Nineteen-seventies feminist and queer cultural products rarely respected traditionally perceived divisions between liberal or radical feminisms, or between categories like "white lesbian" or "lesbian of color," irreverently mixing and matching subject-positions like gay, lesbian, feminist, Asian American woman, Third World, dyke, or Black lesbian and the worldviews associated with each. These breathtaking combinatory moves revealed affinities and overlaps between seemingly opposed feminism frameworks and underscored that feminist and queer ideas, concepts, and values are often far more effective, and *affecting*, on the hearts and minds of audiences when they are set loose from their supposedly proper ideological "homes." Moreover, many so-called liberal feminist goals, like the demand for women's equality, could have radical outcomes beyond legal or economic gains, such as the idea, cogently argued by Dorothy Dinnerstein, that adult human beings of all genders should be equally responsible for the caretaking of children.[40] Conversely, many of gay liberation's most "radical" political strategies, like coming out, could facilitate the increasing recognition and absorption of sexual outlaws into the US social fabric, a decidedly positive liberal outcome. I suggest, then, that what counts as "radical" or "liberal," "single-axis" or "intersectional," "white" or "of color" is sometimes a matter of interpretation and context rather than a categorical fact, and correspondingly, that we do not always need to lead every critique of a given feminist and queer ideology, identity category, or cultural object with a moral judgment about its perceived radicalness or quietism.

Fourth and finally, I attempt to recover the most inventive aspects of the political claims of women's and gay liberation even when the radicalness of those claims were lost in practice, or dulled by conservatisms inherent to both movements. For instance, it remains a stunning contradiction that the movements for women's and gay liberation developed some of the most powerful critiques of gender normativity in US history but also at times exhibited extremely phobic reactions to transsexual participants in their ranks. This interpersonal shunning was both ethically reprehensible and politically puzzling, since many founding documents of second-wave feminism and gay liberation espouse notions of gender and sexual variability, even articulating aspirations for a post-gender world: as early as 1964 the feminist sociologist Alice Rossi argued that equality between men and women could be achieved only through universal androgyny, while in her classic Marxist-feminist polemic *The Dialectic of Sex*, Shulamith Firestone argued for a post-gender world where children are produced in test tubes and all erotic and romantic relationships would be polymorphous; and in his "Gay Manifesto," Carl Wittman developed an analysis of the overlapping ways gender oppression affects gays and lesbians, transsexuals, and women, ultimately declaring that liberation from heteropatriarchy meant freedom for all these groups.[41] Following Janet Halley's encouragement to "split decisions" about our commitments to feminism, I explore what it might mean to recuperate the best ideas of feminist and queer radicalisms in the 1970s while refusing to repeat their most tragic misfirings.[42] When I discuss lesbian separatism, for instance, I unpack and critique the essentialist logic that imagined lesbians as universally ideal feminist subjects, but I reclaim separatism's generative anarchist spirit, its legitimate desire to cut ties with destructive patriarchal arrangements. I believe it is possible to hold women's and gay liberation accountable for their practical failures on the ground, without jettisoning the conceptual power of their most potent ideas.

Today, we have an exceptionally rich vocabulary to describe various kinds of cultural appropriation, violence, theft, erasure, exploitation, and denigration of minoritized life, and the macro- and microaggressions that underwrite them. These terms are intended to identify oppressive institutional structures and interpersonal dynamics in the hope of ameliorating their harm. As powerful and illuminating as these concepts can be, when we relentlessly pursue the project of naming, diagnosing, and critiquing harm, we frequently lose sight of the broader and more revolutionary question of how exactly people come to release or let go of pernicious ideologies; how they jettison attachments to racism, homophobia, sexism, transphobia, and ableism; and how they become more capable of embracing and negotiating difference. In this endeavor, we have shockingly "few respectable conceptual tools" for identifying those cultural practices that might go by the name of mutual exchange, cross-identification, cross-pollination, influence, affinity, sharing, loving, or simply trust and understanding.[43] Far from an easily dismissed lexicon of racist, transphobic, or politically retrograde representations, the cultural archive of 1970s women's and gay liberation provides one of the most sustained attempts to publicly circulate mutually transformative anti-sexist, anti-racist, and anti-homophobic aesthetic forms and feeling states in US history. Rather than running away from the task of representation, the artists, writers, and filmmakers who took up the call of queer and feminist freedom conceived of gender and sexual nonconformity as a formal problem that required creative elaboration to be consciously grasped and meaningfully interpreted by multiple perspectives. These creators never assumed that any single representation of queerness, femininity, gender nonconformity, or sexual diversity could possibly stand in for, or accurately capture, the vastly heterogeneous experiences of women and queers variously construed. Rather they offered up queer and feminist forms as provisional shapes, or constructs, for picturing queerness, first in one way, *then another, then another.* To capture gay cultural politics' imaginative representation of "successive states"[44] of gender and sexuality variety, I put forward a method of interpretation I call *queer formalism.*[45]

Queer Formalism, or the Art of Shapeshifting

Throughout this book I bring the traditional aesthetic concept of *form* to bear on the cultural history of queer and feminist freedom in the 1970s.[46] I define form as the coalescence of an apprehensible material shape, including the molding or crafting of its substance, and the imaginative reconstruction of that shape in the mind's eye. This involves the mental process of forming a picture of something in one's consciousness and imbuing it with conceptual and affective meaning. Aesthetic or cultural forms comprise the entire range of attempts to represent, reproduce, or render the world's existing material shapes in creative expression, through various artistic media and materials. For example, a metaphor is one of the most crystalline expressions of an aesthetic form because it is a literary device that links a recognizable shape, such as a traditional geometric circle, to a concept, like a feminist consciousness-raising session, which placed women into circular discussion groups to pool their experiences of sexism. A *queer* form is any material shape, construct, or pattern that is articulated to, or comes to be inhabited by, some aspect of gender and sexual nonconformity or divergence. This can include the physical structure of a glass dome encircling a utopian collective, which could be imaginatively interpreted as an architectural model for a lesbian separatist commune, or a drawing of a pleasurable gay male sex act rendered within the frame of a traditional square comic strip panel.

Queer cultural forms do not reveal an underlying truth about gender and sexuality or "accurately" represent any individual's precise experience of these categories. They neither uncover the path to total gender and sexual liberation, nor create transparent objects of knowledge that can be used to universally represent particular types or groups of gender and sexual outlaws. Rather, queer forms relentlessly display different *aspects* of gender and sexual existence, thereby making them available to our perception and soliciting collective attempts to produce interpretations of gender and sexuality's manifold dimensions. Although aesthetic forms give provisional order or structure to identities, experiences, bodies, or affects, their primary purpose is not to delimit or restrict the phenomena they represent but provide an adaptable container for meaning-making.[47] Forms establish the conditions for something new to appear in the world, including previously unfathomable expressions and interpretations of gender and sexual being, while cultivating mutual understanding about these categories' extraordinary heterogeneity.

"Form" is an apt term for talking about the political and cultural work of 1970s women's and gay liberation. Feminist and queer activists and scholars from this period regularly described both movements as facilitating the evolution of new "forms" of political association, interpersonal bonds, or consciousness that realized women and queers' shared dreams of a changed world. In his 1971 study of the early days of gay liberation, historian Dennis Altman identified gay communes as a "new form of extended family" that offered a social solution to gays and lesbians' experience of familial homophobia. And in her vivid account of coming into feminist consciousness, Vivian Gornick suggested that feminism is "a profoundly new way of interpreting human experience . . . a new form into which one pours all knowledge, thereby revitalizing and setting into motion anew the sources of psychic energy responsible for growth and change and altered behavior."[48]

The mutually constitutive relationship between feminist and queer social or political forms and aesthetic ones is beautifully captured in a statement made by lesbian musician Jean Fineberg at the inaugural Michigan Womyn's Music Festival in 1976, the first women-only cultural event of its kind: "Imagine a city where women rule. Where all the roads, all the buildings, the plumbing, the hospitals, the restaurants, the stores are run by women. Imagine a city where all the arts . . . are created by women. Imagine a city of thousands of women, where there is no violence . . . no oppression and no fear. This city has existed in only one place in . . . history. We are in that city now. Welcome to Michigan!"[49] While the festival took place within a man-made structure in the style of a rural "village" that people visited and traversed, this was merely the singular material expression of a far more expansive imaginary utopian form, or projected construct, of a feminist cityscape that would embrace, nurture, and value women of all stripes. Though the event later became infamous for its trans-exclusionary policy of admitting only cis women, its original basis in the idea of a fantasized urban ideal encouraged people to contemplate what their own version of such a welcoming feminist and queer metropolis might look like. Thus, the bombastic claim that "this city has existed in only one place in . . . history" was technically true for every person who followed the injunction to "imagine a city," each conceiving a unique feminist paradise of their dreams that had never existed before and could never be replicated exactly again. With this in mind, I submit that the appropriate method for apprehending this synthesis of material forms with feminist and queer lifeways and aspirational ideals is a rigorous *queer formalism*.

I theorize the concept of queer formalism as a dual term that describes, on the one hand, the range of tactics, strategies, and techniques that creative producers deploy to materialize or represent gender and sexual nonnormativity in distinct aesthetic materials and genres; and, on the other, a method of interpretation that treats forms as enabling structures or shapes that powerfully articulate queer genders and sexualities, rather than disciplining or "straightening" them. In *Abstract Bodies*, art historian David Getsy innovates the concept of "transgender capacity" as "the ability or the potential for making visible, bringing into experience, or knowing genders as mutable, successive, and multiple." He continues, "It can be located or discerned in texts, objects, [and] cultural forms . . . that support an interpretation or recognition of proliferative modes of gender nonconformity."[50] By conceiving gender transitivity not only as an identity or lived experience, but as a formal capacity of artistic production, Getsy opens up the possibility of seeing queer genders and sexualities as present in everything from artistic mediums to storytelling conventions to specific art practices. Queer formalism is a method that perceives those instances when queer genders and sexualities, far from being repressed or negated, are actualized in legible but nuanced ways across media and to unanticipated audiences.

Building on previous definitions offered by Getsy and Jennifer Doyle, I characterize a queer formalist as someone who: (a) attends to the overlooked and unexpected presence of alternative sexualities, genders, desires, and intimacies in the material and conceptual forms of cultural objects; (b) explores the "improper" or unorthodox uses of artistic materials and formal techniques to disrupt traditionally received meanings of normative gender and sexuality; (c) shifts the weight of their analysis from understanding how texts represent existing gender and sexual identities toward how they proliferate "figures of the newly thinkable," which provide new ways of apprehending or deploying categories like "woman" or "queer"; (d) develops cultural analyses that can hold together concepts of mutability and change alongside the presence of concrete material shapes or aesthetic constructs; and (e) unpacks how feminist and queer forms are imbued with and transmit diverse feeling states that expand the emotional repertoire of gender and sexual dissidence. Queer formalism is a felicitous term for capturing this range of methodological priorities because, as William J. Simmons argues, it productively weds seemingly incommensurate concepts, including the wildness or rebelliousness of "queer," with the structured logic of "form," without implying that the latter is a disciplining, constraining, or stifling force. Queer formalism, then, intentionally undermines a reigning common sense that has emerged at the nexus of queer theory and some feminist, queer, and trans* social justice discourse, which assumes that the queer critique of LGBTQ identity politics is an argument for understanding all categories of gender and sexuality in formless or fluid terms.

Since its inception in the early 1990s, queer theory has built its self-definition around an intellectual and political resistance to the perceived prohibitive frameworks of identity politics and gender and sexual normativity.[51] Mesli documents how, in queer theory's nascent years, the field opposed itself to the so-called identity politics of 1970s women's and gay liberation, which queer scholars often mischaracterized as uniformly essentialist endeavors to cohere universally shared definitions of gender and sexual identity categories like "woman" and "gay and lesbian." Against this presumed consolidation, the anti-identitarian tradition in queer theory developed an understanding of "queerness" as an unbounded affective force or worldly orientation associated with all types of gender and sexual nonconformity, which can circulate throughout the social field and attach to persons of any sexual orientation or gender expression. Here, queerness is neither an innate characteristic one possesses, nor an identity grounded in sexual orientation or same-sex desire (though it may encompass, or be inspired by, both), but rather a diverse array of practices motivated by perpetual rebellion against heterosexual norms.[52] Accordingly, by the mid- to late 1990s, the field increasingly became concerned with outlining, deconstructing, and strategically combatting the vast ideological structure of *heteronormativity*, understood as the entire network of social and cultural regulations that maintain a heterosexual, reproductive, family-oriented life trajectory as the standard of societal value and belonging.

Across queer theory's intellectual development, then, the field has recurrently located itself on the presumably more politically radical side of a series of mutually reinforcing polarities: in one, queer theory appears as a champion of fluid or boundless conceptions of self against the false unity of essential identities. In the other, queer is that which resists the "stability and immobility" of norms against the lockstep adherence to them. Robyn Wiegman and Elizabeth A. Wilson have argued that by rendering identities and norms as universally "restricting," queer studies unwittingly transforms these categories into the very monolithic unities the field purports to dismantle; this leeches identities and norms of their capacity to function as flexible vehicles for articulating manifold expressions of self or putting forward alternative standards of inclusive, ethical social belonging. Similarly, as Mesli brilliantly exposes, queer studies' summary dismissal of women's and gay liberation as politically myopic, essentialist, putatively white social movements, disavowed the origin and meaning of identity politics as a distinctly Black lesbian feminist analytic; this was a project aimed at accounting for women's multiple, interlocking, identities and proliferating divergent political standpoints *within* feminist theorizing.[53] The field additionally downplayed the integral role radical feminism played in helping to shape gay liberation's, and later queer politics', impassioned critique and rejection of traditional gender and sexual roles and social hierarchies. (This was no better captured than in the fact that the queer studies concept of "heteronormativity" largely replicated 1970s feminists' sweeping analysis of, and revolt against, what they called the system of "heteropatriarchy," despite queer theorists having banished their feminist forebears to political oblivion).

Any cursory look at queer studies' scholarly landscape reveals that the field's dual oppositional stances against static or fixed identities and regulatory norms have also tacitly been applied to the entire realm of cultural production. In a range of queer theorizing from the mid-1990s onward, aesthetic form's shaping quality, its ability to concretize various iterations of gender and sexuality in cultural or artistic expression, came to be seen as analogous to, even a direct extension of, the delimiting or regulatory aspects of fixed identities and prescribed norms. This was evidenced first in the queer theory's aggressive ideological criticism of the relentless homophobia of popular culture and mass media (what Eve Sedgwick famously identified as a field-wide attachment to a "paranoid" style of interpretation, which was obsessed with exposing everything from the novel form's narrative surveillance and policing of sexual deviancy to the heterosexist logics of sentimental literary and film genres like melodrama and romance). Second, in the proliferation of queer theories that denounced the perceived heteronormativity of all teleological structures like temporal rhythms and narrative or conceptual sequences, and procreative figures like the child, which came to be associated with restrictively linear patterns of historical order and reproductive futurity. And third, in the increasing turn away from the study of feminist and queer popular culture toward a near-universal embrace of avant-garde, or experimental media and performance art whose temporariness, ephemerality, and "difficulty" appeared to eschew the assumed constraints of aesthetic form. These more amorphous, evanescent, or formless artistic expressions were seen to disclose the truth of queerness's inherently rebellious spirit against rigidity or fixity in all registers of human experience.

Perhaps no text has come to represent this last approach more than Muñoz's *Cruising Utopia*, which offered an inspired understanding of queerness as a "forward dawning-futurity" that is "in many crucial ways formless," and hence can be registered only as an affectively powerful but ephemeral longing for an anti-homophobic world that nurtures queer existence.[54] As a graduate student years ago, and still today, I found this theorizing extraordinarily empowering because it allowed me to see queerness as a radical potential inherent to all bodies and cultural objects, not simply limited to self-identified gays or lesbians but a potent energy bursting forth from any social, aesthetic, and political practice that breaks the stranglehold of heteronormativity (what Muñoz calls the "prison house" of the present).[55] Yet in researching *Queer Forms*, I have become increasingly dissatisfied with the tendency of this body of queer scholarship to inadvertently underwrite popular discourses of gender and sexual fluidity. Many of my students frequently cite queer theorizing on the performative, affective, or intangible qualities of queer being to argue for the inherent political value of gender and sexuality as infinitely variable substances that exceed all categorization. Ironically, even as these wonderfully curious, queerly oriented young thinkers claim to possess and champion fluid gender and sexual subjectivities, their analyses of culture are often exceptionally inflexible and single-minded; this is epitomized by an almost fetishistic attachment to the idea that every work of art, literature, or popular media can and should offer "authentic," accurate, and inclusive depictions of marginalized identities. Such a stance invariably leads to a recurrent assessment of culture as a repository of stubbornly racist, sexist, homophobic, and transphobic representations, good for morally denouncing, but not for picturing a different world altogether.

What has emerged, then, is a popular *interpretation* of contemporary queer cultural critique that overemphasizes the field's "formless" descriptions of queer (affect, desire, intimacy, sociality, you name it), while conveniently forgetting theorists' long history of imaginative engagement with the material and formal properties of an enormous range of artistic productions. Muñoz's own argument is contradictory on this score, for he foregrounds queerness as a formless "utopian horizon," but always locates it "in the realm of the aesthetic," that very wellspring of cultural forms. Muñoz thus never escapes the power of art and culture to transmit queer affects, values, and ways of life through the formal tools unique to distinct media—and neither do any of the scholars in this tradition, all of whom root their arguments in close readings of LGBTQ and feminist art, literature, film, and music. If queerness is, as Sara Ahmed claims, "about inhabiting the world at the point in which things fleet," this immaterial energy leaves us little to hold on to when it comes to our practical, messy, everyday attempts to shape and do something with our evolving sexualities and genders.[56] This is perhaps why, today, feminist, queer, and trans* social justice "warriors" often passionately declare their commitment to dismantling the gender binary and paving the way for the legitimacy of sexually fluid selves, while also paradoxically clinging fast to the politics of recognition and identity, attempting to counterbalance the increasing destabilization of all gender and sexual categories with a forceful show of self-definition.

Lest I be misunderstood, my critique of "fluidity" is not meant as an attack on queer and gender-nonconforming claims to self-determination or self-nomination, nor as a judgment against categories like non-binary or trans*, which I deeply respect and value as part of the larger endeavor to honor the diversity of contemporary gender and sexual existence. Rather, I question how a legitimate and urgent desire for more flexible, open-ended, and humane ways of describing gender and sexual heterogeneity and change has become hitched to a liquid metaphor that overstates the ease of personal and collective transformation, while also oddly metamorphosing into its own kind of rigid identitarianism. Inevitably, in the name of critiquing totalizing categories or norms of gender and sexuality, the concept of fluidity institutes formlessness itself as a new universal, reproducing what feminist Jo Freeman once provocatively called "the tyranny of structurelessness" to describe the celebrated, but frequently turbulent, nonhierarchical model of 1970s feminist organizing.[57] Thus, in practice, queer cultural criticism's oppositional

binaries of fluid selfhood/essentialism, queerness/normativity, formless-
ness/fixity become mutually constitutive and reinforcing logics that recurrently produce the very constraints they claim to rally against.

In *Queer Forms*, I seek to subvert a dominant style of queer cultural
politics that has emerged at the intersection of contemporary queer
theory and activism, which relies on a foundational commitment to notions of formlessness (or fluid, infinitely labile, identities, norms, and
aesthetics) and whose primary affective stance is a moralizing dismissal
of all material and cultural forms as categorical "prison houses." Cultural
forms have no truck with the foundational oppositions of queer studies. Forms are neither infinitely boundless (because they take concrete
shapes) nor impenetrably bounded (because they allow for expansive
meaning-making). They are neither innately queer (because they require
creative articulation to different expressions of gender and sexual nonconformity) nor are they inherently normative or regulatory (because
they can be imaginatively appropriated and inhabited by anybody). And
because every form is always particular in its specific material shape, its
arrival to new contexts, and its interpretation by each individual reader
or viewer, it can never posit a singular or essential identity *or* confirm
the fluidity of all identities. Aesthetic forms merely offer adaptable
molds, figures, or icons for various expressions of human heterogeneity
to become apparent to our perception and consequential to how we understand the world. The potential radicalness of forms, or their ability to
affect transformative political change, lies not in any quality of fluidity,
but in the exceptionally diverse ways people choose to deploy, interpret,
or circulate them. This open-ended play of formal possibility may seem
like its own kind of fluidity, but this is better understood as a spirit of
flexibility or attunement to variation and change, rather than a commandment to reject all presumably prohibitive shapes and structures by
inhabiting liquid states of being.

Nineteen-seventies movements for women's and gay liberation were
rightly convinced that queerness is in fact here, all around us, and that
it can take countless shapes. For their participants, the present was not
only a prison house but also a creative playground for positing, inhabiting, and setting loose feminist and queer forms in the service of altering the given "system of representation." Against the ideal of fluid,
boundless queer being or its mirror image in a paradoxical type of queer

identitarianism, queer formalism encourages us to inhabit a model of *shapeshifting*. This can be understood both as an affective openness to the measured and meaningful evolution of gender and sexual identities over time, as well as a description of the ways that queer cultural forms disclose new dimensions of themselves as they collide with and are reconstituted in different people's imaginations.[58] Consequently, the method of queer formalism and its preferred orientation of shapeshifting can dramatically shift the ways we understand, study, and interpret feminist and queer cultural representations.

We tend to think of cultural representations as imagined versions of actual people and objects that are reproduced in various media. Queer formalism, however, expands the field of representation to include all attempts to formally capture ideas, fantasies, or felt experiences of gender and sexual divergence. This view encourages us to reorient our interpretations of feminist and queer cultural representations away from their potential ideological meanings, or their perceived authenticity in reflecting the actual lived experiences of sexual minorities, toward their creative capacity to proliferate "new versions of gender, new bodily morphologies [and] the shifting and successive potentials of these categories."[59] In *Transgender Architectonics*, Lucas Crawford critiques the dominant transgender metaphor of the body as a kind of "home" for one's gender expression, arguing that this spatial figure potentially negates the conceptual power of "transing" to point out the constructed nature of all genders, including those of cis men and women.[60] Rather than a proper "home" for our genders or sexualities, Crawford suggests that the body might better be understood as a "short-term lease": "We could see transgender as a more sensible pairing with transient; . . . reread as the *ability* to change."[61] Extending this metaphor to the realm of artistic production, if we see cultural representations of women, queers, and gender outlaws as shapeshifters, we release the need for any single representation to carry the weight of all our political fantasies. Queer forms can then become short-term leases, creative shapes we inhabit variably across time.

This perspective resonates with Gloria Anzaldúa's prescient description of the *mestiza*, or mixed-race Chicana, as someone who "reinterprets history and, using new symbols . . . shapes new myths. She adopts new perspectives toward the darkskinned, women and queers. . . . She surrenders all notions of safety, of the familiar. . . . She becomes a *nabual*, able to transform herself into a tree, a coyote, into another person. . . . A constant changing of forms."[62] As a figure who inhabits "the borderlands," the liminal spaces between many identities, languages, and cultural traditions, the mestiza learns to live productively in those spaces, not becoming fluid but by developing skills at shapeshifting in response to specific cultural contexts.[63] The forms the mestiza takes do not provide a "safe" or "familiar" home for her identity, but rather are temporary or transitional tools to put forward multiple versions of herself across space and time. This was one way that 1970s feminist and gay liberationists conceived of culture, as a fantastical terrain for positing new forms for women and queers to inhabit, but always provisionally, as they pursued an extended journey of self-discovery that required many conceptual strategies, techniques, and models to articulate an evolving self.

In her canonical 1985 essay "Poetry Is Not a Luxury," Black feminist Audre Lorde captured this shapeshifting sensibility of representations when she described the cultural form of "poetry" as a space where we can "train ourselves to respect our feelings and to transpose them into a language so they can be shared."[64] Writing about the necessary role of poetry in facilitating intersectional projects for feminist and queer freedom, she stated, "where that language does not yet exist, it is our poetry which helps to fashion it. . . . [Poetry] is the skeleton architecture of our lives. . . . There are no new ideas waiting in the wings to save us as women, as human. There are only old and forgotten ones, new combinations . . . along with a renewed courage to try them."[65] Lorde suggests that cultural forms like poetry—which encourage the inventive "combination" of and "extrapolation" from existing words, images, and ideas—can provide a linguistic "architecture" that gives shape to our most potent experiences of difference. As an aesthetic expression of highly individual, and subjective "feelings," "dreams," and "visions," poetry allows us to make our singular felt experiences (say of being a Black, disabled, lesbian feminist) public and "shared."[66] For Lorde, cultural representations are not a mirror into which we look to be reflected and recognized. Rather, they are a medium for the transmission of another person's lifeworld so that we might recognize *someone else's* rich complexity, and hence "bridge" emotional and political distances that "fear of the other" has produced between all of us who nonetheless share a common world.

Similarly, Gayle Rubin's discussion of the possibilities and limits of gender and sexual identity categories offers a compelling analogy for an understanding of representations as flawed, yet necessary tools for actualizing diverse expressions of gender and sexuality nonconformity:

> Our categories are important. We cannot organize a social life, a political movement, or our individual identities and desires without them. The fact that categories invariably leak and can never contain all the relevant "existing things" does not render them useless, only limited. Categories like "woman," "butch," "lesbian," or "transsexual" are all imperfect, historical, temporary, and arbitrary. . . . We use them to construct meaningful lives, and they mold us into historically specific forms of personhood. Instead of fighting for immaculate classifications and impenetrable boundaries, let us strive to maintain a community that understands diversity as a gift, sees anomalies as precious, and treats all basic principles with a hefty dose of skepticism.[67]

We can substitute the word "forms" for the term "categories" in the paragraph above, and Rubin's statement would still hold true. Rubin's claim that identity categories "mold us into historically specific forms of personhood," is telling, because it also invokes the shaping quality of cultural forms, the dual fact that they are sculpted by artists while also providing us concrete shapes to inhabit, test out, and interpret. When we understand queer forms as "temporary," "imperfect" outlines that nonetheless meaningfully materialize various feminist and queer ideas, experiences, and feeling states, we can also acknowledge and honor the fact that they are never permanently fixed: this is both because different viewers will interpret a given form or representation in unforeseen ways, and because every one of those constructs will inevitably be complicated, discarded, reinvented, or simply joined by yet another.

Consequently, as Ellen Rooney argues, the true power of form lies not in any given shape it produces, or any property inherent to a given material, but in the complex process of reading or interpretation, when someone creatively translates a work of art for themselves in their mind. She explains, "as the enabling condition and the product of reading, form is neither the external and superficial mold into which content is poured not the inner truth of the text, expressed in its organic shape. . . . Reading is thus corrosive of the facile opposition between form and content, because it must reinvent their relation in every new context."[68] Seen in this light, the need for cultural representations to provide an "external mold" that impeccably replicates a fixed set of progressive political ideals or identities is an abdication of the ethical imperative of reading, because it allows our predetermined categories, political concepts, or analytical frameworks to define the meaning of a text in advance, rather than forming our own original understanding of it. When we give over the task of interpretation, we lose the radically unsettling potential of a text's numerous forms, including the capacity of its characters, symbols, juxtapositions, and techniques to introduce astonishing or startling shapes into our mind that have the potential to "[set] into motion anew the sources of psychic energy responsible for growth and change." In a breathtaking turn of phrase, Rooney reminds us: "When the text bites back, it rewrites [our] assumptions and commitments. . . . Form is its sharpened tooth."[69]

With this insight, we can confirm that the specifically political quality of any given queer or feminist form lies not in its ability to reflect an existing theory, ideology, or analytical concept (say of sexual fluidity, intersectionality, or the performativity of gender), but rather in its incitement to imagine, publicize, and make meaning out of countless expressions of gender and sexuality. When these forms enter people's consciousness, they "bite back" against the many assumptions a reader might have about gender, sexuality, race, embodiment, desire, intimacy, whatever—not only the most pernicious and conservative conceptions of these categories, but also the most tightly held progressive fantasies that attach to them. In one of the most potent and influential acts of reading in feminist history, literary theorist Barbara Smith would interpret the Black female friendship at the center of Toni Morrison's acclaimed 1973 novel *Sula* as a lesbian bond, despite the fact that no same-sex eroticism takes place between the characters.[70] Smith argued that among other things, a distinctly "Black feminist criticism" would be attentive to the presence of lesbian attachments between Black women in US literature, which included both explicit same-sex desire *as well as* any expression of formal rebellion against the normative structures of straight, white, male writing. Smith's essay certainly spoke on behalf of a particular identity group—Black lesbians—by calling out their egregious underrepresentation in literary criticism. But it also conceived of the category of "Black lesbian" as far more than an identity, as a reading practice that "bites back" against feminist literary theory's tendency to pore over the vast terrain of the Western literature only to find evidence of white women's presence. In this sense, Smith called out, and offered an alternative to, a widespread failure of interpretive imagination among literary scholars who refused to "understand diversity as a gift" by bringing a shockingly limited perspective to the study of an inherently diverse US literary tradition. Black feminist criticism was one outcome of 1970s gay cultural politics, not only an analytical tool used by self-identified Black lesbians, but a widely accessible interpretative practice that is rigorously attentive to formal elaboration of gender, sexual, and racial heterogeneity.

In the cultural criticism of Anzaldúa, Lorde, Rubin, and Smith, we can identify a queer formalist impulse that runs through a variety of Chicana/Black/lesbian/feminist theory, which treats both representations and identities as shapeshifting forms rather than immutable categories, universal ideals, or restrictive norms. Moreover, all four were direct participants in the movements for women's and gay liberation, producing their theories out of their lived experiences of coalitional struggles for gender and sexual freedom. Ultimately, the method of queer formalism and the model of shapeshifting that it values celebrates the capacity for representations to multiply, in shape and meaning, just as the movements for women's and gay liberation championed the collective effort of bringing into perception manifold genders and sexualities. When feminist and queer forms proliferate, they begin to approximate the utopian horizon that Muñoz so movingly described by gesturing toward the actual diversity of human gender and sexual expression, which is inexhaustible and boundless, but without collapsing it into undifferentiated formlessness. I offer shapeshifting, then, not only as an intellectually generative affective orientation for studying queer and feminist cultural forms, but as a necessary metaphor for the flourishing of contemporary feminist and queer life, one that provides more heft than queer theory's enchanting but fleeting utopian impulses, unruly assemblages, and ephemeral affects. My wager is that fantasies of fluidity do not serve queer and gender-nonconforming people—at least not nearly as much as we might imagine—because we ultimately still inhabit material bodies and use cultural forms to articulate who we are, what we desire, and what we aspire to become to ourselves and the world. We would do well not to forget Judith Butler's bracing insight that it is precisely the reality of feeling formless, illegible, or unrecognizable that often makes queer and gender divergent existence "unlivable," sometimes fatally so.[71] I would add that while the concept of fluidity often appears as a transparently progressive view of gender and sexuality, it ironically often does not adequately prepare us to cope with the existential reality of contingency and change. And why would it? We are, after all, not yet ether and light.

As Hesford has compellingly shown, our own contemporary attempts to fix the meaning of 1970s women's and gay liberation—which often involves judging them against a present-day ideal of intersectional, fluid, universally inclusive, and social justice–oriented values—has led us to see both as conceptually dead social movements whose radical promise is long past. This too is a failure of imagination. It signals that we have relinquished the responsibility of productively reencountering and interpreting the queer and feminist past, which robs us of the potential to draw rich political and creative resources from our collective history. Yet feminist and queer forms of the 1970s made public concrete alternative expressions of gender and sexuality to US-Americans, not simply to represent women and gays and lesbians or to ideologically "teach" audiences feminist and queer political values, but to provide tools for receiving and responding to genuine human plurality. This is an imaginative capacity necessary for engagement in democratic life. In seeking to highlight and recuperate this radical tradition, the method of queer formalism I offer revivifies one of the oldest projects of feminist and gay cultural politics, the call for greater social, political, and cultural *visibility* of women and queers. But it stresses the importance of cultivating the capacity to register, apprehend, and make meaning of queer genders and sexualities rather than merely counting representations of individual women or gays and lesbians. It is this shift in frame that allows us to see women's and gay liberation as constituting a shared cultural project aimed at enacting what the political theorist Hannah Arendt called "the space of appearance," which describes the ability to make public issues of collective concern that might galvanize the formation of previously unimaginable political associations.[72] In the following chapters, I track the cultural travels of feminist and queer political ideas, strategies, and values whose conceptual force was magnetized to dynamic, playful, strange, and surprising aesthetic forms that transmitted the spirit of queer and feminist freedom to a heterogeneous wider world, in the hopes of forever changing it.

In chapter 1, I explore how 1970s feminist, speculative fiction writers allegorically linked the concept of women's equality to the figure of the female replicant, an android, clone, or ghostly avatar who takes the shape of a woman's body. I analyze how three different literary texts—Levin's *The Stepford Wives* (1972), Russ's *The Female Man* (1975), and Kingston's *The Woman Warrior* (1975)—presented the female replicant as an imperfect or failed duplicate of an "original" woman, who subsequently becomes this original's sustained interlocutor. These writers posited the replicant as an imaginative form whose jarring eruption into narrative space unexpectedly multiplies differences between women, requiring them to fairly compare their perspectives and experiences to discover a common ground. I show how the female replicant functioned as a feminist and queer form that similarly multiplied the meaning of equality itself by recasting it as a project of developing substantial responses to women's heterogeneity, rather than seeking parity or sameness with men.

In chapter 2, I study the avant-garde science fiction films *Zardoz* (1974) and *Born in Flames* (1983). I unpack how they formally depicted the concept of lesbian separatism in the material structure of a walled-off utopian commune or underground cell, where gender and sexual outlaws create their own societies separate from the dominant culture. In both films, the visibly stable architectural form of a bounded separatist enclave is repeatedly revealed to house fierce internal conflict and disagreement between feminists, which productively undermines the lesbian separatist demand for political uniformity among women. Studying *Zardoz* and *Born in Flames* together allows us to see how a similar formal logic of separation and containment of women's political energies runs through a range of feminist projects traditionally seen as opposed, such as lesbian separatism and women-of-color feminisms.

Chapter 3 explores the geometric shape of the circle as a blueprint for the feminist political concept of consciousness-raising (CR). This was a widely adopted activist strategy of organizing women into discussion circles to publicly share and analyze their lived experiences of sexism. I turn to the 1970 gay film drama *The Boys in the Band* to show how the film visually re-creates the experience of a feminist CR session by depicting the explosive confrontation over internalized homophobia between the members of a gay male friendship circle. Throughout *The Boys*, the men sit in a ring while the camera continually rotates between them, encouraging the viewer to inhabit multiple, competing perspectives on the same topic: societal homophobia and its impact on gay male interpersonal love and intimacy. In so doing, the film displayed how the feminist model of CR could be adapted into an everyday practice among a variety of sexual and gender outlaws, including gay men of different racial, class, and generational backgrounds.

Chapters 4 and 5, respectively, explore gay liberation's discourses of coming out of the closet and sexual pluralism as they were represented in the serialized forms of installment fiction and comic strips. In chapter 4, I study the content and reading experience of Armistead Maupin's gay serial fiction *Tales of the City*, which was published in daily installments in the *San Francisco Chronicle* between 1976 and 1977. Drawing on interviews I conducted with original readers alongside close readings of the text as it appeared in the newspaper, I argue that the serialized rhythm of the narrative structurally modeled gay liberation's understanding of "coming out" as a process that takes place over time through repeated public declarations of one's sexual identity alongside personal types of self-fashioning. In chapter 5, I analyze the sequential art of Joe Brainard and David Wojnarowicz, two queer artists who took up the comic strip medium to depict the ways that gay liberation and AIDS activism celebrated sexual pluralism, the value of polymorphous libidinal desires and intimacies. I show how each artist creatively manipulated comic strip form—which relies on serially unfolding visual panels—to render gay sexuality as a ceaselessly unfolding series of erotic possibilities, fantasies, or encounters that cannot be reduced to a single expression or panel. In each of these chapters, serial cultural forms illuminate the broader feminist and queer political project of redefining genders and sexualities as successive states of being that develop through repeated social and sexual encounters across time and space, rather than singular, fixed, or essentially shared identities.

Finally, advancing into the 1980s and early 1990s, chapter 6 explores the metaphorical uses of digestive dysfunction to elicit feelings of disgust with conservative responses to the AIDS crisis. I discuss Tony Kushner's acclaimed drama *Angels in America* (1990–1992) to understand how the play figuratively aligns painful physiological forms of the gut, like stomach ulcers, hemorrhoids, and inflamed bowels, with vile conservative values, thereby creating a formal equivalence between obstructionist, right-wing politics and constipated bowel movements. In so doing, *Angels* worked to reroute public revulsion for the bodies of people with AIDS toward a proper political disgust with government inaction and national homophobia in response to the epidemic. This chapter documents the synthesis of feminist and gay liberationist values in the 1970s into the radical queer politics of the 1980s and early 1990s by exploring how *Angels* links the mutually felt "gut feelings" of gay men and women as a shared intuition that guides their rebellious refusal of the racist, homophobic, and sexist logics of Reaganism.

In his 2019 Emmy award speech, Black queer actor Billy Porter said to his peers: "We as artists are the people who get to change the molecular structure of the hearts and minds of the people who live on this Earth." Porter's metaphor captures how culture can materially and symbolically reshape the way human beings apprehend and sense the world. After all, cultural forms infiltrate our psyches, catalyzing our neural synapses to fire in unanticipated ways as we engage the task of cognitively receiving, interpreting, and responding to new stimuli, including novel ideas that spark our imagination about what we might be or become. Nearly a half-century ago, artists, writers, and filmmakers committed to the values of women's and gay liberation invented queer and feminist forms that translated and experimented with complex political concepts for gender and sexual freedom, projecting them into new contexts and sometimes wholly reinventing them. Because of these forms' materiality, their ability to be rendered both aesthetically and in the mind's eye, they became objects of common concern, collating a shared vocabulary of recognizable yet diverse shapes for sexual outlaws and their potential allies to articulate their varied aspirations for a different world. These were the kinds of cultural experiments that "change the molecular structure of hearts and minds." At its most ambitious, then, this book argues that *taking shape*, rather than becoming fluid, might aid and abet a non-market-driven form of freedom. This is the freedom to become something else in concert with others. If we dissolve into pure fluidity, we are more amenable to being molded by terms external to ourselves. If we seek recognition for a fixed identity at every turn, we lose the psychological capacity to conceive of and enact change by clinging fast to the categories that make us feel most at home. But if we shapeshift, we can grant one another the opportunity to appear and be perceived as an evolving form, not only to claim our visibility, but to be better understood in all our dimensions. *Queer Forms* tracks how movements for gender and sexual freedom think by recuperating their wild imaginations and the many shapes they take.

1

Stepford Wives and Female Men

The Radical Equality of Female Replicants

Human plurality . . . has the twofold character of equality
and distinction. If men were not equal, they could neither
understand each other and those who came before them nor
plan for the future and foresee the needs of those who will
come after them. If men were not distinct, each human being distinguished from any other who is, was, or will ever
be, they would need neither speech nor action to make
themselves understood.
—Hannah Arendt, *The Human Condition* (1958)

I've dreamed of looking into a mirror and seeing my alter
ego which, on its own initiative, begins to tell me unbearable
truths.
—Joanna Russ, *The Female Man* (1975)

Joanna Russ's 1975 feminist science fiction novel *The Female Man* tells
the story of three women from alternate Earths—Janet, Jeannine, and
Joanna—who find themselves transported into each other's realities.
Janet is an interdimensional ambassador from Whileaway, an ecologi-
cal utopia where men have been extinct for a thousand years. Jeannine
is a librarian in New York City circa 1969, in a world where the Great
Depression never ended. Joanna is a writer and academic living in our
version of US-America around 1970, just at the crest of women's liberation. Appearing and reappearing in the contexts of one another's daily
lives, the three women bring dramatically different moods, outlooks,
experiences, and desires to their spontaneous encounters across time
and space, with hilarious and terrifying results. In the book's penultimate chapter, the time travelers are teleported to an unfamiliar world

where they are greeted by Jael, a cybernetically enhanced assassin. She explains: "I suppose you are wondering . . . why I have brought you here. . . . It came to me several months ago that I might find my other selves out there in the great, gray might-have-been, so I undertook—for reasons partly personal and partly political . . . to get hold of the three of you."[1] In the first of the book's two great revelations, our heroines discover that they are all versions of the same woman from alternate dimensions. Using advanced technology, Jael has brought them together to help solve an intractable war between men and women that has raged for half a century on her planet. Like her real-life forebears, the feminists who struggled for women's equality in the 1960s and 1970s, Jeal's first ingenious act is to inaugurate a conversation with herself that might grant new insight about the nature of, and solution to, gendered conflict. Jael is the warrior spirit of second-wave feminism, an imagined figure that gives shape to women's rage at their subordinate status by mobilizing women across worlds into a unified front against patriarchy.

Yet, as any second-wave feminist disappointed by the failure of universal sisterhood can attest, that mobilization is trickier business than anyone might imagine. Once Jael draws her (my)selves together she discovers not sameness or unity but infinite "degrees of difference": "We ought to be equally long-lived but we won't be. We ought to be equally healthy but we're not. . . . We ought to think alike and feel alike and act alike, but of course we don't. . . . Between our dress, and our opinions, and our habits . . . and our values . . . and our experiences, even I can hardly believe that I am looking at three other myselves."[2] The four Js are theoretically equal, Jael tells us—in their existence and shared "genetic pattern"—but not for that reason the same. In Jael's assorted list of distinctions, she articulates a central paradox of late twentieth-century feminist thought and activism: that feminism's most radical political act was the demand for women's universal equality, while its greatest discovery was the fact of women's ceaseless differences, from men, one another, even their own selves. To become a feminist around 1970 was to potentially question every taken-for-granted idea that had shaped one's common understanding and felt sense of gender, and consequently, one's place in the world. In decolonizing one's mind of the singular image of "woman" handed down by patriarchy, the gendered subject would shatter outward into a multiplicity of other identities one might already be or could become. In this process a feminist wouldn't even recognize herself in the mirror: she would see only proliferating "myselves" who might "begin to tell [her] unbearable truths."[3]

Jael and her multidimensional others were one version of the many female replicants that came to populate the stories of 1970s feminist speculative literatures, which included a range of imaginative storytelling modes from traditional science fiction and fantasy to magical-realist life writing. In this period, writers of both popular and experimental speculative narratives—from bestselling horror thrillers like Ira Levin's *The Stepford Wives* (1972) to feminist utopias like Russ's *The Female Man* (1975), from fantasy memoirs like Maxine Hong Kingston's *The Woman Warrior* (1975) to "biomythographies" like Audre Lorde's *Zami: A New Spelling of My Name* (1982)—began to represent female protagonists encountering unsettling alter egos, which turn out to be different beings altogether. In its contemporary definition, the replicant is an android or artificial human, often modeled after an existing person. In feminist speculative writing of the 1970s, the replicant expands into a multitude of figures that represent imperfect duplication, among them lifelike robots, clones, ghosts, and superhuman avatars. If in theory the female replicant is intended to be a perfect simulacrum of a woman, hence the same as her, in practice she is literally another person, someone wholly distinct.

Black feminist poet and theorist Audre Lorde articulates this paradox in *Zami* (1982), when she describes the electrifying but disorienting experience of queer women of color meeting for the first time in 1950s New York City. Despite sharing numerous identities, the Black lesbians Lorde encounters discover far more differences among themselves than similarities: "*Being women together was not enough. We were different. Being gay-girls together was not enough. We were different. Being Black together was not enough. We were different. Being Black women together was not enough. We were different. Being Black dykes together was not enough. We were different. . . .* It was a while before we came to realize that our place was the very house of difference."[4] In her poetic repetition of the refrain "*We were different*," Lorde underscores how she and her new companions realized again and again in each encounter that the only shared reality binding women together as a collective "we" is their inherent variety. For Lorde, the imagined sameness of a replicant—in this instance a Black dyke's mental image of another woman *just like her*, an equal friend, lover, or peer based on shared identity—is always undone by the reality that another queer Black woman has her "own needs and pursuits," her own understanding of what these various identities mean.[5]

The heterogeneity of versions of "replication" across speculative texts and modes in the 1970s required similarly diverse women protagonists to negotiate their relationships to figures both like and unlike them. In these narratives, equality becomes a contingent category, whose meaning is dependent on the particular overlaps and distinctions between a given woman and her ghostly relative, cyborg double, or mythical avatar. As feminist legal theorist Ute Gerhard explains, "[Equality] expresses a relationship between two objects, people, or conditions and determines the respect in which they are to be viewed as equal. . . . [E]quality must first be sought, demanded, and established, and it presupposes the objects being compared are different from each other."[6] In 1970s feminist, speculative literatures, equality is repeatedly presented as something that is "sought, demanded and established," between two distinct "objects," a woman and her replicant. Equality is redefined in these texts not as mere parity or sameness with another person, but as the difficult labor of discovering common ground between two different women that could form a basis for treating them equally—as being of equal value, deserving similar access to rights, or simply having equal claim on the category of the human.

In this chapter, I explore how the female replicant became a dynamic feminist and queer form for grappling with what Joan Scott has called the "paradoxes" of the second-wave feminist demand for women's equality.[7] This included the dual reality that women might constitute a recognizable subordinate class, unified by the social imposition of sexed being on them as a group, while also being radically heterogeneous among themselves. One result is that women have persistently between trapped within a political framework of sameness versus difference: on the one hand, having to make arguments for their political freedom based on the idea that they are fundamentally *the same as* men (for instance, sharing the same capacity for reason and intellectual development); on the other, pressured to pursue claims that women deserve rights because of their unique *differences from* men (including their biological ability to reproduce or the erroneous assumption that women are inherently more compassionate or nurturing).[8] As Scott explains: "Placing equality and difference in antithetical relationship . . . puts feminists in an impossible position, for as long as we argue within [these] terms we grant the current conservative premise that because women cannot be identical to men in all respects, we cannot expect to be equal to them. The only alternative . . . is to refuse to oppose equality to difference and insist continually on differences . . . as the very meaning of equality itself.[9] The female replicant was a "figure of the newly thinkable" that sought to train readers to develop the cognitive capacity to understand the concept of equality in an entirely new way: not as the demand for women to be identical with men, nor only as a plea for equal access to institutional power, but as the political practice of taking account of and negotiating women's numerous differences. Rather than renarrate how women and queers fought for the practical achievement of political, legal, and economic equality, I explore how a specific form, the female replicant, refined the aptitude for apprehending equality in multiplex ways as an imaginative practice of comparing two unlike subjects, thereby repeatedly figuring "the play of differences . . . as the very meaning of equality itself."

The form at the center of this chapter, then, is an apprehensible *figure*, the character type of the female replicant, a double or simulacrum who adopts the distinct shape of the human body to thematize the problem of feminist equality claims. I use both the labels "feminist" *and* "queer" to describe the female replicant because it is a figure that weds feminism's investment in the political freedom of women as a subordinate group with an understanding of the woman (or replicant) seeking equality as a type of gender dissident or rebel, who by her sudden, jolting appearance into narrative space, demands to be accounted for in "some significant way."

According to the *Oxford English Dictionary*, the original Latin meaning of the term "replicant," is "a new applicant," or "replier." In these now obsolete definitions, the replicant is a person who submits themselves as a correspondent to another. These meanings contradict the term's current definition as referring to "an artificial being in the form of a human or other creature . . . who behaves . . . like a replicant, [especially] in imitating or resembling others."[10] What better term, then, to describe that ceaselessly productive paradox of feminist struggle, to make persistent, numerous, and divergent political demands on a patriarchal structure that assumes one's uniform belonging to the essential category of "woman"? Like the replicant's archaic definitions, which return to us as interlocutors multiplying the meaning of a term thought to represent sameness, I conceive of the female replicant as offering us a model of thought for rereading 1970s feminisms' political demands for equality as manifold in their meanings and cultural effects. Simultaneously, I show how this fantastical figure functioned historically as a replicant or replier in its own right, deployed by various writers as way of responding to contemporaneous feminist equality discourses.

Toward this end, I analyze three distinct expressions of the female replicant across the 1970s: in Levin's *The Stepford Wives*, the replicant looms as a potential conformist robot feared to be replacing flesh-and-blood women in an ideal suburban community; in Russ's *The Female Man*, the replicant comes to represent proliferating versions of the same woman from alternate dimensions; and in Kingston's *The Woman Warrior: A Memoir of a Girlhood among Ghosts*, the replicant appears as fantastical shapeshifter, morphing into a variety of women that influence the life of a single Chinese American girl. These authors put forward different versions of female replicants as "new applicants" to a growing feminist and queer political imaginary, cultural forms designed to give shape to equality as an open-ended, flexible, and varied practice of freedom rather than a rigidly established political goal that, once reasonably attained, might be superseded or discarded. Consequently, this chapter elaborates a foundational understanding of forms as enabling structures that expand our cognitive grasp of gender and sexual diversity rather than restrict or delimit the meaning of these categories. Far from fixing the definition of "woman" or positing an ultimate solution to achieving equality, the female replicant offered a labile imaginative container for conceiving these same identities and political concepts as inherently multidimensional.

I begin by briefly glossing the myriad political uses and definitions of equality put forth by 1970s feminists of many stripes. I then explore how three distinct speculative texts used the figure of the female replicant to contribute to a feminist conception of equality as the negotiation of differences, rather than a bid for sameness or identity, with men, a male standard, or other women. Across this chapter, I successively stage encounters with three iterations of this feminist and queer form in order to structurally model the cultural work of the female replicant itself, a figure whose recurrent appearances offered readers a kaleidoscopic view of the problem of equality. The multiplication and narrative arrival of the female replicant's material form or imagined presence in countless fictional scenarios functioned to continually *re*-present this political demand anew as a concept that feminists ceaselessly reinterpreted over time. Each of the readings respectively illuminates a different author's use of the replicant to conceptualize equality as (a) a resistance to sameness or conformity to a male standard, (b) an attempt to acknowledge women's internal heterogeneity, and (c) a problem of translating divergent experiences between women. By creatively figuring equality over and over in the mind's eye, these literary texts themselves became imaginative replicants, or repliers, to movements for gender and sexual freedom, enjoining readers to know women *and* equality as *more than one thing*, and to do something meaningful with that knowledge.

On the Multiplicity of Equality

I begin this book with a meditation on feminist equality precisely because women's demand for equal standing in US public life inaugurated the very possibility of gender and sexual freedom in the 1960s and 1970s. The idea that an entire class of people subordinated on the basis of sex might achieve society-wide value, that their lives, bodies, and desires could become publicly consequential, provided the ground for every subsequent feminist and queer political claim on US society. This encompassed the right to privacy, which granted women access to contraception and abortion, and the demand for social acceptance of alternative sexualities and kinship networks, a precondition for the legal recognition of gay marriage and adoption.

Yet while it has become a commonplace that women's equality was the foundational motive of second-wave feminism, it is also frequently perceived as the movement's least radical political demand or achievement, at times even charged with unwittingly reinforcing a male standard of inclusion in a patriarchal society. As early as 1970, radical feminist Shulamith Firestone, who passionately described nineteenth-century feminist demands for equal civil status under the law as revolutionary, would ironically go on to deride her second-wave equal-rights predecessors as "conservatives" who "concentrate on superficial symptoms of sexism [like] legal inequities [and] employment discrimination" and "stress . . . equality with men . . . rather than liberation from sex roles altogether, or radical questioning of family values."[11] By stripping second-wave feminist equality claims of their revolutionary edge, Firestone inadvertently contributed to what has now become a rigid, and practically cliché, understanding of such demands as representing a liberal, moderate feminism associated with white, middle-class straight women. Subsequently taken up and repeated in countless iterations by socialist, lesbian, and women-of-color feminists, this line of thought shored up what would become the dominant supersessionary narrative of feminist history. As a popular teleological account of feminist political advancement, this narrative relegates equality to a regressive white feminist past that is supplanted by more advanced intersectional feminisms that presumably dispose of reformist equality claims in favor of a dynamic view of women's differences as a basis for coalitional struggle.

As historian Ruth Rosen relates, 1960s feminists did fight for legal equality and access to the material resources available to (white) men, but those activists—including the members of the Presidential Commission on the Status of Women, the founders of the National Organization of Women (NOW), and Black and white women in the Civil Rights Movement—were a diversified group hailing from different racial, class, and educational backgrounds and geographical origins.[12] Early second-wave feminism was intrinsically coalitional, bringing together women who previously never had the opportunity to dialogue, which in turn enabled them to share disparate life experiences and knowledge bases. When feminists demanded universal childcare as a legal right, for example, they were advocating on behalf of working-class *and* professional women across racial lines, whether to have access to a living wage or be freed from the economic burden of childcare services. In this same period, women of color repeatedly underscored the necessity of legal, political, and social equality for Black, Chicano and Latinx, Asian American, and Indigenous women in their writing and activism. Women in the Young Lords Party, a Puerto Rican–led civil rights organization founded in 1968, critiqued the role of the Catholic Church in upholding their unequal status in the home as obedient mothers and wives, while Black feminists deconstructed discourses of Black nationalism that promoted subservient social and sexual roles for Black women.[13] In making equality claims their own, women of color were inspired by earlier feminists' diagnosis of women's subordinate position in the family while participating in developing the second wave's broader critique of normative femininity. And in complementary fashion, the activists who founded women's liberation built their notion of equality on the Civil Rights and Black Power movements, inspired by the struggle for the equal dignity of African Americans. All of these feminisms influenced one another simultaneously, even if some, like the predominantly (though not wholly) white women's liberation movement, gained more immediate political notoriety.

A cursory look at the diverse definitions of equality offered by feminists of many stripes in the 1970s undercuts attempts at securing the meaning or use of the term to a single political group, strategy, or ideology: in her 1964 essay "Equality between the Sexes: An Immodest Proposal," sociologist Alice Rossi argued that the achievement of women's equality in the US would require establishing a completely "androgynous" understanding of gender, where "each sex will cultivate some of the characteristics usually associated with the other." In this view equality involved a society-wide project to dismantle traditional sex roles both through institutional reforms and the wholesale transformation of social and cultural norms. NOW's 1966 Statement of Purpose outlined demands for women's equal access to educational, professional, and economic resources, which would grant women an "active, self-respecting partnership" with men. They went on to articulate women's equality claims to "broader questions of social justice," consequently committing "to give active support to the common cause of equal rights for all those who suffer discrimination and deprivation." Here, equality is understood as the ability to claim shared responsibility for every aspect of public life, which rested on the universal application of democracy to all subjects. In a range of her speeches and essays, Lorde developed a theory of equality as a worldview that grants equal value to women's differences. She claimed, "Now we must recognize differences among women who are our equals, neither inferior nor superior, and devise ways to use each other's difference to enrich our visions and our joint struggles." For

Lorde, equality is not only a legal or institutional goal but an interpersonal practice of treating the lives, experiences, and outlooks of diverse women as equivalently worthwhile. And in an essay for the women-of-color anthology *This Bridge Called My Back*, Chicana feminist Cherríe Moraga defined equality as a social achievement in which women and men come to recognize their shared psychic and bodily vulnerability. She stressed that "it is not really difference the oppressor fears, so much as similarity. . . . He fears [seeing] himself in the bodies of the people he has called different." For Moraga, equality involves a willingness to see one's own susceptibility to pain, violation, or oppression as an existential reality common to others. As these examples attest, the radicalness of feminist equality claims lay both in their willingness to posit the subordinate category of "woman" as, simply, *not less than*, and in their continual incitement to negotiate endless differences—of race, class, age, or sexuality—between the various subjects of a democratic society.

At first glance, the three literary texts I discuss below respectively appear to fit into the commonplace strands of second-wave feminist praxis; however, each goes on to deploy the female replicant to formulate an internal critique of so-called *liberal*, *radical*, and *women-of-color feminisms*, using the very terms of each to question homogenizing or reductive tendencies within them. *The Stepford Wives'* scathing commentary on suburban conformity squarely places it in a tradition of liberal feminism. Yet the novella's corresponding pointed critique of some feminists' obsessive focus on achieving everyday, domestic parity with men urged readers to revivify liberal feminist equality claims as a demand for equal participation in public affairs, rather than the superficial sharing of household chores. As a text with an all-female cast, which also celebrates lesbianism as a potent rebellion against patriarchy, *The Female Man* models the polemical force of radical and lesbian feminisms, which touted "woman-identification" as a way of rejecting "male-defined response patterns."[14] Yet Russ's commitment to rendering women as internally multiplicious, neither equivalent to one another nor undivided within themselves, undermined the utopian belief that women shared an inherent equality by belonging to a universal sisterhood. And in its detailed exploration of the familial history of a second-generation Chinese American girl, *The Woman Warrior* expresses the values of a women-of-color feminism that attends to the particularity of multiply marginalized lives. But by refusing to figure a racialized woman's standpoint as necessarily coherent, unified, or privileged, the memoir questions whether any essential identity could be claimed among women of the same racial, class, and sexual background, even the same family.

If the "Stepford" in Levin's title can also refer to the contemporary perception of different feminisms as a constant "stepping forward" into more advanced iterations, each of these three texts represents a creative interruption of both the lockstep movement of feminist progress narratives as well as reductive conceptions of equality as sameness by critically speaking back to diverse definitions of equality across these traditions. In this way, the female replicants that populate Levin's, Russ's, and Kingston's fictional worlds collectively register the already existing internal heterogeneity of equality discourses across a plurality of feminisms in the 1970s. Moreover, all three texts conceive of equality as a formal problem that necessitates "a creative moment of figuration," the imaginative calling forth of female replicants or repliers who "have preferences like and unlike mine, who see from a standpoint not identical with my own, and whose opinions I am called upon to judge or by whom my own dearly held opinions will be judged and perhaps unsettled even to the point of crisis."[15] After all, every political demand for feminist equality always requires the creative capacity to conceive of, or "represent," other women in the mind's eye, both those who suffer from inequality but also future women who may suffer less or simply be free from the oppressive hierarchies of the present, if not of gender itself. In the context of these feminist political visions, literary representations of female replicants confronting one another in imaginative scenarios gave shape to the fundamental idea of women speaking in many voices in the name of their equal value and humanity.

Stepford Wives

A half-century since its publication, Ira Levin's *The Stepford Wives* remains America's favorite object lesson in the horrors of suburban conformism. The now classic story of Joanna Eberhart's arrival to the seemingly perfect, yet diabolical, New England town of Stepford—where self-aware and "liberated" women are transformed into robot-like "hausfraus" in a matter of months—is so culturally ubiquitous, its title serves as a popular epithet thrown at latter-day housewives who idealize domestic bliss. The "Stepford wife," a stunningly beautiful and buxom domestic who tends to family and home with adoring servility, could not exist without its science-fictional double, the female replicant or robot (created by men) whom audiences of both the book and its film adaptations recognize as the nightmare of Levin's story. In the penultimate scene of the acclaimed 1975 film version of *The Stepford Wives*, a terror-stricken Joanna (played by Katherine Ross) stares into the eyes of her cyborg replacement, who has been sent to murder her. Viewers are left with the chilling image of their heroine about to be choked to death with pantyhose, the symbolic stranglehold of normative femininity made literal.

This scene of patriarchal horror is so seared into our collective psyches that it masks a deep irony: there are no actual robots in Levin's original book. Rather the automaton, or mechanical replacement of the town's women, is a speculative figure imagined by the story's lead characters—aspiring photographer Joanna and her outspoken best friend, Bobbie Markowe—as a possible explanation for the perfect docility and apoliticalness of their new neighbors in Stepford, Massachusetts. These are housewives who so blatantly deny the social transformations enabling US-American women to pursue life beyond domesticity in the 1960s and 1970s, that, according to Joanna and Bobbie, they simply "must" be inhuman replicants. In contrast, the men run an entire civic association, spend most of their time in each other's company, and work a variety of jobs in the growing biochemical and technical industries.

It is only midway through the story, after their once "vivacious" friend Charmaine transforms into an obedient homemaker overnight, that Bobbie suggests the men might be subduing the women chemically, a proposal that fuels Joanna's growing mistrust of her husband and the Men's Association. But Joanna's suspicions are never substantiated, even at the story's conclusion when Bobbie, now reborn as a domestic goddess, offers to cut herself to prove she is human: "Joanna went forward, toward Bobbie standing by the sink with the knife in her hand, so real-looking—skin, eyes, hair, hands, rising-falling aproned bosom—she simply *couldn't* be [a robot], and that was all there was to it."[16] Joanna's story abruptly ends here. The last three pages of the text are told from the perspective of Ruthanne Hendry, Stepford's first Black woman resident who has recently relocated with her family. Walking through the aisles of the local grocery store, Ruthanne approaches the various Stepford wives with a similar air of frustration that Joanna once had: "It still bugged her the way they shopped so languidly . . . as if they never sweated. How white could you get?"[17] Finally, horrifyingly, Ruthanne sees Joanna, now a perfect embodiment of the Stepford wife, proclaiming her newfound love of housework.

Joanna's transformation, one never fully explained, leaves us wondering whether her suspicions of a patriarchal scheme were true, or if upon realizing Bobbie's "humanity," Joanna merely capitulated to the norms of Stepford. Is "all there was to it" the fact that Bobbie bleeds, or does she use the knife to kill her friend, this moment being "all there was" left of Joanna's life? Levin's refusal to finally reveal the Stepford wives as literal robots leaves open the more devastating possibility that Joanna and Bobbie willingly submit to the suburban ideal. The failure of Joanna and Bobbie's feminism to resist the domestic imperialism of Stepford is what allows us to subsequently "see" from the perspective of an African American woman, someone different from the Stepford wives but from Joanna and Bobbie as well. If the specter of the robot double sparks terror in Joanna and Bobbie, Ruthanne is another kind of replicant or potential "replier," whom they have failed to consider as genuine interlocutor, and with disastrous results.

In the early 1970s, *The Stepford Wives* deployed the female replicant to critique a particular version of feminist thought that would come to be called "liberal feminism." This version of feminism is traditionally associated with early second-wave activist efforts to gain legal and economic equality for women by making rights-based claims on the state to access the privileges traditionally afforded white men.[18] The characterization of state-centered reform aims as "liberal" comes with a doubly negative valence: first, that early feminists held a universalist conception of the individual citizen unmarked by race and class, and second, that they invested in achieving a male standard without dismantling it. Yet these negative connotations, captured in the racially inflected phrase "*white liberal feminism*," more accurately name *a popular interpretation of* early second-wave feminism that assumed full equality could be achieved through everyday parity with men, including the sharing of housework and women's limited access to professional fulfillment. At their most aspirational, early second-wave feminists (who composed a multiracial coalition) fought for massive structural transformations—like universal childcare and the Equal Rights Amendment (ERA)—that would have required the state to reorganize every US legal, educational, and government institution to ensure women's equal participation in public affairs.[19] In the everyday context of many white middle-class women's lives, however, equality claims were often watered down from demands for institutional change to an affective stance of resentment toward gender inequality in the home. It was this mainstreaming of feminist equality that the women's liberation movement of the early 1970s vehemently fought against by developing a radical critique of patriarchy. Yet this project was in many ways continuous with, rather than divergent from, the revolutionary energies of early 1960s feminist equality claims.

The Stepford Wives became a bestseller a decade after the publication of Betty Friedan's The Feminine Mystique, eight years after the founding of NOW, and two years after the explosive rise of women's liberation. In this context, the novella was infused with the radical spirit of second-wave feminism across its broader historical arc, using the figure of the replicant to diagnose the loss of the radical edge of early feminist equality claims and their collapse into a more complacent "white liberal feminism" that women's liberationists decried in the early 1970s, but also mistakenly conflated with the activism of their feminist predecessors. The novella trains readers to discern how a repetitively projected anxiety about the female replicant can mask some women's problematic *replication* of a narrow conception of feminism understood as a project of achieving parity with men. Consequently, though the text begins as an explicit argument against homogeneity or conformity of thought within liberal feminism, it ultimately becomes an argument against all types of conformist thinking or logics of "sameness" across a variety of feminisms: Joanna and Bobbie's obsessive need to distinguish themselves from the Stepford wives makes them uniform with one another, in much the same way that radical feminists' need to distinguish themselves from their earlier liberal feminist counterparts flattened the members of each group, discounting their cross-pollination of ideas and practices.

At the core of The Stepford Wives lies the problem that neither Joanna nor Bobbie can imagine a viable politics outside their version of liberal feminism. Their feminism is less a directed program against

patriarchy than a vague agglomeration of ideas about what a "liberated woman" should be: a woman who "gets up petitions" and "pick-
ets," who "meet[s] with other women and talk[s] about their shared
experiences," who has hobbies, and is "not deeply concerned about
whether pink soap pads are better than the blue ones."[20] Despite their
self-identification as card-carrying feminists, both accept their husbands' wishes to move to the suburbs, never publicly protest the sex-
segregated Men's Association, and remain primary childcare providers.
Their main form of feminist resistance, it will turn out, is sustained
commiseration about the backwardness of the Stepford women. *The
Stepford Wives*, then, presents Joanna and Bobbie as emblematic icons
of the mainstreaming of second-wave feminism, who robotically repeat feminist buzzwords with no clear sense of their place in particular
kinds of activist politics. According to the story's bleak conclusion, the
assumption that genuine freedom for women would be an immediate consequence of sharing household duties ("It was Walter's turn to
do the dishes"), parity in family decision-making ("'Do *you* want to
move?' he asked"), or mutually fulfilling sex ("'Was that any good?'
she asked. 'For you?' 'Sure it was,' he said. 'Wasn't it for you?'") is utterly misguided.[21] Whether or not men decide to do the dishes every
once in a while, they still control every major organ of political and
professional life, including the technologies that might be used to turn
women into robots. What becomes clear as the book unfolds is that
both women are invested in the superficial appearance of sex equality
more than either sweeping institutional reform or the reorganization
of gendered relations.

As the book opens, Joanna is interviewed by the "Welcome Wagon
Lady," a sixty-something resident of Stepford who introduces new residents in the local paper:

> "Do you have any hobbies or special interests?"
>
> [Joanna] was about to say a time-saving no, but hesitated: a full an-
> swer, printed in the local paper, might serve as a signpost to women like
> herself, potential friends. . . .
>
> "I'm interested in politics and in the Women's Liberation movement.
> Very much so in that. And so is my husband."
>
> "*He* is?" the Welcome Wagon lady looked at her.

"Yes," Joanna said. "Lots of men are." She didn't go into the benefits-for-both sexes explanation. . . . He's interested in boating and football too," she said, "and he collects Early American legal documents." Walter's half of the signpost.[22]

Here, Joanna presumes that the term "women's liberation" is a uniformly agreed upon "signpost" of certain shared values, so that only those "women like herself" can be considered "potential friends." At the same time, Joanna's commitment to including her husband in her announcement, indicating that he both composes and deserves "half of the signpost," speaks to her one-dimensional conception of parity. The narrative's omniscient view into Joanna's thought process recasts her actions as a kind of liberal feminist virtue signaling, smugly self-satisfied at having included Walter as a coequal partner and presuming they both tacitly share the "benefits-for-both sexes" belief in feminist equality (a belief so taken for granted as to need no explanation or defense). Yet Joanna will soon realize just how much more *she* needs the signpost than Walter. Later that evening, she learns that Stepford already has a well-established Men's Association with no social or civic organization for women. What she initially sees as due fairness to her male partner ultimately masks the fundamental structural inequality of their new home.

Joanna's signpost, however, works exactly as expected. A few days later, her new neighbor Bobbie Markowe thrills at Joanna's write-up and calls her: "They talked about . . . the antiquated sexist unfairness of [the 'men's club']. . . . They talked about the possibility of having a rap session; but they agreed that the women they had met seemed unlikely to welcome even so small a step toward liberation. They talked about the National Organization for Women, to which they both belonged. . . . 'Wouldn't it be great if we could get [together a] NOW chapter . . . and give that Men's Association a good shaking-up?'"[23] Joanna and Bobbie's conversation is defined by a uniformity of opinion not only about shared values and affiliations, but also their interpretation of the Stepford women. In the same breath, they imagine organizing a dialogue with the wives—which might reveal disagreement or alternate views—but then "agree" that the likely outcome will fail to live up to their shared conception of what liberation for women should look like. Their big idea for giving the "Men's Association a good shaking-up" is to create an equivalent women's organization, in the image of perfect symmetry, rather than destroy the men's civic chokehold on the community altogether.

While Joanna and Bobbie complain about the Stepford wives' antisocial behavior, they also refuse to spend time with anyone that doesn't immediately parrot back to them an investment in feminist ideals.[24] In one scene, Joanna visits Barbara Chamalian to ask if she might wish to join a women's consciousness-raising group: "'No,' Barbara said, 'I think you'd better count me out. . . . I'm glad we've met though. . . . Would you like to come in and sit for while? I'm ironing.' 'No, thanks,' Joanna said. 'I want to speak to some of the other women.'"[25] In a rare instance when Joanna is invited to visit with a Stepford wife, she declines because Barbara has not passed her feminist litmus test. Yet Joanna also conveniently ignores other community women who are decidedly *unlike* the wives, including the Welcome Wagon Lady ("sixty . . . but working at youth and vivacity"); Miss Austrian, the town librarian; and Mary Migliardi, a "plump quick-moving white-haired" local caterer.[26] If the wives are irritatingly ageless and beautiful, these women are naturally aging, plugged into local happenings, and in Migliardi's case, irreverent about Stepford's uptight culture. When Mary caters a dinner party at Joanna's house, she explains with chagrin that the Men's Association is a recent civic organization that subdued Stepford's social life.[27] Despite the obvious benefit of getting to know these women as reliable sources of information and potential friends, Joanna never sets up future liaisons with them.

At one point, Joanna conducts research on the town's local happenings and is shocked to discover that a chapter of NOW once existed in Stepford. More surprising, the Stepford women were former participants. Following this discovery, Joanna confronts the defunct chapter's last leader, Kit Sunderson: "'Were the Women's Club meetings more boring than housework?' Kit frowned, 'No . . . but they weren't as useful as housework.'"[28] Joanna's revelation that there once was a Women's Club rattles her, because it posits a political trajectory opposite her image of feminist progress—she cannot imagine a community would transition from "liberation" to conformity, or that her version of feminism might in fact be "boring" or "useless." If a sex-segregated Men's Association was founded *after* the rise and fall of a chapter of NOW, is it possible that Stepford's feminism was not radical enough to upend suburban gender hierarchies? Or perhaps the kind of people who move to Stepford are more invested in the maintenance of traditional domestic harmony than in overthrowing it. Though she reels at this possibility, Joanna inadvertently admits that her life course has been exactly the same: when she says to Walter, "*The [Feminine] Mystique* came out while I was still working," she reveals that nearly a decade after she read this foundational critique of domestic ideology, she chose to quit her job and raise children in suburban Stepford.[29] Even when Joanna finally admits to herself that Stepford is a socially toxic town, the narrator tells us: "She would only want to move, she decided, if she found an absolutely perfect house." The text then repeatedly draws our attention to the fact that Joanna's dogged frustration with the monotony of the Stepford women makes it impossible for her to acknowledge her own propensity for conforming to domestic ideals.

Joanna's most glaring blind spot in this regard is the simple fact that against her stated commitment to supporting the "liberation" of women, she consistently orients her energies toward men. In the book's longest scene, Walter implores Joanna to help him entertain the Men's Association at their house. Despite earlier railing against the "injustice" of the association's men-only policy, she relents: "Give me fifteen minutes and I'll even be an intelligent *beautiful* waitress." (This in contrast to Mary Migliardi's statement, "If my old man was alive he'd have to knock me on the head before I'd let him join!")[30] Joanna captivates the men with her humor and well-formed ideas about encouraging civic engagement: "'And maybe it would get the women out too,' she said. 'In case you don't know it, this town is a disaster area for baby-sitters.' Everyone laughed, and she felt good and at ease. . . . [S]he took part in the talk about them, and the men (except Coba, damn him) paid close attention to her . . . and they nodded and agreed with her. . . . *Move over, Gloria Steinem!*"[31] Joanna performs a bionic femininity for the Men's Association—a perfect combination of attractiveness and intelligence—and receives a recognition she fails to elicit from the Stepford women. Far from seeing herself aligned with feminist figures like Gloria Steinem against patriarchal demands on women, Joanna absurdly imagines herself in competition with Steinem for gracefully influencing men (secretly incensed with Association president Coba's indifference to her).

Among the men who congregate at Joanna's home is Ike Mazzard, a retired pinup illustrator famous for his beautiful portraits of women. When Joanna realizes he has been sketching her throughout the night, she gushes: "Ike Mazzard! Sketching *her*! . . . 'Hey . . . I'm no Ike Mazzard Girl.' 'Every girl's an Ike Mazzard girl,' Mazzard said, and smiled. . . . Try being Gloria Steinem when Ike Mazzard is drawing you."[32] What Joanna perceives of as the men's genuine investment in her is a ruse to draw her attention so that she can be literally drawn by Mazzard, and hence appraised by the male gaze (presumably in preparation for creating her perfect robotic simulacrum). All of Joanna's suspicions about the Men's Association are suspended in the face of this flattering gesture, despite the fact that equality here is doled out by men with power to set the very standard of parity. That parity is based on nothing more than Mazzard's perception of women as all sharing idealized qualities of white, feminine beauty, rather than any material or political equality with men. Joanna's thin conception of equality leads her both to misperceive women's actual diversity (the fact that she and Bobbie, the Stepford wives, and other women in the community like Migliardi, are not all identical, even among themselves), while abetting a male conception of women as all being equal in their sameness.

Ironically, then, Joanna's zeal to find coalition with other similarly progressive minded women who claim to despise traditional domesticity blinds her to possible coalitions across differences of race, age, or sexuality. The arrival of Stepford's first Black woman resident, Ruthanne Hendry, poses a more robust challenge to Joanna's political myopia, functioning as a key symptom of popular liberal feminism's failure to register meaningful differences between women. When Joanna first encounters Ruthanne at the local library, she struggles to spark a conversation: "She wanted to say something friendly . . . but she didn't want to be white-liberal patronizing. Would she say something if the woman weren't black? . . . 'We could walk off with the whole place if we wanted to,' the black woman said. . . . Joanna smiled at her."[33] In this awkward moment, Ruthanne interrupts Joanna's solipsistic fear of being perceived as pandering to a Black woman, playfully suggesting the possibility of a coalition—working together, she implies, they could "walk off with" Stepford itself. The narrative continues:

The black woman smiled. "Is it always this empty?" she asked. . . .

Joanna put her hand out. "I'm Joanna Eberhart," she said, smiling.

"Ruthanne Hendry," the black woman said, smiling and shaking Joanna's hand.

Joanna tipped her head and squinted. "I *know* that name," she said, "I've seen it someplace."

The woman smiled. "Do you have any small children? . . . I've done a children's book, *Penny Has a Plan*," the woman said. "They've got it here; I checked the catalog first thing."

"Of course," Joanna said. "Susie had it out about two weeks ago! And loved it! I did too; it's so good to find one where a girl actually *does* something besides make tea for her dolls."

"Subtle propaganda," Ruthanne Hendry said, smiling.[34]

In this fascinating exchange, the omniscient narrator gives us access to Joanna's shifting apprehension of her new neighbor, first recognizing her as a racialized "black woman," then a universal "woman," and finally as a specific person, "Ruthanne Hendry." The progressive movement of nouns in Joanna's mind directly unfolds from her dawning discovery of Ruthanne's political identity as a liberal feminist. It is only after Joanna realizes that Ruthanne is a feminist children's book writer (reflecting Joanna's own values) that her neighbor suddenly has a name. In this process, however, the particularity of Ruthanne's life experiences as a Black woman professional becomes subsumed into Joanna's generalized notion of "women's lib." Over coffee, Ruthanne begins to express her feelings about the women of Stepford. Before she can finish her sentence, Joanna interrupts: "It doesn't have anything to do with *color*. . . . They're like that with everybody."[35] Joanna preemptively eliminates race as a factor in Stepford's conformist culture, reducing all possible conflict between women to their affective relationship with housework. Joanna's feminism, then, looks nothing like coalition building between different kinds of women (she never socializes with Ruthanne again), or even a critique of the structural logics that make white feminine domesticity the most celebrated form of womanhood. The closest Joanna will get to "equality" with men is sharing their hatred of "women's work."

This stance leads Joanna to misguidedly imagine that her husband Walter is as "interested in Women's Liberation" as she is. Yet nothing in

Walter's actions ever indicates that he is invested in feminism. Rather he echoes back to Joanna what she wishes to hear about their supposed "equal" partnership. When Joanna protests Walter's wish to join the Men's Club, he reassures her: "'If it's not open to women in six months, I'll quit and we'll march together. Shoulder to shoulder.'"[36] And later, when he diminishes her concerns about Bobbie's brainwashing, Joanna asks, "Do you want me to change?" To which Walter replies: "No . . . I'd just like you to put on a little lipstick once in a while. . . . I'd like me to change a little too, like lose a few pounds."[37] In every exchange, Walter makes light of larger structural inequalities—women's lack of civic representation and the unevenness of gendered beauty standards—using a language of false equivalence to give Joanna the impression that they are "marching together" against sexism. Only when Bobbie transforms into an obedient housewife does Joanna finally concede that perhaps Walter had always known Stepford is a town where women are replaced by slavish "dummies." By then, it is too late. Without other women to support her, Joanna appears hysterical in her paranoid rantings about a male conspiracy. Walter promptly denies Joanna access to their children and sets the other men of the town to find her when she sneaks out of a window and flees their house. As she makes her way to Bobbie's house in the snow, her first thought is of Ruthanne Hendry: "Ruthanne had to be *warned*. Maybe they could go together."[38]

It is no small irony that Joanna finally imagines Ruthanne as a potential ally only in the moment that her bonds with white liberal feminists *and* white men unravel. Ultimately, Joanna and Bobbie's demise is the direct outcome of their inability to imagine an entire range of choices outside of the nuclear family: cross-racial coalitions, lesbian affinities, divorce, or simply leaving Stepford (precisely the range of options that feminist politics aimed to make available for all women). Levin underscores that a popular version of white liberal feminism—understood as an affective stance of resentment at domesticity—is not feminism at all, neither an accurate representation of early second-wave feminism, which aimed to install women in permanent seats of political power, nor an expression of women's liberation, which attacked the very foundations of the nuclear family.

The women's desire for equality with men is a pipedream in a world where the means of technological production are owned by men. When

Bobbie finally suspects that the men's employment in various tech and biochemical industries might be linked to the women's transformation into domestic servants, she describes the line of industrial plants where many Stepford husbands work as "poisoner's row." "Even if there's no chemical doing anything," she implores Joanna, "is this where you really want to live? We've each got one friend now. Is *that* your idea of the ideal community?"[39] Here, Bobbie voices the text's most radical claim: namely, that women are figuratively and literally poisoned by a variety of male-dominated institutions. A truly revolutionary response to patriarchy requires women to acknowledge a fundamental disparity in men's and women's access to technological resources and political association, and a willingness to admit that neither the narrowness of suburban domestic life nor a superficial conception of women's parity can be an adequate "idea of the ideal community." That was the position taken by early second-wave feminists, from NOW's unequivocal claim for women's right to full participation in democratic life, to Alice Rossi's argument against the geographical division of labor that relegated domestic women to suburbs while their husbands conducted business in cities, to the broader political lobby for the Equal Rights Amendment.[40]

The Stepford Wives, then, is a text that reveals productive internal heterogeneity within the various traditions of second-wave feminism while assiduously working to dismantle all types of conformist thinking. It criticizes the replication of views between liberal feminists. It is revolted by men's homogenizing of women. And while it takes up elements of both radical and women-of-color feminisms—namely their commitment to dismantling patriarchy and cross-racial and class coalition—it also questions these traditions' tendency to reductively describe the liberal demand for women's equality as bland reformism. Consider that Joanna's easy dismissal of the older and wiser Migliardi, who clearly recognizes the insidious nature of Stepford's placidity because of her long view of the town's history, could be an allegory for radical feminists' flippant disavowal of an older generation of liberal feminists like Betty Friedan, who developed a critique of women's subordination based on their lived experiences growing up in 1950s suburbia. Of all the women besides Bobbie, Migliardi is the most likely to have believed Joanna's suspicions about the men's scheme and perhaps provided allyship in her resistance to Stepford's malevolent influence.

The Stepford Wives thus presents the female replicant as an imaginary form that speaks back to readers, encouraging them to question their own tendency to view equality *as* sameness. It undermines the idea that equality could either mean sameness with men, the sameness of all women, or even the sameness of different types of feminists. When Bobbie asks her fateful question, "Is this your idea of ideal community?" she is also articulating the novella's query to feminists of all stripes: is your idea of an ideal feminist community one where all women share the same political outlook? Levin's cautionary tale tells so-called white liberal feminists they must be far more suspicious of patriarchy, but also of their own attachment to the limited rewards of domestic womanhood. Yet it also makes clear that white liberal feminist fears of a fantasized robotic double that gnaws at the edges of their self-image as "liberated women" ultimately haunts all feminist projects, which invariably produce their own kinds of conformist thinking, making other kinds of productive female replicants across many identities and social contexts impossible to conceive.

This is perhaps why the text ends with Ruthanne's point of view. By inhabiting the mindset of a Black woman professional, the narrator imaginatively compensates for Joanna's failure to see from multiple women's perspectives. What Joanna cannot seem to do, the narrator suggests, we might be able to accomplish with the proper imagination. Yet Ruthanne's future remains uncertain, and perhaps without a "warning" from, or genuine coalition with, women like Joanna and Bobbie, she may be doomed to their fate. For no woman can alter a system of pervasive male domination alone. By revealing Joanna and Bobbie's failure to innovate new political possibilities beyond a bid for equality as sameness, the novella uses the figure of the female replicant to offer a crucial popular critique of the rhetoric of liberal feminism from within its very terms. It compels us to revivify second-wave feminisms' urgent demand that women resist the lock-*Stepforward* movement of normative gender roles and claim full participation in public life, but each in their own way.

Female Men

When readers turn the first pages of Joanna Russ's feminist, lesbian science fiction novel *The Female Man*, they are greeted by a collision of

Js: a series of rapid-fire vignettes introduce three women from alternate dimensions—Janet, Jeannine, and Joanna. The novel opens: "I was born on a farm on Whileaway. When I was five I was sent to a school on South Continent . . . and when I turned twelve I rejoined my family. My mother's name is Eva, my other mother's name Alicia; I am Janet Evason."[41] Our first narrator (one of at least four) initially enters our consciousness as a universal subject, unmarked by gender, race, or sexuality, but born somewhere on an unfamiliar world called Whileaway. Quickly though, we learn this "I" has a shared culture, family, gender, and name ("Evason is not 'son' but 'daughter.' This is *your* translation," Janet informs us).[42] This dramatic rhetorical shift, from the literal birth of an unmarked subject to a particular woman from another planet, also symbolically births a "female man" in our imagination, for on Whileaway, a version of Earth where no men have existed for a thousand years, humanity is synonymous with women. At the peak of their technical innovation, Whileawayans have become time travelers, and Janet is their interdimensional ambassador.

In the following pages, Janet teleports into the lives of the mousy librarian Jeannine and the depressed writer Joanna, scrambling their sense of reality. Though vastly divergent people, Jeannine and Joanna are both trapped by the expectations of proper womanhood. Jeannine secretly despises her sweet but smothering boyfriend, Cal, yet is obsessed with the idea that marriage will grant her self-worth. Joanna is torn between proving her brilliance in male-dominated academia, while desperate to be sexually desired by men. Janet's sudden appearance in Jeannine and Joanna's lives—a woman who thinks men are an inferior species, laughs at sexist insults, cuts her hair off with clamshells, practices martial arts, and has known only women as lovers and friends— literally and figuratively breaks heteropatriarchy's hold on their psyches. Joanna captures Janet's influence on her own life thus:

> Before Janet
> arrived on this planet

> I was moody, ill-at-ease, unhappy, and hard to be with. . . . all I did was
>   dress for The Man
>   smile for The Man . . .

sympathize with The Man
defer to The Man . . .
live for The Man.

Then a new interest entered my life. After I called up Janet, out of nothing, or she called me up (don't read between the lines; there's nothing there) my appetite improved, friends commented on my renewed zest for life. . . . I answered [Janet's] questions; I bought her a pocket dictionary; I took her to the zoo; I pointed out New York's skyline at night as if I owned it.

Oh, I made that woman up; you can believe it![43]

Joanna describes a shift in the social and affective modes of her life from a soul-destroying servility to men, to life-giving dialogue with another woman, who may or may not be her own invention. This shift is rendered visually in the movement from a fixed column of emotional expectations Joanna continually plays out for "The Man" to a return to the flowing paragraph form where events unfold between two characters actively engaged with one another. The effect of this new set of possible relations between women is so powerful it improves Joanna's overall health, renders her a narrating subject speaking in authoritative paragraphs, and unleashes the potential for lesbian desire, an erotic force even Joanna in her new state of feminist consciousness cannot yet fathom ("don't read between the lines; there's nothing there"). In light of Joanna's claim to have "made that woman up," *The Female Man*'s opening line takes on new meaning: Janet is not only literally born on another version of Earth called Whileaway, but is also figuratively born in Joanna's imagination as a feminist and queer form, perhaps conceived while our author visited a farm like those populated by lesbian feminists in the 1970s, where women whiled away the time inventing a new woman-identified way of life.

In *The Stepford Wives*, the female replicant appears as liberal feminists' nightmare of women's replacement by docile robots, a fantasy projection masking the conformity of their own political views. Alternatively, in *The Female Man*, a multiplicity of female replicants appear in the story as versions of the same woman from alternate realities. Here, the replicant returns as a feminist and queer form that represents the symbolic fragmenting of any single woman's sense of self when she comes into radical feminist consciousness. Perhaps unsurprisingly, then, *The Female Man* is an avant-garde work of literature that renders the multidimensional character of women's interior lives through radical experiments with language and narrative. The entire novel is framed by the conceit that we live in a multiverse, where "[e]very choice begets at least two worlds of possibility . . . or very likely . . . an infinite number of possible universes."[44] With this in mind, the novel suggests that when a woman reappraises her own past through the lens of feminist consciousness, she inevitably produces new versions of herself, both in her imagination and in her present lived reality. If a woman suddenly discovers that she could be a lesbian desiring other women (like Janet), she may have to argue against a version of herself that covets heterosexual marriage and domestic bliss (like Jeannine). If a woman begins to realizes that she will have to be in conflict with men to achieve freedom and dignity (like Jael, the warrior assassin who ultimately brings the Js together across time), she may have to grapple with the limitations of her own wish to live in a world without men (like Janet). And if a woman is desperate to stop imitating traditionally "male" behavior to achieve professional success (like Joanna), she may have to draw on the variety of styles, behaviors, and worldviews of all the different versions of herself, rather than subordinating any one of them. The numerous conflicts between the four Js constitute an extended meditation on what happens when any woman comes to grips with her own internal complexity, projected outward as a series of animate, expressive, contentious feminist forms demanding to be given equal weight in a single woman's affective landscape. The narrative framing of a multiverse reveals the impossibility of pure equivalence between different people, decisions, and the infinite timelines these decisions "beget." There is only the continual practice of comparing and judging the relationship between unlike worlds and their influence upon one another (analogous to the practice of comparing women—each a different "planet" or "universe," another "me also").

The concept of infinite parallel universes is manifest not only in the time-slips that lead each of the Js to appear in one another's realities, but also in the proliferation of narrative voices. All four of the Js speak throughout the story, sometimes simultaneously in overlapping, frenetic bursts of speech. This is indicated through parenthetical clauses or dramatic asides where one J distinguishes herself from the others or interjects while someone else is the primary speaker:

> —As I have said before, I (not the one above, please) had an experience on the seventh of February last, nineteen-sixty-nine. I turned into a man.
>
> —I met Janet Evason on Broadway, standing to the side of the parade given in her honor (I was). She leaned out of the limousine and beckoned me in. . . . "That one," she said. Eventually we will all come together.
>
> —Who am I? I know who I am, but what's my brand name. . . . I'm not Jeannine. I'm not Janet. I'm not Joanna. . . . You'll meet me later.[45]

In each of these instances, selves proliferate—with the presence of more and more "I's"—but also stand side by side as interlocutors, dynamically responding to one another. Throughout *The Stepford Wives*, Levin uses parenthetical references following Joanna's speech to enunciate her unspoken disdain for the obedient neighborhood women, ultimately reconfirming her rigid outlook on suburban womanhood. In *The Female Man*, however, parenthetical asides are a formal expression of replication because they literally multiply women's voices on the page while amplifying their grammatical visibility. Moreover, though the four Js frequently take pains to distinguish themselves, many statements in the text could be uttered by any or all at once, so that the narrative oscillates between brief unities of speech ("Eventually we will all come together") followed by continual dispersal ("not the one above, please").

In its narrative framing of a multiverse and concatenation of speaking voices, *The Female Man* formally models what Ann Snitow calls "the feminism of uncertainty," a phrase that captures second-wave feminism's proliferation of multiple, competing, and sometimes contradictory definitions of "woman." Snitow's concept underscores that feminism is a "mixed form, requiring in its very nature . . . inconsistencies," since "one can never stay inside 'woman,' because it keeps moving."[46] Similarly *The Female Man* never stays "inside [the category of] 'woman'" because it proliferates *women* who "keep moving" between worlds.

In one chapter, Joanna and Jeannine visit Whileaway, where they learn about its customs and hear folklore of the women philosophers, scientists, and warriors of this strange world. During their stay, Janet's daughter Yuriko tells Joanna a meandering story about a girl raised by bears in the Whileawayan wilderness. Suddenly Yuriko telescopes the story forward:

> "So the little girl went to school and had lots of lovers and friends . . . and had lots of adventures, and saved everybody from a volcano . . . and achieved Enlightenment.
>
> "Then one morning somebody told her there was a bear looking for her—"
>
> "Wait a minute," said I. "This story doesn't have an end. It just goes on and on." . . . "Anyone who lives in two worlds . . . is bound to have a complicated life" [said Yuriko].
>
> (I learned later that she had spent three days making up the story. It was, of course, about me.)[47]

Yuriko's story performs in microcosm the narrative feat of *The Female Man* itself: it clears space for accounting for the "complicated life" of any given woman by recognizing her fundamental groundlessness. When every preconceived notion of what a woman is, can, or should be is dissolved, a woman's story becomes endless in its conceptual span and lived possibilities. Fittingly, Yuriko's story begins with the young girl being torn away from her mother immediately after birth by an earthquake that separates the ground under their feet. The rending of a common ground between two women is an event that breaks open the possibility of elaborating each of their intricate personal histories without reference to proper origins or developmental telos—not in universal sisterhood, mythical matriarchies, or sacred conceptions of motherhood. Just as Joanna "makes up" Janet (nurturing her but also inventing her as feminist form), so too Yuriko "makes up" a story about Joanna, whose open-endedness models the capacity of one woman to imagine the life of another in the most expansive, nonessentialist terms. And so too, by narrating the four Js' lives in different genres, styles, and tones, Russ grants them all equivalent creative value, while acknowledging the non-*equivalence* of different women's experiences and worldviews.

The iconic figure for groundlessness in *The Female Man* is Whileaway, a richly rendered feminist lesbian utopia. In vignettes interspersed throughout the narrative, Joanna provides readers with detailed, and often hilarious, accounts of Whileawayan history, culture, and belief. She explains: "There's no being *out too late* in Whileaway, or *up too early*, or *in the wrong part of town*, or *unescorted*. . . . You cannot fall out of the kinship web and become sexual prey for strangers, for there is no prey and there are no strangers. . . . While here, where *we* live—!"[48] Whileaway is a necessary fantasy for conceptualizing women's equality without foundational reference to men, maleness, or masculinity. But it also an imperfect one. In the novel's second great revelation, Jael responds to Janet's glib superiority by obliterating any illusions about Whileaway's peaceful origins: "Your ancestors lied about [the plague that killed all men]. It is I who gave you your 'plague.' . . . The war [we] fought built your world for you."[49] Jael shockingly reveals that Whileaway is another version of her Earth, where women won the military conflict with men through biological warfare. The narrative suggests that feminist utopias, which celebrate the idea of a world without men, carry a secret dystopian desire for the extermination of half the species. In light of this discovery, we come to understand Whileaway less as a habitable place, but more a fantastical figure for holding together women's contradictory desires: for freedom *and* violence, for reconciliation *and* separatism, for equality across differences *and* the elimination of differences altogether. It is fitting, then, that the Whileawayan God is a woman whose "whole figure is a jumble of . . . inhuman contradictions [whose visage] becomes in turn, gentle, terrifying, hateful, loving, 'stupid' . . . and finally indescribable. Persons who look at Her . . . have been known to vanish right off the face of the Earth."[50] The Whileawayan God stands in for the most dynamic expression of feminism not as a practice of defining a universal woman, but of grappling with its inherent "uncertainty," even if it means having one's fixed sense of self as a woman "vanish right off the face of the Earth."

This is perhaps why Whileaway appears in so many guises to the various women in the novel as an unexpected but invigorating disruption of their self-understanding, and by extension, why the narrative inhabits a plurality of radical feminisms rather than adhering to any single feminist ideology. To Jeannine, Whileaway is a recurring dream that consumes her waking thoughts: "Why does she keep having these dreams about Whileaway? While-away. . . . To While away the time. . . . If she tells Cal about it, he'll say she's nattering again. . . . Maybe she'll meet somebody."[51] In the context of Jeannine's stultifying relationship, Whileaway is her un-conscious fantasy escape from the demands of heterosexual femininity. It comes to represent an inchoate figure for radical feminism's practice of consciousness-raising, which begins with women's willingness to take their disaffected feelings toward patriarchy—commonly denigrated as "nattering silliness"—seriously as the ground for collective rebellion against it. While Jeannine's hope that "maybe she'll meet somebody" speaks to her delusions of finding a Prince Charming, Jeannine does in fact meet "somebody" that changes her life: *her other selves.*

For Joanna, Whileaway is an endless chain of stories about different women, their adventures, aspirations, entanglements, and achievements, which she both documents and integrates into her self-perception. Joanna's version of Whileaway resonates with women-of-color feminisms, which proposed analytical models for understanding the "complicated" existence of women who "live in two worlds," namely multiply marginalized women who must negotiate inhabiting distinct but overlapping cultural identi-ties and social communities. This approach to women's particularity is crystallized in Joanna's poetic statement that "Whileaway is the inside of everything else."[52] Whileaway is a fantasy of universal harmony that exists within "everything," but that can only ever be particular to, or "inside," each person—for your version of feminist freedom can never be identical to mine even if we share values, goals, or identities, because we literally inhabit different bodies and lives.

Finally, to Janet, Whileaway is simply home. In her very being, Janet is a synecdoche for Whileaway, someone who is effortlessly woman-identified, considers sex with women natural and desirable, and whose entire identity is forged without reference to men. Janet is unraveled by the discovery that Whileaway is a utopia built on genocide, because this reality both frees her from, but also robs her of, her place as an untouch-able feminist ideal. In the figure of Janet, then, *The Female Man* presents us with a feminist and queer form who embodies a seemingly impen-etrable image of lesbian feminist power, only to lovingly shatter this icon and expose its internal contradictions, while putting it in dialogue with a variety of other feminist worldviews. In its depiction of Whileaway as a shapeshifting fantasy of feminist freedom, *The Female Man* irrever-ently tests out the applicability of a variety of feminisms to the lives of different women, even those they were never intended for. Thus, it offers one solution to the homogenizing tendencies of feminist politics *The Stepford Wives* diagnosed, encouraging readers to resist standardizing any of the female replicants they encounter in its pages.

At first glance, it would be easy to interpret each of the Js in one way: Jeannine a pathetic wilting flower, Joanna a self-possessed professional, and Janet a fearless warrior. From this vantage, the three appear as clearly defined points on the progressive trajectory from patriarchal mystification to radical feminism. Over time, it is revealed that each of the women carries deep contradictions that set them at odds with these easy categorizations. Throughout the story, Jeannine's thoughts are most often articulated by Joanna, who denigrates the librarian's apparent meekness by implying Jeannine lacks the ability to speak for herself. At one point, however, Jeannine's voice bursts through the narration:

> I live between worlds. Half the time I like doing housework, I care a lot about how I look, . . . and flirt beautifully. . . . In my other incarnation I live out such a plethora of conflict that you wouldn't think I'd survive . . . but I do; I wake up enraged, go to sleep in numbed despair, face what I know perfectly well is condescension and abstract contempt . . . live as if I were . . . trying to buck it all . . . sometimes laugh and weep within five minutes together out of pure frustration. . . . I dream all over the place.[53]

Jeannine describes her own contradictory reality, constantly torn between an ingrained habit of maintaining feminine ideals and a searing emotional impulse to "buck it all." But this also perfectly describes Joanna's life on the verge of the women's liberation movement, so that both women could be speaking simultaneously. We see here a survival instinct in Jeannine—an ability to withstand "living out a plethora of conflict" and her propensity for "dreaming" of a freer life—born of her unmediated relationship to her feelings, which honestly register that she is being constrained unfairly. Ironically, it is precisely the encounter with this "pre-feminist" woman who "lives between two worlds" that allows Joanna to remember that she too is stuck and requires all the different aspects of herself to see outside her own predicament.

In the final instance, it is Jael, the deliciously vengeful spirit of feminist rage, that dismantles any simple interpretations of her three alter egos.

When Jael first brings them to her timeline, Joanna explains: "She took us topside in the branch elevator: The Young One, The Weak One, The Strong One, as she called us in her own mind."[54] Exactly which of the women is "Young," "Strong," and "Weak" remains unclear, for all three could accurately be described by any of these labels. Janet's combat training makes her physically the strongest, but her emotional fragility in the face of feminist criticism could make her mentally the weakest. Joanna might seem psychologically the strongest (by dint of being able to cognize herself as a "female man"), but in some ways she is the politically youngest of the three, still developing a feminist consciousness. Jeannine is the youngest by age, yet her inner tendency to rebel against her circumstances makes her psychologically the strongest. Jael seems keenly aware of this. At one point, Joanna watches as Jael whispers something into Jeannine's ear: "Something had muddied her timidity. What can render Miss Dadier self-possessed? . . . Jeannine said: 'She asked me if I had ever killed anybody.'"[55] Where Joanna maintains a stubborn fiction about Jeannine's "timidity," Jael sees something in her that is authoritative, a woman capable of unleashing lethal vengeance against those who would denigrate, delimit, or dismiss her. In her flattened view of Jeannine, Joanna reproduces Joanna Eberhart's reductive interpretation of the Stepford wives as passive dupes. Against this logic, Jael treats Jeannine as her equal, reading complexity back into a figure of seeming feminist immaturity. We realize each of these women has the capacity to be many things to themselves and each other, given proper recognition from another woman.

The ultimate expression of women's "equal dignity" in the narrative is the ability to cognize the idea of a *female man*, a state of being that Joanna appears to will herself into by the novel's conclusion. What appears to be an act of will, however, is actually one of creativity, a mental practice of reframing equality not as something to be aspired to or requested, but an existential fact that one simply inhabits. As a citizen of a world where women constitute all humankind, Janet embodies the fantasy of being an already constituted female man. But Joanna is, like us, a person living in a sexist society who must practice projecting herself into the category of "mankind." In the book's final chapter, she explains:

> I'll tell you how I turned into a man.
> First I had to turn into a woman.

For a long time I [was] not a woman at all but One Of The Boys. . . .
I back-slapped and laughed at blue jokes. . . . I thought that surely when
I had acquired my Ph.D. and my professorship . . . when I had grown
strong, tall, and beautiful . . . I could take off my sandwich board. . . . I'm
not a woman; I'm a man . . . I cried . . .

Then I turned into a man. . . .

To resolve contraries, unite them in your own person. . . . Let yourself through yourself and give yourself the kiss of reconciliation . . . love
yourself. . . .

What I learned later in life . . . was that there is one and only one way
to possess that in which we are defective . . .

Become it . . .

If we are all Mankind, it follows . . . that I too am a Man and not at all
a Woman. . . . I think you will write about me as a Man from now on and
speak of me as a Man. . . .

If you don't . . . *I'll break your neck.*[56]

Becoming a female man is a psychic process of asserting one's existence
in the face of every patriarchal demand that one simply *not be.* Joanna
describes the mental gymnastics she performed to maintain her dignity in
a patriarchal world. First, working under the ideological illusion that she
might overcome the inferior label "woman" through professional success;
then realizing the impossibility of escape, with its attendant feelings of
emotional hysteria (not unlike Jeannine's outpouring of anguish against
the constraints of her existence); and finally, forming a kind of second
sight associated with the subordinated, the ability to clearly apprehend the
patriarchal logics that exclude, diminish, and negate her. This last movement is a form of coming into feminist consciousness that echoes a range
of 1970s feminist manifestos and programs, which identified how any
woman desiring to be free of patriarchal constraint finds herself in "painful
conflict with people, situations, the accepted ways of thinking, feeling and
behaving, until she is in a state of continual war with everything around
her, and usually with her self."[57] The Radicalesbians described this process
as one that condenses "the rage of all women to the point of explosion,"
while the Black lesbian feminist Combahee River Collective articulated
"their feelings of craziness before becoming conscious of the concepts of
sexual politics, patriarchal rule, and . . . feminism."[58]

Like these various political diagnoses, what is radical about Joanna's frame of reference is her double movement of first acknowledging her experience as bound up in a structure of patriarchal misrecognition, and then developing her own mode of internal, *feminist* recognition and self-valuation, giving herself "the kiss of reconciliation." That practice produces a wholly different logic of mankind, one in which a woman confers universal human belonging upon herself and publicizes that fact to others rather than waiting for a transcendent authority to grant her permission to do so. As Linda Zerilli underscores, "creating new figures for organizing experience [alters] our sense of the real—not of what we know but what we will acknowledge."[59] In the figure of "the female man," the category of "female" becomes a replicant returning to us with a difference, not simply a term representing what we think "we know" about biological sex or culturally constructed gender, but "acknowledged" as a guarantor of universal recognition.

While it is Joanna who explicitly identifies herself as becoming a female man, as the story concludes, this state of being permeates the lives of all the Js. By the end, Jeannine can literally *see more women* as she walks down the streets of New York City: "Jeannine goes window-shopping. She has my eyes, my hands, my silly stoop; she's wearing my blue plastic raincoat. . . . Jeannine is out on the town . . . saying goodbye to all that. . . . The streets are full of women and this awes her; where have they all come from? Where are they going?"[60] As a result of her time-traveling adventures encountering other versions of herself, Jeannine has both literally and figuratively reoriented her gaze at other women. She is at once less a stranger to herself (taking on the physical qualities of one of her alter egos) and affectively attuned to the presence of other women in their inspiring plurality. And so too do we get a parting image of women (even a single woman) as always legion.[61]

In the book's final scene, the four Js sit in a Manhattan diner discussing their future. As they pay their "quintuple" bill, we are led to believe there are more of them than present:

We went out into the street. I said goodbye and went off with Laur, I, Janet; I also watched them go, I Joanna; moreover I went off to show Jael the city, I Jeannine, I Jael, I myself. . . .

> Goodbye to [Jael] . . . who says . . . always go down fighting, who says . . . die if you must but loop your own intestines around the neck of your strangling enemy. . . . Goodbye to Janet . . . whom we deride but who is . . . our savior from utter despair, who appears . . . in our dreams with a mountain under each arm and the ocean in her pocket. . . . Jeannine, goodbye, poor soul, poor girl, poor as-I-once-was. . . . Remember: we will all be changed . . . in the twinkling of an eye, we will all be free. . . . We will be ourselves.[62]

In this moving farewell, each of the Js briefly inhabits the singular "I," taking charge of the narrative to declare their existence, name and honor their interrelationships, and affirm a solidarity grounded not in sameness but *affinity*. In the various descriptions of the women, as vengeful warriors, idealized (if "derided") lesbian feminist fantasies, and tortured souls, we get a vision of each woman taking independent form, yet all potentially parts of a single woman, herself moving in many directions by activating various parts of a feminist imagination.[63] Equality in *The Female Man* is not a woman's achievement of self-sovereignty, the impossible feat of having unified the various parts of herself. Rather it is arriving at a state of "*being ourselves*," of being together in our equal humanity *and* individual uniqueness, or plurality.

Woman Warriors

If *The Stepford Wives* deconstructs a reductive understanding of feminist equality as sameness, and *The Female Man* formally trains readers to apprehend women's inherent multiplicity, Maxine Hong Kingston's speculative memoir *The Woman Warrior* models the quotidian practice of *translation*, where women imaginatively find ways to speak to one another across their divergent experiences, worldviews, and identities. These strategies of translation produce a provisional equality of perspectives between differently situated women that allow them to gain mutual understanding but also make political claims on one another's behalf. I conclude this chapter with Kingston's widely celebrated text in order to show how it brings questions of feminist equality home, both literally and symbolically, by locating the practice of "making equal," or comparing two different women "who stand in need of being 'equalized' in certain respects and for specific purposes" not in the realm of public affairs, as we might expect, but in the interpersonal life of women in a single Chinese American immigrant family.[64]

The Woman Warrior is a life narrative composed of six interlocking stories, which deploys enchanted elements that blur the lines between reality and fantasy. Each story explores the unnamed narrator's relationship to a different woman who has impacted the formation of her identity. These range from familial ghosts (such as her dead aunt) to mythical figures (such as the Chinese warrior Fa Mu Lan) to the most intimate caregivers (her mother and aunt), whose conflicting expressions of womanhood inspire and confuse our narrator as she struggles to form her own sense of being a Chinese American woman. Inspired by the sheer inventiveness of Chinese myth, its endless production of magical creatures, legendary warriors, and malevolent ghosts, the unnamed narrator of Kingston's memoir recasts members of her own family as fantastical, shapeshifting replicants with whom she must find ways to speak, a task that requires the narrator to "make [her] mind large, as the universe is large, so that there is room for paradoxes."[65] By refusing to identify herself as the narrator, Kingston claims a provisional equality with all other women, who are also storytellers in their own right. Consequently, she proposes that a given woman's sense of identity is necessarily an evolving product of her intricately braided relationship to the other female replicants in her life, so that the name of any one is as complex as the "seven strokes" required to write "the Chinese 'I.'"[66]

The opening pages of *The Woman Warrior* boldly publicize a family secret: "'You must not tell anyone,' my mother said, 'what I am about to tell you. In China your father had a sister who killed herself. . . . We say that your father has all brothers because it is as if she had never been born. . . . Now that you have started to menstruate, what happened to her could happen to you. . . . You wouldn't like to be forgotten as if you had never been born. The villagers are watchful.'"[67] In this startling passage, one woman, our narrator, relays the words of another, her mother Brave Orchid, who is herself speaking about a third "no name woman." This last is a relative who died in disgrace long before the family's arrival to the US as immigrants fleeing Chinese Communist rule. In these first pages, the narrator relates Brave Orchid's brief but devastating tale of this dead aunt, a woman who was punished by her Chinese village for becoming pregnant out of wedlock while her husband lived abroad. In a final act—perhaps of defiance, despair, or "spite"—the aunt drowned herself and her child "in the family well."[68] Brave Orchid's story is intended to protect her daughter against a similar fate should she behave in ways that would cause her to lose the shelter of their community. Yet the original contexts in which this story might have made sense to Brave Orchid's daughter, including the particular social taboos of a Chinese village, no longer exist for the family. US born, raised in a single-family home in Stockton, California, our narrator cannot live out the same fate as her aunt.

Faced with this "no name woman's" submerged history, the storyteller is forced to make sense of an unlikely female replicant whom she has never met and can only ever imagine. She explains, "Whenever she had to warn us about life, my mother told stories that ran like this one . . . to grow up on. She tested our strength to establish realities. Those in the emigrant generations who could not reassert brute survival died young and far from home. Those of us in the first American generations have had to figure out how the invisible world the emigrants built around our childhoods fits in solid America."[69] In the following pages, this need to "figure out" an "invisible world" of parables and myths exported from China leads our storyteller to combine her own uneven knowledge of Chinese history and her talents as a writer to creatively fill in the gaps of her dead aunt's past. In a series of counterfactual speculations, the narrator wonders if her aunt had been raped by a fellow villager; or if she had been abandoned by a lover; or, perhaps less likely, if she was a "a wild woman" shirking Chinese custom.[70] With each "perhaps," our narrator constructs a different interpretation of this family ghost, to "figure out" what insights the vengeful spirit of a banished aunt might hold for her "American life," for "[u]nless I see her life branching into mine, she gives me no ancestral help."[71]

Like the warrior scientist Jael, who draws together her other selves to learn from their unique perspectives, our unnamed narrator directly translates her mother's words on the page to elicit her readers' opinions. Shortly after relating Brave Orchid's cautionary tale, the narrator directly addresses her Chinese American readers: "Chinese-Americans, when you try to understand what things in you are Chinese, how do you separate what is peculiar to childhood, to poverty, insanities, one family, your mother who marked your growing with stories, from what is Chinese? What is Chinese tradition and what is the movies?"[72] The narrator asks a particular segment of her readership: what are the imaginative strategies you deploy to make sense of your "Chineseness" when there are so many versions of it being offered to you? The question undermines the very idea of any singular, unified, or coherent Chinese culture that could be handed down in an unbroken line by family, education, or popular culture—each of these sources is simply another "peculiar" perspective that informs one's own. Similarly, no definition of "woman" within the feminist imagination could possibly explain the heterogeneous experiences of unevenly situated Chinese and Chinese American women in a single family across time and continents. Like the shock of groundlessness in *The Female Man*, the surprise of *The Woman Warrior* is the fact that not even a shared cultural heritage or the bonds of family can provide a solid basis for mutual understanding between women. Rather than speaking from a position of self-righteous certainty as a "Western feminist," as some critics have claimed, the storyteller "crowdsources" fresh perspectives on the meaning of a family legend, thereby treating multiple points of view on a single woman's life as all potentially equally valuable.[73] This was the skill Joanna Eberhart lacked, which diminished her capacity to see other women as dynamic correspondents, braided knots of history, affect, experience, and desire with whom one must engage in countless acts of translation.

For our storyteller, every such encounter always begins with the incommensurability of two different women's life experiences, which requires comparison to forge a provisional equality between them, a sense of "getting the shared world in view."[74] One potent strategy the narrator draws upon is *projection*, the creative practice of imagining oneself standing in the place of, or seeing through the eyes of, another woman (as when she attempts to inhabit the potential lifeworlds of her long lost aunt). The most sustained example of projection in the text appears in the second story, "White Tigers," which relates the narrator's long-held fantasy of becoming Fa Mu Lan, a mythical Chinese "woman warrior" who trains for years as a master fighter to defend her village from despotic warlords and free China from their illegitimate rule. The narrator's fantasy is a response to the transmission of mixed messages about the proper social trajectory of Chinese girls: "When we Chinese girls listened to the adults talk-story, we learned that we failed if we grew up to be but wives or slaves. We could be heroines, swordswomen. . . . [A] swordswoman got even with anybody who hurt her family. Perhaps women were once so dangerous that they had to have their feet bound."[75] The narrator grows up hearing Chinese myths about the heroism of warrior women, but simultaneously experiences the devaluation of Chinese girls, who are expected to maintain humble obedience to family and husbands. This contradiction is redoubled in US culture, where the presumed equality and freedom of women in a democratic society runs up against unrelenting demands to approximate an ideal of submissive white femininity: "Walking erect (knees straight, toes pointed forward) . . . and speaking in an inaudible voice, I have tried to turn myself American-feminine."[76] In both contexts, the storyteller is acutely aware that women hold great power—including the ability to effect social change, fight injustice, and leave a legacy for their families and communities—but that that power is everywhere delimited and suppressed.

The storyteller is left to find ways to draw from those aspects of Chinese tradition that leave openings for women's unlimited potential, while adapting the meaning of those traditions to her everyday life in a US context. She explains:

> My mother told [stories] that followed swordswomen through woods and palaces for years. Night after night my mother would talk-story . . . her voice the voice of the heroines in my sleep. . . . At last I saw that I too had been in the presence of great power, my mother talking-story. After I grew up, I heard the chant of Fa Mu Lan, the girl who took her father's place in battle. . . . I had forgotten this chant that was once mine, given me by my mother. . . . She said I would grow up a wife and a slave, but she taught me the song of a warrior woman, Fa Mu Lan.[77]

By taking the place of her father in battle, Fa Mu Lan is a Chinese woman who unexpectedly comes to inhabit the traditional space of male power. This provides a creative model for conceiving of Chinese women in new roles, both in their surprising rebellion against traditional expectations of dutifulness, as well as US stereotypes of Asian women's presumed passivity. The magical ability of women to become warriors is literalized in the capacity of actual Chinese women like the narrator's mother Brave Orchid to tell multiple, sometimes conflicting, stories about their lives and cultural histories—this includes Brave Orchid's surprising disclosure that she went to medical school in China, becoming the first woman doctor in her village years before she emigrated to the US. In the image of Fa Mu Lan's warrior path, and her mother's remarkable past as a trained physician, the narrator grasps that even within the matrix of a patriarchal Chinese tradition there exist a variety of stories (imagined and real) in which women are capable of being, quite simply, *more than one thing.* Unable to reconcile patriarchal custom with the countless stories of Chinese women's warrior skill, the narrator instead projects herself through Fa Mu Lan's fantastical power, her mother's talk-story, and her own writerly skills, forming a lineage between them that honors both their shared experiences and particularity.

To "grow up to be a warrior woman" in the US context, then, involves our narrator herself becoming a storyteller who circulates a prodigious myth about what Chinese women can be, which is the prismatic set of tales we hold in our hands. As an adult, the storyteller is able to see that even though she and Fa Mu Lan do not share a particular life, they do share an ethical orientation. Both are rebels against a range of injustices in their respective worlds. As the story concludes, the narrator reassesses her relationship to Fa Mu Lan: "I went away to college—Berkeley in the sixties . . . and I marched to change the world. . . . What [the swordswoman and I] have in common are the words at our backs. The idioms for revenge are 'report a crime' and 'report to five families.' The reporting is the vengeance—not the beheading . . . but the words. And I have so many words—'chink' words and 'gook' words too—that they do not fit on my skin."[78] It is only in hindsight, from the vantage of a college-educated activist, that our narrator recognizes the symbolic weight of the story of Fa Mu Lan. It is no longer only a tale about a woman's skillful wielding of physical power, but more importantly, her readiness to bear testimony for the collective experience of her people. Who counts as one woman's "people" shifts in relation to her specific social and political contexts. As a Chinese American woman who went to "Berkeley in the sixties," the storyteller speaks with, and on behalf of, multiple oppressed groups, from African and Asian Americans battling against entrenched racisms to Third World peoples struggling to overthrow the yoke of colonialism. Against the violent, reductive force of racist "'chink' words and 'gook' words," she uses a vast vocabulary of feminist replication, a counterdiscourse, to create an imaginative context in which her readers can potentially project themselves into the experience of one Chinese American girl and the women who make up her life, even if only partially. That is the condition for conceiving of others as equal: the ability to conceptually link or fairly compare one person (or form) to another, to create an equality between them, despite their manifold differences.

It is telling that the storyteller invokes her experience of "marching to change the world" as a precursor to her enlarged perspective. It is in and through her encounters with large-scale political movements for the universal equality of various oppressed peoples that the narrator is able to reapproach the life histories and worldviews of the women in her family as all equally valuable. The storyteller's experience echoes contemporaneous women-of-color feminist accounts of the transformative effects of coming into feminist and queer consciousness in the 1970s, which many claimed granted them new insight into the historically situated conditions of the women in their life. In *This Bridge Called My Back*, Moraga recounts, "It wasn't until I acknowledged and confronted my own lesbianism in the flesh, that my heartfelt identification with and empathy for my mother's oppression—to being poor, uneducated, and Chicana—was realized."[79] In the same collection, Asian American feminist Mitsuye Yamada wrote, "Earlier this year, when a group of Asian Pacific American women gathered together in San Francisco . . . to talk about feminism, I was struck by our general agreement on the subject of feminism *as an ideal*. We all believed in equality for women. . . . Through the women's movement, I have come to truly appreciate the meaning of my mother's life and the lives of immigrant women like her . . . and through her I have become more sensitive to the needs of Third World women."[80] While similar racial, gender, or class experiences, and common cultural heritages provide some shared vocabulary between these women and their mothers, those factors alone do not foster effortless understanding. Rather Moraga and Yamada describe how their own evolving feminist and queer consciousness about the multiple, overlapping inequalities faced by women of all stripes has given them conceptual tools for "see[ing] connections" between their particular experiences and those of their mothers, without collapsing them. Consequently, in the wake of her own transformative encounters with feminist and Third World movements, what the narrator of *The Woman Warrior* retains from the original story of Fa Mu Lan is not a coherent Chinese tradition to be transmitted to her readers, but rather the fable's fantastical incitement for women to *imagine what it is like to be someone else.* By refusing to narrate her life as universally representative of Chinese women's experiences, however, the storyteller's solicitation to, in Kandice Chuh's words, "imagine as the other" also encourages readers to "imagine the other differently," to see the category of Asian woman as plural and particular to every person who inhabits or claims affinity to it.[81]

Fa Mu Lan is only one of the many feminist forms the narrator projects herself into to expand the limits of her own identity, construct her complex lineage to other women storytellers, and rebelliously claim images of Chinese women's power. Another of the most recurrent figures in *The Woman Warrior* is the dragon. In traditional Chinese culture, the dragon is a mythical creature, often depicted as a giant, multicolored lizard with wings, associated with extraordinary strength and the qualities of achievement and excellence. In the storyteller's rendition of the Fa Mu Lan legend, the dragon appears in a multitude of guises. The warrior's ability to discern a dragon in the wild comes with maturity and skill: "I needed adult wisdom to know dragons. . . . Dragons are so immense, I would never see one in its entirety. But I could explore the mountains, which are the top of its head. 'These mountains are also *like* the tops of other dragon's heads,' the old people would tell me. . . . The dragon lives in the sky, ocean, marshes, and mountains; and the mountains are also its cranium . . . sometimes the dragon is one, sometimes many."[82] The storyteller's multiplex description of the dragon is a compelling analogy for the expanding category of "woman," whose meaning was no longer self-evident by the mid-1970s, proliferating at "a breathless pace" as various expressions of feminist activism and political thought revealed the infinite variety of women's experiences. Through the practice of figuration, Maxine adapts a Chinese icon to describe and explain the complexity of women, who exist everywhere ("[living] in the sky, ocean, marshes, and mountains"), who provide so much of the foundation for the social world she moves through ("solid and immobile"), yet whose figurative "heads" are also only ever "like" one another, but never identical.

Maxine's reconceptualization of the dragon as a distinctly feminist figure allows her to tailor its most magnificent qualities to a moving description of her mother's fortitude in the face of extraordinary personal challenges, including the death of her first-born children, attending medical school, and living through World War II, all before arriving to the US: "My mother may have been afraid, but she would be a dragoness. . . . During danger she fanned out her dragon claws. . . . Danger was a good time for showing off."[83] Just as the narrator had projected herself *backward* through the lineage of women beginning with Fa Mu Lan all the way through her mother, the master storyteller, so in parallel fashion, she draws from the Fa Mu Lan story a shapeshifting figure of immense power and intricacy, the dragon, that she projects *forward* through the prism of contemporary feminist thought. Consequently, like the influence of feminist and queer consciousness on Moraga and Yamada, which granted them new insight into their mothers' experiences, the dragon becomes symbolic of the narrator's "adult wisdom" in recognizing qualities of strength, resilience, even panache in Brave Orchid that she had once mistaken for coldness, insensitivity, or opacity. The storyteller's adept practice of figuration, where Chinese icons like the dragon come to describe, or sit productively beside, contemporary feminist understandings of the category of woman, suggests a supple understanding of Chinese tradition and feminist thought as mutually influencing. Figures like Fa Mu Lan and the dragon are not secondary to so-called Western feminist discourse, but in fact precede it, offering historical examples of inchoate feminisms from the Chinese tradition that are simply revivified and translated to a US context.

Throughout *The Woman Warrior*, the stakes of translation are exceptionally high, for it involves nothing less than the possibility for mutual understanding. The failure of translation can have terrible psychic consequences, including feeling invisible or negated, an outcome that redoubles both the Chinese immigrant experience of US racism and the Chinese American girl's sense of being devalued by her family. In the final chapter, our narrator recounts a terrible moment of childhood conflict with her mother. One night, she explodes at Brave Orchid:

"[The Teacher Ghosts] tell me I'm smart, and . . . I can get into colleges. . . .
I am not going to be a slave or a wife . . . I don't want to listen to any more
of your stories; they have no logic . . . I can't tell what's real and what you
make up." . . .

My mother, who is a champion talker, was, of course, shouting at the
same time. "You can't listen right. I didn't say I was going to marry you
off. . . . Can't you take a joke? . . .

"When I get to college, it won't matter if I'm not charming. And it
doesn't matter if a person is ugly; she can still do schoolwork."

"I didn't say you were ugly."

"You say that all the time." . . .

"That's what Chinese say. We like to say the opposite."

It seems to hurt her to tell me that . . . and suddenly I got very con-
fused and lonely because I was at that moment telling her my list, and in
the telling, it grew. No higher listener . . . but myself.[84]

In this heartbreaking encounter, our narrator's list of resentments
against her mother's many expectations betrays a fundamental misun-
derstanding of Brave Orchid's worldview. The daughter's rage is understandable, as she lacks the full context required to properly translate the
meaning behind Brave Orchid's words; yet so is Brave Orchid's frustration, as she realizes that her daughter's US-American upbringing has
failed to provide a shared frame of reference between them. In Brave
Orchid's perspective, criticizing her daughter's appearance is actually a
compliment, because "saying the opposite" is a humble way to indicate
her daughter's beauty in Chinese tradition. Similarly, her lack of praise
for her daughter's scholastic achievement is meant to strengthen her resolve and set exceptional standards for excellence. And in her fantastical stories, Brave Orchid expresses the playfulness and exhilaration of
Chinese myths to her children. By claiming that Brave Orchid's stories
"have no logic," the narrator effectively negates her mother's form of
rationality, which leads to a sense of isolation born out of the experience
of speaking past other women, rather than with them.

As the storyteller grows older and becomes more aware of the racism
and sexism of US society, the neat distinction she has produced between
a superstitious and "confusing" Chinese culture and a rational transparent US culture disintegrates. Both societies, she realizes, merely offer

STEPFORD WIVES AND FEMALE MEN | 99

different attitudes on the world, both carry conservative *and* progressive possibilities, both are hypocritical and contradictory, and neither can be relied upon to provide her a stable sense of self. As an adult, the storyteller looks back on the fateful night she screamed her list of grievances at Brave Orchid and reflects: "I had to leave home in order to see the world logically. . . . I learned to think that mysteries are for explanation. . . . Shine floodlights into dark corners: no ghosts. . . . I continue to sort out what's just my childhood, just my imagination, just my family, just the village, just movies, just living."[85] In this poignant meditation, the storyteller finally reconstructs the origins of her own worldview. She sees in hindsight that her dogmatic attachment to a US-American logic of rationality and transparency is not universal but simply a "new way of seeing" that revels in exposing myths and smugly speaks in the name of "reality" over fantasy but is no less invented than Chinese myth. To expose, simplify, and scoff at Chinese tradition, and the women shaped by it, is to "make it less scary" by freeing oneself of the difficult labor of interpreting its intricacies. Yet the very stories we hold before us testify to the narrator's recognition that "logic" cannot provide an adequate way to "sort out" what aspects of her Chinese American identity were shaped by the presence of different women, the idiosyncrasies of her family, or the messages of US popular culture. Ultimately, these stories are no more and no less than the skills one Chinese American girl develops to understand the female replicants in her life, to create some sort of equivalence between herself and her mother, sister, friends, even her dead aunt, in the absence of universally shared contexts for meaning-making.

Far from being the product of any single lineage of feminist thought or activism, the various strategies the storyteller invents to reach across distances of history, language, experience, even temperament and habit, reflect multiple, overlapping feminist ideals. All involve some aspect of pooling the experiences of different women, which looks like the radical feminist practice of consciousness-raising. All demand an accounting of the manifold, overlapping identities that Chinese women inhabit, which echoes women-of-color feminists' commitment to valuing and learning from "multiple identity standpoints." And all place equivalent value on the dramatically variegated life experiences, worldviews, and personal idiosyncrasies of different women, which models the project of feminist equality discourse.

The storyteller's debt to a variety of feminist lineages is under-scored when placed alongside the grassroots writing and theorizing of Asian American feminists in this period. In 1971, a diverse group of Asian American students at UC Berkeley—hailing from Chinese, Japa-nese, Vietnamese, Indonesian, and Arab backgrounds—collaboratively edited a groundbreaking collection of feminist writing titled *Asian Women*. They organized more than forty entries exploring everything from the history of Chinese women indentured servants to Asian Amer-ican popular culture and Third World feminisms. It is no small coinci-dence that, like the storyteller of *The Woman Warrior*, the anthology's editors went to "Berkeley in the sixties," using the knowledge they had gained in ethnic studies classrooms, feminist working groups, and Bay Area Third World activism to develop strategies for making sense of their multiple identities. Through historical research and interviews, the writers *reconstructed* the lives of their mothers and grandmothers and *projected* themselves into a variety of Asian pasts. In reappraising the contemporary lessons to be learned from spiritual disciplines like Tai Chi and Taoism, they *translated* Asian traditions into contempo-rary feminist contexts. And in short stories and poems about numerous kinds of Asian women, contributors produced new imaginative *figures* that feminists of all stripes might identify with. As Laura Kang explains, the collection's myriad genres, voices, and methods underscored that early Asian American feminism was not a unified theory or activist practice aimed at defining an essential Asian female identity. Rather it was an amalgamated set of strategies for doing justice to the complex lives of Asian women that adapted and reinvented concepts from a plu-rality of feminisms.[86]

Like the feminist projects that preceded it, *The Woman Warrior* captures this earlier moment of inchoate possibility in its unorthodox blending of multiple feminist worldviews and its refusal to ultimately fix the meaning of "Asian American woman." The outcome is not only a complex portrait of Chinese American women's multiplicity, but also of their affinities with other multiply marginalized women, an equality born of shared experiences rather than essential traits. Near the conclu-sion, the narrator relates a conversation with Brave Orchid about her tireless labor in California's tomato fields: "'Every woman in the tomato row is sending money home,' my mother says, 'to Chinese villages and

Mexican villages and Filipino villages and, now, Vietnamese villages, where they speak Chinese too. The women come to work whether sick or well. 'I can't die,' they say, 'I'm supporting fifty,' or, 'I'm supporting a hundred.'"[87] Through a kaleidoscopic portrait of one Chinese American girl's network of female replicants, the storyteller comes full circle back to the broader collective experience of women from around the globe, who despite their innumerable differences, encounter one another in the shared context of migration. Each has a distinct version of "village," family, and language, and each has a singular outlook born of her unique history. But in their geographical convergence in the US, in their collective labor in California's tomato farms, in their shared responsibility to a transnational web of kinship, those individual histories now converge to tell a larger story as immense as any dragon.

* * *

Across the arc of this chapter, I have followed the imaginative travels of the female replicant through three speculative narratives to show how this figure provided a feminist and queer form for thematizing the project of equality as a continual practice of negotiating women's differences. In *The Stepford Wives*, the female replicant comes to represent an anxiety about women's mechanical duplication and replacement by robots but goes on to become a potent warning about the threat of conformist thinking in all varieties of feminism. In *The Female Man*, the female replicant transmutes into a metaphor for the generative fragmentation of a single woman's identity into countless "other selves," demanding that we cognitively apprehend all women as having rich and variegated interior worlds. And in *The Woman Warrior*, the female replicant returns as a strategic shapeshifter taking on countless guises in an attempt to translate different women's life experiences as a basis for meaningful exchange between them.

At first glance, it would be easy to see *The Stepford Wives*, *The Female Man*, and *The Woman Warrior* as collectively charting a trajectory from a myopic white liberal feminism to a radical lesbian feminism, and finally to an intersectional woman-of-color feminism. This view would conveniently shore up the dominant supersessionary history of 1970s feminisms, but it would also demand its own kind of myopia. We would have to ignore *The Stepford Wives'* demand that feminism account for

Black women's perspectives. It would mean overlooking *The Female Man*'s inchoate intersectional approach to women's "complex lives," and dismissing *The Woman Warrior*'s commitment to consciousness-raising about Chinese women's oppression as a mistaken attachment to "white feminism." My point has been to trouble that narrative, by revealing how, even as each text builds its version of the female replicant from the position of particular women, each then continues to draw from a variety of feminist concepts, practices, and theories across the span of their stories. In their irreverent mixing and matching of different feminist ideals, these texts trained readers to see the problem of equality from plural dimensions and perspectives, to see how variously situated women might use the same feminist tools and concepts differently or choose to invent new approaches to equality altogether. The female replicant functioned as a feminist and queer form by repeatedly returning multiplicity both to *women* as a heterogeneous group and to *equality* as a multifaceted concept: whether in the majestic face of the Whileawayan God or the manifold forms of the dragon.

It is these many faces or aspects of equality, understood as the dynamic and engaged negotiation of differences, that is often lost to contemporary social justice discourse. Of course, present-day feminist, queer, and trans* liberation projects frequently take up equality claims to demand such things as women's right to equal pay and reproductive health, gays and lesbians' ability to marry, adopt children, and be free from sexual policing, trans* people's access to gender-affirming medical care and legal self-nomination, and all these groups' freedom from discrimination. These movements share many political interests and their participants frequently hold overlapping commitments across all three. Yet every bid for equality made by distinct constituents of gender and sexual outlaws always starts as a specific demand that requires the comparison of two unlike subjects "who stand in need of being 'equalized' in certain respects and for specific purposes." All women and queers should live equally under the law, but not all women and queers need to be *equalized* to the same degree in relation to the exact same variables (e.g., everyone should be free to access the bathroom that accords with their gender, but cis women and queers may not need to be equalized around this issue as urgently as trans folks. Then again, they might, depending on the context. One would have to make the case through careful comparison in particular instances). Yet social justice discourse also often conflates equality, which simultaneously recognizes and mediates between differences in their distinction, with the presumed value of *universal inclusion*, a tacitly shared goal of a world where every single human being is accepted and nurtured regardless of their identity. No progressive-minded person could disagree with the spirit of this aim. Yet, whereas equality requires discernment, the ability to tell differences in order to meaningfully account for them, inclusion is a conceptually nebulous value that requires no apprehensible forms to make political claims on behalf of an amorphous mass called "everybody." This is perhaps why the term sits comfortably within the network of "formless" signs or concepts that accumulate around the celebrated ideal of gender and sexual fluidity. Like the paradigm of infinitely mutable, fluid selfhood, the fantasy of universal inclusion has the potential to leap too swiftly past the necessary labor of giving shape to our differences, juxtaposing and adjudicating their meaning across infinitely variable locations and circumstances.

The female replicant continues to matter today as a feminist and queer form that can teach us to resist the twin pitfalls of (a) a rigid conception of the feminist and queer past, which would reductively circumscribe the manifold meanings of equality to an easily dismissed bid for sameness within a bankrupt normative standard, and (b) the tendency to seek utopian escape from the difficult process of perpetually representing and working out our differences in the present. That the same figure could be rendered in such a multitude of ways, offering so many perspectives on the concept of equality, suggests the richness of the female replicant as a cultural form for transmitting new ideas about feminist equality claims in the 1970s and after. In turn, the female replicant offers us a model for our own reappraisal of historical projects for gender and sexual freedom by enjoining us to reconceive the feminist and queer past not as a fixed set of ideologies, "waves," or conflicted camps, but as diverse, yet equal interlocutors, demanding that we ceaselessly look back, listen, and reply.

2

Entering the Vortex

Breaching the Boundaries of the Lesbian Separatist Frontier in Avant-Garde Science Fiction Film

The fact that men took control of the earth and changed it from a peaceful productive world into a conglomeration of societies founded and continued on rape, war, exploitation and destruction is not an accident: By their very nature, by their emptiness of female qualities, men are a death-force.
—Gutter Dyke Collective, *Dykes & Gorgons* (1973)

The gun is good. The penis is evil.
—The Stone Head, in *Zardoz* (dir. John Boorman, 1974)

At the end of her explosive 1967 polemic, *The S.C.U.M. Manifesto*, the sex worker, playwright, and feminist revolutionary Valerie Solanas boldly proclaimed: "If all women simply left men, refused to have anything to do with any of them—ever, all men, the government, and the national economy would collapse completely."[1] Three years before the official formation of a women's liberation movement in 1970, Solanas articulated the foundational, anarchist proposition of what would soon be called *lesbian separatism*, a feminist politics based on the ideal of complete divestment from men and male-dominated society. To reread *S.C.U.M.* (Society for Cutting Up Men) today is to encounter one of the most incendiary and thrilling performances of political rage in the history of late twentieth-century radical writing. Pulling no punches, Solanas founds a politics based on nothing but complete identification and alliance with women as an oppressed group, whose inherent superiority to men entitles them to cut ties with, and ultimately violently destroy, patriarchy. She arrogantly offers a total theory of male domination, identifying men as the root cause of all modern evils, from war, violence, and disease to the everyday indignities of boredom, conformity, and elit-ism; a total theory of gender, arguing that "the male is an incomplete female, a walking abortion . . . deficient, [and] emotionally limited"; and a total theory of overthrowing patriarchy, based on the anarchist principle of women banding together to "[take] over the country . . . by systematically fucking up the system, selectively destroying property, and murder."[2] The polemical force and conceptual power of *S.C.U.M.* lay in Solanas's unilateral reversal of the logic of male power. Inhabiting a godlike voice with unquestioned legitimacy to make universal claims about the nature of gender and male domination, Solanas radically pro-posed that everything we think we know about "women"—the culture's assumptions that they are overly emotional, physically weak, lacking in ambition or original thought—would "collapse" when "groovy females" finally and decisively separated from the men who blocked all possible avenues for their flourishing.

The S.C.U.M. Manifesto was shockingly ahead of its time, vehe-mently demanding that women abandon men at all levels of society two years before radical women in the New Left officially began to leave the movement and develop their own theory of gendered oppression. *S.C.U.M.* would come to have special meaning to lesbian feminists in the early 1970s, who found themselves negated and despised by a patriarchal society, but also painfully shunned by straight women in the feminist movement and gay men in gay liberation. In 1977, lesbian separatist writer and activist Charlotte Bunch reflected back on the ex-perience of many lesbians who were forced to leave women's liberation because of virulent homophobia: "The [women's] movement had been our family. . . . When we began to proclaim our love for one another . . . most of us did not realize how savagely we would be disinherited by our 'sisters.' Lesbianism is not only a threat to men, but also to many het-erosexual women. It suggests that women do not inevitably have to love men, or to love them at any cost."[3] Lesbian separatism, then, emerged as a double-edged response to an unrelenting experience of both politi-cal and interpersonal rejection. It was simultaneously a *defensive* poli-tics based on protecting lesbians from the psychological and physical harms of heteropatriarchy, and a boldly *offensive* politics that forcefully asserted the innate value of a "woman-identified" or uniquely lesbian orientation to the world. This stance was understood to be inherently

anti-patriarchal by virtue of lesbians' affective, erotic, and political disinterest in men.[4]

At the core of this logic, separatism sought to ask and answer what
was arguably the most radical speculative question ever posed by
second-wave feminism: what could women possibly be or become
without men? This question presupposed the concept of form or taking
shape. After all, it is the work of form to separate, distinguish, and mold
uniquely defined objects of perception that can then exist in relation to
one another. By willfully detaching from male-dominated society, separatists sought to clear space for the formation of an emergent subject, the
lesbian feminist, while imagining that this new political being would be
capable of radically altering the course of human civilization by destroying patriarchy. In Solanas's incendiary vision, for example, she imagined
that women's separation from male-dominated society would enable the
coalescence of a unique category of "females," anarchist feminists who
would compose a "Society for Cutting Up Men" committed to exter-
minating the male species. In this sense, lesbian separatism provided
the paradigmatic logic of all left-wing identity politics in the 1970s and
after, which aspired to a world where different oppressed subjects could
distinguish and define their uniquely marginalized identities, potentially
granting them a newfound insight on how to dismantle the sources of
their subjection, and perhaps even all others'.

In this chapter, I explore how the affective and conceptual logic of
lesbian separatism was visually represented in experimental science fiction cinema of the mid-1970s and early 1980s. Specifically, I analyze John
Boorman's dystopian film *Zardoz* (1974), which narrates the tragic collapse of an ideal separatist commune, and Lizzie Borden's speculative
documentary *Born in Flames* (1982), a fictional account of a future lesbian army composed of numerous guerilla cells that battle a patriarchal,
socialist US government.[5] I argue that these films dramatized and gave
concrete form to two distinct but interrelated versions of separatism
that emerged over the span of the 1970s. In *Zardoz*, we see separatism
enacted as a total program in which a single community of "Eternals,"
or evolved humans, seals itself off from the outside world. Throughout
the film, the concept of separatism is repeatedly thematized in a series
of physical structures that contain, delimit, or circumscribe the collective and their wealth of psychic knowledge, such as impenetrable dome

shields, diamond-like crystals, or labyrinthine halls of mirrors. This version of separatism echoed an early 1970s lesbian feminist ideal known as the "Lesbian Nation," a loosely affiliated series of all-women communes, farms, and collectives, which were conceived as bounded geographical spaces meant to encompass and nurture lesbian feminist lifeways and values.

Alternatively, in *Born in Flames*, separatism functions as a contingent political strategy taken up at different moments by the various members of a Women's Army in order to regroup one's social energies, develop new methods of protest, or simply think through and sort out one's varied political commitments. Instead of an all-encompassing ideology, separatism reappears as the *impulse to separate* or get distance from the sources of one's oppression, even from one's own political allies. This separatist impulse is repeatedly figured in the film's proliferation of numerous delineated visual units or cells that formally model the organizational structure of the Women's Army: these include the enclosed spaces of radio recording studios or living rooms that house lesbian feminist consciousness-raising (CR) meetings; a string of concentric circles used to describe the modular cells of the Women's Army; and the physical frame of the camera itself, which frequently outlines the talking heads of individual members of distinct feminist collectives. While *Born in Flames* contrasts dramatically with *Zardoz*—in its racially diverse cast, multiple forms of feminist praxis, and realist setting in a modern-day New York City—the film significantly draws from elements of early 1970s separatist politics, but adapts them to a multiracial, coalitional context.

Both films develop a formal lexicon or vocabulary of lesbian separatism in its many historical expressions, providing viewers a multiplicity of figures, images, or icons of separation at varied scales—whether as a collective divestment from a dominant patriarchal culture, or in countless types of interpersonal withdrawal from toxic relations with men and other women who misrecognize one's existence. Rather than home in on a single form, then, this chapter pursues the *formal logic* of splitting off and containment as it is materialized in a variety of apprehensible shapes—from a sealed dome encircling a utopian commune to the networked structure of a guerilla army—that are articulated to lesbian separatism as a *political logic* of women's separation, enclosure, and self-definition. In the previous chapter, I unpacked how feminist and queer forms can operate as enabling structures that amplify our ability to conceive gender and sexual diversity in the mind's eye. Here, I argue that forms can also serve a historical function by illuminating new dimensions of the feminist and queer past and making them available to cognition. The proliferating lesbian separatist forms of *Zardoz* and *Born in Flames* allow us to trace the surprising and unexpected continuities that exist between an essentialist and often white, lesbian separatist political vision, and more coalition-based socialist and women-of-color (WOC) feminisms that have traditionally been understood as radically opposed. By doing so we can better acknowledge the significant influence that a seemingly anachronistic and widely dismissed lesbian separatism has had on contemporary left-wing identity movements, while simultaneously honoring Black and other WOC feminisms as fundamentally lesbian-inflected traditions of radical thought that are not antithetical to separatism but have been central co-creators of it.

As film scholar Damon Young has shown, the 1970s signaled a moment when the dominant "male gaze" of Hollywood cinema was giving way to a more expansive visual imaginary that included the increasing presence of new kinds of gender and sexual subjects, including sexually empowered women and explicitly out queers on screen.[6] In this context, lesbian feminist visions of the future could be more fully fleshed out and creatively tested in the cinema, especially as men, once representing the unmarked universal "eye" of the cinematic apparatus, increasingly became the object of the filmic gaze, literally and figuratively undressed, objectified and scrutinized by the camera much as lesbian feminism ideologically scrutinized maleness and patriarchy. Science fiction cinema was a particularly fertile ground for exploring the political possibilities and limits of lesbian separatism across the 1970s because of separatism's affinity to utopianism, the impulse toward conceiving a fully realized ideal world. The social and political desire for complete separation from men and male-dominated society was in many ways a speculative fiction or aspirational dream that would require a monumental transformation in gender hierarchy to be actualized. Separatist cultural critic Jill Johnston underscored the magnitude of this project in her bestselling collection of feminist writing, *Lesbian Nation* (1973): "The aim is an end . . . to sexual duality or the two-sex system and a gradual evolutionary movement through ... homosexuality back to true parthenogenetic species. All men start off as women and that's the way they'll end up if they don't destroy us first."[7] Johnston's statement saw the flight from male society as potentially having the world-historical effect of destroying the gender binary altogether, and by extension eliminating "man" as a biological or social category of being. In its most extreme expressions, separatist ideology included a variety of feminist fantasies such as attempts to discover the secrets of parthenogenic or virgin birth, recovering evidence of prehistoric matriarchal cultures, and the constitution of a fully autonomous Lesbian Nation.[8] While separatists succeeded in creating a number of women-only collectives and communes, and developed a nationwide "Amazon Network" of lesbian print culture, many of these hopes for a completely self-sustaining lesbian way of life, and a total revolution in gender relations, could exist only in one's reveries.[9]

Despite its utopian promise separatism has, since nearly its inception, been the perennial bad object of second-wave feminism, perceived as an essentialist identitarian politics grounded in the fantasy of a universally shared lesbian orientation to the world that seamlessly knits together the erotic and political dimensions of any woman's lived experience. *As if.* With the ascendancy of postmodern and intersectional feminist approaches to identity, which refuse essentialism and acknowledge the complex interlocking nature of race, class, sexuality, and ability, lesbian separatism today often looks like a tragic relic of a failed (white) feminist past. It is perhaps unsurprising, then, that separatism was forcefully challenged in its own historical moment by women-of-color feminists, most explicitly in the Combahee River Collective's Black Feminist Statement, which criticized lesbian separatists' exclusive focus on sexuality as the root of all other oppressions, thereby downplaying or altogether ignoring the central role played by race and class privilege in women's subordination. Accordingly, the most common critiques tell us that separatism relies on an essential notion of lesbian identity that is putatively white, able-bodied, thin, and educated; denies the necessity of political coalition across differences; reduces the radicalness of feminist political aims to a narrow and naïve fantasy of creating a shared women's culture; and engages in a withdrawal from the primary sites of collective political struggle that is ultimately self-defeating and ineffective in dismantling patriarchal institutions.

The power of these criticisms lies in their profound *rightness*: on any intellectual score, they are simply correct. Affectively, however, they frequently ring hollow. Lesbian separatisms' monolithic analysis of patriarchy as an omnipotent unified conspiracy against women may in reality be wrong, but it certainly *feels* right; and in similar fashion oppressive systems like white supremacy, capitalism, or heteronormativity may be complex and unevenly distributed, but for many of us, they certainly *feel* as though they are insidiously everywhere.[10] Despite the critical purchase of arguments that have made separatism a feminist anachronism, none have ever adequately been able to dissolve the nagging fact of separatism's galvanizing emotional force, its articulation of genuine rage at patriarchal domination, and its creation of a ground for women's legitimate claim to moral righteousness in the face of their shared oppression. As lesbian philosopher Sarah Hoagland explains: "To withdraw or separate is to refuse to act according to the system's rules and framework. . . . Separatists tend to have more anarchist sensibilities— distrusting institutional power of any kind, wanting new value to emerge from small groups engaged in creating new ways of being."[11] That spirit of rebellious refusal runs through a vast array of contemporary left-wing political programs, from identity-based projects for racial, gender, and sexual freedom, to campus social justice activism, to feminist movements against sexual assault, which hitch their utopian ambitions to a definitive separation from the monstrous systems of domination that daily oppress marginalized people. The collective "we" of a broad activist and academic left are, in this sense, far more indebted to the political imagination of lesbian separatism than we know or are willing to admit.

Consider that despite their categorical dismissal of separatism, the Combahee River Collective went on to explain their own motivation for separating and developing coalition among women of color by stressing: "Above all else, our politics initially sprang from our shared belief that Black women *are inherently valuable*, that our liberation is a necessity not as an adjunct to somebody else's but because of our need as human persons for autonomy. . . . This may seem so obvious as to sound simplistic, but it is apparent that no other ostensibly progressive movement has ever considered our *specific oppression* or worked seriously for the ending of that oppression. . . . We believe that the most profound and potentially most radical politics comes *directly from our*

own identity, rather than working to end somebody else's oppression"
(my italics).[12] Overlooked in contemporary analyses of the Collective's
statement is the fact that its conceptual framing nearly exactly reiterates
Bunch's 1972 description of lesbian separatist practice: "Many women
turned to separatist groups apart first from men, and then from others
within the women's movement . . . to develop an analysis of *one's particular oppression* and force its recognition by others; *to build pride* and
self-dependence away from those who downgrade or ignore you . . . and
to build a political ideology and strategy . . . *with those who share certain
oppressions* and/or ideological positions" (my italics).[13] Though WOC
feminists would frequently distinguish their activities as stemming from
the "need for autonomy" or self-determination rather than separatism,
lesbian feminists like Bunch, Marilyn Frye, and Hoagland fundamentally understood the choice to separate from patriarchal oppression *as*
an exercise of women's autonomy. The rhetorical and political echoes
between Bunch and the Combahee River Collective help us register the
unexpected but productive continuities between separatist logics and
women-of-color feminisms in this period, which despite having different historical origins and competing analytical frameworks, shared parallel aspirational and affective logics.

First, both separatists and women-of-color feminists endeavored to
produce a comprehensive political analysis of systemic oppression based
in their distinct identities—including lesbian, Black and brown, or Third
World subjectivities—that could also ultimately be applicable to, or account for, *all* women.[14] Second, both separatists and women of color theorized versions of identity politics that they each believed could explain
the totality of different oppressions experienced by any given woman.
In their 1973 newsletter, the Gutter Dyke Collective asserted: "*We see
sexism as being the basis of all our oppressions*—all the other 'isms' that
continue to perpetuate themselves (capitalism, nationalistic socialism,
imperialism, racism, classism, etc.)."[15] Black feminist Beverly Smith contested this line of thought with her criticism that "[o]ne of the problems
with separatism is that I can't see it as a philosophy that explains and
analyzes the roots of all oppression and is going toward solving it."[16]
Yet the very terms of Smith's dissatisfaction with separatism suggested
that there is or could be some philosophy that would "explain and analyze" the roots of all oppression (for her, separatism simply wasn't it).

Indeed, Smith contributed to the Combahee River Collective's project to put forward such a wholistic analysis of the "interlocking nature" of dominations when they claimed: "If Black women were free, it would mean that everyone else would have to be free since our freedom would necessitate the destruction of all the systems of oppression."[17] Though the Collective offered a more complex analysis of power than separatists, theorizing what Rostom Mesli has called "multiple identity standpoints," they were equally eager to discover a unified theory of structural inequality and locate an ideal political figure—in their case the Black lesbian—as the potential harbinger of total liberation. Third and finally, both separatists and women-of-color feminists thought critically about the kinds of divestments they needed to make to politically thrive under the inhumane conditions of patriarchal subordination. Just as lesbian separatists articulated a need to break away from male-dominated society and the homophobic and sexist elements of women's and gay liberation, women-of-color feminists also chose to disengage from the racist elements of the women's movement, distanced themselves from sexist cultural nationalisms, and sometimes cut interpersonal ties with white feminists who failed to address their own racism and classism.[18] It was these very separations that made it possible for emergent categories like lesbian feminist, Black lesbian, Third World feminist, Black dyke, womanist, womyn, and more, to take distinct form and speak back to both dominant structures of power and left-wing movement cultures.

To make these comparisons is in no way to collapse distinct strands of feminist thought and praxis that often operated with radically different assumptions and terms.[19] As Mesli underscores, it was the Black lesbian feminists of Combahee who specifically invented the term "identity politics" in 1977, intending it as a concept that could account for the unique insights that particularly situated marginal subjects might offer to broader struggles for political freedom. Yet by understanding some aspects of women-of-color feminisms as expressions of separatism, we can see how the seemingly narrow, identity-based logic of a predominantly (though not wholly) white lesbian separatism potentially might describe a shared logic of separation and self-valuation at the heart of all left-wing identity politics. In both, a certain will to universality is ever present: the desire to make the particularity of one's social position speak to all others, coupled with a forceful refusal of dehumanization through the elevation of one's own identity to a revolutionary calling. Both goals sprang from a utopian desire at the core of 1970s feminist identity politics, an almost fantastical wish to do justice to the totality of oppressive forces that women faced. Mesli reminds us that there is nothing about identity politics tout court that necessarily engenders one to treat identities as essential, universal, or fixed. Rather identity politics is founded on the bedrock assumption that a person's sense of self, born out of a specific social location, simply offers one valuable and unique perspective on the world. The essentialist qualities of identity politics, what leads in other words to *identitarianism*, is the will to transform the injurious qualities of one's structural position within a society into a total program or conceptual roadmap to universal liberation. This is an impulse that no identity movement has ever truly overcome since the very concept of identity politics was invented.

By tracking the surprising travels of lesbian feminist forms in the narrative and aesthetic projects of experimental science fiction films of the 1970s and early 1980s, I aim to show how the desire to separate, in its countless expressions, remains a compelling, potent, and sometimes self-destructive conceptual force in contemporary left-wing aspirations for a more just future—whether those aspirations go by the name of intersectional, queer or trans* critique, critical race theory, social justice, being "woke," creating safe spaces, defunding the police, or otherwise. Like these movements' intensified focus on liberation from systemic oppression, lesbian separatism enabled women to conceive their identities, desires, and political commitments divorced from the sources of their suffering, thus inhabiting thrilling new forms of selfhood; but it also permanently tied women to their pain and resentment at the wounds inflicted upon them by a patriarchal culture.[20] Without a clear-eyed appraisal of our own enactments of a disavowed separatist politics today, we lose the capacity to discern when progressive attempts to separate contribute to building the egalitarian world we fight for, or further alienate us from the shared universe we inhabit with others. Consequently, I propose that the figure of the Vortex, the name given to the commune in *Zardoz*, can function as an analytical tool that holds together a central paradox of separatist logics. On one hand, a vortex captures the vertiginous, or spiral-like, logic of early lesbian separatism, in which the search for a fantasized pure or authentic lesbian feminist identity led many to aggressively enforce a single shared communal ideal. On the other, it embodies the propulsive force of the separatist flight from patriarchy, a dynamic whirlpool of intensity powerful enough to launch us into new identities, unimagined lifeworlds, or realms of political possibility. We too must from time to time self-consciously reenter the lesbian separatist vortex to harness its impassioned desire for "systematically fucking up the system," while learning again and again how not to be sucked down into the abyss.

"The gun is good. The penis is evil": Separatism as Vortex in John Boorman's *Zardoz*

In the opening sequence to John Boorman's 1974 dystopian science fiction film *Zardoz*, viewers witness a giant stone head floating across a landscape of rolling green hills. The head bears the face of a rage-filled, bearded old man with a gaping mouth exposing jagged teeth, as if permanently frozen in a primal scream. A gathering mass of horseback-riding men gallop across the hills toward the head, shooting guns into the air. All are dressed in the same uniform—blood-red loincloths and bullet holsters crossing hirsute chests—and all are worshipfully yelling toward the floating monument a single word: "*Zardoz!*" As the stone head descends, we see many of the men donning red-and-white, Janus-faced masks bearing the image of the vengeful god. Finally, a booming roar issues forth from the stone head's mouth: "Zardoz speaks to you, his chosen ones. You have been raised up from brutality to kill the brutals who multiply. To this end, Zardoz, your god, gave you the gift of the gun. The gun is good. The penis is evil. The penis shoots seeds and makes new life to poison the Earth with the plague of men. But the gun shoots death and purifies the Earth of the filth of brutals." With these final words, a cascade of guns and bullets spew from Zardoz's open mouth, covering the ground. As the worshipers celebrate these gifts, one among them looks directly at us, raises his revolver, and shoots between our eyes (figure 2.1/plate 2).

This bizarre and fascinating scene presents a near-perfect allegory for patriarchy as it was described by lesbian separatists in the 1970s: "a wilderness of chaos and destruction"[21] populated by a monstrously violent "death-force"[22] whose seemingly universal reach stretches far into the

Figure 2.1. Top to bottom: The Stone Head descends toward its worshipers in the opening shots of *Zardoz*; Zardoz bellows to the Exterminators: "The gun is good. The penis is evil"; Zed raises his gun and shoots directly between our eyes. *Zardoz*, dir. John Boorman (20th Century Fox, 1974).

past and aims to control the future. Here, the "God" of patriarchal culture is condensed into the frozen countenance of old white male fury, a literal and figurative monolith that also covers the faces of its worshipers, flattening their individuality into the singular essence of male domination. As feminist historian Dana Shugar explains, "the discourse of separatism shifted the emphasis of blame in theory from a social ill (sexism) to its perceived social agent (men). . . . [M]en were seen as the inherent cause of every destructive aspect of life on earth."[23] Accordingly, when the unnamed gunman looks at us and shoots, he asserts his patriarchal power both by controlling our gaze and symbolically inaugurating the narrative we are about to watch.

In the following tale, however, we learn that Zardoz is a false god invented by Arthur Frayn, a member of a utopian commune called Vortex 4, to maintain control of a chaotic "Outlands." The Outlands is a postapocalyptic zone of lawless violence where the last remnants of humankind are picked off or enslaved by "Exterminators," the red-clad men whom Zardoz equips with their weapons. Alternatively, the Vortex is an idyllic, egalitarian community of "Eternals," highly evolved beings gifted with superhuman intelligence, telepathy, and immortality who have lived together for two centuries attempting to discover "the unsolved secrets of the universe." The Vortex is, symbolically speaking, the ideal lesbian commune, a material expression of the separatist fantasy of "the lesbian nation as a psychological, spiritual, and emotional entity, as well as a . . . physical goal."[24] Zardoz tells the story of how Zed, a "mutant" Exterminator from the Outlands (the same one who "executes" us in the opening scene), infiltrates the Vortex by stowing away in the stone head where he shoots Frayn, effectively killing his own god. In entering the Vortex, Zed seeks answers about his origins and the secret to immortality, but his presence inadvertently brings to the surface roiling tensions between the Eternals, inspiring a revolution that leads to the commune's explosive demise.

At first glance, nothing about Zardoz would lead one to consider it a feminist film, and certainly not a lesbian separatist fable. In a 1974 review of the movie for Film Quarterly, film scholar Marsha Kinder describes Zardoz as "liberated and experimental in form, but fascist and sexist in content."[25] She is not wrong. From one angle, the film is about a sexually aggressive male predator who violates a utopian community, foments internal dissent that leads to its destruction, and takes one of its leaders as his figurative bride. The plot would seem to prove Johnston's essentialist view that "[t]he world in the 20th century is a spectacle of the gross amplification of the insecure man. . . . Man is completely out of phase with nature. Nature is woman. Man is the intruder."[26] Yet I will argue that this obvious lesbian feminist reading of the film—as a story of one man's savage intrusion on ideal "nature"—is exactly what *Zardoz* sets out to parody and deconstruct. By setting up a rigid formal division between a seemingly boundless Outlands populated by brutish male "exterminators" and a rigidly bounded Vortex inhabited by "feminized" and intellectually superior "Eternals," *Zardoz* replicates the foundational logic of separatism as a defensive politics that seeks to protect women from the harms of patriarchal society while elevating them to the status of supremely evolved beings.

The film's critique of separatist logic lies in the revelation that the stone head is a fake deity invented by a member of the commune. Through this ingenious plot device, the film suggests that the seemingly clear-cut moral and intellectual division between the Outlands and the Vortex is, at least partly, an ideological fantasy perpetuated by the Eternals to legitimize their separation from the outside world. And in parallel fashion, the lesbian separatist imaginary required a view of male nature as fundamentally barbaric, "egocentric," and "incapable of empathizing or identifying with others"[27] in order to develop an equally essential characterization of women "as nurturing, life-giving, cooperative rather than competitive, connected with all living beings, nonhierarchical, nonoppressive, and . . . 'inherently collectively oriented.'"[28] As the story unfolds, Zed's infiltration of the Vortex looks less like a self-evident invasion of a utopia and increasingly like a moment of reckoning in which the members of a separatist collective must contend with their own internal dissensus and contradictory desires.

Zardoz, then, can be read as allegory for the logic of lesbian separatism in the mid-1970s that gives figurative and literal shape to separatist ideals. Figuratively, the plot explores the social and interpersonal consequences of separatism if it were taken to its logical extreme. Literally, the film presents a wide range of material shapes, in the form of enchanted objects and devices—from information-storing crystals to mirrored dining tables, from flying stone heads to inflatable synthetic bubbles—that concretize different aspects of separatist ideology, including the investment in social and political sameness, or *mirroring* of values and interests, between women. As we have seen, the stone head, the gun, and the Vortex are all part of this visual lexicon, respectively providing rich figural analogies for the concepts of patriarchy, male sexual violence, and lesbian ideological purity. But perhaps the most obvious separatist form in *Zardoz* is the transparent dome that protects the Vortex from the outside world. At one point, Zed runs toward the Vortex perimeter and forcefully presses himself up against the shield only to find his face smashed against its surface. The shield becomes the ultimate metaphor for lesbian separatism as a program of division and protection, a physical manifestation of the ideological borderline between women and a patriarchal society that also traps, and literally flattens, an essential definition of "man" within its walls.

"Coinciding with Ourselves": Zardoz *as Separatist Allegory*

But what exactly does Zed discover within those walls? Visually, the Vortex looks like a psychedelic hippie commune: there are hydroponic green houses, communal areas for weaving and baking, and gardens where Vortex members engage in collective chanting. The Eternals dress in gender-neutral clothing, including low-cut macramé halter tops, billowing harem pants, and Cleopatra-like headdresses. Considering that the commune is mixed in gender and borrows from the styles of 1960s and 1970s countercultural movements—including the hippie appropriation of Near Eastern and South Asian fashion—it may seem odd to read the Vortex through a lesbian separatist lens, a political ideology committed to all-women spaces and resolutely against the heterosexual bias of the US counterculture. Ideologically speaking, however, the Vortex models a lesbian separatist ideology on at least three fronts.

First, the Eternals view themselves as an evolved version of humanity biologically and intellectually superior to the "brutals" that populate the outside world. Their evolved status parallels a variety of separatist arguments that women are innately superior to men. Physiologically, the Eternals have gained superhuman abilities that allow them to transform traditional human functions like eating, sleeping, and communicating to facilitate their collective mission to explore "the unsolved secrets of the universe." They require no sleep, devoting every waking moment to scholarly research and artistic production. They are telepathic, capable of conveying the full depth of their thoughts and feelings unmediated by language.[29] And they are immortal and nonreproductive, gifted with unlimited time to pursue their crafts without fear of overpopulation. The Eternals conceive of their way of life as a natural outcome of having achieved what they call "total consciousness," a state in which their "waking and unconscious lives" are perfectly unified. For lesbian feminists, an initial separation from patriarchy through a systematic "withdrawal of energy"[30] from men, was similarly imagined to lead to an ultimate "unity," both psychologically *within* any single woman and politically *between* different women, what the Radicalesbians called a state of "coinciding with ourselves."[31] Thus, having achieved total consciousness, a woman would be expected to reorganize every aspect of her social, political, and erotic life around a primary attachment to other women.

As a consequence of their evolutionary superiority, however, the Eternals have lost the capacity to empathize with the inhabitants of the Outlands, deeming them inferior animals or "brutals," incapable of feeling or consciousness. When one of the Eternals expresses pity for their "suffering," another flippantly replies, "You can't equate their feelings with ours. It's just entertainment." One of the signal rhetorical features of 1970s separatist political writing was the performance of a vitriolic verbal assault on men in the form of name-calling, denouncements, and character assassination: Solanas famously claimed that "maleness is a deficiency disease"; the Gutter Dyke Collective called men "parasitic penis-brains"; and the Collective Lesbian International Terrors (or C.L.I.T. Collective) asserted that men exhibit "natural stupidity" and "aren't human."[32] Separatists took up the same violent and demeaning language used to describe women in a patriarchal society, but used it to describe the monstrous behaviors of men. This reverse discourse provided a thrilling affective ground for a new kind of misandry, or hatred of men, by allocating to lesbians the moral authority to be savagely uncivil toward the sources of their oppression. It is this authority that allows Consuella, the Vortex's putative leader, to offhandedly command May, a scientist studying Zed's "breeding potential," to "kill it," when debating how to deal with the intruder. Consuella literally enacts Solanas's dictate that "[t]he elimination of any male is a righteous and good act . . . beneficial to women as well as an act of mercy."[33] While spellbinding in its will to power, misandrist discourse relied on the idea that, for women to construct primary psychic and sensual bonds with one another, they had to deny compassion and understanding for men. The Eternals provide a crystalized expression of this conundrum, a group of supposedly perfected beings sharing a highly developed psychic link that requires the violent subordination and exclusion of an entire category of Others to maintain its equilibrium. Indeed, when May refuses to execute Zed, Consuella implores her to reconsider, "For our love."

Second, the Eternals share a collective consciousness, and function on the basis of "complete equality," including the egalitarian distribution of labor and government by consensus. This approach to collective life models the philosophy of the lesbian "back to land" movement, which sought "to acquire rural spaces [where women could] live in nature as equal members of a women's community (and not as man's 'property') [and] 'remove' the effects of relations of ownership from the land."[34] These values are frequently on display in the Eternals' collective care for local wildlife and communal food preparation. When Consuella discovers that Arthur Frayn has been manipulating Outlanders into "growing wheat," she immediately protests: "I've always voted against forced farming." This egalitarianism extends to the Vortex's psychic life: the Eternals communicate telepathically, and every thought or feeling each has is stored in a crystal called "the tabernacle." Each wears a crystal ring, which functions as a miniature version of the tabernacle, a supercomputer that houses a seemingly limitless archive of historical and scientific information, and psychological data, about the collective. Unlike a traditional engagement or wedding band, which symbolically seals the heterosexual bond, the crystal ring is a quasi-mystical metonym for the collective's hive mind, literally drawing their energies together much as lesbian separatists repeatedly demanded that women's "energies must flow toward [their] sisters."[35] This distribution of "energies" within a crystalline construct is understood as an extension of the collective's pledge to egalitarianism in all relationships, which is why they frequently debate and vote on matters of shared concern. Yet, because the thoughts and feelings of any member are collectively experienced, those who disagree with the majority are perceived as enacting "psychic violence" and punished. Throughout the film we are witness to "the trial of George Saden," a scientist who has "studied [the Vortex's] social and emotional substructures for 140 years." Saden's "constructive" criticisms of the collective have led him to be "accused of transmitting a negative aura." Finally, when Zed expresses surprise that there are "no police [or] exterminators" to punish misbehavior in the Vortex, the rebellious misfit known as "Friend" explains, "Ah, but we discuss it endlessly, every little sin and misdemeanor raked over and over."

The collective's obsession with anticipating and mitigating psychic harm through consensus performs a hyperbolic parody of the endless lesbian "processing session," in which women engage in sustained recognition of, and engagement with, one another's emotional needs. Lesbian separatist ideology often conceived of women's same-sex erotic desires as an organic physical expression of innately shared emotional orientations and political commitments among women. Throughout *Zardoz*, mirrors often function as material containers for the Vortex members' collective consciousness, literalizing the separatist value of sameness, or reflecting, of political values. The lesbian feminist conception of women being naturally attuned toward one another's affective needs placed an undue burden on separatism as an ideology that could both explain women's subordinate status and also minister to their individual psychic and spiritual well-being, including the elimination of painful disagreements among women. For example, the authors of *The Amazon Report* stressed the importance of seeing separatism as a total theory that could bind women across "differences [of] race class, age, life styles, etc." They explained: "It is important to see these things as differences, not divisions, to . . . provide a framework which leads to understanding and the eliminations of these differences being oppressive to any of us."[36] And the members of the Gutter Dyke Collective embraced separatism as a refuge from the psychic "negativity" of group conflict: "We want to withdraw from . . . oppressive, negative situations . . . to avoid a lot of fighting . . . as well as support each other in our agreements."[37] Consuella models this logic exactly when she says to May, "You are hurting me," after the scientist refuses to eliminate Zed, recasting May's failure to mirror her feelings as emotional injury. By placing such a premium on women's universally shared consciousness, separatists persistently perceived internal dissension between lesbians as "a [form of] false consciousness learned from so many years of patriarchal conditioning," rather than an outcome of genuine divergences in thought, experience, and desires.[38]

Consequently, the increasing rebelliousness of various members of the collective upon Zed's arrival is repeatedly interpreted as an expression of internal, "destructive tendencies" or problematic "under-thoughts" that must be contained and rooted out. When May attempts to sway the collective to vote for keeping Zed alive, Consuella retorts, "Now she wants to bring in this animal from the outside. . . . Remember the delicate balance we must maintain. . . . May is a great scientist, but she also has destructive tendencies." The "animal" in question is not only Zed, but also what Consuella sees as May's "male-defined response patterns,"[39] which are perceived as an unnatural by-product of "outside" forces. Similarly, in one of the film's most disturbing scenes, Friend is telepathically subdued by the collective when he refuses to join them in "second-level meditation" while seated together for dinner. As punishment, the Eternals all direct their hands toward him, projecting a psychic assault so powerful he loses control and involuntarily admits: "I will not be one mind with you. . . . The Vortex is an obscenity. I hate all women." Friend is forced to admit to harboring patriarchal thoughts as the underlying root of his refusal to be "one mind" with the Vortex, which leads to his expulsion from the community.

Third, and finally, a direct outcome of the Eternals' arrival at total consciousness is their transcendence of both erotic desire and reproductive potential. They are essentially androgynous and lack the capacity for sexual arousal (what Consuella describes as a "violent . . . act which [once] debased women and betrayed men") or reproduction. Instead, throughout the film, we see Vortex members gestated and rapidly regenerated in hydroponic bubbles after being harmed or killed. These fascinating images provide one version of the lesbian separatist fantasy of parthenogenic birth, the ability of women to mentally will the reproduction of female babies without sex with men. As the Gutter Dyke Collective proclaimed: "[W]ithout using our female bodies to make more of the rapists, the males would all die out. . . . We are the means by which we continue ourselves."[40] While the project of reclaiming women's sexuality from patriarchal control was sound in theory, in practice it led to the de-eroticization of lesbian sex in favor of women's intense

emotional bonds, the phobic exclusion of bisexual women, a rigid policing of lesbian gender expression, and even a rejection of male children
from separatist gatherings.[41]

The Vortex members uncannily reproduce this separatist logic: despite having no erotic desire toward one another, the Eternals are fiercely
co-dependent, demanding complete interpersonal loyalty. As the trial
of George Saden makes clear, any hint of intercommunal criticism is
punished by group shunning. In fact, we soon learn that despite appearing to exist in universal harmony, the Vortex is also home to two outcast
communities, the "apathetics" and "renegades." Apathetics are Eternals
who suffer from an entropic disease spreading its way through the Vortex that enervates their entire being; they stand stationary like zombies
with a dazed look in their eye, incapable of feeling and communication. Alternatively, the renegades are Eternals who have been punished
for dissidence by being aged to senility. They live in the remains of a
former nightclub called the Starlight. The elderly men dress in frayed
tuxedos while the women prance around in garish prom dresses. These
two communities perfectly complement lesbian separatism's most derided categories of sexual identity: the bisexual woman and the butch or
femme lesbian. Hardline separatists often described bisexuality as a lack
of feminist political will, an expression of a woman's inability to fully
commit to lesbianism. Like apathetics, bisexuals were perceived as an
ideological plague that leeched energies from lesbian feminist political
projects. As Johnston put it, "Bisexuality is a state of political oblivion
and unconsciousness."[42] Separatists similarly relegated butch-femme
roles to an anachronistic lesbian past—associated with "aging dykes"—
that was indicative of lesbians' unselfconscious absorption of artificial
heterosexual gender roles.[43] The renegades' appearance as mentally deranged octogenarians who dress up in costumes that "ape the normative
institutions" of masculine and feminine gender roles brilliantly captures
the lesbian separatist perception of butch-femme roles as a kind of pathetic drag performance.

Taken together, the Eternals' evolved status, their collective consciousness, and their transcendence of erotic and reproductive functions align
the Vortex with the fantasy of an ideal lesbian separatist community.
The film's hyperbolic parodying of these qualities sheds light on separatism's will to power as an attempt to wrest control of patriarchy's arbitrary

domination of women through a logic of radical reversal. This included upending the perception that men are biologically superior to women, that women's primary psychological attachments were with the opposite sex, and that women's natural role was to be man's sexual vessel. The problem with the lesbian feminist project lay not in its aim to flip the patriarchal script, but in its assumption that lesbian-identification was the self-evidently superior alternative. Even as it promised the tantalizing possibility of a world without gender hierarchy, separatism often merely inverted it, placing women (and lesbians) on top. The persistence of hierarchical thinking within a lesbian separatist enterprise that claimed to value egalitarianism and equality could then be simply blamed on the vestiges of patriarchal conditioning, rather than on women's own will to power.

To Look Behind the Mask

No better is the lesbian will to power represented in *Zardoz* than in the ceaseless competition of gazes, which dominate the film's visual landscape. Eyes are everywhere in the Vortex, and for a community of telepaths, looking is never merely an innocent act of observing, but a way to judge, punish, and psychologically control others. As Friend explains to Zed early on: "Ever hear the expression, 'If looks could kill?' Well here they can." At the same historical moment of *Zardoz*'s release, feminist film theorist Laura Mulvey published her now canonical analysis of the male cinematic gaze, "Visual Pleasure and Narrative Cinema." Mulvey famously argued that classical Hollywood cinema relied on a tacit assumption that the viewing subject of any film narrative is male, thereby "cod[ing] the erotic into the language of the dominant patriarchal order."[44] Consequently, in Mulvey's formulation, the pleasure gleaned from film spectatorship was a distinctly masculine one that repeatedly presented women's bodies as objects of fetishistic sexual fascination or else sadistically degraded women as a way of subverting their potential to disrupt the primacy of the male viewpoint. Mulvey's feminist project, like the political goals of separatists, was to expose this dominant male looking position, "to analyze [its] pleasure," in order to "destroy it."[45] *Zardoz* takes Mulvey's analysis a step further, enacting a visual reversal in which the traditionally all-powerful masculine look of the cinematic apparatus is replaced by an unyielding feminine stare capable of penetrating the male body.

If *Zardoz* opened with Zed staring aggressively into the camera, exercising the power of a patriarchal male gaze that looks at and violates its audience, that power is utterly lost upon his entry into the Vortex. When May first discovers Zed on the shore of a lake inside the Vortex, a shot/reverse shot captures them locked in a battle of unwavering glares. As Zed lifts his gun to shoot her, May's eyes widen, and a piercing boom interrupts the scene, bringing Zed to his knees. The sound announces May's psychic attack on Zed, which overturns his previous control of the visual field. Finally, an extraordinary long shot captures the two at opposite ends of the screen, held in tension as May interrogates Zed about his arrival to the Vortex (figure 2.2/plate 3). The back of May's head is foregrounded to the far right while she appraises the intruder, whose body appears to the far left, dwarfed in size and cowering from her telepathic assault. Between them is a long forest of trees whose vanishing point ends at May's head. May's gaze becomes homologous with that of the viewers so that she (and we) take the place of the male look while staring down at the "inferior" Zed. At the same time, the forest between them appears to emanate from her glare, so that May's perspective is literally aligned with the natural world.

In *Zardoz*, then, Zed, played by a hirsute and highly sexualized Sean Connery, comes to take the symbolic place of "woman" in the cinematic gaze. Following his first encounter with May, various members of the collective stare intently at Zed, psychically "penetrating" him, surveying his genitals, and using their crystal rings to x-ray his body (in one suggestive scene, May directs her ring at Zed's retina and demands that he "open, open, open" his mind to her). Accordingly, the Eternals seem to believe that, because they have the apparatus to analyze, study, or see through Zed, they necessarily understand him or can adequately assess his intentions. This misperception maps onto the lesbian separatist assumption that a feminist analysis of patriarchy necessarily revealed the universal truth of men, their intentions, and their essential nature.[46] Thus, the formal reversal of the gaze without an equivalent dismantling of the hierarchy of looks means that women simply violate men (as men have traditionally done to them), while framing that violation as a legitimate destruction of patriarchal domination.

Figure 2.2. Top to bottom: May trains her powerful female gaze at Zed; Zed is incapacitated by May's telepathic assault; May takes in the sight of Zed, her look aligned with the natural world. *Zardoz*, dir. John Boorman (20th Century Fox, 1974).

Yet almost as soon as Zed infiltrates the Vortex, his seemingly adamantine performance of aggressive male sexuality fractures under scrutiny: repeatedly subjected to the powerful gaze of the Vortex members, Zed's virile male body becomes intensely objectified and feminized. Against all the Eternals' assumptions, rather than being aroused by stereotypical pornographic images of women, he is stimulated by Consuella, one of the most erudite and powerful members of the Vortex. The Eternals discover Zed is highly intelligent and curious about practically everything related to their way of life. And he ultimately comes to question every ideological assumption they hold dear. Zed's presence sends a shockwave through the Vortex not because he "pollutes" the Eternals' thoughts, but because he defies their limited expectations of what the "brutals" of the Outlands are and can be. This is perhaps no better captured than in the revelation that Zed is a mutant. While studying Zed's physiology, May discovers he is a highly evolved being, perhaps even more advanced than the Eternals, but also possibly another species altogether. May's description of Zed as a "mutant" borrows one line of 1970s separatist thought, which claimed that "the male . . . developed as a mutation . . . from a natural catastrophe . . . and the y chromosome is really a broken x," therefore making men "inferior physically [and] psychologically" to women.[47] *Zardoz* duplicates the language of genetic deviation, but resignifies the meaning of "mutation" not as a pathology but as productive form of divergence or multiplicity. At the moment that Zed becomes branded a mutant, he is no longer a "man" by any traditional definition, but an unpredictable wild card, an "open form"[48] that comes to represent a vast range of surprising outcomes of feminist thought.

From one angle Zed is everything that "man" *could* evolve into if he encountered, and was transformed by, feminist ideals; from another, he represents the variety of critiques of separatism, including the many intersectional arguments made by both straight and lesbian WOC feminists who sought to tear down the impenetrable ideological shield of separatist essentialism. As though to impress this point upon us, throughout the film Zed is repeatedly visualized as a disruptive figure that crosses sealed thresholds, punches through sacred objects, and breaches established physical and psychic boundaries. And when he finally discovers the location of the tabernacle in a diamond-like crystal, it pronounces, "You have penetrated me." By separating himself from the brutal Outlands and infiltrating a series of lesbian feminist forms—among them a sealed dome and a sentient crystal—Zed himself becomes a distinctly *queer* form, mutating the meaning of maleness before our very eyes. In a great irony, then, it is precisely by upsetting the equilibrium of a separatist commune that Zed comes to embody lesbian separatism's most radical expression as a type of feminist anarchy that willfully demolishes the hallowed hierarchies of the gender binary.

Zed reaches his full potential as a mutant anarchist at the stunning moment when May, having discovered his unique genetic structure, probes his mind to unveil the secret behind his arrival in the Vortex. Zed reveals that during a routine hunting expedition, a masked figure lured him into an old library, where he was taught how to read: "I learnt all that had been hidden from me. I learned what the world had been before the darkness fell." One book radically altered Zed's consciousness: *The Wizard of Oz*. Perhaps the greatest US-American fairy tale, L. Frank Baum's *The Wizard of Oz* is a fable about the duplicitous machinations of an old white man who fools the simple-minded inhabitants of an Emerald City into believing he is a sorcerer god. *The Wizard of Oz* is a story about ideology because it uncovers how human beings invent false deities. The plot details how a group of ordinary people (a young girl, Dorothy, and her three very queer companions, the Cowardly Lion, the Tin Man, and the Scarecrow) band together and expose the Wizard as a base illusionist: "They looked behind the mask and found the truth. I looked behind the mask and I saw the truth. . . . Zardoz." Zardoz, then, is a god that carries the secret of its fraud in its very name. It is this discovery that leads Zed to "look behind the mask" by entering the Stone Head, killing Arthur Frayn, and infiltrating the Vortex.

But this account alone is not enough for May: probing deeper into Zed's thoughts she demands he admit his motives: "What was your purpose? . . . To penetrate the Vortex? . . . To destroy us? . . . You wanted revenge." He replies, "We wanted the truth!" To which May counters, "Truth or revenge?!" Finally, Zed collapses in her arms sighing out, "*Revenge* . . ." Holding him close, she admits: "I remember feelings such as those, they stir in me." *The Wizard of Oz* is a fairy tale that teaches Zed how to read past the ideological ruse of white masculinity, which inspires him to seek out the truth of his origins. In complementary fashion, lesbian separatists saw their own myth about the existence of ancient matriarchies and the inherent superiority of women as providing a coherent narrative frame for, and ideological analysis of, innate male backwardness that would allow women to see through the lie of patriarchy. It is no surprise that the capacity to "look behind the mask" is gifted to Zed by a member of the Vortex, for as Bunch argued, it is precisely a lesbian feminist consciousness that had the potential to alter the hearts and minds of men if lesbians were willing to release proprietary hold on their political worldview.[49] Zed is that unexpected mutant remainder of lesbian thought, a "man" who learns the lessons of separatist ideological critique so well that he sees past both patriarchy *and* the limits of the separatist analysis that aims to destroy it. Hence, when May coerces Zed to admit his motives were driven by revenge, rather than a search for truth, she projects her insecurity about harboring "feelings such as those" in herself. After all, in her zeal to study Zed, May wanted to discover more about the truth of "man" but also potentially exact revenge on the Vortex for keeping it from her.

As Zed's revelation is transmitted to May, his memories radiate throughout the collective's hive mind, catalyzing the Vortex's implosion. If the first half of *Zardoz* documented the various material forms that make up the Eternals' separatist lifestyle, the second half narrates the spectacular dissolution of those structures in the commune's collapse. Enraged at May's betrayal and Zed's inadvertent destruction of the collective's psychic equilibrium, Consuella leads a party of vengeful Eternals to find and kill the mutant agitator. May and her devoted followers hide Zed, telepathically gifting him the store of their knowledge in exchange for his "seed" to breed a new species. And the exiled Friend leads the apathetics and renegades into open rebellion against the Vortex, engaging in spontaneous sex and ending their immortality in a suicidal orgy of death. Amid this upheaval we are told the story of the tabernacle: it is revealed that the Eternals' collective consciousness was originally created by a group of middle-aged white male scientists obsessed with preserving the knowledge of Western civilization, who became bored and disaffected with eternal life and were ultimately banished as "renegades." This discovery reaffirms the separatist assumption that the failures of any lesbian collective were always due to the persistence of "male-defined response patterns" among its members,

Figure 2.3. Zed faces his alter ego in the form of a violent Exterminator and shoots to kill. *Zardoz*, dir. John Boorman (20th Century Fox, 1974).

rather than any of their willful actions or character defects. The mutant Zed becomes the only person who can break the hold of the tabernacle on the Eternals' psyches, granting them freedom from a stultifying immortality, which we now see as a life spent studying and rehashing white, Eurocentric culture and values. Zed ultimately faces the tabernacle in the form of a diamond-like crystal, psychically "penetrates it," and discovers inside a hall of mirrors where the faces of the Eternals refract into infinity. Finally, Zed encounters an image of himself as an Exterminator wearing the Janus-faced Zardoz mask. Reversing the logic of the film's opening scene, Zed looks directly at his mirror image, raises a gun and shoots himself in the heart (figure 2.3). Thus, he destroys the tabernacle, frees the Vortex members, and symbolically "kills" his former self.

If we were to inhabit the traditional logic of lesbian separatism, we could interpret this series of events in just one way: a brutal, violent male is briefly subdued by the egalitarian, feminine energies of an evolved collective. He overcomes the collective's power by exploiting the patriarchal desires within its members, irrevocably damaging their unity. Finally, he reclaims the gun to "penetrate" their communal consciousness, thus destroying their way of life. The various self-destructive tendencies of the collective members would then be read as evidence of the persistence of patriarchal thinking within women who have yet to come into full consciousness (even if they believed they had). Yet my point has been to show how *Zardoz* parodies this rigid ideological reading to reveal its inadequacy in explaining the more unpredictable effects of lesbian feminist political ideals. This includes the radical possibility that women might become *anything* separate from men; that men themselves might evolve or mutate if they encountered lesbian feminist values; and that a true separation from patriarchy might mean that the categories of "woman," "man," "lesbian," and "feminist" would unravel or become unrecognizable. By shooting his own reflection in the monolithic image of the violent Exterminator, Zed performs the lesbian separatist fantasy that men might self-annihilate, but does so symbolically, freeing himself both from patriarchy *and* separatism's limited conception of "male" nature. Seen in this frame, the film can be reread thus: a bearer of the violent male gaze willfully separates from a brutal, patriarchal world and encounters a radically different lesbian feminist culture. This way of life penetrates his being, revealing his mutant capacity for radical evolutionary change. As a result, he discovers that this culture's ideas about him are themselves rigid and limited. He sets about taking on a new form as a mutant agitator, ultimately encouraging Vortex members to question their own assumptions and pursue divergent paths to liberation. This would also be a lesbian feminist reading, but one that acknowledges the anarchic qualities of separatist thought as a mode of critical consciousness that deconstructs the assumptions of all gender binaries, including within oneself.

On the surface, the final scenes of *Zardoz* may seem to undermine this claim. Having "inseminated" May and her followers, Zed blesses them as they tearfully leave the Vortex on horseback. The apathetics and renegades are slaughtered by Exterminators Zed leads into the Vortex.

Finally, Zed takes Consuella as his symbolic wife and they flee the carnage of the Vortex by hiding in the wreckage of the Stone Head. In the final shots, a rapid-fire montage depicts Zed and Consuella birthing a child, growing old, withering, and dying, while their progeny leaves their care to enter an unfamiliar outside world. Kinder has argued that the last scene reconstitutes the heterosexual nuclear family against the idyllic communal life of the Vortex.[50] Yet the conclusion is far more ambivalent than this reading admits. After all, before the constitution of any kind of "nuclear family," we see what looks like an Amazon tribe led by May going off into an untamed wilderness, bearing offspring whose mutated genetic makeup carries the potential for a completely different social order. In their seemingly nihilist death wish, the apathetics and renegades exercise a powerful agency, demanding freedom from the essential identities socially imposed upon them by the Vortex. Finally, Zed's union with Consuella rapidly ages and decays, while their child, an androgynous boy, outgrows their care, and deliberately leaves behind Zed's gun, the last vestige of male aggression. In sum, a nonviolent androgyne goes off into uncharted territory where he might encounter the mutant offspring of an all-woman Amazon tribe: a queer anarchist vision indeed. From this perspective, the film suggests that, precisely because of its anarchist qualities, lesbian separatism is bound to spin out many unpredictable queer forms that could finally break away from gendered logics altogether. While the various incoherencies of the film's political narrative can easily be chalked up to failures of filmmaking and scriptwriting, they might also productively be understood as everything that falls out of lesbian separatist orthodoxy, including the possibility that a so-called man might contribute to feminist revolution.

The limits of lesbian feminist orthodoxy were not lost on separatists themselves, including one of its founding figures, Bunch, who wrote as early as 1972: "[Separatism] has led too often to more fragmentation, followed by a retreat from responsibility. . . . We romanticize oppression. . . . Our problems came . . . from the impression we gave that only lesbians could fight male supremacy, rather than that lesbian/feminist consciousness was crucial to the struggle. To avoid the dead ends of separatist purity, we must act out on the belief that revolutionary consciousness is possible among all people: men can [fight] for an anti-sexist world; whites can struggle to end racism; middle class women can combat classism."⁵¹ The problem with separatism, then, lay less in the impulse to be liberated from oppressive structures of domination—a utopian aspiration central to all left projects for political freedom—and more in its presumptive claim to know in advance the outcome of such freedom should it be achieved: namely, the emergence of an authentic lesbian identity in all women, which would provide for an unshakable unity among them. This was a paradox that would permanently haunt lesbian separatist philosophy and practice: a stated investment in clearing ground for women to become *anything*, combined with a laser-focused insistence that the lesbian was the only truly revolutionary thing to be. In its final depiction of multiple unpredictable flights from the Vortex, *Zardoz* modeled separatism's most radical potential, the collective project of divesting from everything we know or think we know, in order to discover what unexpected forms of life might emerge on the other side. The power of lesbian separatism lay not in its total program but in its speculative claim to separation, which could potentially be taken up by anyone. That deviation, or splitting away, was perhaps the most common story of all left identity movements, but especially feminists of color, who developed some of the most effective identity politics of the late twentieth century by willfully separating not only from white supremacy and patriarchy, but, when necessary, their white sisters in the struggle. It was in the process of undertaking these many separations that the very category "women of color," and the figure of the Black lesbian feminist, came into being. If *Zardoz*'s Vortex gave shape to lesbian separatism as a total program in the mid-1970s, by the early 1980s, Lizzie Borden's *Born in Flames* would materialize the situational separatism of women of color in the form of the radical activist cell.

"Five hundred mice can do a lot of damage and disruption": Separatism as Cell in Lizzie Borden's *Born in Flames*

Early in the feminist science fiction film *Born in Flames* we are introduced to a twenty-something, Black lesbian radical named Adelaide Norris and her mentor Zella Wiley, a former lawyer turned militant. Adelaide is the nominal leader of an incipient Women's Army, a loosely affiliated series of radical feminist groups that begin to coordinate in New York City ten years after a socialist revolution sweeps the nation.

Despite the revolution's claim to granting universal economic freedom, an anti-feminist and racist backlash rolls back the gains of women and minority workers. Midway through the film, Adelaide helps organize a march through New York City that includes a diverse cross-section of left political groups, including Third World women, gay liberationists, Black, Asian, and Latina feminists, and labor unionists. Afterward, she laments to Wiley: "These three thousand women were so separated. It wasn't even unified. If it was altogether it would be a lot different than a group of women here, and this meeting [over] there." Wiley rejects Adelaide's logic: "I always say if you were the army and the school and the head of the health institutions and the head of the government, and all of you had guns, which would you rather see come through the door: one lion unified, or five hundred mice? And my answer is five hundred mice can do a lot of damage and disruption." Indeed, *Born in Flames* is a film that documents how a group of disparate women—"five hundred mice"—contribute to a growing feminist guerilla movement by pursuing distinct strategies of "damage and disruption" to a corrupt socialist regime.

Wiley's eloquent metaphor for feminist political resistance might seem radically opposed to the lesbian separatist fantasy of essential unity between women. Yet this image of the dispersal of feminist energies draws its conceptual force from another aspect of 1970s lesbian feminist politics, the anarchist impulse to diverge or break away from dominant systems of power. The more hardline separatist project parodied in *Zardoz* was defined by a fantasy of a single definitive split with patriarchy materialized in the structure of an impenetrable shield or Vortex. Eight years later, Wiley's conception represents a different kind of separatism marked by the perspective of women-of-color feminisms. This might be understood as *a million little separations* that would enable an equally numerous series of productive, but contingent, coalescences of women in their particularity. Responding to widespread attacks on lesbian separatism as myopic, dogmatic, and putatively white feminist politics in the late 1970s, lesbian philosopher Marilyn Frye would contend: "Feminism seems to me to be kaleidoscopic—something whose shapes, structures and patterns alter with every turn of feminist creativity. . . . [T]he theme of separation, in its multitudinous variations, is there in everything from divorce to exclusive lesbian separatist communities, from shelters for battered women to witch covens, from women's studies programs to women's bars."[52] Frye's expanded conception of separatism freed the act of separation from the ideological grip of a total program, redefining it as feminist ethos of multiple, situational divestments of differing magnitudes and intensities.

In both its narrative trajectory and its visual form, *Born in Flames* gave shape to the impulse to separate on a variety of scales, beginning with women's broader defection from a morally bankrupt Socialist Party, followed by the formation of local, independent working groups and grassroots activist cells, and finally lived out through a series of interpersonal decisions to refuse recruitment into any one political project. When the Black feminist radio DJ Honey encourages her neighbor in public housing to consider joining the Woman's Army, the tenant replies: "Nah, I'm not gonna join anybody. I got my own forces." And so too, as the resident disc jockey of Phoenix Radio, Honey has her "own forces" in an unseen audience of potential fellow travelers who tune in and take up her call to "sound off and defend all women." While a coalition of anarchist women does finally emerge to wage guerilla war against a recalcitrant government, it is only by first organizing their "own forces" and "getting it together" in their own "heads," (what separatists described as "directing our energy toward ourselves") that the various women in the film—including the Women's Army organizers Adelaide Norris and Hillary Hurst, the DJs Honey and Isabel, and the white women editors of the *Socialist Youth Review*—move toward a feminist consciousness informed by the particularities of race and class struggle. In so doing, the women of *Born in Flames* practice a contingent separatism not as a creation of an impenetrable bubble, but as a series of multiple autonomous cells that strategically detach from the sources of their oppression.

Born in Flames would be released at the very moment when Black lesbian feminism and socialist feminism were at the height of their political and intellectual power, and lesbian separatism was in terminal decline.[53] While many separatists still held to the values of women-only spaces, women-run businesses, and a shared lesbian culture, separatism as a total program was roundly critiqued as essentialist, racist, and unsustainable for long-term social transformation.[54] In a keynote speech at the 1981 Michigan Womyn's Music festival, Black feminist organizer Bernice Johnson Reagon offered one of the most compelling retorts to separatist thinking when she asserted: "We've pretty much come to the end of a time when you can have a space that is 'yours only.' . . . [T]here is no such thing. . . . Give it up."[55] In her address, however, Reagon also acknowledged the historical conditions that had forcibly separated various oppressed groups from mainstream US-American culture. This was a primary political exclusion that compelled distinct groups to *willfully* separate and organize around their own political interests, what she called "little rooms" of political solidarity: "Now these little rooms were created by some of the most powerful movements we have seen in this country. [The] Civil Rights movement . . . was the first one . . . once [Black folks] did what we did, then you've got women, you've got Chicanos, you've got the Native Americans, and you've got homosexuals, and you got all of these people who also got sick of somebody being on their neck. And maybe if they come together, they can do something about it."[56] Even as Reagon ultimately argued for the value of coalitional politics, she acknowledged the historical necessity of distinct groups starting from their immediate social locations, demanding rights on the basis of their own identities. In *Born in Flames*, this turn toward identity politics is lampooned by the radio DJ Isabel when she sarcastically responds to news of an emergent Women's Army with the statement: "Lesbianism, faggotism, niggerism, honkyism." Like Reagon's wry description of "little rooms," Isabel pokes fun at the ways that identity movements forge entire ideological projects or "isms" from the very terms of their subjection. Separation, then, whether forced or chosen, was practically an existential reality of all identity politics—after all, to coalesce or be in coalition with meant the provisional coming together of separate political entities for common interests, not their melding into final unity.

Many straight and lesbian feminists of color took issue with a predominantly white lesbian separatism not only because of its essential framing of lesbian identity, but also because it seemed to celebrate willful separation from mainstream society while ignoring the traumatic reality of those who were a priori excluded from access to public life on the basis of their race or ethnicity.[57] And yet this was also how lesbian separatists described their relationship to patriarchy, a system that by default separated women from political power and social legitimacy. Despite what seemed like a definitive split between a putatively white lesbian separatism and WOC feminisms, both models emerged out of the shared experience of being left out (or forcibly separated from) a white heterosexual ruling class as well as emergent left revolutionary projects that did not ultimately account for the full range of human differences, and perhaps never could.[58] The difference between an orthodox lesbian separatism and the political designs of women-of-color feminists often lay not in any one group's decision to separate or organize their own but in differing ideas about the purpose and utility of separation. Where hardcore separatists touted permanent retreat from patriarchy as both ultimate strategy and goal of feminist politics, women of color saw separation as a context-specific tactic that could be deployed by different groups to clarify their political commitments before working with others to remake the society. Black political organizer Gwendolyn Rogers captured this latter sensibility when she argued, "I think it's very important to organize among Black Lesbians, Lesbians in general, and gay males. I also think it's very important to bring the issue of Lesbian and gay oppression to the overall movement."[59] Decades later, film theorist Lucas Hilderbrand placed *Born in Flames* in the context of Rogers's and other feminist of colors' coalitional projects, noting: "Coalition across races and sexualities was central to *Born in Flames'* vision of revolting against the state's institutionalized oppression and continued economic disparities to create a new order."[60]

While film theorists and Black feminists alike have celebrated *Born in Flames* for its rebellious depiction of "organizing among Black lesbians, lesbians in general," and women of many colors and class backgrounds, the film neither summarily leaves separatism behind, nor disavows the electric thrill of cutting ties that might result in the organic coming together of a wholly new political community unrecognizable to the powers that be. Working with and against existing readings of the film that see it as a resolutely post- or anti-separatist text that centralized "coalition across races and sexualities," I draw out those moments when an anarchist separatist impulse symptomatically explodes into the narrative, revealing the productive *synthesis* of lesbian separatist and WOC feminisms. We can see that impulse in Wiley's metaphor of "five hundred mice," but also in various characters' increasing militancy and woman-identification. Whereas DJ Honey first describes Phoenix Radio as "a station not only for the liberation of women but the liberation of all," following escalating attacks on women's social and economic security, she pivots to calling it a "station dedicated not only for the liberation of women, but a station dedicated to sound off and defend *all women.*" Honey's rhetorical shift from celebrating "the liberation of all" to promoting the defense of "all *women*" captures what is perhaps the most explicitly separatist aspect of the film, one rarely acknowledged by critics: its commitment to a cross-racial, cross-class form of "woman-identification." Consequently, I take up Jayna Brown and other scholars' claim that *Born in Flames* represents a rich cacophony of competing but equally productive feminist commitments, while including lesbian separatism among the many meaningful forms of feminist politics displayed in the narrative. And in fact, the film encourages us to do so by providing viewers an iconic figure for separatist values, the DJ of Radio Ragazza, Isabel. While the coalitional, Black lesbian–led Women's Army starts to cohere, Isabel remains a resolutely independent, anarchist lesbian, rejecting organized activism and committed to a vision of women's spiritual evolution through music. Isabel embodies a white lesbian separatist outlook that places its faith in a universal "women's culture" that might, in her words, "redesign the mindscape of an alienated" society. The film never rejects her worldview out of hand, suggesting that she carries an incendiary spirit crucial for galvanizing women's political rage against the system. "We are being murdered out there in the street," Isabel tells her audience as the government cracks down on women's resistance, "And if you're gonna sit back and watch it happen sister, you better get it together and wake up!"

"It's going to be a very difficult task getting women to think along that same line": Separation as Preparation for the Revolution

Throughout *Born in Flames* the term "separatism" accrues many meanings, but it is most often deployed as an epithet for describing someone's politics as narrow or single-issue. According to the FBI agents surveilling Adelaide and Hillary's movements, the Women's Army was "started . . . as a radical separatist vigilante group." Here, separatism is associated with an anarchist project of women taking the law into their own hands. Yet at the very moment that we hear the FBI agent make this claim, the camera takes us into a feminist-of-color community meeting led by Adelaide, in which participants are discussing the potential closure of a local day-care center. What the FBI describes as "separatist vigilantism," the film re-presents to us as a local practice of "organizing one's own." Alternatively, according to the *Socialist Youth Review* editors, separatism "hurts our struggle for the equal advancement of all parts of society." In this frame, separatism is a limited, even selfish, form of "identity politics" that indicates a reckless "splitting" away from the Socialist Party. When the editors reject Adelaide's attempt to recruit their support, they explain: "If we support a demonstration by one group it's separatism. We risk splitting the party at a time of major crisis." Ironically, this is one way that 1970s Black feminists described a putatively white lesbian separatism, as "a narrow kind of politics [that] seems to be only viably practiced by women who have certain kinds of . . . white-skinned privilege, class privilege."[61] In *Born in Flames*, this same label is projected back onto Black lesbian feminists, whom the editors paradoxically describe as "a group of women who only emphasize discrimination based on sex as opposed to race or class." The political incoherence of the term "separatism" as it appears throughout the narrative suggests that, by the time of the film's making, the word had transformed from a description of a distinct kind of lesbian feminist praxis to a vague floating signifier, or epithet, used to describe any politics that could be perceived as anarchist in spirit, and hence antithetical to ideals of political unity.

Ironically, the broad coalition that emerges by the end of the film is achieved precisely because each of the women activists we follow first operates separately from the rest, finding common cause only through a process of refining independent political commitments. This is what Honey's neighbor describes as the endeavor of "personally . . . [coming] together before you can get together with any group." As Hillary admits to Adelaide when they first discuss the potential of armed revolt, "I think it's going to be a very difficult task of getting women to think along that same line." In fact, the first half of the movie documents a series of failed attempts at coalition building. When Adelaide first approaches DJ Honey about using Phoenix Radio to advertise the Women's Army, Honey apologetically replies, "You know I would like to say yes, but I'm working with some other women right now, and I wouldn't want to commit myself or them." Similarly, Isabel of Radio Ragazza outright refuses to work with the Women's Army because it is not radical enough for her political tastes: "It's all talk and no action, it's all rhetoric . . . we're doing enough in the community by putting out our music." These various encounters reveal that the inability to unite between different feminists was not always or only due to strictly ideological divisions but could also be chalked up to simple interpersonal conflicts or differing political dispositions.

In *Zardoz*, the Eternals share a collective consciousness and are of one mind; they separate from the larger world but not from one another. In *Born in Flames*, women activists and organizers represent many minds, multiple ideologies, and distinct social locations separate from one another, but occupying the same political landscape. This is formally captured in the film's frequent visual use of talking heads, which literally frames numerous women—radio DJs, political organizers, newspaper editors, and guerilla militants—as discreet entities inhabiting divergent positionalities within a broader network of political agents (figure 2.4/plate 4). Throughout the film, we repeatedly see close-up shots of DJs Isabel and Honey performing feminist monologues during their broadcasts, which are intended to politically galvanize their radio audiences. Unlike the thundering, bellicose voice of the Stone Head in *Zardoz*, which speaks in one god-like tone to its worshipers, Isabel and Honey represent women of different races who exhibit distinct political affects, vocal ranges, and musical tastes. Where Isabel boldly preaches in prophetic terms about a coming political revolution, Honey delivers her speeches in a measured, comforting tone that encourages political involvement. Where Isabel plays aggressively political rock and punk songs filled with lyrics about "[setting] the vast conglomerates aflame," Honey plays buoyant soul and R&B music whose lyrics invoke images of collective love and harmony (such as the Staple Singers' "I'll Take You There," whose utopian refrains imagine an escape from a present wracked by sadness and grief). As Brown argues, the visual and aural shifting back and forth between Honey and Isabel allows us to inhabit, and viscerally feel, distinct styles of feminist cultural politics without having to choose one over the other. If in *Zardoz*, the crystal tabernacle converges the psychic energies of an entire collective of Eternals, in *Born in Flames*, competing networked radio stations disperse the distinct feminist energies, styles, and tonalities of DJs Isabel and Honey outward to countless women.

Figure 2.4. DJs Isabel and Honey speak directly to their radio audiences. *Born in Flames*, dir. Lizzie Borden (First Run Features, 1983).

This separatist impulse, captured in the visual partitioning and dissemination of feminist positionalities, is continually enacted in different ways throughout the film: for example, the camera frequently inserts us into the middle of ongoing feminist CR sessions led by Adelaide and Hillary, allowing us to feel like participants in a variety of feminist debates. Similarly, the increasing radicalization of the white women editors of the *Socialist Youth Review* is presented in a series of close-up shots where each member of the editorial collective argues with her peers about the political vision and tactics of the Women's Army. The film then depicts both individual feminists and competing feminist ideologies as distinct cells or visual units juxtaposed side by side even as they are edited separately from one another. At one point, an FBI agent investigating the Women's Army explains to his superior: "It's subdivided into small cells, each one of which selects its own leader on a rotating basis. . . . About every two or three months, a leader is selected from *those* leaders for the entire organization. And this is the problem, we don't know how to figure out at any given time who is in charge" (figure 2.5). The FBI's description of the Women's Army as a cellular structure presciently describes the aesthetic form of *Born in Flames* itself, a film whose visual gaze is always shifting between political groups, activist leaders, and ideological frames on a "rotating basis." The agent's drawing of smaller adjacent circles surrounding a larger unity also offers viewers a visual blueprint for the Army's strategic oscillation between separating and coalescing. For the film to finally land on any single woman activist or cell would be to decide on a unilateral definition of feminist freedom, or a single representative for the category of "woman," or just one version of the Women's Army. But the film never allows us "to figure out at any given time who is in charge," always choosing to visually and ideologically split off more perspectives for us to contend with.[62]

On the ground, the Woman's Army appears as series of separatist collectives pursuing distinct avenues for political transformation. Some arms of the movement function as feminist CR groups while others pursue direct-action activism, leafleting, and picketing. And a few engage in vigilante action protecting women from street harassment and assault. A variety of cut-scenes throughout the film show different members of Women's Army units engaging in karate lessons, learning to shoot, and even roughing up men who are abusing women. The film thus directly

Figure 2.5. Top to bottom: The camera takes us inside the everyday workings of a Women's Army CR session led by Adelaide Norris; FBI agents develop a diagram of interconnected cells to describe the decentralized structure of the Women's Army. *Born in Flames*, dir. Lizzie Borden (First Run Features, 1983).

represents the lesbian separatist claim, "We want to continually raise our own consciousness, as well as our physical ability . . . to fight . . . and perform all primary functions ourselves."[63] Throughout the narrative, however, we see the increasing radicalization of women from all demographics, as they begin to realize the potential necessity for guerilla violence against a state that has demoted them to a permanent state of political and economic inferiority. At one point, a Black feminist community activist describes the government's refusal to respond to women's protest against the reallocation of social services "to rehabilitate rapists." She says to Hurst, "And they've been cutting back on everything else. Like the victims, you know, women, they've received nothing. . . . So the women in the unit met recently. They are ready to move. Ready to escalate what we been doing." Here, an activist committed to local coalitional politics, community education, and direct-action protest begins to synthesize a more hardline separatist approach that is a strategic response to the government's complete lack of accountability to women. The Women's Army, then, is a "mixed form," which knits together the lesbian separatist values of self-sufficiency, anarchism, and woman-identification with the feminist-of-color investment in community organizing and political education.

Perhaps the most powerful fusion of separatist and women-of-color politics in the film can be found in the way that the category of "woman" emerges as a politically significant term to various political actors. As we have seen, hardcore 1970s separatists frequently embraced "woman" as an essential category of belonging seamlessly binding together those included under its name. Yet even as women of color fought for inclusion within the category "woman," they questioned the term's presumed universality, demanding an accounting of women's multiplex identities and experiences. In *Born in Flames*, a shared sense of common cause or woman-identification between different activists, laborers, and cultural producers emerges out of the very particular conditions of women being singled out by the socialist government. In an attempt to appease rioting white and Black men, who "claim that women and other minorities receive preferential treatment in the real job market," the government issues pink slips to women laborers in a number of male-dominated professions. Protesting their arbitrary removal from paid employment, a group of women construction workers organize outside their former labor site, telling their male co-workers: "We want you to join us . . . we'll all work together." But the men refuse this political invitation, choosing their own economic interests above the collective good of the laboring classes. The double betrayal of women by the government and their male co-workers is what convinces many women that they live "in a fake socialist state [that] denies the basis of true Socialism, which is constant struggle and change." Responding to this reality, DJ Honey declares on air, "Every woman under attack has the right to defend herself. And in situations where we are constant victim of brutality, we must take on the whole armor and defend ourselves." Women come to a separatist position—which includes disengaging from men, refusing ineffective government reform, becoming woman-identified, and arguing for the right to violence—not because they simply want to, or because they hate men, but as a strategically necessary response to existing political conditions.

Similarly, the role that lesbianism potentially plays in binding different women together is situational, rather than an innate unifying force. Early in the film, the FBI agents following Adelaide and Hillary speculate that the affinities forged between members of the Women's Army "may have to do with their lifestyles"; and indeed, lesbianism as a contingent fact of some women activists' lives does play a role in drawing women together, erotically and socially. But the film never presents lesbianism as a transparent ground for political community, rather simply one site among many for potentially meeting fellow travelers. The film's attention to the distinct contexts from which various political actors and their bonds emerge is what keeps its separatism honest and nonessentialist, providing a model for the cross-pollination of separatist and feminist of color values. Seen in its particular context of political struggle, the coalition that emerges between different women across the arc of the film is itself an outcome of a collective divestment, or separation, from patriarchy, but not one based in any inherent or universal quality in women. Separatism and coalition, then, become mutually constitutive categories (and strategies), neither conceptually or politically owned by white women or women of color alone.

In fact, the joining together of all the feminist political actors in the film is catalyzed not by any innately shared characteristic of "womankind" but by a particular situation of collective trauma: the murder of

Adelaide Norris by police and FBI agents. As the Women's Army gains more followers, Adelaide is abducted by FBI agents under false charges and kept overnight in a jail cell where she is found dead under mysterious circumstances the following day. The government's blatant cover-up of Adelaide's death, followed by bombings of the Ragazza and Phoenix Radio stations, convinces all the women in the narrative of their shared interests in exposing government corruption by making their collective voices heard among the masses. In a final, decidedly separatist move, the various feminist factions of the Women's Army, the *Socialist Youth Review*, and the fugitive radio stations both independently and collectively decide on the necessity of forcibly taking over media outlets in order to "have control of the language . . . of describing ourselves." As Wiley explains to members of Adelaide's former Women's Army cell: "The most important thing is . . . our media. . . . See that it can't be quieted." The editors of the *Socialist Youth Review* finally turn against the party, openly questioning Adelaide's death as a government plot in a front-page exclusive; simultaneously, DJ Honey dedicates a broadcast to Adelaide, bringing widespread attention to the loss of a Black lesbian political hero. Finally, and most explosively, when the government puts forward a plan to pay women for housework in an attempt to defuse radical feminist energies, members of the Women's Army enact an armed takeover of a local television station. They interrupt regular programming to broadcast a statement by Wiley, in which she tells thousands of viewers: "Adelaide Norris . . . was murdered because she stood against the betrayal of women. We are being sold down the river, at home, at work, and in the media. And now the president wants to pacify us with wages for housework."

The emergent necessity of claiming control over the media echoed a central aspect of separatist politics in the 1970s, namely the importance of lesbians using print and visual media outlets to control popular definitions of lesbian identity. As the C.L.I.T. Collective argued: "We evolved as a group . . . to counterattack recent media insults against Lesbians. . . . Right now the Media State . . . is defining what a lesbian is to the people of America as if lesbian was a new word. . . . The Media Mindfuck is their false plea for acceptance of the lesbian from the people when it is the Media State which has always been the oppressor of lesbians."[64] In her public message, Wiley takes up the separatist critique of media and government institutions' "false plea for acceptance of the lesbian," but she refuses the separatist demand "that all Lesbian-feminist writers and readers not . . . publish in, read, or buy the straight press."[65] Just prior to Wiley's broadcast going live, we see many ordinary women—mothers and wives unaffiliated with the Women's Army—watching television with their families. The camera then indicates the broad spectrum of people that will witness Wiley's radical statement, underscoring the importance of feminist ideas being heard by as wide an audience as possible. Finally, when Wiley does appear on air, we see her talking head appear on DJ Honey's television set; Honey speaks back to the screen in solidarity, "All right! Go right ahead." Earlier, Honey had similarly been mesmerized by the sight of the *Socialist Youth Review*'s front-page exclusive on Adelaide's murder, which she runs across while walking past a newsstand on the street. When she circulates this devastating headline to her production crew, one of them declares, "We've gotta do something about this" (figure 2.6/plate 5).

In each of these moments, Honey is directly hailed by different feminist activists she was previously working separately from. The recurrent drawing of Honey's gaze to newspapers and television screens allows us to witness the everyday process by which formerly independent feminist actors begin to converge by mutually influencing one another across media platforms. As Brown describes, "Dissenting currents form in the film as women take over the airwaves and redirect them. A counterpublic coheres and disperses, sonically, through music, poetic manifesto, and polemic address. Wherever they are—on the subway, in the streets, in the kitchen—women turn their dials and tune in."[66] In these various public addresses, figures like Wiley and the editors of the *Socialist Youth Review* attend to what Black lesbian feminist Tania Abdulahad identified as "an ongoing problem of Black women's organizing" in the early 1980s, namely the struggle to expand "what kinds of commitments will people make to challenge themselves to be political." She continues, "People define politics very narrowly in terms of elections. . . . But every waking moment of your life is about some political decision or . . . act that you're making." When Wiley challenges her audience to see "every waking moment" of their lives as political, she asks them to examine the government's false progressive narrative. Wiley's takeover of the media, then, brings both women-of-color *and* lesbian separatist politics home

Figure 2.6. Honey's gaze is repeatedly drawn to the media statements of different feminists in her extended circle of fellow travelers. *Born in Flames*, dir. Lizzie Borden (First Run Features, 1983).

by entering people's private spaces and redefining the media narrative around one Black lesbian's political legacy as a first step in ensuring the freedom of all women from patriarchal rule.

Without question, *Born in Flames* advances significantly from the rigidity of hardline lesbian separatist politics in the early to mid-1970s. This is especially the case in the film's depiction of women laborers, organizers, and activists who productively oscillate between separation and coalition, and its turning away from a more orthodox separatist attachment to women's cosmic harmony as a spiritual shield against the psychic injuries of patriarchy. In *Born in Flames*, women of many races, ages, classes, and temperaments vehemently argue, disagree, and disappoint one another, yet they still manage to live and act together in the same political universe, even if they sometimes choose to do so separately. The signal power of *Born in Flames* lies not only in its rare and extraordinary depiction of a multiracial anarchist feminism, as so many critics have rightly celebrated, but also in its constant ability to split decisions. The film takes up separatism's anarchist spirit of divesting from virulent systems of domination, but it refuses its call for a permanent geographical flight from the scene of political struggle. It releases separatism's hold on the ontological priority of the "lesbian," but aspires to separatism's universality, seeking to "deconstruct and reconstruct all the laws that suppress and oppress all of us." The narrative embraces a women-of-color identity politics grounded in the material conditions of women's lives, while refusing to criticize or disavow those who choose to separate and go their own way. And finally, it stresses the necessity of communication between woman-identified women, but it releases preexisting notions of who might count as a woman, comrade, or friend in the struggle. In so doing, *Born in Flames* transforms a certain affective desire for revenge endemic to lesbian separatist misandry into a desire to *avenge injustice*.

Born in Flames can be understood then not as a narrative of rupture or supersession from an essentialist lesbian separatism, but as a narrative of provisional continuity, in which earlier separatist ideals are adapted and evolved for new circumstances and emergent revolutions. Feminist literary scholar Elaine Cannell contends that *Born in Flames* leaves its viewers with the following radical lesson: if we should find ourselves left out of one revolution that claims to speak in our name, we must simply diverge and make another.[67] As Isabel says to her listeners following Adelaide's death: "It is all of our responsibilities as individuals and together to . . . reexamine everything, leaving no stones unturned." Similarly, Honey commands her audience: "Black women, be ready. White women, get ready. Red women, stay ready, for this is our time and all must realize it." Isabel and Honey implore their listeners to "get ready" for the revolution as individuals *and* together, as distinct or separate groups of women *and* as all women united. This is brilliantly captured in one of the film's final images. In the wake of the bombings of Radio Ragazza and Phoenix Radio, Isabel and Honey join forces at a local U-Haul depot. We see them hotwire two moving trucks, pack up their existing equipment, and drive off the lot to launch fugitive radio stations broadcasting from the road. Throughout, Black and white lesbians help each other start their engines and begin to drive, while Honey's voice tells us: "Phoenix and Ragazza are now on the move." Shot from above, they appear as two mobile units or cells taking flight together. In these parting scenes, the film lovingly parodies the stereotypical image of the "lesbian U-Haul truck," which pokes fun at lesbians' tendency to hastily fall in love and move in together overnight. Now, however, U-Haul's iconic tagline, "Adventure in Moving," comes to describe a coalitional lesbian politics that commits hard but is always "on the move."

Truth or Revenge? The Affective Legacies of Lesbian Separatism

By all accounts, lesbian separatism has left the building. And, many might add, "good riddance." As Clare Hemmings tells us, in many contemporary narratives of feminist historiography, lesbian feminism (especially its separatist varieties) often stands in for the monolith called "white feminism," a myopic project that is always firmly rooted in the past and happily overcome in the present. Elizabeth Freeman has written about the ways that separatism now functions as a political anachronism, returning to us from a mythical 1970s in the haunting image of a recalcitrant essentialist lesbian who symbolically drags down the gender anarchy of queer political projects. And Jennifer Nash has unpacked how the rise of intersectionality as both an established Black feminist analytic and a buzzword in left social justice discourse is often understood as a venerated corrective to dominant white feminist conceptions of power and social stratification.[68] And certainly, when separatism has made brief appearances in the forty years since its initial efflorescence and demise, it is often in its most tenaciously essentialist varieties: this includes separatists' sex-phobic alliance with anti-pornography feminists in the 1980s; the Michigan Womyn's Music Festival's decision to maintain their ban on admitting trans-women, disagreements over which led to the eventual termination of the event after nearly four decades; and the highly publicized "gender critical" stance of so-called trans-exclusionary radical feminists or "TERFs," a recently coined term used to describe feminists who maintain a rigidly biological definition of "woman" and accordingly reject trans-women's claim to belonging within that category.

And yet, in my preceding analysis, I have tried to show how separatism functioned in the 1970s as a rich speculative project of seeing what forms women might take in the absence of patriarchy. Despite the many egregious missteps of separatist practice, its conceptual architecture provided an exceptionally powerful motivation for the convergence of feminist energies around a commitment to value women, divest from patriarchy, and imagine a world beyond the gender binary. If these latter values are some of the defining qualities of lesbian separatism, as I believe they are, then separatism is all around us today, even when we don't know it. After all, if lesbian separatism is a highly refined identity politics aimed at ameliorating harm by producing an analysis of hierarchal power in the hopes of destroying its malevolent hold on oppressed people, then it precisely describes nearly every major left-wing intellectual and activist project for political freedom since the radical movements of the 1960s. Mapping the continuities between early separatist thought, women-of-color feminisms, and more recent intersectional social justice movements is an urgent task that has the potential to reveal much about what Wendy Brown has called the "wounded attachments" that underpin present-day left identity politics.

In an effort to lay the foundation for that inquiry, I want to conclude by providing a provisional sketch of some of the unexpected sites where separatist impulses powerfully emerge in contemporary interdisciplinary scholarship and self-described intersectional activism. In her sweeping assessment of "the field imaginary" of women's studies, Robyn Wiegman has argued that a central motivating force which underwrites the progress narratives of feminist theory is the desire to finally land on a key term, concept, or method that would make the analysis of women's oppression synonymous with their political freedom. In this logic, women's studies' abandonment of the falsely homogenizing category of "woman" in favor of the more labile and inclusive term "gender," or the denouncement of a one-dimensional white feminism in favor of an intersectional approach to oppression, signals a desire to replace one set of failed universals with concepts or terms that seem more attuned to human complexity, and hence more capable of doing justice to their objects of analysis.[69] And yet this was exactly the promise of lesbian separatism in the 1970s: to produce an analysis of patriarchy so powerful it could deliver women the highest form of justice by once and for all freeing them from the sources of their subjection. Indeed, separatists themselves were convinced that the "lesbian" was a both a politically disruptive force against patriarchy and a unifying category for all women, in ways that surprisingly echo the contemporary uses of terms like "queer," "gender," "trans*" and "women of color," each of which seek to unseat entrenched universals (straight, male, cis, white), but sometimes merely replace them with the promise of simply including more people within their terms.

Similarly, we see the separatist will to power in a variety of theoretical moves in the interdisciplines. At various points in the intellectual histories of women's studies, Black studies, queer studies, and transgender studies, scholars in each of these fields have forcefully argued for the ontological priority of their own categories as concepts that can ultimately explain all other oppressions. In doing so, they echo separatists' earlier claim that the lesbian represents the constitutive outside of patriarchy, the social and sexual type that a male-dominated society both defines itself against and fundamentally rejects; thus, as we have seen, separatists argued that lesbian identity provides the foundational paradigm for, and political solution to, all other forms of social hierarchy. With this in mind, we might recall Lee Edelman's now famous conception of "queer" as a philosophical category representing the radical negation of the social order as it stands, which supersedes (even denatures) every traditional mode of political protest; or consider recent Afropessimist theorizing, which reconceives "Blackness" as an existential experience of abjection (rather than a racial identity) that stands permanently outside the human, and hence is the most radically "fugitive" of any minoritized forms of being. Similarly, Marquis Bey extends this logic to "transness," seeing Blackness and transness as "differently inflected names for an anoriginal lawlessness that marks an escape from confinement and a besidedness to ontology."[70] Despite their different objects of analysis and their putatively anti-identitarian aims, each of these intellectual projects reperforms the lesbian separatist logic of elevating a single category of being to the place of an inescapable cosmic force or imperative. Hence, each respectively grants queerness, Blackness, or transness nearly un-limited explanatory power to illuminate vast structures of domination or normativity, while reinventing all as concepts describing an existen-tial status of total *separateness* from the social.

At the same time, a variety of projects existing under the ban-ner of contemporary social justice politics—including queer-of-color performance, campus student activism, and feminist anti-violence campaigns—often share an almost identical conceptual and affective structure to 1970s lesbian separatism. In his inspiring recent article "Re-volting Self-Care: Mark Aguhar's Virtual Separatism," James McMaster argues that queers of color often perform highly refined expressions of separatism as a meaningful way to express their revulsion toward domi-nant logics of white supremacy and transphobia. Discussing the digital separatist tactics of the queer-of-color trans performance artist Mark Aguhar on Aguhar's heavily trafficked blog, McMaster explains that "her extraordinary aesthetic projects emerged . . . as so many dismissals of whiteness, masculinity, thinness, and all things hegemonic while affirm-ing brownness, femininity, and fatness for herself and others . . . who might slowly be suffocated otherwise."[71] McMaster's reading builds on queer theorist Roy Pérez's description of Aguhar's digital art practice as a form of "critical flippancy," which involves a deft "switching [of] regis-ters . . . from confessional, to theoretical, to capricious, to sneering," in order to, "[mock] a hater while empowering the one who dared to laugh it off."[72] Aguhar's distinctly queer-of-color mode of "critical flippancy" looks unmistakably like the forms of "'mocking' one's oppressor" per-fected by lesbian separatists in the 1970s, who "empowered" themselves by identifying men as "penis-brain" "walking abortions." And indeed, McMaster explicitly names Aguhar's practice a form of "virtual separat-ism," identifying it as a mode of survival for those who might "slowly be suffocated otherwise." McMaster's choice of words is striking, as it nearly replicates the lesbian feminist description of separatism as an answer for "how to stop choking to death," which was the title of a foundational 1973 separatist position paper. Despite McMaster's chance citation of this lesbian feminist rhetorical flourish, and his explicit use of the term "separatism" in the title to his article, he never discusses a putatively white 1970s version of separatism. Instead he identifies a tradition of feminist and queer-of-color separatism that can be traced back to Audre Lorde's now-canonical essay "The Uses of Anger" through to Sara Ahmed's recent figure of the "feminist killjoy." Like *Born in Flames*, which reveals an existing synthesis between lesbian separatist and WOC values, McMaster's argument reconfirms the presence of separatist perspectives, strategies, and figures in the long history of feminist and queer-of-color political thought, further undermining any illusions we may still hold that separatism is a property only of white women.

Finally, contemporary student movements on college campuses commonly focus on protecting students from sexual assault, encouraging the creation of safe spaces for minoritized students, and seeking to identify and punish microaggressions. Yet even as they aim to establish more integrated college campuses that support the flourishing of all students, these movements frequently rely on some of the most problematic aspects of 1970s separatism to make their political claims. Sociologists Bradley Campbell and Jason Manning have described contemporary campus activism as a "victimhood culture," which often functions as a kind of "purity spiral" of moral recrimination in its aim to destroy systems of oppression.[73] These movements often position the student as a subject who is always already defined by existing or anticipated trauma, similar to separatists who figured women as existentially wounded by men. So too, just as lesbian separatists claimed moral authority on the basis of their status as victims of sexual and gender subordination, campus activists often seek to reverse stubborn hierarchies of arbitrary racial, sexual, and class privilege by "emphasizing the moral worth of victims and their allies, while condemning the vice of privilege and the evil of oppression."[74] And finally, in their demand for safe spaces, student movements take up the separatist call for creating collective living spaces, community centers, or farms where women could interact with like-minded people in relative protection from the psychic harms of patriarchy. As a result, campus activists sometimes conflate the necessary and ethical value of more inclusive and accessible colleges and universities with the aim of ensuring each students' affective experience of feeling recognized in every campus space in which they appear. The measure of these movements' success then becomes an impossible standard of universal and unwavering psychological well-being.

If these comparisons feel uncomfortable, perhaps it is because the association with lesbian separatism threatens to taint any contemporary left intellectual or political project with the mark of racism, exclusion, essentialism, and transphobia. Yet to outright deny the separatist impulses at play in a variety of left-wing identity projects—as Barbara Smith did when Adrienne Rich suggestively compared lesbian separatist practices with those of women-of-color feminists in 1982—is a refusal to admit our own legitimate desires to get distance from the sources of our oppression, as well as our own capacity for essentializing and universalizing in the name of our political freedom.[75] Looking in the mirror, like Zed at the heart of the tabernacle, might force us to reckon with the fact that many of our own affective desires for a changed world carry the ambivalent structure of lesbian separatism, an ideology torn between seeking the *truth*, by exposing the ideological structures that enact endless injury, and exacting *revenge*, by debasing the categories of the oppressor and elevating our own. The search for truth in contemporary left social justice projects is everywhere apparent in concepts, terms, and strategies that demand ever greater precision in naming our complex identities and the forces that relentlessly work to diminish or do damage to them. But the desire for revenge obtains in the need to have our once denigrated identities now take moral, political, and existential priority, and in the emotional thrill of public takedowns and callouts. After all, the Me Too movement has created an unprecedented collective forum for victims of sexual assault to narrate their personal experiences online, thereby exposing the truth of rampant sexual violence. Yet this structure of publicly airing grievances exacts an intoxicating revenge in the communal pillorying of individual perpetrators of assault and harassment. And likewise, campus activists often seek to punish people responsible for inflicting microaggressions upon students by demanding university administrators intervene and fire or denounce faculty, student groups, or visiting speakers for harmful speech.

My goal is not at all to dismiss the legitimacy of these desires—as the "accountability queen" of my friendship circle, I am no stranger to the intense affective pull of making others account for their actions, especially within the larger project of social transformation and equity in an unjust world. Rather, my point is that when we refuse to acknowledge the separatist impulse at play in these various projects, when we deny that *at least some of the time*, our claim to social justice is also a righteous claim to vengeance, we cannot tell when our strategies of separation move us toward freedom or permanently bind us to the sources of our suffering without effecting genuine change. Consider once more that Me Too's encouragement to publicly disclose experiences of harassment and abuse recognizes and amplifies the commonly neglected voices of sexual assault survivors in the mode of mutual solidarity; yet, by its very rhetorical structure, the phrase "Me Too" automatically interpolates any potential movement participant as someone who has experienced sexual trauma, implying that women's voices can be heard most effectively *only or primarily* when they speak from a position of woundedness, injury, and violation. Simultaneously, the vengeful takedown of sexist public figures can often hinder structural change by punishing single "bad apples" instead of dismantling patriarchy. And while student movements rightly denounce hate speech on university and college campuses, their reliance on administrative decree to remedy student harm can make them complicit with the most conservative forces of the neoliberal university. Moreover, what we now routinely identify as transphobia among some 1970s separatists and radical feminists—namely the refusal to acknowledge trans-women *as* women—was (and sometimes still is) understood by these activists as a legitimate defense of cis women from perceived male harm and abuse. In this logic, trans-woman are viewed, however misguidedly, as actually cis men attempting to appropriate, claim, or manipulate cis women's "authentic" experience of their bodies and lives; this, just at the moment that cis women seemed to have finally found their political voice. Even as contemporary queer, feminist, and trans* social justice projects rightly denounce this essentialist view of biological womanhood, they frequently reproduce its defensive posture, by conceiving all kinds of marginalized identities as both defined by perpetual exploitation and mistreatment, but also culturally sacrosanct, proprietary commodities owned by distinct groups, and thus needing to be rigidly guarded against appropriation, influence, or adaptation. In each case, these movements unwittingly borrow lesbian separatism's most problematic elements but tend to jettison its visionary dimensions, including its anarchist impulse to divest from dominant systems of power. As Wiegman reminds us, "The problem, then, is not what we cling to but the way we convince ourselves that we don't."[76] And indeed, the fact that contemporary left thought and activism persistently return to the universalism of classic separatism, its politics of recrimination, its critical flippancy and moralizing, and its intoxicating rage, even when they claim their ground in progressive intersectional thought, is a profound denial of what we cling to.

Truth or revenge? If we, like Zed, could face our own mirror images, our wounded attachments, perhaps we could answer this question differently: neither truth, nor revenge, but *divergence*.[77] The lesson we have to learn from separatism is this: the promise of separation will always fail if we use it in the hopes of discovering some universal, cosmic ground of identity or moral authority that binds us together against our oppressors. But it can be a potent part of our varied projects for political freedom if it is wielded as the endless impulse to diverge, to do something different, to split off and take new forms. As Gloria Anzaldúa reminds us, "At some point, on our way to a new consciousness, we will have to leave the opposite bank, the split between the two mortal combatants somehow healed so that we are on both shores at once. Or perhaps we will decide to disengage from the dominant culture . . . and cross the border into a wholly new and separate territory. Or we might go another route. The possibilities are numerous when we decide to act and not react."[78] Returning to lesbian separatism involves learning from the possibilities and pitfalls of this utopian project, which is nothing more nor less than the practice of *splitting decisions*. What if we separated when necessary, but never for good? What if we valued our identities but didn't elevate them to the status of universal priority? What if we named injuries but refused to make them the basis for coalition? What if we projected different ideas of who we wish to be in the political future, but never decided in advance where we will land? What if we made passionately ethical arguments on behalf of the oppressed, without presuming to lay claim to a definitive moral high ground? "The possibilities are numerous" when we "choose to go another route."

If, like *Zardoz* and *Born in Flames*, we could see separatism not as the reductive image of the anachronistic white lesbian feminist (though we can show her love too), but as a labile feminist and queer form that travels, we can finally reckon with its power. In its most ideologically rigid expressions, lesbian separatism ultimately could not imagine reconciliation with any perceived dominating system or those who claimed its privileges. In this sense, separatism spoke to a deep anxiety at the core of all left political struggles: the nagging possibility that no identity group could ultimately provide a purely welcoming home for anyone. From this vantage, lesbian separatism poses such an intense problem for our current political imagination not only because of its ideological or analytical missteps, but because it relentlessly forces us to confront our own impossible desires for a final, stable, shared identity to liberate us from the endless, painful negotiation of difference. Perhaps instead of seeking that identity in the midst of a roiling vortex of ideological purity, we could inhabit lesbian separatism's anarchist spirit and simply take flight.

3

"Beware the Hostile Fag"

Acidic Intimacies and the Gay Male Consciousness-Raising Circle in The Boys in the Band

Speak Pains to Recall Pains
—the Chinese Revolution
Tell It Like It Is
—the Black Revolution
Bitch, Sisters, Bitch
—the Final Revolution
—New York Radical Women meeting poster composed by
Kathie Sarachild (1968)

I need to be together with other gay men. We have not been together—we've not had enough self respect for that. . . . We need to recognize one another wherever we are, start talking to each other. . . . We need consciousness-raising groups and communes. Our gay souls have nearly been stomped to death in that desert called America. If we are to bloom, we can only do it together.
—Gary Alinder, "My Gay Soul" (1970)

In November 1968, Kathie Sarachild, a founding member of the women's liberation group the Redstockings, presented an outline for a new feminist political practice at the first national Women's Liberation Conference. She dubbed this practice "consciousness-raising" or "CR." Consciousness-raising was a collective exercise of publicly speaking personal truth to uncover shared experiences of patriarchal oppression. In Sarachild's words, CR required women to meet in "rap groups" or "bitch sessions," in which they would "recall and share [their] bitter experiences" of sexism.[1] In making those recollections public, consciousness-raising would create a space for "evaluating [women's] feelings" and provide the context for "cross-examination," in which women could interrogate and formulate judgments about their relationship to structures of gendered inequality.[2] Such an activity, it was theorized, would link the personal with the political in the most systematic and immediately visceral way, encouraging women "to look for explanations for each part of [their] history in terms of the social or cultural dynamic created by sexism—rather than in terms of the personal dynamic."[3] Having recently made the radical decision to cut ties with the New Left and the liberal wing of the National Organization for Women, leaders of women's liberation were keen to develop a model of internal critique that could provide women with tools to make many more such decisions for their political freedom.[4]

Six months before Sarachild's speech in April 1968, Mart Crowley's explosive play *The Boys in the Band* appeared Off-Broadway. Without precedent, the play depicted a group of gay men engaged in a series of fiery debates about the nature of gay desire, identity, and social life that unfold across a single evening at a party gone awry. At a "smartly appointed duplex apartment in the East Fifties" of Midtown Manhattan, an eclectic circle of eight gay men—among them a bookstore clerk, a fashion photographer, a public-school teacher, and a luxury antiques dealer—convene to celebrate the birthday of their mutual friend Harold.[5] When Alan, a homophobic former college roommate of the host, Michael, crashes the event, his presence brings repressed tensions among the group to the surface. These tensions overwhelm the convivial party atmosphere, resulting in a series of painful revelations about the men's internalized self-hatred, experiences of unrequited love and sexual shame, and individual forms of resistance to a heteronormative society. If Sarachild's speech articulated the form and content of a developing practice of feminist consciousness-raising rooted in collective public dialogues, *The Boys* appeared to enact an early version of this activity directly in front of theater audiences by displaying one of the longest and most searing public "bitch sessions" ever performed on the US-American stage.

Just as feminist CR centralized the importance of group process in the form of a women's conversation circle as a generative site for "pooling" experiences of sexism, the second half of *The Boys in the Band* similarly presents a group of gay men arranged in a circle, passionately sharing experiences of homophobia. Whereas feminist CR underscored the value of women's feelings as a source of knowledge that might allow them to speak truth to power, so too the members of this gay male group are driven by feelings of rage, bitterness, and sadness to rail against homophobia's power to constrain their social existence. And finally, where one of feminist consciousness-raising's central goals was the production of concepts for analyzing the logics of male domination that underwrote women's lives, in the bitchy and hilarious witticisms that the gay male characters of *The Boys* sling at one another and at the straight world that shuns them, they articulate concepts they have developed to identify and frustrate the heterosexist logics that underwrote *their* lives.[6]

With the 1970 film adaptation of Crowley's play, *The Boys in the Band* became not only the first explicitly gay movie distributed to a mass audience but also arguably the only Hollywood film to visually represent and model consciousness-raising as it was taken up and adapted by different publics, including urban gay men. By the time of the film's release in March 1970, CR had been a staple of radical feminist organizing for more than sixteen months, while CR practices had been introduced to the Gay Liberation Front, the vanguard organization of the gay liberation movement, by the Redstockings member Karla Jay in November of the previous year.[7] When Jay and coeditor Allen Young published *Out of the Closets: Voice of Gay Liberation*, the first US anthology of LGBTQ political writing, in January 1972, the collection included A Gay Male Group's "Notes on Gay Male Consciousness-Raising." This was a modified version of Sarachild's CR program tailored for gay male group process that, according to the writing of other contributors, was indicative of the forms of CR gay men had been engaging in since 1970.[8] If the 1968 theatrical version of *The Boys* anticipated the moment of consciousness-raising's ascendancy in feminist practice, the 1970 film appeared on the other side of CR's full institution in both women's and gay liberationist circles. Far from being out of date by the time of its release, the film adaptation of *The Boys* debuted at exactly the moment when feminist and gay CR began to diffuse into the wider culture. The widespread appeal of CR as a quotidian practice of personal storytelling created more everyday opportunities for women and queers to articulate their distinct experiences of sexism, misogyny, and homophobia to one another and consequently develop shared standards for adjudicating meaningful responses to their unjust subordination. In this context, the film accrued a host of new meanings beyond its theatrical version, now not only portraying the seeming fractiousness of gay men as a group but also documenting gay men's heart-wrenching emotional labor to negotiate newly "liberated" identities and social worlds *despite* the societal homophobia that continued to plague their lives.

Moreover, the ready adoption of feminist CR by gay liberationists revealed that, for many politicized gay men, the radical feminist critique of patriarchal gender norms provided the basis for their growing awareness of homophobia as a stigma against perceived gender, rather than erotic, deviancy, captured in the widely shared stereotypical view of gay males as "failed" or "incomplete" men.[9] This required gay men to see themselves as aligned in some way with women as a subordinate group, and hence to expand their criteria for judging sexuality within the broader structure of patriarchy.

This chapter reinterprets the film adaptation of *The Boys in the Band* as a text that indexes the early adoption of radical feminist political strategies within the gay male social culture of the late 1960s and early 1970s. In the "truth game" the friends play in the film's second half, the characters are positioned in a circle, while engaging in a protracted "bitch session" in which they "recall and share [their] bitter experiences" of unrequited love. These recollections of trauma around same-sex desire, homophobia, and their social consequences enable both the characters in the film and its viewers to take into account a broader range of gay male experience than either institutional homophobia or internalized self-hatred allow for, thereby enacting feminist CR's stated conceptual goal of "building a collage of similar experiences . . . by pooling description of the forms oppression has taken in each individual's life."[10] In the movie, this practice of "pooling" multiple, often incommensurate lived experiences or perspectives on the world—what the political theorist Hannah Arendt identifies as the foundation of "enlarged" or "representative thinking"—involves members of the group verbally relating their distinctive stories, but also the camera's canny visual movement between them, so that we "see" each character both figuratively and literally in a way that provides a kaleidoscopic view of gay male lived experience.[11] It is from this position of "enlarged thinking" that the men inch toward a new set of standards for making critical judgments, ones that equip them to better understand their social and psychic location in an emergent and increasingly heterogeneous urban gay male collectivity. The struggle to arrive at those standards is the film's version of CR. It results in the characters' uneven movement to new locations in relation to their experiences of, and responses to, homophobia; but it also solicits viewers to formulate their own judgments not only about each character and their conflicted interactions but also about the broader social consequences of heterosexism, that is, to "form an opinion . . . by taking account of other views."[12]

This process is depicted in the movie as emotionally (even sometimes physically) violent and intellectually demanding. The breathless pace of barbed speech suggests the level of cognitive and verbal skill required to navigate the complexities of gay male emotional bonds, variously organized around feelings of smugness and superiority, loneliness and intense desire for community, and love tempered by insecurity and self-doubt. Yet the film's version of CR—impassioned, angry, unpredictable, and uncensored—revealed some of the unexpected volatility that this political form could unleash (a volatility feminists often assumed they could control through the elaborated rules set forth by the Redstockings' original CR manifesto).[13] *The Boys in the Band* underscored the necessity of formulating an equally powerful practice of *critical judgment* within all forms of social interaction—not merely the aspects of one's life amenable to politicization—where critical judgment is understood as the ability to distinguish claims motivated by insecurity, unrequited desire, or misdirected blame from claims that accurately identify social injustice. The film allows us to see how political forms like the feminist CR program and its imagined circle of interlocutors could provide a powerful analogy for lived social forms like the gay male friendship circle; in turn, the movie's ability to use cinematic technique to visualize such overlaps allows it to function as a potential cultural transmitter of consciousness-raising in both its structure and its values. My contention is that this practice, as the film presents it, empowers its participants to develop more effective judgments of one another as well as the systems of power that oppress them, consequently strengthening social bonds between queers, women, and sexual and gender outlaws—bonds that became newly imaginable at the very historical moment when members of the women's and gay liberation movements were abandoning the known worlds of sexism, homophobia, and self-hatred in search of an uncharted territory of freedom, sexual liberation, and rich sociality.

Acidic Intimacies

The Boys in the Band has been lambasted by critics for its judgmental, bitchy tone and for the vitriol that the characters, particularly Michael, spew at their supposed friends and intimates. As films scholar William Scroggie recounts, "In 1971, gay liberationist Dennis Altman called *The Boys* 'Crowley's portrait of unredeemed misery,'" and "another gay liberationist, Peter Fisher . . . wrote '*The Boys* . . . presents a stereotypical picture of unhappy people unable to come to terms with themselves.'"[14] One year later in *Out of the Closets*, co-editor Young would claim that *The Boys* "depicts a sad collection of stereotypes . . . designed to win pity and perhaps tolerance from liberals."[15] The by-now-clichéd criticisms of the film's negativity, however, fail to explain the conceptual power of the movie on three fronts.

First, by focusing on the alienation such hostility among the guests implies about late 1960s gay male experience, critics ignore the powerful and sustaining intimacy that underlies the conflicted engagements depicted in the movie. Despite the frustrations the men express about their social and sexual lives, *The Boys in the Band* is a showcase in *acidic intimacies*, or painful but deep-rooted social bonds, rather than an exposé of gay male anomie. These intimacies are acidic in the sense that they register the bitterness or sting of relationships cemented through shared knowledge of another gay man's insecurities, manipulations, and character flaws. Early in the film, Michael tries to align himself with Alan's genteel values by piously claiming to his friend and former lover Donald, "Believe it or not, there was a time in my life when I didn't go around *announcing* I was a faggot. . . . I didn't come out until after college," to which Donald retorts, "It seems to me that the first time we tricked we met in a gay bar on Third Avenue during your *junior year*." "Cunt," Michael responds with a sarcastic smile. These instances of barbed retort, dotting the entire narrative, display the double edge of shared lived experiences that also make all parties vulnerable to being called out for self-deception and evasion.

Second, critics' condemnation of the film's portrayal of regressive gay male stereotypes willfully subordinates both the formal structure of the narrative and the communal scene into which the characters are placed, in favor of reading the movie as a decontextualized presentation of rigid or stock caricatures. Across the narrative, we witness or hear about numerous forms of gay male sociality. The film opens with a kaleidoscopic montage of the characters as they go about their daily lives—working, shopping, cruising—followed by a panorama of a gay bar packed with men socializing. This long shot provides visual evidence of a vibrant and diverse gay male public culture in late 1960s and early 1970s New York City. The scene visually echoes and contradicts the famed 1964 *Life* magazine photo spread "Homosexuality in America," which opens with a foreboding image of the darkened interior of a gay leather bar with a group of shadowed faces amid the crowd of "deviants." A far cry from this "sad and sordid world," the bar in *The Boys in the Band* is brightly lit and overflowing with smiling, laughing faces, a site of convivial flirtation (figure 3.1).[16]

Throughout the film we hear conversation detailing the social conventions of gay bathhouses, reminiscences about the communal experience of Fire Island, furtive visits to gay bars with closeted college chums, the circulation of shared cultural references between gay friends (from Bette Davis to Tennessee Williams), and globe-trotting sexual adventures. These experiences indicate the expansive range of gay male sociability across differences of race, class, and sexual and cultural taste, rather than isolation or homogeneity. Moreover, the intimacies between the characters are strikingly varied: we see gay best friends (Michael and Harold), ex-lovers (Michael and Donald), former college roommates (Michael and Alan), former tricks (Donald and Larry), the polyamorous couple and the ménage à trois (Larry and Hank), and of course, the loosely knitted, but deeply affectionate gay friendship circle itself. Even as each of these bonds potentially presents a categorical "type" of relationship that has stereotypical features—the stranger sociality of gay men who trick together like Donald and Larry or the performative intensity of the effeminate "screaming queen" like Emory—the particular ways each character inhabits these types in relation to others become the basis for the film's depiction of a crisis in judgment. The film asks, how does one form objective opinions, and make definitive claims, about a

Figure 3.1. Top: *The Boys in the Band* depicts the lively, upbeat social life of a New York gay bar in 1970. *The Boys in the Band*, dir. William Friedkin (National General Pictures, 1970). Bottom, and facing page: *Life* characterizes the dark interior of a gay leather bar in 1964 as a "sad and sordid world."

HOMOSEXUALITY

A secret world grows
open and bolder.
Society is forced to look
at it—and try
to understand it

These brawny young men in their leather caps, shirts, jackets and pants are practicing homosexuals, men who turn to other men for affection and sexual satisfaction. They are part of what they call the "gay world," which is actually a sad and often sordid world. On these pages, LIFE reports on homosexuality in America, on its locale and habits (*pp. 66-74*) and sums up (*pp. 76-80*) what science knows and seeks to know about it.

Homosexuality shears across the spectrum of American life—the professions, the arts, business and labor. It always has. But today, especially in big cities, homosexuals are discarding their furtive ways and openly admitting, even flaunting, their deviation. Homosexuals have their own drinking places, their special assignation streets, even their own organizations. And for every obvious homosexual, there are probably nine nearly impossible to detect. This social disorder, which society tries to suppress, has forced itself into the public eye because it does present a problem—and parents especially are concerned. The myth and misconception with which homosexuality has so long been clothed must be cleared away, not to condone it but to cope with it.

Photographed for LIFE by BILL EPPRIDGE

A San Francisco bar run for and by homosexuals is crowded with patrons who wear leather jackets, make a show of masculinity and scorn effeminate members of their world. Mural shows men in leather.

way of life that has become so extraordinarily expansive and diverse, yet still so irreducibly particular?

The Boys in the Band responds to this question through a relentlessly dialogic narrative driven by ceaseless, rapid-fire talk, which produces a ballistic experience of constant call and response, witticism and reply, argument and rebuttal. The hatefulness and ridicule expressed by characters are feelings performed in the company of others and invite fierce riposte. Acidic speech is repeatedly named as such—as when Harold describes Michael's barbs as "hateful"—and those who utter it are called out for their actions. Some, like Michael, exhibit an almost manic drive

to be held accountable by others—confronted and forced to respond to criticisms of one's actions—which is understood as a potentially therapeutic outcome of being fairly judged. Michael plays his level of hostility toward the group to Harold's absolute limit, attacking his friend so aggressively (even after Harold warns, "I know this game you're playing. . . . I can beat you at it. So don't push me"), it is as though he unconsciously seeks to elicit a response that would refuse, and thereby provide insight about, his bitterness.

No guest leaves Michael's apartment until the very end of their "hostile" dialogue, committing to the psychic and social consequences that might unfold from their sparring. Equally crucial, upon evening's end, Harold's parting words to Michael are "Call you tomorrow," while Donald affirms he will be back next Saturday to "spend the night." Despite what Harold calls the "fervor with which [Michael] annihilate[s]," Michael's antagonism toward his company is strangely *productive* of their social relations. By the closing shot, we know more about each character, they know more about one another, and they have explained themselves and their experiences with greater depth than ever before. Yet knowledge of Alan's "true" sexuality, of whether the evening's events will alter his homophobic views, or if the men will leave politically enlightened remains open. In this way, the film embraces the power of dialogic engagement in the form of consciousness-raising but presses back against the radical feminist assumption that the consequences of such a practice could or should be predictably coordinated as a linear movement toward left political commitment.

Third, and finally, critics' willful overlooking of the film's social dimensions has led to a related failure to account for its rebellious, antihomophobic spirit. In the characters' bombastic refusal to accept the specter of homophobic judgment (either in external sources like the heterosexual superiority of Alan or internal ones like Michael's disgust at his friends' flamboyance), they embody the spirit of radical feminist and gay liberationist politics *affectively*. My reading of the film takes seriously the idea, central to feminist and gay CR, that gay men's feelings about their oppression might function as a source of political knowledge. The film argues that we might learn something fundamental about how homophobia functions from these angry "screaming queens" precisely because they are willing to scream about its painful consequences. In 1968, Sarachild wrote, "We're saying that when [women] had hysterical fits, when we took things 'too' personally, that we weren't underneath our feelings, but responding with our feelings correctly to a given situation of injustice."[17] Echoing this logic, A Gay Male Group's "Notes on Gay Male Consciousness-Raising" opens by acknowledging that "*Gay males feel pain.*"[18] Both statements recognize that one's emotional responses to sexism and homophobia, rather than being merely subjective or indulgent, can be legitimate evidence of the unjust workings of patriarchal power. The text's willingness to represent painful affects onstage and on-screen has led many critics and viewers to dismiss *The Boys* as depicting the worst aspects of gay male identity and experience. Yet this interpretation colludes with a homophobic and sexist logic that views intense emotionality as immature or "hysterical," denigrating the possibility that negative feelings might be an acute register of injustice and, consequently, a rebellious act against it.[19] Against this reductive frame, *The Boys* honors a fundamental conceit of CR practice, that no marginalized group can know or grasp their oppression, let alone conceive their version of liberation, without a sense of shared reality about it. This is possible only through the exchange of perspectives on the same experiences, whether of homophobia and familial shunning or their alternatives in gay male sexual freedom and camaraderie. What critics decry as the film's negativity and regressive stereotypes, then, are a byproduct of its honest attempt to render the common features of whatever we might call *the gay male experience*, but from multiple, particular standpoints, so that every individual can ultimately make their own informed decision about how they wish to respond to the conditions of their subjection.

Consider a scene near the conclusion of the film: after various members of the group have narrated stories of unrequited love, Michael confronts Alan about his cruel shunning of their mutual college friend Justin. Justin is a gay man with whom Alan purportedly had a romantic friendship. As Justin tells it, when he openly expressed his gay desires Alan permanently cut him off. Speaking in his friend's defense, Michael rages, "You ended the friendship, Alan, because you couldn't face the truth about yourself. You could go along, sleeping with Justin, as long as he lied to himself and you lied to yourself and . . . dated girls and labeled yourselves men. . . . But Justin finally had to be honest. . . . You couldn't take it and so you destroyed the friendship. . . . [To] this day he still remembers the treatment—the scars he got from you. . . . Call him and apologize." This moment is easily dismissed because of the questionable motives behind Michael's demand and the potential misfire of his assumption that Alan is gay. Yet in the context of gay liberation's bold refusal of "marriage, family, and home that our society holds up as normal," what could possibly be more courageous than a gay man demanding accountability from a straight man for his homophobic violence against another gay man?[20] This demand is the outcome of Michael's consciousness being raised over the course of the evening, even if unwittingly, for he begins the night committed to maintaining the secret of his gayness from Alan, and ends it audaciously refusing to hide behind heterosexual norms or grant Alan the privilege of leaving his own homophobic actions unacknowledged. Like Sarachild's injunction for women to see their feelings as a guide to a theory of their oppression, Michael takes Justin's emotional "scars" as an opening to theorize and call out the heterosexist logics that allow Alan to "label himself a man" and exploit the false legitimacy of that identity.

This bold representation and validation of gay men's feelings was enabled by CR practices in both women's and gay liberation that embraced the value of cross-examination. Dialogic exchange allowed participants to develop a voice within a collectively organized political practice and worked to deconstruct resistances to CR, which, according to the original feminist CR program, included "false identification with the oppressor," "rugged individualism," and "excusing the oppressor."[21] Yet *The Boys in the Band*'s conceptual innovation of feminist CR was to refuse the premise that consciousness-raising must take place in a nonjudgmental space; it understood that for sexism and homophobia to be appropriately judged, those who might best be equipped to offer such a critique would need to work through their own conflicted judgments about themselves and one another. Perhaps most daringly, the film catalyzes this necessary but difficult struggle by materializing the force of homophobia in an actual figure, Michael's ex-college roommate Alan. Where feminist CR imagined patriarchy as an abstracted oppressor a given group would identify and analyze from an initial location of relative psychic safety, in *The Boys*, homophobia is embodied in an actual person who aggressively inhabits the space of the gay gathering, demanding not merely abstract analysis but substantive response in the form of critical judgments about the men's relationships to homophobic privilege and power.

Performing Judgment

The Boys in the Band is a relentlessly judgmental text. From one angle, the characters' painful exposures of each other's personal failures and inadequacies are directly opposed to the founding feminist CR principle of nonjudgmentalness. As Pamela Allen explained in her description of CR group process in 1969, what is important "is the fact that someone listens and does not ridicule. . . . Unless women are given a non-judgmental space in which to express themselves, we will never have the strength or the perception to deal with the ambivalences which are a part of us all."[22] In *The Boys*, the men's judgmentalness and ridiculing of one another, the domination of the conversation by a single member of the group (Michael), the use (and abuse) of alcohol and other mood-altering substances, and the interruptions of one another's testimony are all elements that shirk the value of nonjudgment in a "safe" space. Moreover, the baldly misogynistic language used by many of the characters—including sexist terms like "slut," "cunt," and "bitch"—alongside the femmephobia that Alan, Michael, and Hank exhibit, might seem to immediately undercut the film's performance of feminist practices and ideals. Yet such qualities uncomfortably, but frankly, register the lingering power of internalized homophobia among gay men—captured in the fear of being seen as "incomplete" or "womanly" men—while also suggesting the repurposing of sexist terms as part of the playful, bitchy, acidic intimacies developed within gay male communal life. From another angle then, the stated commitment to nonjudgmentalness in feminist CR avowed a naïve utopian wish that group process might uncover an essentially conflict-free female experience for women to draw on in achieving their political goals, thereby downplaying women's own potential lingering feelings of resentment, meanness, or insecurity toward other women.

Unsurprisingly, testimonies from practitioners of feminist and gay CR in this period reveal that the lived experience of consciousness-raising groups rarely achieved their lofty ideals of nonjudgmentalness, often exposing significant emotional conflicts and inequalities between members. Describing one of the Redstockings' first CR meetings, Karla Jay recalls Kathie Sarachild's overzealous interruptions and negative evaluations of participants' testimony as undermining Sarachild's own CR program injunction to *listen to other women*. In an account of gay male CR in the first gay men's living collective in New York City in 1971, John Knoebel explains how jealousies, unacknowledged racism and classism, and conflicting political commitments led to the breakdown of the collective's relationships despite their consistent engagement in group process. And in an inspiring description of participating in a six-month-long CR group in New York City, June Arnold documents an epiphanic moment when disagreements about each woman's view of her sex life led to the following exuberant exchange: "'I guess we're not going to get to any conclusions from this session—we're all saying completely different things!' 'Beautiful! Maybe that's what liberation really is.'"[23] These testimonies show how consciousness-raising unleashed unexpected and messy conflicts in the attempted movement between the personal and the political for women and gay men alike. Feminist CR's disavowal of judgmentalness had the downside of potentially silencing the necessary act of *judging*, that is, forming an opinion about and developing substantive responses to other women's ideas, experiences, and behaviors. The conflicted aspects of the men's dialogue in *The Boys* encourage viewers to develop their own critical faculty of judgment, in order to parse different forms of criticism precisely, from the most personal character assassinations to the most generative rebuttals of entrenched thinking.

The film produces a distinction between the cultivated practice of gay male *judgmentalness* (or "bitchiness") and the faculty of *critical judgment*. Yet it does not place these categories in a developmental narrative, in which an individual evolves out of the former into a mature, "adult" capacity for objective judgment. Rather, *The Boys* acknowledges the conceptual power of both judgmentalness *and* judgment in gay male social life, while stressing the importance of distinguishing them. In the narrative, judgmentalness ironically functions as a form of gay male community building. It is a highly developed code of verbal sparring that requires common cultural references and the recognition of others' personal characters. When deployed outside the gay male collective, judgmentalness is a useful weapon against homophobia, a cultivated condescension toward straight culture and its banal, normalizing force; within the gay male social milieu, it often functions as a loving form of social antagonism among friends that implies an intimate "knowingness" of one another's flaws. This is exhibited in A Gay Male Group's "Notes on Gay Male CR," whose lengthy catalog of different forms of "resisting consciousness" (more numerous and specific than those named in Sarachild's original program) admitted a willingness to lodge judgments against gay men's habits of evasion, including "continual use of drugs and drink during meetings" (think Michael), "coming late to meetings or missing them with no excuse" (think Harold), and "not revealing physical attractions" (think Donald).[24] There is something undeniably bitchy about this catalog of resisting consciousness that suggests an insider's knowing side-eye to often unaccounted-for gay male bad behavior. *The Boys* takes this willingness to express judgmentalness to the extreme, making accountability, rather than nonjudgmentalness, its central value.

Early in the film, as Michael readies for his guests, he asks Donald, "What are you so depressed about? Other than the usual *everything*, I mean?" When Donald refuses to answer, Michael sarcastically replies, "Well, if you're not going to tell me, how can we have a conversation *in depth*—a warm, rewarding, meaningful friendship?" Michael sardonically calls out Donald's melancholic tendencies, while couching his barb in genuine care for his friend's anxieties. Even as he pokes fun at social "depth" amid the pervasive superficiality of gay social culture, he lovingly elicits the emotional confession he denigrates: Donald finally divulges his struggles over his gay identity and its potential rootedness in parental disappointment and "a neurotic compulsion not to succeed." Donald's miming of the clichéd narrative of abnormal childhood development, supported by his psychologist (and by a homophobic US culture), enables Michael to subject this story to critique: "Christ, how sick analysts must get of hearing how Mommy and Daddy made their darlin' into a fairy." The exchange presents gay male judgmentalness as an alternative value system that cannily sees behind and deconstructs the clichés of pathologizing definitions of gay male identity, consequently producing more humane bonds between gay men (while brilliantly turning the accusation of homosexuality's "sickness" back onto the psychotherapists who enforce these stories).

If gay male judgmentalness can produce alternative intimacies outside the gaze of societal and clinical homophobia, *critical judgment* serves as a tool for holding other gay men accountable for their speech and actions. Critical judgment involves the capacity to take in multiple viewpoints on the same circumstances to form substantive opinions about them that have qualitative weight—that is, not simply pointing out inadequacies or problems but suggesting what should be done about them.[25] As Knoebel recounts about the 95th Street Collective's group process, "Whenever there was a disagreement between any of us, everyone would gather together. . . . Everyone's opinion was solicited. Grievance usually meant that one or both parties were asking the other to change . . . so we always use these instances to try to . . . understand what criticism or self-criticism was being offered. A sense of group process arose out of this."[26] Critical judgment then, is about the production of normative standards of social conduct. If a certain loving bitchiness brings gay men together, a clear-eyed critical judgment allows them to stand apart, call one another out, and hold others accountable. According to *The Boys in the Band*, both are crucial to the maintenance of heterogeneous community; it is their conflation, or the inability to distinguish between them, that is destructive of collective life.

The movie's array of personalities presents the audience with many vantage points from which to look on the evening's events, yet the film frames this larger set of views within three primary models for judging the content of the party, embodied by its three central characters. In the naïve all-American blueblood Alan, the cynical and insecure Michael, and the self-effacing Harold, the film presents distinct types of judgment that take different founding criteria and have varied consequences for queer communal life. These can be understood respectively as the *ideological*, the *ambivalent*, and the *judicious*. The film typologically reduces Alan, Michael, and Harold to each of these corresponding models but sets them in dynamic interaction, with explosive and unpredictable results.

The Boys in the Band presents Alan, Michael's former college roommate and a Washington, DC, patrician, as an allegorical figure for societal homophobia. His judgment against homosexuality precedes his physical presence at the gay male gathering. When Michael explains to Donald his squeamishness about introducing Alan to a group of "screaming queens," he explains that Alan and his "social type" have "certain standards" that "we have to acknowledge." Those standards are aligned with normative heterosexuality, proper gender performance, and discretion regarding sexual impropriety; as Alan later explains to Michael, "I couldn't care less what people do—as long as they don't do it in public—or—try to force their ways on the whole damned world." In his view, "the whole damned world" is presumptively straight, and the performance of nontraditional masculinity or same-sex desire constitutes that norm's forceful violation.

Alan, then, represents a judgment informed by the belief in universally shared (heterosexual) standards by which all external realities can be measured. These "standards" are so pervasive that, as Michael's declaration confirms, "*we* have to acknowledge them." It is no surprise that Alan experiences a visceral revulsion at Emory's exaggerated femininity, privately explaining to Michael with barely restrained disgust, "he just seems like such a goddamn pansy." Alan's rage toward Emory is an outcome of Emory's daring refusal to acknowledge or affirm the assumed value of Alan's heterosexual privilege. Alan repeatedly invokes the universality of his position when he entreats Michael with the phrase "you know" to indicate their presumed shared beliefs regarding the public, flamboyant sexuality Emory represents: "Oh, come on, man, *you know* me—*you know* how I feel—your private life is your affair" (my italics). Invoking a transparent understanding between "men," Alan rhetorically constitutes the essential nature of his position by presuming similitude of feelings across personalities and social positions. Though Michael initially presents Alan's stance as understandable, even justifiable, their private conversation unhinges his initial alignment with heteronormative propriety. Against Alan's repeated invocations of the commonly recognized norms he holds dear, Michael engages in an act of cross-examination—a central practice of feminist CR—that reorients the assumed universality of Alan's worldview toward the particularity of his social location. In response to Alan's assumption that Michael knows his viewpoint, Michael coldly replies, "No, I didn't know that about you," and demands to know, "Why are you here?" and "What were you crying about on the telephone?" These requests reduce Alan to the specificity of his own actions.

In Michael's cross-examination, he exhibits a second form of judgment best described as ambivalent. Michael is undoubtedly the most judgmental character in *The Boys in the Band*, bringing down world-rending condemnations against every party guest, including himself. Yet Michael's claims flicker between a biting moralism, exhibited in his cutting judgmentalness, and a righteous quest for justice, exhibited in his critical judgment of homophobia. These positions compete as contradictory motives animating Michael's speech and action and are embodied in his concept of the "Christ-was-I-drunk-last-night syndrome." He explains: "You know, when you made it with some guy in school, and the next day when you faced each other there was always a lot of crap about 'Man, was I drunk last night! Christ, I don't remember a thing!'" Michael uses this phrase to indicate both an immature form of self-loathing instilled in gay men about their sexual desires, requiring them to pretend their liaisons never happened, and the lies that straight men use to deny their sexual activities with other men. The slogan captures the element of CR group process that Pamela Allen called "analyzing," in which participants respond to their aggregated experiences of sexism by developing concepts that describe and illuminate the social conditions of women's oppression.[27] Yet whereas feminist CR imagined a pure progression from sharing experiences to conceptual analysis that always landed on the side of women as an oppressed class, Michael's concepts for identifying homophobic lies are ambivalently produced in the thick of living life as a gay man in uneven relationship to others who share his sexual identity. A concept like the "Christ-was-I-drunk-last-night syndrome" is ambivalent in the sense that it reveals feelings of bitterness toward, and a desire to expose, both the privilege of heteronormative ideology *and* the hypocritical self-deceptions of gay men.

Michael's obsessive pursuit of "the facts" in all things leads him to assume that certain truths—for instance, Alan's potential homosexuality—merely need to be uncovered through forceful revelation. This zealous truth-seeking reveals Michael's continued commitment to universal values, though perhaps reconstituted ones organized less by heterosexism (like Alan's) than by gay moralism. In one instance, Michael harangues Harold about his self-torturing beauty regimen: "Standing before a

Figure 3.2. "Summer 1968." *The Boys in the Band*, dir. William Friedkin (National General Pictures, 1970).

bathroom mirror for hours and hours. . . . And looking no different after Christ knows how many . . . ointments and creams. . . . Yes, you've got scars on your face—but . . . if you'd leave yourself alone you wouldn't have any more than you've already awarded yourself." Michael's ambivalence is apparent in his simultaneous judgmentalness toward his friend's unhealthy vanity and his critical judgment of the pernicious cultural beauty standards that oppress women and gay men alike. It is Michael's increasing inability to distinguish between these positions—brought on, in part, by the contradictory demands of a homophobic society—that mark him as a "hostile fag." Rather than villainize that hostility, *The Boys in the Band* presents it as a dynamic force that can potentially bring into being new forms of consciousness.

Michael's ambivalence is on the cusp of the revolutionary. Throughout the evening, Harold comically calls Michael's frenzied attacks a form of "turning," a symbolic centripetal revolution producing enough tension to spin outward yet remaining tightly coiled. Moreover, throughout the first half of the movie, Michael is repeatedly filmed standing before a wall on his patio chalked with the words "Summer 1968," referencing the year of the New Left's political implosion and fracturing into a new spate of radical movements (figure 3.2). Michael's figurative "turning" presents him as poised to jettison one set of toxic universal values but unable to imagine what the world might look like devoid of another set of ideals decoupled from gay moralism (hence his investment in the Catholic Church, what Harold calls his "insurance policy" against life's unpredictability). Harold at one point flatly states, "Michael, . . . you don't know what side of the fence you're on. If somebody says something pro-religion, you're against them. If somebody denies God, you're against *them*. One might say you have a problem in that area."

Harold breaks the deadlock of the "problem" of judgment that Michael's ambivalence and Alan's universalism produce. Irreverent and self-deprecating, Harold has no time for truths that do not help a life flourish. His battles with internalized homophobia have literally scarred him, and his response to both self-inflicted and societally imposed mutilation is, quite literally, to *laugh*. Harold enters the narrative immediately after Alan's violent assault on Emory midway through the party, walking in on a spectacle of homophobic rage. Instead of reacting negatively to the events, he calmly reads Emory's birthday card—a hilarious injunction to "roll over and play dead" (read: be "banged" by the cowboy hustler whom Emory has purchased as his gift)—and explodes into raucous laughter that undercuts the gravity of Alan's actions. When Michael scolds Harold, "What's so fucking funny?" Harold retorts, "Life. Life's a goddamn laugh riot. You remember life." Harold's willingness to laugh at even at the most bitter aspects of gay experience indicates his openness to being amused by "life" and its over-the-top ridiculousness, while also functioning as a critical weapon that equalizes the playing field between gay and straight. By hyperbolically vocalizing his immense pleasure at Emory's gift, an offering that would traditionally be deemed distasteful in more "straight" settings, Harold values Emory's flamboyance while debasing Alan's hysteria, which appears embarrassingly out of step with gay male conviviality and playfulness. Unlike Alan and Michael, Harold is eminently self-critical and disparages the value of exposure, recognizing the social limitations of acts of cruel revelation. When Michael lobs his acidic criticism of Harold's beauty regimen, Harold replies, "You'd really like me to compliment you now, for being so honest, wouldn't you? . . . Slut." In an act of counterexposure, Harold reveals the ruse of a certain kind of "truth telling" that speaks in the name of authenticity and justice but is in fact self-serving.

Unlike Michael, whose main conceptual move is to unmask, Harold wields a form of judicious critical judgment that discerns which truths should remain private and which deserve public airing. Harold's discernment is evident in his investment in maintaining a realm of private intimacy among friends, which is the foundation for love in the face of fierce criticism. When Larry asks Harold to tell the group what Michael has engraved on his birthday gift (a photograph of Michael in a silver frame), Harold holds back: "Just . . . something personal." Despite Michael's airing of Harold's dirty laundry, Harold remains committed to distinguishing between those intimacies that need to be made public and those that should be held close to the heart. Harold is never framed as inherently morally superior to Michael. As Harold points out, he and Michael "are a match" because of how well they "play each other's game." Rather, the film suggests that Harold's judicious attitude toward *this* particular evening's events is a consequence of his position relative to Michael's emotional implosion—that is, Harold's capacity for judiciousness emerges in the context of a dialogic and combative evening of social engagement.

The film argues that judiciousness might be one radical consequence of being forced to take into account multiple viewpoints, which Harold is able to do only by witnessing recognizable aspects of his own identity inhabited and performed by others. In light of the perspective this view affords, it is unsurprising that, when Michael finally holds Alan accountable for his actions by demanding he stay for the truth game, Harold says, "Revolution complete." What Harold initially considers Michael's ceaseless, insular "turning" becomes a revolution both figurative and literal—an act of rebellion against Alan indicating Michael's momentary but decisive jettisoning of his ambivalence—that Harold's balanced viewpoint can discern. In this sense, Alan is the material instantiation of the patriarchal and homophobic ideologies that feminist and gay CR sought to identify, resist, and dismantle, while Michael, who, in the words of "A Program for Gay Male CR," "identifies with the oppressor," is the ideal subject of consciousness-raising. The moment Michael turns his critical judgment upon Alan signals the completion of a conceptual circle of thought that in turn produces the actual circle that organizes the game the men play.

"Revolution Complete"

If Alan, Michael, and Harold embody various models of judgment, the truth game that unfolds over the second half of the film sets them in motion by borrowing a dynamic political form, the consciousness-raising circle. Michael sets up a game in which each group member must call the person he has loved most and confess his feelings to them. Every participant is judged by a scoring system that distributes points based on how close he comes to revealing his true feelings to the object of his affection. Though the game seems organized around the mere admission of love, it results in various group members explaining the contexts in which a specific attachment came into being and the prohibitions that prevented its fulfillment. The game's coercive aspect unwittingly produces the conditions under which gay men's feelings are treated as a source of "truth" about lived social relations. Yet this reality is infused with Michael's ambivalence. On the one hand, by publicizing the repeatedly failed trajectory of same-sex desire, Michael seeks to ridicule his friends' naïve hopes for sentimental love in the face of societal homophobia. On the other, by legitimizing the concrete fact of gay love, he appears intent on eliciting from Alan a dual confession of closeted homosexuality and repressed feelings for Justin. Following a classical model of feminist CR, Michael seems to imagine that the game can produce such a powerful sense of universally shared experience of gay male shame that its force will make visible and destroy Alan's hetero-patriarchal edifice. Yet the necessarily dialogic nature of the game Michael sets up means that he is unable to predict the content, delivery, or outcome of the stories that are told in the circle; consequently, the game ends up exposing the truth of gay male *heterogeneity*, rather than essential identity, while also acknowledging the complexly shared and uneven effects of heterosexism.

This expansive view of gay male heterogeneity models a form of "enlarged thinking" that can respond to conflicted circumstances in the absence of universal standards for adjudication. This notion of "enlarged" or "representative thinking" is captured by Arendt when she explains that critical judgment requires that "I form an opinion by considering a given issue from different viewpoints, by making present to my mind the standpoints of those who are absent. . . . The more people's standpoints I have present in my mind . . . the stronger will be my capacity for representative thinking and the more valid my final conclusions."[28] In the truth game's multiplicious view of who gay men are and how their experiences and desires might alter what counts as "normal," it becomes a living rebuttal to Alan's universalism. The game transforms CR from a practice striving toward false unity into a process that demands substantive responses to diversity, which, according to writers like Jay, Arnold, and Vivian Gornick, was often what the lived experience of CR practice was felt to be. Gornick elaborates: "Coming together, as they do, week after week for many months, the women who are 'in a group' begin to exchange an extraordinary sense of multiple identification. . . . Like shaking a kaleidoscope and watching all the same pieces rearrange themselves into an altogether other picture."[29]

As various members of the group begin to divulge stories of teenage longings crushed by homophobic rejection, college affairs swept under the rug, and adult relationships on the rocks or gone sour, the fine-grained distinctions between gay men's "kaleidoscopic" experiences of same-sex desire become apparent, just as much as widely shared trends of disavowal, ostracization, and shunning come to the fore. The game highlights differences of sexual habits and romantic outlooks (the desire for monogamy versus polyamory); differences of race and ethnic identity (Bernard's complex negotiation of Black gayness in a predominantly white and Jewish friendship circle); divergent responses to homophobia (Emory's flouting of homophobic scorn versus Michael's adherence to norms of respectability); differences in class background, mannerisms, and psychological struggles. In so doing, the game necessitates the proliferation of multiple, competing contexts for, and perspectives on, gay male experience.

This cultivation of "multiple identification" is captured in the tortured exchange between Larry and Hank, in which they overturn numerous expectations about monogamy, proper masculinity, and intimacy. Larry and Hank are the only romantic couple in the group. As handsome, gainfully employed gay men with a rich sex life, they seem to embody a companionate ideal many of the group members long for. Yet from the moment Hank and Larry are introduced in the movie's opening shots, their relationship appears strained by jealousies and miscommunication. We first see them together when an irritated Hank shoves his way through a crowded gay bar to pull Larry away from one of his flirtations. And later, when Michael demands that the two take their turn in the game, they are forced to articulate seemingly contradictory outlooks on committed gay love.

Hank is attached to monogamy and marriage as the foundation for a secure emotional bond between lovers, while Larry believes in polyamory as a release valve that allows long-term relationships to work by granting partners freedom to explore their sexuality with others. Rather than opposing these views, the narrative contextualizes each. The script suggests that Hank's attachment to monogamy may be the outcome of multiple circumstances: his insecurities entering a sexually promiscuous gay male culture after living most of his life as a monogamously partnered straight man, his nostalgic memories of marital stability, or perhaps simply habit. Alternatively, Larry explains his desire for polyamory as both an expression of his natural sex drive and an extension of his social life among gay men, an alternative site of personal fulfillment from marriage. He exasperatedly admits: "I can't take all this let's-be-faithful-and-never-look-at-another-person routine. If you want to promise that, fine. . . . But if you *have to* promise it, as far as I'm concerned, nothing finishes a relationship faster because it just doesn't work." What is required is not relinquishing either position but the ability to see from each other's perspective to develop meaningful responses to different contexts for inhabiting gay desire.

The scene of Hank and Larry's argument accomplishes three conceptual movements that characterize the truth game more broadly. First, it exposes significant differences among the group members, in this instance about what a proper romantic relationship looks like for gay men, but in other interactions differences in responses to homophobia, approaches to racial sensitivity, and awareness of class disparity. Second, the game publicizes homophobic conditions that prevent the expression of same-sex love. Alan's normative standards of judgment are potentially undone by the collective stories told but especially by Hank's narrative. When Alan vehemently refuses to acknowledge the reality of Hank's homosexuality, calling it "disgusting" and referring to heterosexual affairs as "normal," Hank replies, "It just doesn't always work out that way, Alan." Like Larry's claim that the "let's-be-faithful routine . . . just doesn't work," Hank's admission that things "don't always work out" in the way of a universally presumed heterosexuality boldly refutes Alan's illusions not only of Hank but of normative heterosexuality. For Alan, to see an effeminate man like Emory claim gay identity is no surprise, but Hank poses an impossible paradox, namely, that a man who appears just like himself—clean-cut, masculine, and with an unassuming affect—could also be a "goddamn pansy."

Moreover, the film visually holds characters like Alan to account for their homophobic reactions by rigorously tracking their expressions of confusion and disgust when they seek to disengage from difficult conversations about same-sex desire. In the exchange between Hank and Alan about Hank's homosexuality, Alan abruptly turns away when Hank admits, "I left my wife for Larry." As Alan turns, he states, "I'm really not interested in hearing about it," to which Michael responds, "Sure you are. Go ahead, Hankela, tell him all about it." When these two lines are spoken, the camera follows Alan's distressed face but keeps Hank and Michael in view behind him. Both Michael and the camera disallow Alan to disconnect from the conversation. Shortly after, Larry calls Hank's answering service on Michael's kitchen telephone to tell Hank he loves him from across the room. A series of shot/reverse shots show Alan standing in the eyeline of both men as their gazes lock from opposite ends of the apartment; even as Alan refuses to identify with the men in the circle, the camera actively locates him in the line of same-sex desire (figure 3.3). This camera work—in which conflicted interlocutors are persistently held together on screen—doubly formalizes the dialogic work of consciousness-raising that the game is analogous to, holding the characters visually accountable to the unfolding dialogue, while reminding viewers that they too are potential participants in the circle.

Finally, the game allows for internal critique among the gay male members of the group, both creating the space for telling stories and allowing each member to hold others answerable for how they tell their stories. When Hank relates his sad tale of a failed marriage and a life upended by coming out, Larry refuses Hank's self-pitying portrait: "Why am I always the goddamned villain in the piece?! If I'm not thought of as a happy-home wrecker, I'm an impossible son of a bitch to live with! . . . It's my right to lead my sex life without answering to anybody. . . . Numerous relations is a part of who I am!" Larry refuses

Figure 3.3. Top to bottom: "It just doesn't always work out that way, Alan"—the camera keeps Alan's face in view, even as he tries to turn away from Hank's revelation; Alan stands directly in the line of Hank and Larry's gay love. *The Boys in the Band*, dir. William Friedkin (National General Pictures, 1970).

the normalizing narrative that reduces gay male promiscuity to a destructive force, instead telling a different story about sexual freedom as a meaningful way of relating to others that exceeds any given sexual orientation. By articulating his worldview in a shared space, however, Larry elicits a range of opinions, from those like Emory, who undercuts

Larry's lofty paeans to sexual freedom by reminding him of his fickle erotic tastes and "wantonness," to those who, despite Larry's character flaws, broadly agree with the value of free gay erotic expression.

All three of these outcomes—the highlighting of gay men's' differences, the articulation of homophobia's multiple contexts, and the opportunity for internal critique—are similarly magnetized in the stories of Bernard and Emory, who respectively inaugurate the first two rounds of the game. If the conflict between Hank and Larry brought to the fore "multiple identification," allowing various members of the group to project themselves into different positions around the question of nonmonogamy, Bernard and Emory's tragic tales of homosexual rejection put in relief the limitations of effortless cross-identification between urban gay men along lines of race, class, and gender expression. Bernard is the only African American gay man in the group, while Emory is the circle's most flamboyant member. It is fitting that Bernard and Emory are, like Michael and Harold, "a match," not only as two of the group's fondest members, but as those who are figuratively positioned farthest from the center of normative white, straight-passing masculinity—as a result, they enjoy the privilege of sharing a unique language of biting mutual mockery built on trust, but perhaps also self-deprecating defensiveness in the face of gay male racism and sexism. (Early on, Emory directs an exoticizing joke at Bernard: "Hi, Bernadette, Anyone ever tell you you'd look divine in a hammock surrounded by . . . lots of lush tropical ferns?" To which Bernard laughingly retorts, "You're such a fag.") Their thick skin notwithstanding, the bitter aftertaste of Bernard and Emory's participation in the game—including the other members' inability to understand the uniquely racialized, classed, and gender-marked aspects of their lives—underscores the variety of entrenched racisms and sexisms that deeply afflict gay urban men (all of which were explicitly identified by "A Program for Gay Male CR" as detrimental aspects of gay male socialization requiring open discussion and systemic deprogramming).

Under pressure from Michael, Bernard reluctantly tells the group a story about the first and only time he made love to Peter Dahlbeck, the white son of his mother Francine's employer, Mrs. Dahlbeck, as a teenager. The recollection reveals that Bernard's first experience of unrequited love took place within a context of multiple marginalization, as a Black gay son of a working-class woman. The object of his desire, then, is an especially cruel one, because Bernard has spent his life in love with an unavailable white, putatively straight man who is heir to the family Bernard and his mother have lived in financial and social subordination to for decades. However, when Bernard calls his one-time paramour up (knowing that Peter has now been divorced three times), it is Mrs. Dahlbeck who picks up the phone. Though Bernard was originally emboldened to make the call among his gay male peer group, in this moment, he is suddenly mortified to realize that this action could jeopardize his mother's employment and social standing in the context of the Deep South. In Michael's zeal to force Bernard to "go ahead . . . make the call" and admit "that [you've] always loved him," he recklessly overlooks the potential social and economic consequences that might unfold for Bernard's family should the truth of his gay desire come out. Michael's myopic gay liberalism is captured in his smug side comments to Bernard throughout the conversation, like encouraging Bernard to refer to himself as Francine's "*son*, not boy." He arrogantly assumes that a powerful show of gay self-confidence alone could cut through entrenched structures of race and class hierarchy. Unsurprisingly, Bernard is emotionally obliterated by the event, not only reminded of what he cannot have (Mrs. Dahlbeck telling him that Peter is, once again, out on a date with a new woman), but thrown under the bus by his supposed friends, who despite their frustrations with Michael, fail to intervene on Bernard's behalf.

Unlike Bernard, who is peer-pressured into playing Michael's game, Emory, now visibly drunk, forcefully demands to take his turn. Though inebriated, he lucidly relates a story about his teenage love of Delbert Botts, a successful college-aged dentist in New York City whom Emory had admired in high school. Emory recounts how just before his prom, "I called him and asked if I could see him alone. . . . I was so nervous . . . I just stared straight ahead . . . and I asked him to be my friend. He said he'd be glad to be my friend. . . . And the next day I went out and bought him a gold-plated cigarette lighter. . . . And I wrote him a card that said, 'From your friend, Emory.'" Though Botts pretends to appreciate Emory's kindness, he goes on to spread gossip to the entire school about Emory's queerness, humiliating the young man before his peers. The story appears to confirm Emory's foolishness and naïveté before his friends, yet it also depicts the visibly "gayest" person in the circle as simultaneously the bravest and most authentic member of the group.

Emory's complex combination of intense emotional vulnerability and brazen display of gay desire performatively echoes his combination of feminine and masculine qualities, a network of seemingly contradictory social signs existing in one body that elicits dramatically divergent emotional responses from his peers. As Emory relates his story the camera cuts to each party guest's reaction: Alan is palpably uncomfortable, Michael radiates disdain, and Bernard expresses righteous sympathy for his friend's suffering. Emory's story, then, both astonishes and threatens the members of the group, who simultaneously appear jealous of his nerve yet cannot face their own internalized homophobia and self-hatred. Emory's story overturns the easy ability to make negative judgments about the flamboyance of gay men because it reveals such traits as empowering in the face of societal homophobia. And indeed, though in his worst moments Michael viciously denigrates Emory as undesirable ("Who would want to go to bed with a flaming little sissy like you? Who'd make a pass at you?"), Emory is consistently an object of fascination, admiration, and attraction for the other men, especially the winsome Larry who *does* make countless passes at Emory throughout the night. In the public context of the truth game, this contradictory blend of collective revulsion at *and* attraction to Emory's unique gender expression exposes the group members' internalized sexism alongside their deep affinity for feminine masculinities.

In the heartbreaking examples of Bernard and Emory, the truth game functions precisely like a CR session, bringing to light the ingrained racism, and internalized sexism and homophobia, of the gay men gathered at Michael's apartment. At one point when Bernard tries to dissuade Emory from telling his story, encouraging him to preserve his "dignity," Michael explodes: "Well, that's a knee-slapper. I love your telling him about dignity, when you allow him to degrade you constantly." Bernard bites back: "He can do it, Michael. I can do it. You can't. . . . I let him do it because it's the only thing that, to him, makes him my equal." In this moment of radical honesty, Bernard admits to a sense of shared subordination with an effeminate gay man. In so doing, he verbalizes a commonly unspoken truth, that multiple forms of marginalization are reproduced within the elaborate hierarchies of gay male social culture, where normatively handsome, muscular white men remain the ideal objects of desire. Bernard and Emory share analogous, though not identical, oppressed positions within that hierarchy, as well as a kind of mutual understanding, or negotiated trust, that allows them to banter, tease, and poke fun at one another's racial identities and gender expressions with greater latitude than someone like Michael, who is oblivious to his relative privilege within the pecking order. Such a negotiation is by no means liberatory or even politically palatable, but rather an interpersonal necessity carved out of adverse conditions.

In this sense, the forced public airing of grievances demanded by the truth game reveals not only differences between the players but also what Brian Norman calls "imperfect analogies" between various subordinate groups: "CR documents from women's liberation often offer analogies between the personal experience reported and that of other groups. . . . These analogies . . . seek alliance with another group who might be sympathetic to the example accessed through noticeably imperfect analogy."[30] In Bernard and Emory's relationship we see a quotidian version of the "imperfect analogy," where mutual experiences of race and gender-based oppression overlap, creating potent sites for the formation of common cause, friendship, and mutual care.[31] Such comparisons do not solve the twin problems of racism and sexism within the group as a whole, but they make them intensely visible, allowing these damaging logics to be scrutinized and potentially worked on not only by the party guests but by the film's viewing audience.

In *The Boys in the Band*, the multiple stories, interpretations, and reactions that unfold from the truth game undermine feminist CR's desire for concrete political outcomes of group process, but simultaneously reveal the power of enlarged thinking to forge associations in the absence of universally shared standards of judgment. Though Michael hopes to shake the foundations of Allen's seemingly unyielding attitude toward homosexuality, he himself desires the men in the room to articulate a universally shared woundedness about the gay experience. And indeed, rejection, isolation, and homophobia are recurrent elements in the stories shared, but certainly not the only elements, nor the defining ones. Michael is trumped by his own plot, for what emerges in the course of the night is a multidimensional view of gay existence that itself produces new conditions for making judgments from an expanded perspective on the heterogeneous experiences of gay male life: this includes the unique positions of a Black gay professional, a sexually libertine photographer, a flamboyant, out-and-proud antiques dealer, a staid schoolteacher, and more.

Harold, despite recusing himself from the game, is the character who appears most often in the background of scenes throughout its unfolding. Harold's distanced on-screen presence—highlighted by his literal seat outside the circle—alongside his handful of comic interjections to the men's stories, signals his mediated engagement in the game, rather than his complete removal from it. As the political theorist Linda Zerilli states, drawing on Arendt, "Judging involves neither becoming identical with you, nor . . . with myself, but 'thinking in my own identity where actually I am not.' . . . Outsideness suggests that we understand and judge from a position that is neither identical nor incommensurable but . . . at once separate from and related to that which we judge."[32] Harold's decision to position himself in such a way that he is like the participants (a gay man) but unlike them (a nonplayer) is exactly what allows him to absorb the multiple viewpoints articulated throughout the evening and formulate a judgment on the basis of those views, rather than any universally predetermined set of values.

As a result of staking out this position, by evening's end, Harold confidently "takes his turn" at the game and renders the following judgment, one that responds to Michael's violent exposure of other characters' inadequacies but also binds him and the other members of the gay male circle together collectively: "Now it's my turn, Michael. And ready or not, here goes. You're a sad and pathetic man. You're a homosexual and you don't want to be. But there is nothing you can do to change it. Not all your prayers to your God, not all the analysis you can buy in all the years you've got left to live. You may very well one day be able to know a heterosexual life if you want it desperately enough—if you pursue it with the fervor with which you annihilate—but you will always be homosexual as well. Always, Michael. *Always*. Until the day you die." In this breathtaking speech, Harold delivers a critical judgment born from his careful viewing of the night's events and his willingness to inhabit an "insider-outsider" position that allows him a more impartial, but not fully deracinated, view of the scene. He is keen to make public the shared condition of internalized homophobia that can motivate "hateful" speech

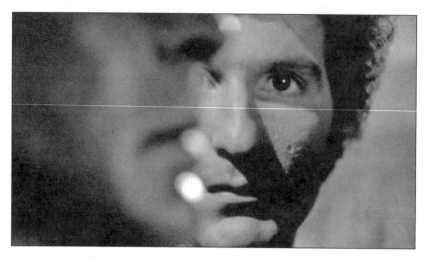

Figure 3.4. Harold's judgment. *The Boys in the Band*, dir. William Friedkin (National General Pictures, 1970).

like Michael's, while deploying that exposure not to humiliate or destroy but to hold another accountable *and* to reaffirm that other's social belonging. In reminding Michael that he will *always* be a homosexual, Harold counters Michael's ambivalent desire to belong, but not to a category so denigrated and despised as homosexuality. Thus, Harold names Michael "one of us" to remind him that no matter what source he seeks out to define his condition—God or psychotherapist—he will always be part of the gay social circle he has shamed.

At the moment when Harold begins this speech, Michael, in utter abjection after his failed attempt to out Alan, has literally turned away from the scene of emotional carnage he has orchestrated. Once again, the camera refuses to allow Michael his disengaged solitude. We follow Harold's gaze as he walks across the room to confront his friend, until he stands directly beside Michael, speaking at the side of his face. Finally, in the film's most intimate shot, Harold delivers the last two lines of his speech in a tight close-up, Michael's profile silhouetted against Harold's visage (figure 3.4). The dramatic image of Michael's profile bisecting Harold's face figuratively suggests the overlapping nature of their psyches, while also distinguishing them, since their actual profiles face different directions. This double movement of comparison and distinction, the oscillation that defines representative thinking, is underscored by the fact that the close-up highlights Harold's pockmarked cheek. This visual feature reminds us of the physical scars that *his* self-hatred has wrought. He and Michael are indeed similar, but the circumstances of the evening, which allowed Harold to step out of his insider position, have also made it possible for him to exercise his newly raised consciousness by making an informed judgment that creates distance for the sake of holding another accountable, but simultaneously reasserts the continuity of gay community amid difference and disagreement. Hence, even in the "face" of Michael and Harold's clash, Harold's parting words are, "Call you tomorrow." What the content of that conversation might be remains entirely open to possibility.

"We Argued about Everything": Reclaiming the Transformative Power of Queer Conflict

This chapter has sought to make two claims about *The Boys in the Band* and its continued relevance to the study of gay and feminist social formations in the twenty-first century. First, its depiction of furious collective dialogue between gay men offers one avenue for exploring the rich connections between the social and political conflicts that animated women's and gay liberation movements. The gay male friendship circle takes the form of a consciousness-raising group. The men's shame about their homosexuality is framed in terms of their failures to live up to traditional gender roles and beauty standards. The hateful speech that dominates the conversation echoes the personal attacks that Jo Freeman would call "trashing" within the women's movement.[33] And the forms of evasion and refusal to answer for one's actions enacted by each character model the many types of "resisting consciousness" that Sarachild detailed in her "Program for Feminist 'Consciousness Raising.'" These and countless other links suggest the need to develop a stronger account of the complex interaction between the social and political valences of women's and gay liberation, one attentive to the role of *culture* as a site where the political innovations of these movements were expressed in creative terms. Reading the film as an embodiment of feminist CR practice illuminates how aesthetic forms, even one as ancient as a standard geometric circle, can function to transmit and test the conceptual limits of political forms by placing them into new and unexpected contexts and imagining a wider range of publics for their use. Moreover, CR's affectively laden philosophy and format, which took gender and sexual dissidents' feelings seriously as a meaningful basis for cultivating political values and community, demands that we consider consciousness-raising as one largely overlooked origin for contemporary affect studies, which has, with few exceptions, neglected feminism's second wave as a potentially rich source of theorizing about feminist and queer emotional experience.[34]

This latter fact is vividly captured in historian John D'Emilio's moving recollection of his participation in the early days of the Gay Liberation Front. In his forward to the 1992 reprint edition of *Out of the Closets*, D'Emilio recounts:

> First, we argued about everything. The intensity of feeling that characterizes many of the documents in *Out of the Closets* was expressed among us. . . . We were discovering, even inventing, our identities. . . . We fought over sexuality, over feminism, over the name and purpose of the organization, over how to draw more lesbians into the group. . . . Second, we had meetings, seemingly all the time. They were general meetings . . . men's caucus meetings . . . consciousness-raising group meetings. . . . I felt as if I were making a whole new host of friends. I was awed by the audacity of Martha Shelley's angry polemics . . . I was struck by the raw power of the "Woman-Identified-Woman." Reading the achingly personal testimony . . . of the other gay male contributors, I tapped into reservoirs of old pain from my own years of struggling to come out. This book was a cathartic experience.[35]

Rereading *Out of the Closets* two decades after he first encountered its galvanizing content, D'Emilio experiences the book itself as one outcome of a collective practice of feminist and queer consciousness-raising. The anthology's amassing of multiple queer and feminist voices, speaking in dramatically different tones but all with great force, becomes a cultural model of the lived intensities of activist gathering. The latter involved a relentless mode of queer engagement or conflict born out of the twin experiences of shared sexist and homophobic trauma alongside the newly granted opportunity to publicize and transform such suffering into productive political ebullience and action. Though some of the contributors, including Allen Young, decried *The Boys in the Band* as a repository of negative stereotypes about gay male life, D'Emilio's electric description of gay liberation activists as people who "argued about everything," who expressed an extraordinary "intensity of feeling," and who lovingly registered each other's "pain" looks like nothing so much as the fiercely demanding, caustic, but transformative night of arguing at Michael's "smartly appointed apartment . . . in the East Fifties." It is perhaps no surprise, then, that in his forward, D'Emilio admits: "I saw a performance of *The Boys in the Band* [in the late 1960s], and though the gay liberationists would attack the play as self-hating and oppressive, to me it was sweet as nectar."[36]

Second, in an era when gay male social formations have attained unprecedented political, economic, and cultural power in the modern US with no formal ties to feminist politics, *The Boys in the Band* remains one of the most compelling refusals of affirmative gay identity politics in twenty-first-century popular culture. Notwithstanding the undeniable continued force of homophobia and the religious right's bolstering of anti-gay legislation, legal victories for same-sex marriage, the repeal of "Don't Ask, Don't Tell," and gay men's explosive visibility and active participation in the production of US media content have lifted this social group's status to new heights. Out of these perhaps limited successes, urban gay men have jettisoned previous commitments to self-criticism grounded in a feminist political practice of CR, while largely disavowing their shared political and social lot with women.

Here I speak as a participant more than a scholar, taking the injunction of feminist CR practice to treat feelings as knowledge by relying on my felt experience of navigating metropolitan gay male public cultures. From this standpoint, I suggest speculatively that in the wake of increasing public acceptance and accessibility to the privileges of normative US society, middle-class urban gay men have found numerous ways of courting validation from inside and outside their community, responding to decades of homophobia with an ecstatic show of capacity: the ability to maintain beautiful bodies and exceptional creative careers and to flexibly manage the celebrated institutions of marriage, child rearing, and home ownership, *as well as* open relationships, circuit parties, and gay cruises, all the while exhibiting no anger or frustration in the face of societal heterosexism. Gay men's feelings, which in the context of gay liberation and AIDS activism were valued for their ability to register the pain and violence of homophobia, are increasingly valued only if they embody the range of positive affects that come with demanding and achieving successful middle-class life or mastering the variety of sexual liaisons and pleasures that come with having access to money, men, and travel. We may now express indignation only at the denial of civil liberties, while genuine anger or frustration directed toward other gay men for their attachment to bankrupt politics and a broader culture of homophobic and racist violence can be understood only as bitterness (i.e., those who rage are simply losers who did not get their share) rather than as a productive registering of inequalities that can and should be addressed.

Perhaps the most powerful way in which such feelings have been made illegitimate is by the de-eroticization of anger and rebellion among gay men: it is no longer sexy to dissent, to disagree, to demand something politically from one's interlocutors as it was at the height of gay liberation and AIDS activism. This seems apparent in everything from the condemnation one might receive for critiquing the narrow political achievement of gay marriage to a simple disagreement of how one chooses to interpret a movie. While writing this chapter I accidentally ran into a man at a San Francisco café who had previously pursued me energetically on an online sex and dating application. When he learned I was revising a chapter on *The Boys in the Band*, he expressed his disdain for the movie's depiction of the most stereotypical aspects of gay male "bitchery." Internally I bristled at this clichéd critique—and smelled the whiff of not a little internalized homophobia at his hyperbolic miming of the characters' effeminate affect. But he was cute, and I wanted to know more. I explained my sense that the movie's depiction of rebellious gay men engaged in fierce debate represented a bold and progressive form of consciousness-raising, and I characterized its critical camp irony as being courageous. He countered that camp irony was *not sexy*—it was not possible to see the men in the movie as sexually desirable because of their flamboyant excess. We concluded our conversation on a friendly note, yet this man who had consistently sought me out for two weeks online never reached out to me again during my travels. The possible reasons for this are infinite. But questions lingered: did associating myself with the loud, audacious, and demanding spirit of this movie desexualize me? Had I bruised his ego by opposing his interpretation of the film, and did a bruised ego mean instantaneous loss of sexual interest? Surely, chemistry alone might have dictated the outcome; but I could not shake the feeling that the contentious experience of disagreement, even over something as simple as a movie's content, had marked me as "difficult," and hence unsexy—difficult in the way the men of *The Boys* are difficult, and hence dangerous. I wondered if the contemporary meaning of male homosexuality has become a "desire for the same" not only in terms of the presumed gender of one's sexual object choice but also in terms of political values, so that gay male erotic life requires mind-numbing similitude across every scale of embodied and political life to remain secure in its sexual identity. I wondered too how consequential gay men's participation in the future of US democratic life could be, if gay male culture's litmus test for the social and political significance and legibility of any subject is how erotically desirable he is: in other words, what does it mean to extend care, investment, and value to anyone and anything you do not want to fuck?

And yet . . . who is to say the preceding analysis is an accurate critical judgment of contemporary urban gay life, rather than an expression of resentful judgmentalness born from my own painful personal experiences of rejection? Would a queer social justice activist today necessarily agree that impassioned expressions of political rebellion are, in fact, undesirable or unsexy? What about the experience of seemingly wealthy, attractive, married gay men struggling with addiction, depression, or social ostracism? Do the external trappings of normative middle-class life for queer people necessarily grant universal privilege, happiness, and security? Surely, "urban gay male culture" is an exceptionally unstable category, collating queer hipsters, muscle queens, techies, avant-garde artists, gay intellectuals, disability rights activists, retired professionals, same-sex families, and much more. And how do we account for the emerging solidarities between queers of color, the transgender community, intersectional feminists, and Native and Indigenous queers? The feelings of frustration and disappointment that first lead me to conceive my own critique of gay male collectivity are meaningful and insightful . . . up to a point. For, like every feeling state, outlook, or interpretation, they are also limited and partial. The vantage where I stand can be enhanced or corrected only through encounters with countless other perspectives—both from within and without my version of "queer community"—which, taken together, can help me "get the shared world in view." Thus, in the wake of this minor rejection, I kept mulling, I met another man for dinner and conversation, and I rewatched *The Boys in the Band*.

Nearly half a century since its original cinematic release, *The Boys in the Band* continues to provide a compelling alternative to the culture of gay male affirmation. It is, in this sense, a radically "new" narrative in the context of contemporary gay identity politics because it validates those worldviews and feeling states most commonly seen as antithetical to gay upward mobility, social advancement, and validation, such as negativity, bitterness, anger, depression, self-loathing, confusion, ambivalence, and frustration.[37] The film embraces the generative aspects of bitterness, its ability to lay bare formerly suppressed emotions and the unfairness of gay life. It also suggests that other meaningful affective investments might be involved in a loving critique of gay male culture, including calls for accountability, impassioned mutual conflict as much as unconditional support, ethical standards of conduct, and collective dialogue without end. Above all, *The Boys in the Band* demands that we keep speaking to one another, keep turning toward each other, until our revolution is complete.

4

Queer Love on Barbary Lane

The Serial Experience of Coming Out of the Closet with Armistead Maupin's Tales of the City

We should own the mythology of homosexual reproduction, because imagining a world in which *more* homosexuals are welcome is essential to producing a world in which *any* homosexuals are welcome.
—Valerie Rohy, *Lost Causes* (2014)

Some queers were flabbergasted that their secret lives were being laid out in the daily newspaper. Because the assumption was you could live that lie and nobody would think about it. . . . In some ways I was outing the city culturally.
—Armistead Maupin, interview with the author, August 1, 2015

On Monday, May 24, 1976, the *San Francisco Chronicle*—the Bay Area's highest-circulating newspaper—published the first installment of Armistead Maupin's serialized gay fiction *Tales of the City*, a daily soap opera narrating the social and sexual (mis)adventures of a cadre of queer San Francisco neighbors living on Russian Hill.[1] The series opener drew readers in with the titillating headline, "She's 25, Single And Mad for S.F." Any reader who chose to heed this siren call would, in short order, meet Mary Ann Singleton, a straitlaced, independence-seeking Clevelander dead set on making a move to the city by the Bay, where somehow, in just five days of vacation, she has become convinced she belongs. From the outset, *Tales* hooked its audience with a title that reads like a personal ad announcing a very queer sort of desire: a young woman, single, rashly in love—perhaps insanely so (lunacy often bearing the mark of queerness in the homophobic imagination)—with a city, but perhaps also with an unknown person, whose initials, S.F., could indicate a lover of any gender, ethnicity, or sexuality. The narrator tells us, "On the fifth night [in San Francisco] she drank three Irish coffees at the Buena Vista, realized that her Mood Ring was blue, and decided to phone her mother in Cleveland. . . . 'Mom, I called to tell you something . . . I'm not coming home' . . . When it was over, Mary Ann . . . walked through Aquatic Park to the bay . . . drunk with the prospect of an undefined future."[2]

Nearly a year later, following a series of disastrous affairs with men, joining a chosen family among her neighbors at 28 Barbary Lane, surviving a deranged serial killer, and gaining the mentorship of her transsexual landlady Anna Madrigal, Mary Ann would turn to her gay best friend, Michael Tolliver, and say: "'I feel that I'm on the verge of something . . . really wonderful. . . . I'm changing a lot, aren't I?' He nodded smiling, 'It's called coming out.'" To which she replies: "'A girl can come out? I mean, if she's straight and all?' 'Uh huh. Straight and all.'"[3] Of course, Mary Ann had already come out hundreds of serial installments prior, when she called her mother like so many queer people had before and since, in a classic scene of frightened disclosure, unsure of what consequences might unfold from her declaration that she "loved" the wrong object: not heterosexuality, Cleveland, or marriage, but S.F. Readers' first entry into Tales was a coming-out story that instilled in its audience, "straight and all," the affective feeling of an "undefined [queer] future" that might unfold from a sudden reorientation of anyone's desires to a city like San Francisco and its queer cultural values in the radical 1970s.

Within weeks, Tales of the City became a citywide sensation. In the sex lives of the uptight, straight, Midwestern migrant Mary Ann Singleton, the gay romantic Michael Tolliver, the bisexual hippie Mona Ramsey, and the failed civil rights activist Brian Hawkins, readers from every sexual orientation and social status found characters to identify with, learned about San Francisco's many subcultures and sexual scenes, and encountered complex interpersonal relationships between gay and straight city dwellers. For San Franciscans waking up Monday mornings after a weekend of nightlife, sex, and camaraderie in places as varied as bathhouses and roller discos, each Tales installment provided a literary map of their own social and erotic awakening.

In the language of 1970s gay liberation, "coming out of the closet" was a public declaration of an evolving personal awareness about one's sexual orientation that required repeated performances over time. Gay city supervisor Harvey Milk underscored this point in his widely memorialized speech at the 1978 San Francisco Gay Freedom Day Parade:

> Gay brothers and sisters . . . you must come out . . . to your parents, your relatives. I know that it is hard and will hurt them but think about how they will hurt you in the voting booth! Come out to your friends. . . . Once and for all . . . destroy the lies and distortion. . . . If Briggs wins . . . there will be no safe closet for any Gay person. So break out of yours today; tear the damn thing down once and for all.[4]

Milk's impassioned plea was made in the context of the impending California vote over the Briggs Initiative, a ballot measure that would make it legal to remove out gay public-school teachers and other civil servants from their jobs. Milk demanded that queer people of all stripes come out repeatedly as a regular part of combatting homophobic political initiatives nationwide. In so doing, he framed coming out less as a purely private act of self-disclosure promising a fuller sense of self, and more as a collective practice of political freedom enacted in numerous contexts whose multiple performances could help create an anti-homophobic world.

Similarly, in its oscillation between immediate installments and unfolding storylines, *Tales of the City*'s serial narrative provided a creative form for exploring this double movement of "coming out" as declaration and duration—that is, as something one expresses in a single statement ("I'm gay") but then must live out repeatedly in sexual and social acts across time. By the time of Milk's speech, *Tales* had fictionally documented countless coming-out narratives across more than 280 serial entries: from Michael Tolliver's heart-wrenching coming-out letter to his evangelical parents, to Anna Madrigal's story of her transformation from World War II military officer to eccentric San Francisco landlady. From Mona Ramsey's acknowledgement of her bisexuality after years of dating men, to spoiled heiress DeDe Halcyon's confession that she is pregnant with interracial twins, the product of an affair with her Chinese American grocery boy. Such fictional revelations, of crossing sexual, gender, class, and racial boundaries and unapologetically pursuing intimacies denigrated by the dominant culture, taught readers day by day how to "tear the damn thing down once and for all," destroying whatever closet locked them away from the life they wished to lead.

In this chapter, I explore how serial narrative—fictional storytelling presented in installments over time—functioned as a potent form for disseminating heterogeneous expressions of gay identity as well as new kinds of queer social bonds to public audiences in the 1970s. I take as my case study the content and reading experience of the most popular 1970s serial gay fiction, Maupin's *Tales of the City*, which first appeared in daily installments in the *Chronicle* between 1976 and 1977. I argue that the serialized rhythm of the narrative formally modeled gay liberation's conception of coming out about one's sexuality as a process that unfolds through repeated encounters with new erotic possibilities that have the potential to fundamentally alter the composition and meaning of urban subcultures and social worlds.

To provide evidence of this link between serial format and the reorganization of urban communal life, I draw on interviews I conducted with living San Francisco readers of Maupin's original text as well as the author himself. I consider how the text's expanding narrative about 1970s queer cultures and the actual experience of reading it daily alongside other San Franciscans functioned as a material expression of one's coming-out process, allowing individual readers to disclose their sexuality to others through recurrent public reading and ongoing engagement with each character's sexual awakenings. As one interview subject, Michael Thorburn, recalled "[I] remember those early days sitting on the bus reading it. And looking around, seeing who else is reading it . . . and going from, maybe I see one or two other people . . . to more and more people . . . to where it became a point of discussion on the way down. And people didn't talk on the bus. I mean, you could have your crotch in somebody's face and you wouldn't talk. But *Tales* was a reason to . . . engage in this kind of conversation."[5] Thorburn humorously captures how the shared experience of encountering a mass-circulated print cultural form directly altered the way people interact in public space: from the awkward, silent intimacy of an overcrowded bus to enthusiastic verbal interactions about the lives of fictional queer characters. Perhaps most compelling is Thorburn's suggestion that to simply read *Tales* openly on trains, busses, and sidewalks was a way to come out of the closet, not simply as gay or lesbian (though often just that), but as a distinct kind of San Franciscan affectively amenable to the city's queerness, a receptivity that in turn elicited positive attention and investment from strangers.

That affective openness was similarly modeled in the logic of serial narrative. Because *Tales of the City's* ongoing story was indefinite in span and circulated in public, it lent itself to non-teleological storytelling. Its creative investments lay in the open-ended development of countless, surprising interpersonal and erotic relationships between former strangers, rather than the final consummation of any of those bonds in the idealized arrangements of (gay or straight) marriage, family, home ownership, or child rearing. Just as the series opened with Mary Ann *not* telling her mother she had found a good man to settle down with, confounding the traditional logic of the marriage plot,[6] so too the provisional conclusions that punctuate each of *Tales'* first two years of publication both end with Mary Ann and Michael together contemplating an "undefined future" in the wake of painful breakups, dramatic emotional growth, and a recommitment to their chosen queer kinship on Barbary Lane.

Yet while literary theorists have traditionally understood serial narrative as formless—a storytelling mode with an indeterminate beginning, middle, and end—the serial movement between daily installments and long-term storylines could easily be given a concrete shape, or pattern, in the imagination: as serial blocks of texts visually encountered in the paper; as a sequence of interrelated scenes or interactions between characters across time; or as a notational rhythm with dots or periods representing discreet entries and curved arcs indicating extended plotlines. One outcome of *Tales'* formal elaboration in people's minds was that readers from all walks of life could begin to picture the development of their own sexual, gender, racial, and political identities as a *serial process*, unfolding in both immediate moments of personal revelation (or single installments) and extended practices of community building (or networks of stories), much like Mary Ann and Michael's shared social evolution. Across the arc of this chapter, I explore how serial narrative functions as a queer form in relation to three aspects of *Tales*: the unpredictable unfolding of its plots, the evolving rhetorical voice of its narrator, and the creation and maturation of its distinctly queer character types. As a formal logic, or rhythm, based on the indefinite unfolding or expansion of narrative, seriality conferred an open-ended potential for each of these variables of the text to become distinctly queerer as the story developed over time.

Nearly a half-century since its debut, *Tales of the City* remains among the most popular serial narratives of the twentieth and twenty-first centuries. Even at the time of its original publication, its influence quickly exceeded the scope of the San Francisco Bay Area. First, in the thousands of newspaper clippings local readers collected and mailed to their friends and family around the country. Next, achieving international recognition as a series of bestselling novels published between 1978 and 2014 (of the nine novels, the first five collect installments that initially appeared in the *Chronicle* and later the *San Francisco Examiner*). And finally circulating in numerous media forms including widely acclaimed PBS (1993) and Showtime (1998, 2001) miniseries, a stage musical, a BBC radio series, and a revival as a Netflix series (2019).

Beyond its broad influence and persistence, the original serial narrative remains an astonishingly rich archive of 1970s San Francisco cultural history, documenting the sociological effects of the convergence of the hippie counterculture, the New Left and student movements, and women's and gay liberation in the Bay Area. This includes the series' unprecedented frankness about recreational drug use (especially marijuana, psychedelics, and amphetamines), its frequent discussion of public sex spaces, its near-anthropological descriptions of gay and straight sexual subcultures, fashion, and social habits, and its attention to class stratification in contemporary San Francisco. One former reader, Mark Giberson, explained, "[*Tales*] was just so cutting edge. . . . The liberation that was going on, you were talking about things that people had never talked about before. . . . There was that whole thing of drugs and hippies and San Francisco. I think that to me *Tales* . . . was an acceptance of all that. . . . A big reason why everyone talked about it was because it . . . was a real reflection of the changes that were happening in society."[7]

Despite its cultural longevity and historical value, *Tales of the City* remains one of the most understudied works of US-American popular culture broadly, and LGBTQ literature specifically. The paucity of scholarly attention paid to *Tales* might be attributed to the story's uneasy fit with contemporary progressive left cultural politics, namely the characters' seeming apoliticalness and the narrative's glaring whiteness.

On one hand, the characters generally embrace progressive ideas about gender and sexual freedom (Brian Hawkins is even a former ACLU lawyer), develop forms of alternative kinship that model feminist and queer social values, and voice their disagreement with conservative political movements (as when Michael decries Anita Bryant's homophobic "Save Our Children" campaign to repeal SF county civil rights protections for LGBTQ people). On the other, none of the characters could be remotely described as "street queens," the colloquial term used by San Francisco gay liberationists to describe radical anti-establishment activists;[8] nor do they seem aware of monumental political events such as Harvey Milk's successful 1977 campaign for the board of supervisors. Moreover, while *Tales* presents readers with an ever-expanding cast of characters richly diverse in sexual orientation, gender expression, class background, and geographical origin, its early years fail to offer any characters of color in central roles. These realities make it easy to dismiss *Tales* as a nostalgic text with little enduring political value, at best amusing beach reading, at worst a relic of gay white liberalism's racist claim to universality.

Against this assumption, I argue that *Tales of the City* offers one of the most generative and successful models of queer political transformation in contemporary US culture, not only as a project of changing hearts, minds, and votes, but of creating the broadly shared affective conditions for the flourishing of queer life. *Tales* performs its politics through serial form and a distinct storytelling voice, particularly Maupin's frequent use of the free indirect style, a mode of narration that gives readers intimate entry into the private thoughts and feelings of various characters. Rather than frame gay and feminist politics as a set of explicit ideologies or programs for action, Maupin presents queerness as a type of narrative multiplication unfolding across serial installments, the steady expansion of a fictional world that attends to those lives, loves, and desires existing at a slant from heterosexual normativity. Emerging onto the cultural scene in 1976, six years after the explosive arrival of the women's and gay liberation movements in New York City and San Francisco, *Tales* is the story of what happens to ordinary people who live in the wake of those movements' dissemination into the wider culture. Simultaneously, it transmits to readers what it affectively feels like to inhabit queerer and more feminist modes of life when they become available to you at the level of the everyday. The great revelation of the story is that all lives, not just those of LGBTQ-identified people, are fundamentally queer, which in turn requires new kinds of kinship forms outside the nuclear family to ensure collective thriving.

My aim is to recuperate the queer promise of *Tales of the City*—its formal elaboration of what Valerie Rohy calls "homosexual reproduction," the bringing into being of more self-proclaimed gender and sexual dissidents—without absolving the story of its frustrating inability to incorporate cross-racial identification and coalition into its project. Yet by placing more weight on *Tales'* formal innovations than its representational failures, I underscore that the limits of Maupin's own racial imaginary in the early years of his writing are not ultimately synonymous with the limit of *Tales'* broader cultural capacity to account for queer-of-color life. That capacity inheres in both the narrative's seriality, which offers a model of ceaseless growth and inclusion through indefinite storytelling, and in Maupin's creative commitment to the use of free indirect style or discourse, which opens up the possibility of thinking and feeling alongside people who are radically different than oneself. That the later novels and recent Netflix series significantly integrate queer-of-color and trans* experience testifies to *Tales'* creative expansiveness and political adaptability, at once indicating Maupin's personal evolution as a white gay man who accidentally became San Francisco's queer bard across a half-century of the city's history, as well as the narrative's ability to respond to, and encompass, the realities of its diverse audience across time.

In this chapter, I build on Robyn Warhol's trenchant claim that *Tales of the City*'s "serial format . . . enabled the series to accomplish significant antihomophobic cultural work," to argue that serial storytelling in the context of the unfolding gay and women's liberation movements of the 1970s functioned as both a theory of, and affective vehicle for, queer and feminist social transformation.[9] In a rare, foundational study of *Tales*, "Making 'Gay' and 'Lesbian' Household Terms: How Serial Form Works in Armistead Maupin's *Tales of the City*," Warhol shows how *Tales* reinvented the sexually conservative model of the nineteenth-century, domestic Victorian serial to make space for queer ways of life. She explains, "*Tales of the City* is . . . the first serialized domestic novel addressed to a mainstream audience that explicitly attempts to reconfigure public and private assumptions about . . . gay sexuality. . . . It serves as an example of what Lauren Berlant and Michael Warner call . . . 'the queer project' whose goal is . . . 'to support forms of affective, erotic, living that are . . . accessible, available and sustained through collective activity.'"[10]

To unpack *Tales*' "queer project," I study the original installments as they first appeared in the *Chronicle*'s "Style" section, which helps us better understand how the daily presence of complex, playful, and intimate representations of queer people in the newspaper made meaning in the larger context of a decidedly non-queer mass market publication with nearly half a million subscribers.[11] By locating the serial within its broader print ecology, we can see how *Tales* came to be structurally in dialogue with the *Chronicle*'s increasing press coverage of local and national queer life during a period of heightened social and political visibility for LGBTQ people. Most importantly, I conduct close readings of the fictional text itself, to illuminate how Maupin's writerly style contributed to the serial's particular affective force, namely its transmission of an emotional receptivity to queerness. To aid in this endeavor, I add to my analysis the testimony of readers who followed *Tales* in its original print run as Bay Area residents.

Over the course of two summers living in San Francisco between 2016 and 2017, I interviewed twenty-nine original readers of *Tales of the City* who encountered the serial upon its initial publication from varied subject positions and in myriad social contexts: as a feminist UC Berkeley undergraduate poring over the daily newspaper at the student union; as a closeted Stanford graduate student in a weekly reading group; as a pregnant housewife in Oakland enjoying a morning diversion before chores; and as photographers, writers, dancers, and filmmakers living in collective housing where the *Chronicle* circulated around the breakfast table.[12] My intention was to collate enough testimonies to get a sense of the shared language followers of *Tales* used to describe their material reading habits, their emotional attachments to different characters, and the long-term impression the serial left on their lives.[13]

My findings showed that readers often had similar felt experiences of the text, even in divergent reading contexts, while also seeing *Tales* as a repository of queer particularity. According to many, it was Maupin's canny ability to simultaneously describe shared experiences of San Francisco's many alternative lifestyles and progressive ideals, while grounding them in the idiosyncratic lives of queer characters, that attracted its audience. Readers consistently found themselves *partially* identifying with various characters' personalities or behaviors (Mary Ann's resilience or Michael's sexual freedom), while voicing the many ways they did *not* see themselves reflected in the central cast. This complex structure of identification, counteridentification, or nonrelation to characters belies Maupin's own stated claim of San Francisco's queer transcendence—the idea that the city's queerness dissolves differences of race, class, gender, or ability—but also challenges critics' charge that *Tales* elevated a distinctly white gay version of San Francisco to a universal experience.[14] Both white and Black readers of the serial told me they never assumed the story accurately captured what queer life was like for most LGBTQ people in the city regardless of race or class identity, but rather offered a compelling slice of the queer world that resonated across differences without standing in for all of them.

Readers' accounts of their encounter with *Tales of the City* allow us to see how gayness, commonly understood as attaching to the erotic and social lives of LGBTQ people, circulated far beyond either activist circles or the coming-out narratives of individual gays and lesbians. Rather, by the mid-1970s gayness could be apprehended as an exuberant affective orientation toward the world influencing the hearts and minds of putatively straight subjects who felt affinity with and desired to be transformed by gender- and sexual-nonconforming ways of life. Instead of treating readers' testimonies as unadulterated truth or subjecting them to ideological critique, I conceive of their claims as alternative perspectives that stand alongside and add dimension to my own interpretations. I interweave direct statements from my interview subjects and paraphrase recurrent claims made by them to give a sense of the shared lifeworld of readers as it collided with the fictional lifeworld of Maupin's creative universe.

I begin by exploring how 1970s gay liberation framed coming out of the closet as an unpredictable and potentially revolutionary strategy for disseminating queerness throughout the social body by acts of public declaration about one's sexuality and gender. *Tales of the City* harnessed the affective power of such disclosure by making personal revelations about gender and sexual nonconformity the driving force of its plots; in so doing, Maupin repeatedly circulated knowledge about the queer cultural practices of San Francisco's citizens, while training readers to receive any expression of coming out, regardless of its form or content, with nonjudgment and love. Next, I focus on three central characters in the narrative—Mary Ann Singleton, Michael Tolliver, and Anna Madrigal—each of whom came to represent different versions of coming out. I show how the personal evolutions of each character—as a straight woman influenced by San Francisco's queer culture, a gay man coming into political consciousness, and a trans-woman growing her chosen family—resist attempts to identify a biological or cultural explanation for gayness, instead defining it as an affective and erotic force for good that spreads across social relations through willful acts of trust and intimacy. Finally, I query the limits of this formal elaboration of queer life in accounting for LGBTQ people of color by analyzing the widely cited moment when Mona's African American, lesbian lover D'orothea Wilson "comes out" as white after years of passing for Black. This storyline registers a queer desire for cross-racial identification that is undermined by Maupin's concern that race, unlike gender and sexuality, may not be as culturally malleable a category, and hence that a white gay man cannot fairly represent a Black woman in literary form. Ultimately, I argue that cross-racial, gender, and sexual identifications *are* possible within the unpredictable affinities coming out invites, and that *Tales'* own spirit of queer reproduction provides a transferable model for such bonds beyond the representational pitfalls of Maupin's original creative universe.

"No seasoned homosexual ever served as my mentor. But . . . I wish someone had": On Queer Reproduction

Three weeks into *Tales of the City*'s first year of publication, Mona Ramsey—long-term tenant at 28 Barbary Lane, the "ramshackle, two-story structure made of brown shingles" housing our cast of characters on Russian Hill—checks in with her beloved friend and landlady, Anna Madrigal, about the new renter, Mary Ann Singleton. Mona asks, "Did you get a chance to talk to her privately?" Madrigal replies: "Just for a few minutes. In my bedroom. She saw the picture on my dresser. . . . She thought it was Mr. Madrigal. My husband, that is." "Bizarre!" Mona exclaims. "Well, it's a logical conclusion, Mona," Madrigal retorts. "The poor thing's from Cleveland for heaven's sake. She's not prepared for those kinds of possibilities."[15] To any seasoned reader of *Tales*, "those kinds of possibilities" include the fabulous discovery (revealed months

208 | QUEER LOVE ON BARBARY LANE

later in the first series' then-shocking conclusion) that Madrigal is a transsexual, served as a military officer in World War II, and had a "sex-change operation . . . in Denmark" before moving to San Francisco twelve years prior to start a new life.[16] Yet at its moment of publication, Mona and Madrigal's exchange demands the reader to consider: "Am I as *bizarrely* provincial as Mary Ann and, if so, what does that say about me?"

Tales of the City's primary cultural work in the mid-1970s was to transform its readers into the kinds of people prepared for, even desiring of, the queer possibilities that Madrigal's secret embodies. It was not merely that *Tales* introduced its audience to a diversity of queer characters—gay men, transsexual women, and queer, questioning, and closeted folks of many genders, classes, and generations—but that its serial narrative, predicated on the ceaseless and pleasurable production of mystery and revelation in future installments, instilled its readers with the proper emotional orientation toward positively receiving the queerness of others. As one former reader, Mary Richardson, exuberantly declared to me, "I wanted to be Maryanne [*sic*]. . . . A single, swinging gal in the big city where the world was my oyster. Where people being DIFFER-ENT was the norm."[17] Growing up two hours outside of San Francisco in rural Ukiah, California, Richardson identified with Mary Ann's inexperience as a sheltered Midwestern girl, while longing for an expansion of her worldly knowledge of human differences, a longing *Tales* fulfilled. In this sense, *Tales* gave both formal shape and affective force to the gay liberationist value of coming out of the closet.

In the early 1970s, coming out emerged as one of the most radical, and effective, strategies for politicizing gay identity. Today, coming out is commonly imagined as a scene of intimate disclosure, often between a parent and child, in which a vulnerable "closeted" person verbally professes their gayness to a loved one in hopes of expressing a more authentic sense of self. Alternatively, in the 1970s gay liberation originally conceived of coming out as a process of both individual *and* collective transformation that might have revolutionary public consequences. As one gay liberation activist stated on the *Dick Cavett Show* in 1971: "Gay people, when they first realize that they're gay, have a process of coming out, that is, coming out sexually. We've extended that to the political field. We feel that we have to come out politically, as a community which is aware that it is oppressed and which is a political power bloc feared by the government."[18] In this view, coming out is understood first as the process of coming into one's own sexual freedom through a series of intimate personal acts—from the thrilling pursuit of gay sex to the formation of queer friendship circles—which are then declared or enacted in countless public settings (including a national late night talk show); this process forged bonds between those who claim a shared identity through repeated public expressions of their gayness, thereby making them a visible and numerically significant political force.

Underscoring this link between self-actualization and revolutionary potential, activist and writer Allen Young stated in 1972, "As I develop a gay identity . . . I am swept up in a process of change which allows me to define myself in terms other than some masculine ideal. I have a growing awareness of myself and my relationships to other people which is exhilarating. . . . I dance more, I laugh more, I am learning how to listen to others. . . . I am finding out how to love my brothers and sisters, how this love is the vital revolutionary force we all need."[19] In Young's account, the interpersonal effects of embracing one's sexuality are not ancillary to grounded activism but provide a blueprint for the kind of world one wants to create through political engagement. To "come out" by dancing, conversing, and having sex with other gay people can inaugurate "exhilarating" new feelings toward queer existence as a positive social good that improves one's everyday associations with a growing network of potential friends, intimates, or chosen family while also galvanizing political commitment to an anti-homophobic world. In both personal and civic conceptions of coming out, the verbal declaration of one's sexuality to someone else is merely the most local expression of a much larger collective transformation. Moreover, for lesbian feminists, coming out also had the potential to dismantle patriarchy, because it involved the reorientation of women's erotic, social, and political investments toward other women, undercutting the traditional roles of wife and mother within the heterosexual family. Far from reducing the inventive aspects of forging a gay "way of life" to the simple exposure of a presumed "inner truth," coming out became a radical theory of queer reproduction. It was a way to materially spread difference from heterosexuality through the indefinitely repeated and collectively shared publicization of living and desiring at a slant from heterosexual life trajectories, thereby offering one expression of French philosopher Michel Foucault's appeal "to use one's sexuality . . . to arrive at a multiplicity of relationships."[20]

LGBTQ historian John D'Emilio sums up this "reproductive" potential of coming out for gay liberation when he states, "Coming out . . . became the key strategy for building a mass movement. When gay women and men came out . . . we relinquished our invisibility . . . and became personally invested in the success of the movement in a way that mere adherence to a political line could never accomplish. Visible lesbians and gay men . . . served as magnets that drew others to us."[21] The logic of coming out presumed that the declaration of one's gayness would attract others, consequently becoming one way to literally propagate *more gay people*, and hence reproduce a coherent gay and lesbian culture. Yet this process necessarily revealed queerness, the vast range of expressions of gender and sexual nonconformity, to be infinitely heterogeneous, so that any sense of a unified gay identity or community was continually, and productively, made contingent by the countless styles, forms, and expressions of coming into queer ways of life.

Rohy theorizes the concept of "homosexual reproduction" as "encompassing both the social reproduction of really existing, material gay and lesbian cultures and identities and, antithetically . . . the [queer] proliferation of difference. . . . Gay and lesbian identities and cultures reproduce or 'cause' themselves, but queerness is reproduced or 'caused' by its abjection from heteronormative culture. . . . Homosexuality multiplies . . . but queerness divides."[22] The political effectiveness of coming out lay both in its ability to hail a growing public of self-identified gay people, and its capacity to spontaneously call forth, and build affinity between, all those who diverge "from heteronormative culture." Moreover, because coming out took myriad shapes and forms—as a verbal declaration or demand, a series of social or political acts, or simple sexual exploration—it could produce a near-infinite array of effects. This included heightening intimacy and trust between people, motivating others to come out, or eliciting rejection or violence, which in turn might encourage queer solidarity in the face of such attacks. The unpredictably of coming out, its capacity to provoke so many possible outcomes, gave it a radically anarchic edge that had the potential to undo the social order as it stood, including the transformation of putatively "straight" people into incipient queers.

In the mid-1970s, *Tales of the City* modeled what the politics of gay liberation might look like when coming out of the closet was translated from a revolutionary political act to an everyday interpersonal form for forging relations of deep intimacy among members of a "logical" (or chosen) kinship rather than the presumptive filial bonds of a hetero-sexual family. As Mona Ramsey admits to her former lover D'orothea, "I'm not sure I *need* a lover. Sometimes I think I'd settle for five good friends."[23] Good friends, the narrative tells us, are the bedrock of queer life, a social relation built not on putatively shared blood ties, gender, racial, or sexual identities, or class background, but on trust developed from mutual vulnerability. I call this *Tales'* "sexual politics," by which I mean the text's developing vision of an ethical relationship between one's interpersonal life and one's public, civic life. That vision was rooted in both gay liberation's politicization of sexuality in the 1970s and Maupin's own coming-out process.

Arriving to San Francisco in 1972 as a Southern-raised, Republican journalist, Maupin found that the city's gay sex scene disorganized his political commitments:

> So, San Francisco, with this population of straight people that was more comfortable with my sexuality than I was really changed everything, in-cluding my politics. . . . When I dragged guys home from Polk Street . . . my picture of me shaking hands with Nixon in the Oval Office was not a bonus. . . . They looked at me like I was Jeffrey Dahmer. . . . And then I had to really start examining my politics and think, "All right, if you've been oppressed by this mindset, what about . . . other people? What about the people of color? What about women? What about . . ." San Francisco was my teacher in that regard.[24]

Maupin describes how his quotidian, serial sexual encounters came to have broader political significance in the cultural context of a city that encouraged such liaisons, seeing them as the basis for communal joy as well as potential opportunities for identification and coalition building across racial, gender, class and sexual differences. For Maupin, coming out was a mutually constitutive experience of becoming an out gay man *and* a politically progressive, queer San Franciscan. *Tales'* poli-tics, then, lay less in any stated commitment to activist programs, and more in its spirit of queer kinship articulated through its serial narrative form, which appeared (like Maupin's sexual adventures) as a series of perpetual conversations between characters, and between the narrator and readers, regarding the existence and positive value of sexual diversity. This sexual politics reframed the affective relationship of readers toward queerness on two fronts: it made the encounter with queer genders and sexualities, as well as alternative sex cultures, not only mysterious and gripping, but pleasurable and desirable. And it hailed its reading audience as a distinctly queer public, thereby forcing readers to become, even briefly, unfixed from their personal sexual or gender identities. *Tales'* sexual politics took shape in three conceptual moves.

First, as Michael's statement to Mary Ann that, indeed, straight girls can also "come out of the closet" underscores, *Tales of the City* understood coming out as a broadly accessible practice available to people far outside the boundaries of "gay" and "lesbian" identity. The purpose was to show that people of all sexual orientations and gender expressions often fail to live up to heteronormative ideals, thereby inadvertently "coming out" as queer. At various points in the narrative, Mona Ramsey, a hippie, advertising copywriter and long-time friend of Michael Tolliver, "comes out" as a "fag hag" and a self-proclaimed failed lesbian, and later discovers she is the daughter of a trans-woman. The discovery of Anna Madrigal's transsexuality is but one of countless revelations that enrich her narrative of gender transformation: she confesses to her lover Edgar Halcyon that she grew up in whorehouse in Winnemucca, Nevada, and later explains to her tenant Mona that she is, in fact, her father. And DeDe Halcyon Day, the unhappily married daughter of the aristocratic Halcyon family, comes out as a "liberated" woman, first as the mother of interracial children born out of wedlock, and later as the intimate friend of D'orothea, with whom DeDe will later raise her children. Coming out also takes many rhetorical forms. Characters come out through personal dialogue, letters, the narrator's omniscient narrative voice, and, most importantly, through extraordinary plot twists, in which the punchline of a particular installment or narrative arc is the unexpected admission of one sort of queerness or another.

In this way, *Tales of the City* articulated the lived practice of coming out to the central formal conceit of installment fiction, the *cliff-hanger*. Serial narrative requires the continual production of mystery, followed

Plate 1. Thelma and Louise "keep going." *Thelma & Louise*, dir. Ridley Scott (Metro-Goldwyn-Mayer, 1991).

Plate 2. Top to bottom: The Stone Head descends toward its worshipers in the opening shots of *Zardoz*; Zardoz bellows to the Exterminators: "The gun is good. The penis is evil"; Zed raises his gun and shoots directly between our eyes. *Zardoz*, dir. John Boorman (20th Century Fox, 1974).

Plate 3. Top to bottom: May trains her powerful female gaze at Zed; Zed is incapacitated by May's telepathic assault; May takes in the sight of Zed, her look aligned with the natural world. Zardoz, dir. John Boorman (20th Century Fox, 1974).

Plate 4. DJs Isabel and Honey speak directly to their radio audiences. *Born in Flames*, dir. Lizzie Borden (First Run Features, 1983).

Plate 5. Honey's gaze is repeatedly drawn to the media statements of different feminists in her extended circle of fellow travelers. *Born in Flames*, dir. Lizzie Borden (First Run Features, 1983).

Plate 6. "If I could attach our blood vessels in order to anchor you to this present time I would." David Wojnarowicz, James Romberger, and Marguerite Van Cook, *7 Miles a Second* (Seattle: Fantagraphics Books 2013 [1996]). Courtesy Estate of David Wojnarowicz; and James Romberger and Marguerite Van Cook.

Plate 7. Left: Joe Brainard, "If Nancy Was a Boy," 1972. Courtesy Tibor de Nagy Gallery, New York; Ron Padgett; and the Colby College of Museum of Art; Right: Joe Brainard, "If Nancy Was a Sailor's Basket," 1972. Courtesy Tibor de Nagy Gallery, New York; Ron Padgett; and the Colby College of Museum of Art.

Plate 8. Joe Brainard, "If Nancy Knew What Wearing Green and Yellow on a Thursday Meant," 1972. Courtesy Tibor de Nagy Gallery, New York; Ron Padgett; and the Colby College of Museum of Art.

Plate 9. Joe Brainard, "If Nancy Was an Underground Comic Character" (1972). Courtesy Pavel Zoubok Gallery.

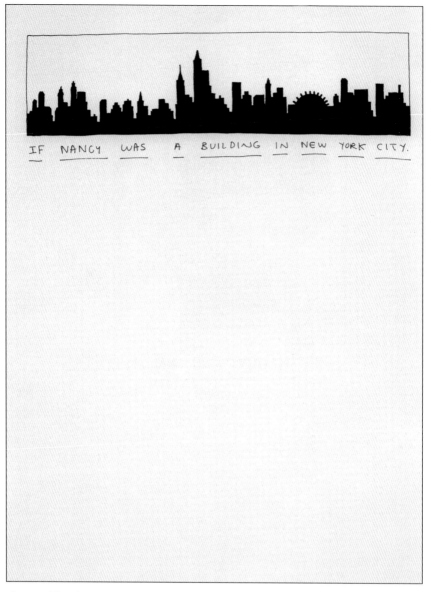

Plate 10. (above) Joe Brainard, "If Nancy Was a Building in New York City" (1972). Courtesy Tibor de Nagy Gallery, New York; Ron Padgett; and the Colby College of Museum of Art.

Plate 11. (facing page) "We are born into a preinvented existence within a tribal nation of zombies." David Wojnarowicz, James Romberger, and Marguerite Van Cook, *7 Miles a Second* (Seattle: Fantagraphics Books 2013 [1996]). Courtesy Estate of David Wojnarowicz; and James Romberger and Marguerite Van Cook.

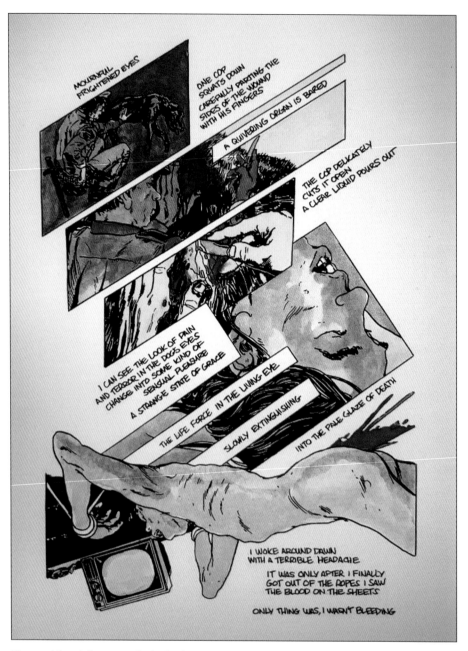

Plate 12. (above) "I can see the look of pain and terror in the dog's eyes change into some kind of sensual pleasure . . ." David Wojnarowicz, James Romberger, and Marguerite Van Cook, *7 Miles a Second* (Seattle: Fantagraphics Books 2013 [1996]). Courtesy Estate of David Wojnarowicz; and James Romberger and Marguerite Van Cook.

Plate 13. (facing page) "And I'm carrying this rage like a blood-filled egg." David Wojnarowicz, James Romberger, and Marguerite Van Cook, *7 Miles a Second* (Seattle: Fantagraphics Books 2013 [1996]). Courtesy Estate of David Wojnarowicz; and James Romberger and Marguerite Van Cook.

AND I'M CARRYING THIS RAGE LIKE A BLOOD-FILLED EGG AND THERE'S A THIN LINE BETWEEN THE INSIDE AND THE OUTSIDE A THIN LINE BETWEEN THOUGHT AND ACTION AND THAT LINE IS SIMPLY MADE UP OF BLOOD AND MUSCLE AND BONE AND AS EACH T-CELL DISAPPEARS FROM MY BODY IT'S REPLACED BY TEN POUNDS OF PRESSURE TEN POUNDS OF RAGE AND I FOCUS THAT RAGE INTO NONVIOLENT RESISTANCE BUT THAT FOCUS IS STARTING TO SLIP MY HANDS ARE BEGINNING TO MOVE INDEPENDENTLY AND THE EGG IS STARTING TO CRACK AND AMERICA SEEMS TO ACCEPT MURDER AS SELF-DEFENSE AGAINST THOSE WHO WOULD MURDER YOU AND IT'S BEEN MURDER ON A DAILY BASIS FOR TEN COUNT THEM TEN LONG YEARS AND WE'RE EXPECTED TO PAY TAXES TO SUPPORT THIS PUBLIC AND SOCIAL MURDER AND WE'RE EXPECTED TO QUIETLY AND POLITELY MAKE HOUSE IN THIS WIND-STORM OF MURDER BUT I SAY THERE'S CERTAIN POLITICIANS THAT BETTER GET MORE COMPLEX SECURITY ALARMS AND THERE'S RELIGIOUS LEADERS AND HEALTH CARE OFFICIALS THAT HAD BETTER GET BIGGER FUCKING DOGS AND HIGHER FUCKING FENCES AND QUEER BASHERS BETTER START DOING THEIR WORK FROM INSIDE HOWITZER TANKS BECAUSE THE THIN LINE BETWEEN THE INSIDE AND THE OUTSIDE IS BEGINNING TO ERODE AND AT THE MOMENT I'M A THREE HUNDRED SEVENTY FOOT TALL-ELEVEN HUNDRED THOUSAND POUND MAN INSIDE THIS SIX FOOT FRAME AND ALL I CAN FEEL IS THE PRESSURE ALL I CAN FEEL IS THE PRESSURE AND THE NEED FOR RELEASE

I'M SEEING MY HANDS AND FEET GROW THOUSANDS OF MILES LONG AND MILLIONS OF YEARS OLD AND I'M EXPERIENCING THE EXERTION IT TAKES TO MOVE THESE PROGRAMMED LIMBS

I AM CONSUMED BY THE EMPTINESS LYING BENEATH EACH AND EVERY ACTION I WITNESS OF OTHERS AND MYSELF, EACH LITTLE GESTURE IN THE MOVEMENT OF THE PLANET IN ITS CANYONS AND ARROYOS, IN ITS SUBWAYS AND CITIES, IN THE MOTIONS OF WIND AND LIGHT, EACH LITTLE ACTION CONTINUING THE SLOW DEATH OF OURSELVES, THE SLOW MOTION APPROACH OF THE UNVEILING OF OUR ORDER AND DISORDER IN ITS ULTIMATE CLIMAX, BEGINNING WITH A SPARK SO SUBTLE AND BEAUTIFUL THAT TO TRUST IT IS TO TRUST OUR OWN STUPIDITY

IT SPARKS IN THE INVERSION OF WIND THEN FLOWERS OUT MOMENTARILY IN BLACK PETALS OF SMOKE AND LIGHT. VIBRATING IN THE MIST THAT EXUDES FROM ITS CENTER A HUGE FAT CLOCKWORK OF CIVILIZATION. THE WHOLE ONWARD CRUSH OF THE WORLD AS WE KNOW IT ALL THE WALKING SWASTIKAS YAPYAPPING CARTOON VIDEO DEATH LANGUAGE A MALFUNCTIONING CANNONBALL FILLED WITH BONE AND GRISTLE AND KNIVES AND BULLETS AND GEARS AND PISTONS AND LIGHTNING, SPEWING LANGUAGE AND MOTIONS AND SHIT AND ENTRAILS IN ITS WAKE. IT'S ALL SWIRLING IN EVERY DIRECTION SIMULTANEOUSLY.

SO IT'S NEITHER GOING FORWARD NOR BACKWARD NOT FROM SIDE TO SIDE EMBRACING STASIS BEYOND THE STILLNESS ONE WITNESSES IN A DECAYING CORPSE THAT LASTS MILLIONS OF YEARS IN COMPARISON TO THE SENSE OF TIME, THIS THING OPERATES WITHIN

Plate 14. (facing page) "I'm seeing my hands and feet grow thousands of miles long and millions of years old." David Wojnarowicz, James Romberger, and Marguerite Van Cook, *7 Miles a Second* (Seattle: Fantagraphics Books 2013 [1996]). Courtesy Estate of David Wojnarowicz; and James Romberger and Marguerite Van Cook.

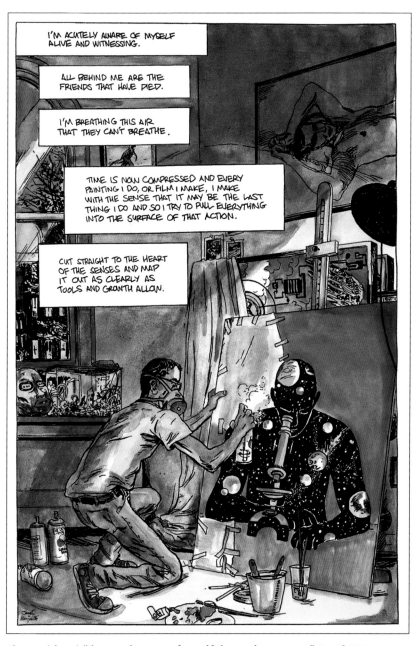

Plate 15. (above) "I'm acutely aware of myself alive and witnessing." David Wojnarowicz, James Romberger, and Marguerite Van Cook, *7 Miles a Second* (Seattle: Fantagraphics Books 2013 [1996]). Courtesy Estate of David Wojnarowicz; and James Romberger and Marguerite Van Cook.

Plate 16. Top to bottom: Juan carries Chiron aloft in the waters of the Atlantic Ocean; Kevin cradles Chiron's head against his shoulder in *Moonlight*'s final scene. *Moonlight*, dir. Barry Jenkins (A24, 2016).

by spectacular revelation, to maintain its readers' attention. In *Tales*, the characters' various disclosures become both an occasion for the unfolding movement of plots as well as a satisfying affective experience of being attuned toward various forms of surprise. This is captured in the bombastic titles of many individual installments, including such gems as: "The Landlady Confesses," "Edgar Shares: The Awful Secret," "Mary Ann Is Forced to Spill the Beans," "Beauchamp Confesses to DeDe," and "Tinkerbell Stands Revealed." Maupin's hyperbolic titles draw from the sensational tone of tabloid headlines and pulp fiction to render interpersonal disclosure and its public consequences both the driving force of the narrative and the source of its emotional pleasures. In fact, among the many descriptors that interviewees provided of their reading experiences, the two most commonly named were *joy* and *surprise*. Readers explained that despite *Tales'* many disturbing plot twists (including one about a deranged, transphobic serial killer), the narrative fundamentally elicited feelings of exuberant hope about queer social relations and, more broadly, the radical 1970s as a period that would inaugurate a political and cultural reinvention of US society. Speaking about the serial quality of the narrative, former dancer Michael Bluegrass stated: "having it spread out like that made it more joyful."[25] Bluegrass recounts how his ebullience sprang from the experience of waking up to the daily possibilities of 1970s San Francisco life as a young gay dancer cohabiting with other artists, a feeling of potentiality accentuated by the arrival of the paper each morning with a new story. Simultaneously, readers collectively commented that the affective engine of the plot was the thrill of surprise, both the perpetual spinning outward of shocking plot twists but also unexpected discoveries about various characters' lives. Ironically, most of the great "secrets" unveiled in each serial entry are intimate, quotidian realities about the characters' health or mortality (Edgar's impending death), sexual and gender identities (Madrigal's transsexuality), or harmless foibles (Mary Ann's affair with a married man). What we grow to thrill at is not simply astonishing narrative turns, but the endless wonder of other people's interior complexity.

As these discoveries accumulate across the series, the text distinguishes between playful, benign admissions and those that require the building of trust over time. When Madrigal first invites Mary Ann to her apartment for dinner three weeks into the series, she carefully considers whether or not to share the truth of her identity (and by extension with us, the audience). Looking at a photo of a young man in military uniform perched on Madrigal's dresser, Mary Ann inquires: "'Is that Mr. Madrigal?' The question came out sounding harsh. Mary Ann's face turned crimson. Mrs. Madrigal looked at the secretary for a moment, apparently weighing a decision of some sort. Then she sat down on the edge of the bed and began to laugh. . . . 'There was no Mr. Madrigal. Or Mrs. Madrigal, for that matter.' 'I'm afraid I don't understand.' 'I made it up. Isn't it a lovely name?'"[26] In this moment, the narrative voice gives us insight into both interlocutors' positions—we are at once privy to Mary Ann's indiscretion in approaching other people's private lives (she blushes at her faux pas), but also aware of Madrigal's calculation about Mary Ann's capacity to handle some unknown truth, which we will later find out is Madrigal's transsexuality. Despite her larger-than-life presence, Madrigal here appears both powerful and vulnerable: on one hand, we are reminded that someone in her position must think critically about the consequences of disclosing her queerness to the wrong person at the wrong time. On the other, Madrigal's confident claim to have "made up" her own name will gain greater meaning after we learn about her trans identity, suggesting that coming out for Madrigal is a means of self-invention. In this instance, gender itself, and the agentic act of transgender self-nomination, becomes analogous to serial narrative, a story one "makes up" and elaborates over time. The fact that Maupin decides not to give us access to this information at this point in the story reminds us that, like Mary Ann, we too must evolve into someone capable of receiving Madrigal's personal history with openness and understanding.[27] The narrative transforms the discovery of potential queerness into the very mysteries of its plotlines, so that we both desire to know, but also desire to be the kind of person who *deserves to know*.

Because *Tales* was read communally, both broadly among Bay Area residents but also between family members, roommates, and co-workers, the story circulated the intimate experience of surprise across its audience, transforming the practice of reading publicly into a collective "coming out." Over and over again former readers stressed the community aspect of reading *Tales* daily: living in a communal house of gay artists, Bluegrass describes, "at first we couldn't believe that something that gay was actually going to be published in *The Chronicle*. . . .

It was fun to get up in the morning. Somebody would go get the paper and they'd bring it back and everybody would pass it around and read it." And commenting on the political nature of *Tales*' publicness, Randy Alfred astutely observes, "I mean the thing that makes it different . . . was this communal event, it was a shared thing. And telling people that straight people can talk in public about getting laid . . . well then gay people can [too]. So it's political in . . . the way the word 'political' is used in feminist discourse."[28] Alfred links the classic feminist adage that "the personal is political" to the public nature of *Tales*' cultural address, namely the ways it "treat[ed] gay sexuality and straight sexuality with this equal[ly] sardonic . . . yet accepting" tone, which made both straight and gay sex life topics of shared conversation.

Perhaps most revealing is Tonia Schulberg's recounting of the ways that *Tales of the City* "was a mechanism for conversations . . . that allowed me to express my values and to talk to my parents about it."[29] An Oakland schoolteacher and civil rights activist, she explains the effects of reading and discussing the serial daily with her parents, who lived farther south in San Lorenzo, California:

> [My] father was pretty homophobic at the time, but he read the column and we would talk about it and I think it changed . . . his outlook. He was very active in community theater . . . and he knew a lot of gay guys because of the theater, but he was always a little standoffish. And the more we read the column, and the more we talked about it, the less standoffish and the more open he became. . . . [And] when we found out about Mrs. Madrigal . . . [I remember] a very shocking conversation with my mother who wanted to know how [a sex change] could be possible, and I was trying to explain to her . . . what it meant to be trans. . . . I know that my mom would have conversations with [my father], and he would be open to having conversations with me, and I think that's what brought about . . . this change in his life.[30]

Schulberg describes one of the ways that literary production can have a materially transformative effect on readers' affective orientation to the world. In this account, such change happens under unique conditions, when a work of literature is read repeatedly over time by people in geographic proximity, while appearing in a print media like the daily newspaper where information of common concern is circulated. In the case of *Tales*, the story made gender and sexual diversity a regular object of collective interest that elicited conversations, in this case among family members, that affectively worked on and altered people's worldviews over time. In this way, the reading process became an expression of the coming-out process. Political activist Paula Lichtenberg goes so far as to suggest that *Tales'* normalization of queerness may have been an important factor in influencing the outcome of the Briggs Initiative, which was struck down by a landmark vote in 1978. As she explains, activists canvasing against the bill "had little cards" that read, "'You just interacted with a gay person and if you vote for Prop 6, you're hurting me.' That's why . . . *Tales* was so important, because [it] mention[ed] . . . gay people as normal people." She continues, if you were a regular reader, "you've got to know . . . Michael's a nice guy. . . . I don't wanna go against him, so it was really [an] important part of the campaign that this was appearing in the newspapers."[31]

Second, alongside *Tales of the City*'s social expansion of coming out, the story functioned as a font of queer knowledge, offering a primer on LGBTQ life as well as the diverse heterosexual sex cultures of 1970s San Francisco. In case you hadn't known that co-ed bathhouses were offering the "World's Cleanest Orgy," you'd be informed on day two of reading *Tales*, when Connie Bradshaw, a sexually liberated flight attendant, hands Mary Ann a magazine graphically detailing the rise of straight "swinging" sex spaces. We soon learn about the Social Safeway, a "local tradition every Wednesday night," where gay and straight singles cruise for sex and dates; the mixed crowd of the Stud bar, one of the few locales where a gay man and his straight male friend can score on the same night; the Come Clean Center, a laundromat fit more for picking up casual sex than cleaning your underwear; and Tuesday nights at a South San Francisco roller skating rink. "Tuesday night is Gay Night," Michael explains to Mona in one story. "It's the damnedest thing you've ever seen. Two hundred dudes on roller skates. A regular Sodom and Gomorrah on wheels."[32] It would be difficult to overstate the exceptional rarity and radicalness of the dissemination of queer knowledge to audiences of a mass-circulated daily newspaper, even today. This knowledge had material effects, as it not only "outed" particular subcultures of gay and straight San Francisco to mass audiences but also potentially recruited countless curious readers into the city's growing social and sexual cultures.[33] Artist Beth Grace Silver recalled her fortuitous discovery of *Tales* around the time of her arrival to San Francisco in 1978: "[At] the age of twenty-five, I moved from Detroit to San Francisco to restart my life. . . . I had NO friends and I had never met a gay person. (All that changed quickly.) . . . I remember reading my first *TOTC* column. . . . I used it as my personal guide to 'How to Be a Single Person in San Francisco.' Marina Safeway? Went there. Buena Vista? Done. . . . All of this made me feel like I really belonged. . . . *TOTC* has been a blueprint for me."[34]

As the seemingly omniscient purveyor of this knowledge, *Tales of the City*'s unnamed narrator functions as someone universally "in the know," sometimes explicitly explaining to readers the complex mores of class, gender, and sexuality in San Francisco's various social scenes. Simultaneously, *Tales* unapologetically named the average straight reader as a "boring" or ill-informed type lacking cultural competence. When Mary Ann considers moving back to Cleveland, "'where people are steady and predictable and a little bit old fashioned,'" Michael retorts: "And boring. . . . Why do you have to go to Cleveland for boring people? We have plenty . . . here. Haven't you ever been to Paoli's at lunchtime?"[35] And when Michael's conservative parents decide to visit San Francisco on Halloween, a gay "high holy day," Michael thinks to himself, "If he was . . . very careful . . . he could . . . protect their fragile, Reader's Digest sensibilities from the horror of The Love That Dares Not Speak Its Name."[36] By consistently decentering the dominant US-American reading subject and their "fragile Reader's Digest" sensibility, *Tales* rerouted the cultural logics that attached shame, guilt, and disgust to queer life, instead associating those same affects with the middlebrow reader unable to evolve with the times. In so doing, Maupin transforms the traditional understanding of a queer subject position from one of immaturity or deviance into a desired position of canny knowing. *Tales*, then, hailed a mass public readership, presumed to be majority straight, *as if it were* a distinctly queer counterpublic.

Michael Warner explains that a counterpublic is an audience that is self-consciously aware of its alienation from a dominant culture. A counterpublic's members "are socially marked by their participation in this kind of discourse; ordinary people are presumed not to want to be mistaken for the kind of person who would participate in this kind of talk or be present in this kind of scene."[37] He continues, "Within a gay or queer counterpublic . . . no one is in the closet: the presumptive heterosexuality that constitutes the closet for individuals in ordinary speech is suspended. . . . The expansive nature of public address will seek to keep moving that frontier for a queer public, to seek more and more places to circulate where people will recognize themselves in its address."[38] *Tales* called upon "ordinary people" to willingly be "mistaken for the kind of person who would participate in this kind of [queer] talk" about gay ways of life. And incredibly, it met not with "intense resistance," but with abiding love and investment from both gay and straight readers.[39] As Paul Quin explained, "Not that I don't believe anyone would think someone gay just because they were reading *Tales* but any [eye] contact would be more the hip position. . . . Non-gay people were totally addicted to *Tales* as much as any gay audience."[40] Quin suggests that the mere fact of reading *Tales* in public could mark one as potentially gay, but that the signaling of glances between readers could also indicate a "hipper" (read queerer) worldview among straight fans. Consequently, the text "[kept] moving the frontier for a queer public" by making its audience aware of the difference between merely knowing cultural trivia about LGBTQ people and a more substantive understanding of the felt experience of living queerly in a world organized by heterosexual logics.

Across the story's first two years of publication, the *Chronicle*'s reporting on LGBTQ issues grew exponentially, nearly tripling from ten short articles in 1976 to twenty-nine articles in 1977: this included extensive coverage of Bryant's "Save Our Children" campaign and Milk's successful bid for city supervisor, a slew of stories about the murder of gay gardener Robert Hillsborough by local teenagers, and the record-breaking attendance of two hundred thousand people at the 1977 Gay Freedom Day Parade. The *Chronicle* also published articles on the widening influence of gay culture on everything from Valentine's Day cards to men's fashion to the sudden popularity of sex therapy. These articles, as well as the more properly political reporting, by and large presented a sympathetic view of queer people and their cultural impact on US society.[41] The appearance of *Tales* in the daily "Style" section of the newspaper—sitting alongside fashion and sex advice columns—relegated the story to the more lowbrow, "feminine" topics, but also firmly linked *Tales* with

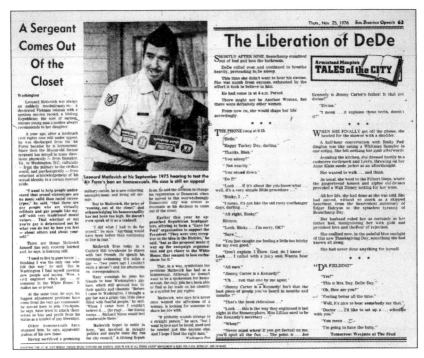

Figure 4.1. The unanticipated arrangement of a *Tales* installment alongside reporting about gay social interest stories. *San Francisco Chronicle*, November 25, 1976.

practical knowledge necessary for navigating contemporary urban sexual cultures.

The juxtaposition of *Tales'* serial entries with stories about gay culture, politics, and social life could produce unexpected connections between gender and sexual outlaws variously construed. In one fascinating layout, the Thursday, November 25, 1976, installment of *Tales*, titled "The Liberation of DeDe," appeared side by side with a short article, "A Sergeant Comes Out of the Closet," which recounts the struggle of a formerly Republican military officer to publicly acknowledge his homosexuality, consequently alienating him from his political party (figure 4.1). In the *Tales* entry, Maupin describes DeDe's decision to keep her pregnancy from an illicit affair, a willful choice shaped by her budding feminist consciousness. The visual placement of a news story about a real-life conservative military officer's coming out (as both gay and a

Democrat) alongside a fictional socialite's decision to bear an interracial child out of wedlock creates an fortuitous analogy between different versions of gay and feminist "liberation," both bound together by the coming-out narrative. It would not be an exaggeration to say that by 1977, *Tales* had anticipated and laid the groundwork for the *Chronicle* to come out of the closet as a queer newspaper. So much so that one exasperated reader wrote to the editor in June 1977, "Will you please stop writing articles concerning homosexuals! . . . Every time I read your newspaper a huge article regarding these abnormal people glares at me."[42] Such phobic reactions were themselves figured as "abnormal," published as oddball outbursts out of touch with the paper's generally liberal attitude. From its inception, then, *Tales* functioned less as an obvious fiction separate from the news, but as another kind of reporting from the field, documenting the lived experiences that attended the increasing visibility and influence of queer life on the city.

Finally, and most subversively, *Tales of the City* offered a public model for the reproduction of queerness without making any recourse to the origins of homosexuality. In more than 280 entries between 1976 and 1977, Maupin never once broaches the question of whether homosexuality is genetically inherited or culturally conditioned. On Friday, September 2, 1977, one month before the second series' conclusion, an article titled "When Your Child Tells You 'Mom, I'm a Homosexual'" appeared in the *Chronicle*. On the question of "what makes a person gay," the psychiatrist Charles Silverstein is quoted: "'Homosexuality unfolds. We don't understand how. . . . 'Coming out is a process,' not a one-shot conversation."[43] To any regular *Tales* reader, this statement would have appeared both patently true and banally obvious, because the idea that "homosexuality unfolds" was built into the very form of *Tales*' serial "process." Queerness, then, is never materialized in proof of genetic gayness, or even belonging to a distinctly queer subculture (leather queens, clones, dykes, or faeries), but merely in the event of being hailed as potentially "one of us."

This is impressed upon readers in the series' first week of publication. When Mary Ann accepts the offer for her new apartment at 28 Barbary Lane, Mrs. Madrigal tells her: "'I knew you were one of us.' . . . Mary Ann studied the woman's face for a moment and came to the conclusion that it was quite beautiful. . . . There was something puzzling, though, some ill-concealed secret that surfaced on Mrs. Madrigal's face."[44] Against Mary Ann's unself-conscious transphobic look, which seeks to "expose" some "ill-concealed secret" in Madrigal's face, Anna lovingly returns a piercing insight about Mary Ann's *own* ill-concealed secret, that she is "one of us," a queer in the making. If in the classic homophobic conceit "it takes one to know one," *Tales* suggests that we are all capable of bearing witness to the queer potential in one another regardless of our presumed sexual orientation or gender expression; this takes place not through a straight person's condescending claim to "read" queerness in someone's behaviors or facial features, but through generous acts of attentiveness to other people's capacity to be or become something different than normatively heterosexual subjects. This loving attention can bring into being countless queer communal forms, like the chosen family at Barbary Lane.

Arguably the most courageous and inspiring expression of the will to queer reproduction in *Tales of the City* can be found in Michael's coming-out letter to his Evangelical mother in the series' second year of publication:

No, Mama, I wasn't "recruited." No seasoned homosexual ever served as my mentor. But, you know what? I wish someone had. I wish someone older than me and wiser . . . had taken me aside and said, "You're all right, kid. You can grow up to be a doctor or a teacher just like anyone else. You're not crazy or sick or evil. You can succeed and be happy and find peace with friends . . . who don't give a damn who you go to bed with. Most of all, though, you can love and be loved, without hating yourself for it." But no one ever said that to me, Mama. I had to find it out on my own, with the help of this beautiful city that has become my home. . . . San Francisco is full of men and women, both straight and gay, who ignore sexuality in considering the worth of another human. . . . Being gay has taught me tolerance, compassion and humility. . . . It has given me people whose passion and kindness and sensitivity have provided a constant source of strength. It has brought me into the family of man, Mama, and I like it here. I *like* it.[45]

The force of Michael's "Letter to Mama" is twofold: rather than defending against the myth of homosexual "recruitment," Michael stresses the value of more experienced gay people guiding and supporting young queers. The analogy to this mentorship is *Tales* itself, a story that has taught its audience to be able to view Michael as a member of "the family of man." *Tales* hails its seasoned readers, regardless of their stated sexual identity, as those potential recruiters of future generations of gender and sexual outlaws, even providing them a script for articulating love and commitment toward the flourishing of queer life in the absence of a commonly shared, gay-affirming discourse. Second, in his letter, Michael frames homosexuality not as an identity, but as a set of values that fuels the production of new social relationships among members of "the family of man" variously construed—gayness, Michael explains, is the basis for friendship, and far from being reviled and detested, it is to be "liked." This is one of the most powerful cultural expressions of the gay liberationist view that "gay is good" that *Tales* offered its readers in the 1970s, and it called upon those readers as people with the power to make *more gay people exist, and exist happily, in the world.*

"You must always give people the opportunity to surprise you": On Queer Becoming

So far, I have argued that *Tales of the City*'s most powerful cultural innovation in the 1970s was to transform the practice of coming out by expanding its coordinates beyond gay and lesbian identity, while training its readers to be affectively open to receiving the possibilities of its disclosure through the structure of serial narrative. Here, I further elaborate this claim by arguing that *Tales* gains its greatest capacity to reproduce queerness through Maupin's skillful use of a single literary technique, the free indirect style, arguably the most widely cited literary innovation associated with the rise of the novel. Free indirect style, speech, or discourse describes a mode of storytelling in which a narrator expresses the thoughts and feelings of a character so directly to the reader, it as though they *are* that character thinking aloud, rather than an omniscient speaker. Literary scholar D. A. Miller explains it thus: "In free indirect style, narration comes as near to a character's psychic and linguistic reality as it can get without collapsing into it. . . . In the paradoxical form of an impersonal intimacy, it grants us . . . the experience of a character's inner life as she herself lives it, and an experience of the same inner life as she never could."[46]

But what does this look like? Take two screamingly queer instances of free indirect speech in *Tales of the City*: when Michael's parents make a surprise visit to San Francisco, the narrative reads, "Look, son, your Mama and I want to take you out to dinner tonight. Why don't you show us one of your favorite places?' *Peachy. We'll just boogie on down to The Palms, sip Blue Moons in a window seat, and watch the Cycle Sluts wave leather dildos at the traffic cops.*"[47] And later, when Brian, the straight playboy of Barbary Lane, invites Michael to hang out: "'I've got some Maui Zowie. I thought you might like to smoke some and . . . rap for a while.' Rap. Such a quaint word, thought Michael. Straight people *still* longed for the Summer of Love."[48] In these two moments, *Tales'* urbane omniscient narrator slips into Michael's mind so intimately that, in effect, its voice speaks in the idiom of his thoughts and impressions—no quotations required, we are shunted into the ironic outlook of a gay man navigating the often dull, cliché waters of "straight people."

Regardless of any reader's sexual orientation, these moments can facilitate sudden and intense identifications with queer characters, while dislocating us from our own subject positions: if we happen to be those straight people who wish to "rap" with our gay friends, we embarrassingly realize just what they might think of us. Free indirect style, then, is a very queer sort of narrative mode, because it consistently comes out of the closet on two levels: it is narration that publicly "confesses" the inner life of fictional characters, but in its uncomfortable closeness to those characters' psyches, also admits its own wish to abandon the omniscient voice for the promise of becoming a "full social being," in this case, a particular kind of gay man.[49] Maupin deploys the free indirect style to impart his partial but canny insider's knowledge of LGBTQ culture to a mass audience. But in doing so, he also admits his genuine desire to inhabit the lifeworlds of other people; thus, the free indirect style becomes an imaginative and aspirational practice that, like coming out, experiments with making public new and unexpected intimacies in the hopes of altering the self and the social world. Three characters typify the use of free indirect style in *Tales*—Mary Ann Singleton, Michael Tolliver, and Anna Madrigal—while also embodying three distinct forms of coming out.

Despite being our polestar, the character with whom we enter the larger imaginative world of *Tales of the City*, Mary Ann is arguably the most troubling figure of the series. In granting us access to Mary Ann's immediate psychic impressions of San Francisco, Maupin repeatedly reveals her attachment to delusional fantasies of heterosexual romance, her negative judgments of free sexual expression, and her naïve relationship to toxic masculinity. Mary Ann's judgmentalness becomes a narrative staple early on. When Mary Ann's former high school classmate Connie Bradshaw takes her to the Social Safeway to pick up men in the series' second installment, Mary Ann is so put off by the demonstration of public cruising that she dramatically wheels her cart away: "Connie could go practice her pagan mating ritual. Mary Ann intended to shop. Period."[50] Weeks later, after a failed attempt at a do-it-yourself face mask treatment (for a girl with no names on her dance card), Mary Ann sits despondently in her tub: "You look like a giant Shake 'n Bake pork chop. And for what? . . . For Dance Your Ass Off? . . . For Michael what's-his-name down the hall? For a married man who's married to a wife, a family, *and* a job?"[51] Shifting from second-person narration to free indirect speech, the string of resentful questions Mary Ann asks herself reveals what little value she places on public dance and cruising spaces, as well as her dismissiveness toward gay men like her neighbor Michael whom she can only see as obstructing her access to romantic possibilities. The narrator then gives us special insight into Mary Ann's psyche, not simply describing what she thinks, but speaking in the voice of those thoughts. This grants us direct access to the affective tone and feel of her Midwestern judgmentalness.

As readers get hip to Mary Ann's outlook over time, free indirect style not only expresses her inner thoughts but also provides a meta-critique of them, particularly as they relate to her naïve relationship to dysfunctional straight men. When Beauchamp Day, the unhappily married son-in-law of her boss Edgar Halcyon, seduces her, the narrative reads: "Suddenly he seemed terribly vulnerable like a small boy about to be spanked and Mary Ann felt an overwhelming urge to cradle him in her arms."[52] And later, when Mary Ann meets inspector Hank Tandy, a middle-aged police officer with whom she pursues a short-lived relationship: "Something about his soft brown eyes and bearish frame made her think of home . . . of Cleveland."[53] Upending Mary Ann's seemingly innocent view of these bumbling, childlike men, we will soon find out that Beau-champ is an emotionally manipulative, closeted lothario, and Tandy a serial murderer and rapist. The exposure of Mary Ann's inner life allows us to see how deeply invested she is in normative masculinity, but also betrays a particular version of heterosexual femininity that is willing to risk losing one's personal dignity, the bonds of queer kinship, and even one's life in exchange for male affection. Maupin uses Mary Ann to forward a two-pronged feminist judgment against heteronormativ-ity: he simultaneously forces all readers, regardless of their gender or sexual identity, to access the fictional world of *Tales* through a primary identification with a single, independent, working woman, while also unabashedly critiquing that character's failure to be adequately woman-identified or queerly oriented herself.

Mary Ann's most damning offense is enacted in the story's eleventh hour. Three installments before the conclusion of the series' first year of publication on New Year's Eve, the Tinkerbell serial killer, a recur-ring menace who murders a variety of supporting characters (includ-ing Connie), is revealed as Hank, the police officer Mary Ann has been having an affair with and who is also investigating the case. Shortly before Tandy's confession to having committed the murders, he "outs" Madrigal as a transsexual and weaves a lie that she is the real killer. For a split second, Mary Ann believes him: "Devastated, Mary Ann stared at the unflinching face of Anna Madrigal. . . . [She] felt her flesh crawl as she stared into the face of the woman she had trusted for so long."[54] Here, all of Mary Ann's former ill-conceived judgments about Madrigal's "beautiful," "careworn," but "mannequin"-like visage con-verge in an instant of transphobic judgment, where the falsehoods of a murderously delusional straight man against her loving landlady are taken at (literal) face value. The narrative impresses this reality upon the reader in both its content and its visual form. The installment titled "Tinkerbell Stands Revealed" has the highest word count of any entry in the first year of *Tales*' publication. The majority of the text appears in highly compact blocked paragraphs primarily composed of Tandy's megalomaniacal monologue. Maupin then formally renders the con-cept of "mansplaining"—a distinctly male type of patronizing toward women—as a visual wall of text, unbroken by the flow of reciprocal dialogue common to the text's queer interpersonal exchanges or by free indirect speech, whose narrative intimacy is summarily blocked by Tandy's incessant talking.

Within the space of two sentences, Tandy's plot is unraveled. Yet what "stands revealed" about Tinkerbell is not simply the mystery of a malevolent character's machinations, but more broadly the ways in which transphobia coheres at the nexus of police power, misogyny, and straight women's complicity with patriarchy. After all, we cannot easily forget Mary Ann's momentary willingness to buy the transphobic, narcissistic fantasy of a psychotic police officer above the genuine care of her landlady, who had unconditionally included her as a member of her queer family. It is telling that in Maupin's own personal recollections of his queer awakening to San Francisco, he explained that many of his sexual partners looked at him like he was "Jeffrey Dahmer," the infamous gay serial killer and cannibal, after learning of his conservative political origins. In both Maupin's own lived experience, and his fictional storytelling, the serial killer—a sadistic, life-negating type that literally annihilates the bodies of women and queers—becomes a terrifying metaphor for societal homophobia and transphobia. Through Mary Ann, Maupin suggest that all those who live in an anti-gay world—even the most naïve or innocent among us, like a good Midwestern girl—are susceptible to such murderous impulses and must work tirelessly to dismantle their complicity with the violent logics of gender and sexual hierarchy.

Indeed, what ultimately redeems Mary Ann is her ability to internalize the critiques of her friends and chosen family, and to make measured and meaningful change to her worldview and behaviors over time. In the series' second year, Mary Ann turns to her boyfriend Burke and describes her first meeting with Michael at the Social Safeway: "'He was so cute . . . but I was furious at him, because he was with this guy that I really liked and all night long I just kept saying to myself, 'What a waste.' . . . I believed that, too . . . that he had gone wrong somehow. I told myself I felt sorry for him, but I was really feeling sorry for myself. I found out that all the Mr. Rights weren't made for me, and I couldn't handle it." Burke consoles her: "It's OK. People change."[55] In this touching moment, Mary Ann retroactively reads her own thoughts (ones that were provided to readers a year before through Maupin's use of free indirect discourse) as stemming from a homophobic and self-serving perspective that presumed the privilege of a world made for the fulfillment of her straight desires. It is Mary Ann's ability to make this cognitive leap that signals her true coming out. In this sense, no *Tales* character better represents coming out as a *process* than Mary Ann, for her maturation into a queer San Franciscan is hard won, requiring many clumsy encounters with gay ways of life, a variety of failed attempts to recuperate heterosexuality, and, quite simply, substantial time for "working on it" by internalizing her new experiences and evolving in responses to them. These lessons were not lost on readers like Mary Richardson, who claimed that "Maryanne [*sic*] had a big impact on reinforcing the belief that I didn't have to marry a cowboy and spend my life in a small town." The narrative transformation that allows Mary Ann to become an imaginative figure for liberated femininity is a slow and imperfect one, but it is partly facilitated by Mary Ann's unexpected encounter with Michael, who would evolve from her anonymous gay neighbor into her beloved best friend, Michael "Mouse," in the course of her first year in the city by the Bay.

As *Tales of the City*'s central gay male character, Michael embodies the most classic form of coming out as the public assertion of same-sex desire. He is the character who normalizes gayness for readers through his ebullient, loving presence as a straight woman's best friend, and a misguided but relatable romantic whose obsession with finding everlasting love echoes Mary Ann's. Yet through the adroit use of free indirect discourse, Maupin reveals the psychological burden Michael carries to live up to the unrealistic masculine ideals of gay male social and sexual life, as well as the constant emotional labor he shoulders to manage his straight friends' conflicted feelings about gay existence. Through repeated encounters with Michael's inner life, readers not only gain an understanding of the humanity of gay men, but also witness the deep pain and emotional exhaustion that someone like Michael (and perhaps by extension Maupin himself) feel at having to constantly reassert that humanity to others.

In the series' first year, Michael echoes Mary Ann in his near-manic drive to find romance with an ideal "masculine" white man. Michael's first official introduction as a regular cast member appears in an early installment titled "Looking for Mr. Right": "As he scanned *The Advocate*'s classified section . . . [his] favorite item was this: **Clean-cut,**

**straight-looking court reporter, 32, sick to death of bars, baths and
bitchiness, seeks . . . A REAL MAN who's into white water rafting,
classical music and gardening. No fats, fems or dopers, please. I'm
SINCERE. Ron.** Well, who the hell isn't, thought Michael. Was there
a single goddamn gay man in all of San Francisco who didn't, in his
heart of hearts, lust after a Potrero Hill cottage for two . . . ?"[56] By reproducing a personals ad from a widely circulated gay publication, the
Advocate, Maupin makes this genre of gay male discourse available to a
mass audience that would normally never access it on their own. But he
is also giving readers insight into Michael's reaction to the ad's content.
Perhaps even more discomforting than Ron's sexism and internalized
homophobia is Michael's unselfconscious attachment to the ad's normative ideals. By explicitly giving voice to his knee-jerk defensiveness
toward the ad, the free indirect style reveals Michael himself as a man
who is simultaneously exhausted by the impossible hunt for the perfect
domestic gay life but still erotically bound up in its idealized promise of
sexual fulfillment *and* social belonging.

As Michael later admits to his neighbor Brian: "'I meet . . . some
guy . . . at a bar or at the baths, and he seems really . . . what I want. A
nice mustache, Levi's . . . somebody you could take back to Tallahassee. . . . Then you go home with him . . . and you try like hell not to go
to the bathroom, because [it's] the fantasy-killer . . . that goddamn little
gold pedestal dish full of colored soap balls!"[57] Just as Mary Ann finds
herself seduced by Hank's "bearish," bumbling masculinity, so too Michael organizes his erotic fantasies around the iconic signifiers of macho
manhood in the hopes that they might somehow usher his reentry into
his hometown, Tallahassee, as a legitimately coupled success story. The
odd intertwining of Michael's sexual fantasies with his aspiration to return home with a properly masculine boyfriend reveal something powerful to readers about the stranglehold of normative masculinity and
heterosexuality on queer and straight people alike: underlying the frantic gay male need to police the boundaries of erotically desirable masculinity (e.g., Michael's spinning out about soap balls!) is a deeper desire to
be welcomed back into the fold of home and family.

In one of the most explicit instances of free indirect style in all of
Tales of the City, Michael prepares to go to a costume party dressed as
the Greek god Pan, after his current love interest, the gynecologist Jon

Fielding, turns down an invitation. Dismissing his disappointment with Jon's decision, Michael looks at himself in the mirror: "And he looked damned good. . . . For once, he was proud of himself. . . . Remember this moment and hold your head up later . . . when your parents call from Tallahassee and wonder if you've met any 'nice girls' . . . when someone at the tubs says, 'I'm just resting right now' . . . when the beautiful and serious-minded Dr. Jon Fielding burrows his Byronesque brow . . . and declines a costume party that 'might be a little freaky.' OK, Jon. Eat your heart out."[58] In this equally heartwarming and heartbreaking moment, free indirect discourse explains a complex social reality otherwise unbeknownst to straight readers: that the building up of gay men's physical beauty (in impossibly muscular physiques and butch fashion) is a direct response to the social and cultural devaluation of their identities—by homophobic family and friends, but just as cruelly, by other gay men whose countless forms of interpersonal rejection and judgment can destroy one's self-worth. Michael's willful "bucking up" in the face of so many disappointments reveals a deep vulnerability at the heart of gay male identity, to be loved and desired as much by one's family as one's peers.

But just as Mary Ann comes to develop a critical stance toward her own myopic straight worldview, Michael also increasingly realizes that no amount of work on the self will successfully win him happiness within the logic of gay male macho identity. Months after this scene, "as [Michael] walked down Divisadero, [he] reflected sadly on the way that Madison Avenue rules the libidos of lost people. When the soul is dead . . . the trademark is everything. A collegiate shoe. A lumberjack shirt. . . . A handful of blue glitter. Even a psychotic killer needs a badge of identity."[59] Once again, free indirect speech shows us how a distinctly gay perspective, when taken as a critique of heteronormative society, can dismantle a range of assumptions about gender and sexual identity, including the suspect attachment to butch style, which Michael finally comes to acknowledge is a superficial gender performance based in commodity culture. That performance, Michael realizes, is not that structurally different than a serial killer's signature (in this case, the distinctive "handful of blue glitter" the Tinkerbell murderer throws on his victims' bodies), a bid for validation that disregards the humanity of those other bodies it solicits and violently rejects.

Fueled by the increasing public awareness of Bryant's "Save Our Children" campaign, in its second year *Tales of the City*'s narrative voice increasingly expresses Michael's struggle to provide gay social and sexual knowledge to his straight friends while simultaneously wanting to be genuinely seen by them. His relationship with Mary Ann, especially, is strained by her frequent inability to understand the everyday lived experience of being an out gay person, including fear of social shunning and homophobic violence. In the third installment of *Tales*' second year, Mary Ann and Michael pack for a cruise to Mexico: "Mary Ann sighed and sat down on the edge of the bed. 'I used to be a Y-Teen. Mouse . . . now I'm smuggling dope into Mexico.'" He quips: "And traveling with a known homosexual." To which Mary Ann replies flatly: "Yeah." The narrative continues: "Michael sat down next to her and held her hand. He stared at the black light mandala that Mona had left when she took off for D'orothea's. 'That's a funny phrase, isn't it? Known homosexual . . . you never hear about . . . known insurance salesmen. And when you're not a known homosexual, you're an admitted one. Mr. Diddly-Squat, an admitted stockbroker, was found stabbed to death in Golden Gate Park.'"[60]

Despite their growing friendship, rather than laugh off Michael's joke, Mary Ann obliviously responds in the affirmative, painfully revealing her own residual embarrassment at being associated with homosexuality (and, by extension, illicit drug use). Michael takes Mary Ann's hand in a gesture of comfort, yet in the same instant, the narrative lets us know that he is thinking of Mona, the one friend who truly understands him. Torn between guiding Mary Ann through her ongoing process of "loosening up" and wanting the validation of a companion who needs no guidance in loving queer people, Michael's internal conflict leads him to verbally pontificate about the unfairness inherent in homosexuality as a distinctly marked category that people claim to label and "know," even as they remain ignorant of the lives lived under that banner. In the context of the newspaper, Michael's joke about the imaginary stabbing of "Mr. Diddly-Squat" is deadly serious. After all, it is precisely "known homosexuals" who are the regular targets of violent assault in San Francisco, a sociological reality documented in the *Chronicle*, including its months-long reporting on the murder of gay gardener Robert Hillsborough—stabbed to death by a homophobic teenager screaming

"This is for Anita!"—only twelve weeks after this installment. Here, Michael becomes a stand-in for Maupin the author, a gay man who has held his readers' hands through the process of queer socialization, while perhaps wishing he didn't have to anymore. From the outset of the second series, Maupin begins to use the free indirect style to demand more than mere liberal allyship from readers, namely the ability to viscerally inhabit the lifeworlds of the queer people they claim to support and love.

This is perhaps why Michael himself, already openly gay to his circle of friends, finally chooses to explicitly come out of the closet to his parents midway through *Tales'* second year. By his declaration, Michael claims accountability toward, and aligns himself with, the loud, flamboyant "Marys" that have long existed on the outside of his fantasy ideal of the mustached, flannel-shirted hunk. As Mary Ann has often been to Michael (a loving but sometimes "out of it" friend), so Michael has been to non–traditionally masculine gay men (supportive in theory, but never in practice; always gay, but never a "faggot"). In his 1970 coming-out call to action, "A Gay Manifesto," gay liberationist Carl Wittman explained this logic: "'Closet queen' is a broad term covering a multitude of forms of defense [and] self-hatred. . . . We are all closet queens in some ways, and all of us had to come out. . . . We must afford our brothers and sisters the same patience we afforded ourselves. . . . They alone can decide when and how."[61] Through his delayed "official" coming out, Michael retroactively becomes the iconic model of the sexually libertine but politically disengaged "closet queen" who ultimately decides "when and how" to escape the trap of heterosexism.

This becomes clear a few entries after Michael writes to his parents, when he shares a poignant conversation with Mary Ann: "'I wish [Anita Bryant] could know you. . . . You aren't extreme, Mouse.' 'What if I were? Would you love me any less?' 'Well, no, but I . . .' 'Those so-called extreme ones are the ones who've suffered all these years . . . and we've let them. . . . Those of us who could fake it have ducked our heads and butched it up with the bigots. We're to blame for the prejudices of people like Anita Bryant. As long as we coast along leading our discreet, tortured little lives, we're not going to be free.'"[62] Up to this point, Michael has indeed been the playful and lovable gay man that we, like Mary Ann but unlike Bryant, have been lucky to know and love. Through Maupin's narrative voice we have been given intimate access to "those discreet, tortured lives" of the gays who marginally pass and that Michael now vehemently refuses. Michael's ultimate coming out, then, is not as a gay man, but as a *politicized* gay person, who sees his identity as the basis for solidarity with other gender and sexual outlaws. Through its serial unfolding, *Tales* "affords our brother" Michael, and its vast Bay Area audience, "the same patience" Wittman argues we must grant all people as they evolve into sexually and politically free subjects. Yet the historical context of Michael's coming out, as Bryant was capturing the hearts and minds of homophobic US-Americans everywhere, was urgent enough to demand an acceleration of this process. Through these exchanges, Maupin sought to hold his audience accountable too, presenting readers a dialogic model not only for enacting love and sympathy toward their queer friends, but being politically responsible for their thriving.

Mary Ann and Michael's friendship models an authentic, if painstaking, transformation that results from the persistent exchange between gay and straight companions as they share their most private fantasies, reckon with the consequences of their desires, and mutually develop new social aspirations grounded in solidarity across difference. Yet if, in Mary Ann, readers encountered a naïf migrant to a queer San Francisco (perhaps not unlike themselves), and in Michael met a brash Romeo daring to navigate the competitive world of gay sex and dating (perhaps not unlike how confident readers aspired to be), in Anna Madrigal, *Tales of the City* offered readers a fully formed mother-figure who builds alternative family through trust, rather than patriarchal power or maternal loyalty. Madrigal is the person we ethically *need to be* to bring about the queer world that gay liberation so compellingly set out to create in the 1970s. It is conceptually fitting that Madrigal is (a) a landlady, someone who curates an intimate living community among strangers (not unlike Maupin himself in his hailing of a reading public as "one of us," sight unseen); (b) a transsexual, someone who has experienced the world from multiple subject positions as male and female, as a biological father and figurative "mother" to her renters, as a one-time husband, estranged son, *and* rediscovered daughter; and (c) an established woman in her fifties, that is, someone with life experience (one of those very kinds of people that Michael wished had taken him under their wing). These qualities mark her as arguably the most aspirational and pedagogical personality in *Tales*, someone whose current place in life has been achieved over time, by her movement through a range of identities and experiences that have each functioned to give her a greater worldly perspective.

Unlike Mary Ann and Michael, who spend so much of the narrative defending their identities against all sorts of threats to their egos, from swinging singles to screaming queens, Madrigal lives by the modus operandi "include, include!" Very early in the series' second year, the narrative relates: "She smiled . . . at herself . . . an aging sentimental oddity who had walked serendipitously into paradise. This was hers. This earth, these bricks, these brave old trees bursting with . . . She swept an alien dog turd off the edge of the courtyard. That was hers, too. . . . And every other tawdry cast-off of the philistines who came to gawk at the Murder House."[63] Free indirect speech gives us insight into Madrigal's distinct outlook on the world, one that acknowledges, and takes responsibility for, everything that appears within its sight. Hers is a queer spirit of valuing that which is devalued, "cast-off," and abused. In the broader narrative, this includes taking as her lover Edgar Halcyon, an aging member of the San Francisco elite whose impending death has made him lose his self-worth ("Because I wanted you to remember who you were then. Something tells me you're not to too happy with who you are now"); Michael, when his lover Robert dumps him; and Mary Ann, when her world falls apart as failed affairs, murdered acquaintances, and faltering friendships dissolve her utopian fantasies of San Francisco life. In our interview, artist Daniel Goldstein stressed the power that Madrigal held in gay readers' imagination: "I love[d] [her] worldliness and all-knowingness. . . . There was . . . something about a woman of an older generation totally being accepting. . . . I came out to my parents that year, in 1977. I think all of us were looking for a parent figure who would completely embrace us and accept us. And who would be wacky as well. . . . She was . . . that ideal parent."[64] From this perspective, we might say that Madrigal's parenting style is defined by radical acceptance of queerness, taking as bedrock the assumption that "it is worth imagining a world in [which] we recruit, we choose, we increase."[65]

Throughout *Tales*, Madrigal seems to have a kind of "second sight" into the other characters. She "sees" or divines their struggles or else identifies their extraordinary potential for transformation even when they cannot perceive it themselves (as when she claims to have known that Mary Ann is "one of us . . . from the minute [she] walked in"). It would be easy to initially categorize Madrigal as a classic "oracle" figure, a "magical queer" who exists merely to illuminate the lives of others, while remaining a flat character devoid of her own inner life. Yet free indirect style repeatedly show us that Madrigal's insight is in no way mystical but lies simply in her genuine curiosity about the world. Upon their first accidental meeting at Washington Square Park, Anna encourages Edgar to share the story of his first sexual experience. He admits that he lost his virginity at seventeen to a sex worker named Margaret at the Blue Moon Lodge in Winnemucca, Nevada: "Anna Madrigal bit her forefinger meditatively. She was weighing something, analyzing Edgar's face for clues to his character. Finally, she said, 'Margaret was a very good person.' . . . 'I beg your pardon?' 'Margaret was a good person,' Anna repeated. 'She read me all the Winnie the Pooh books. . . . My mother ran the Blue Moon lodge. . . . I grew up there.'"[66] Having never met Edgar before in her life, and knowing nothing about his intentions, Madrigal dares to trust him with the revelation of her intimate history with the Blue Moon Lodge. That dare, however, is based on Madrigal's thoughtful, though swift, intuition of Edgar's inner playfulness, indicated by his own willingness to tell a stranger about his "first time." As opposed to Mary Ann, who initially sees the mysteries of others as potentially suspicious, even malevolent, Madrigal is the iconic figure of trust and compassion: she discloses, and elicits disclosure from others, thereby making them potential members of her social family.

When Mary Ann sheepishly admits to Madrigal that she might go on a date with Beauchamp, her boss's married son-in-law, she expects the landlady to react as her mother would by reprimanding Mary Ann for making a disastrous personal decision. Instead, Madrigal drolly retorts, "'I'm not Dear Abby, Mary Ann. You should do what you want to do. . . . If you want to enjoy [life], you have to grab it by the . . .' Mrs. Madrigal stopped herself, remembering the delicacy of her audience. 'You have to take a firm hold on it.'"[67] Once again, adeptly reading the room, Madrigal models a spirit of nonjudgment, encouraging Mary Ann to live fully, make mistakes, and see where they lead her. But she does so in Mary Ann's language. Much like Michael, Madrigal models for readers the loving emotional labor that queer people frequently perform to guide their straight friends toward a more sexually free life; but her nimble approach also functions pedagogically, training readers of all stripes how to be equally supple at navigating others' unique temperaments, aesthetic tastes, and varied senses of humor. It is fitting, then, that in the 2019 Netflix revival of *Tales*, Madrigal, played by a luminous Olympia Dukakis and still a feisty, loving landlady edging into her nineties, imparts her greatest bit of wisdom to a young Latinx trans-man: "You must always give people the opportunity to surprise you." Madrigal's distinctly queer worldview stretches across generations and identities as a sensibility defined by an affective openness to other peoples' particularity and unpredictability.

That openness to surprise is what makes queer kindship and cross-identification—between a transsexual woman and a cis-woman, between a straight woman and a gay man, between gay and straight men—both possible and enduring, even in a phobic world. When Mary Ann discovers that Connie has been murdered by the Tinkerbell killer, she emotionally unravels before Anna. Prior to hearing this devastating news, the landlady says: "'Do you want to tell mother about it?' Mother. The word jarred Mary Ann at first, but the landlady's face shone with honest compassion. Suddenly, the floodgates burst. . . . Mrs. Madrigal scooped the sobbing secretary in her arms. 'Oh God, Mrs. Madrigal! It's . . . so hard to be a woman.' . . . 'I know what you mean, dear.'"[68] In this moment Mary Ann finally recognizes authenticity in Madrigal's face, her previous suspicion of Madrigal's intentions crumbling before a genuine intimacy based in shared experience: to be women in a world that is violently murderous toward women.

By the end of *Tales*' second year of publication in late 1977, this intimacy had grown so deep that free indirect style could make us privy to one of Mary Ann's most beautiful thoughts: "God bless Mrs. Madrigal. . . . She was the only constant in Mary Ann's life. Lovers came and went . . . but Mrs. Madrigal endured forever."[69] It is not so much that Madrigal, the person, endures forever (for she is as mortal as the rest of us), but that her spirit of inclusion provides a distinctly queer model of loving that persists past all forms of romantic attachment. It is in this sense that Madrigal is the single character that comes closest to representing serial narrative itself: a form of indefinite unfolding that, conceptually speaking, has the potential to live on forever.

That capacity to endure—which might also be understood as the capacity to "recruit" people into queerness—is exquisitely captured in

Madrigal's most triumphant moment of queer mythmaking, in which she renarrates the history of San Francisco, and its contemporary inhabitants, as a story of queer migrants fortuitously reunited in the city by the Bay. Lying in bed with Edgar, she expounds:

> "There's a theory . . . that we are all Atlanteans . . . Us. San Franciscans." Edgar grinned at her indulgently, bracing himself for another of her yarns. . . . "In one of our last incarnations, we were all citizens of Atlantis. All of us. You, me, Frannie, Dede, Mary Ann. . . . We all lived in this lovely, enlightened kingdom that sank beneath the sea a long time ago. . . . Now we've come back to this special peninsula on the edge of the continent . . . because we know, in a secret corner of our minds, that we must return together to the sea."[70]

In her tall tale, Madrigal upsets all San Francisco origin stories based in colonial histories of westward expansion and the white monied classes—rather she addresses all the city's citizens, a collective "Us," from its most established elites to its most rebellious, queer transplants, as people who always belonged here and have simply returned home.

It is telling that Madrigal relates this story to Edgar Halcyon, arguably the most "straight" figure in all of *Tales*, a rich, white, cisgender, heterosexual, married patriarch. Edgar potentially represents the most recalcitrant kind of reader of *Tales of the City*, that member of Maupin's audience who would, if discovered reading this soap opera, vehemently deny attachment to it. But the intimate vulnerability of the scene, in which this very kind of reader is literally in bed with a trans-woman, destabilizes this subject position: for all it takes to be queer is to be hailed as "one of us." And, repeatedly called upon as a queer member of Anna's family, Edgar cannot deny that "[f]or reasons that . . . he couldn't explain . . . Anna Madrigal was becoming very important to him."[71] And so too, for all those former Atlanteans returning home—including every reader of Maupin's tales—San Francisco had become very important to them. In Madrigal's deft hands, queerness—that radical force that will shake the foundations of San Francisco like an earthquake—becomes its own origin story, requiring no explanation aside from its mere existence and glorious capacity to forge bonds of love and affection among people, "straight and all," wherever they are from. In so doing, she offers her own "tale of the city" that aligns with the radical claim of gay liberation that "[g]ay revolution will produce a world in which all social and sensual relationships will be gay and in which homo- and heterosexuality will be incomprehensible terms."[72]

* * *

It is tempting to end here, with the utopian force of Madrigal's queer San Francisco myth. But to do so would be to overlook one of the most conspicuous, and illuminating, failures of the free indirect style to actualize Maupin's vision of queer kinship across difference in the 1970s. I refer here to the mysterious character of D'orothea Wilson, who represented Maupin's most sustained, but ultimately aborted, attempt at rendering Black lesbian identity in *Tales of the City*. In the final instance, Maupin negated D'orothea's Blackness through a bizarre plot twist in which the lesbian model "comes out" as white. By doing so, Maupin turned away from the full implications of her character, including the potential of modeling cross-racial coalition between gender and sexual outlaws, as well as sharing the unique perspective of one Black woman just as much as any white, gay, or trans* character. Rather than repeat the same flight, I conclude this chapter by reckoning with the implications of this creative choice, which I argue remains a highly instructive object lesson in the pitfalls of essentialist versions of contemporary identity politics.

It is fair to say that the logic of queer reproduction, which is *Tales of the City*'s greatest political gift, fails to extend to race in the series' original incarnation. This is true at the level of representation—including *Tales'* noticeable lack of substantive characters of color, queer or otherwise—but also at the level of plot. In the one instance when a character makes a public declaration about their racial identity, the coming-out process does not materialize meaningful interpersonal outcomes or influence the narrative's trajectory. If Michael's famed letter to Mama worked to multiply queerness throughout the social field, D'orothea's coming out as a white woman from Oakland has the opposite outcome, reducing people of color in the central cast from one to zero, while foreclosing the possibility that racial difference might be one valuable site of social and erotic connectivity between queers variously construed. In the wake of

D'orothea's politically compromised form of coming out, no other white character can ever convincingly "come out" as someone with sincere cross-racial affinities without appearing to appropriate racial categories not properly their own. Why do gender and sexuality appear to be such flexible categories for Maupin—who places a transgender woman at the center of his fiction—while race remains less amenable to transitivity, affinity, and cross-identification?

One well-established historical answer to this question has been the claim that coming out is a political practice grounded in a predominantly white middle-class rejection of the heterosexual nuclear family and is less easily available to racialized subjects for whom thick family networks are a necessary social anchor in a racist US society. As Trinity A. Ordona underscores in her history of Asian American lesbian organizing in the Bay Area, "'Coming out' publicly or to family was especially problematic for Asian and Pacific Islanders, given that the prevailing paradigm emphasized separation, and even rejection of family as a necessary, but 'healthy' price to pay for accepting one's homosexuality. . . . The culturally proscribed heterosexist bias and fear of rejection of their families were insurmountable barriers at the time, so most [Asian American] women remained closeted to their families during these years."[73] Similarly, historian Horacio N. Roque Ramírez has documented how Latinx gays and lesbians in the San Francisco Bay Area found themselves torn between commitments to their cultural heritage and a desire to express gay sexuality, which was paradoxically more viable in predominantly white queer spaces, even as these space were suffused with racism. Ramírez quotes Diane Felix, a founding member of the Gay Latino Alliance (GALA), the first Bay Area social and political organization of LGBTQ Latinx: "The minute I came out it was my own *Raza* [Chicanos, Chicanas and Latinx generally] that threw me out 'cause I was queer. It was always a contradiction for me: Why are they [whites] more liberal?"[74]

These experiences suggested that a particular version of coming out—as rebellious verbal public declaration—often did not allow for a synthetic integration of queer identity with ethno-racial belonging because it centralized divestment from existing networks of care based in heritage and tradition. Yet as we have seen, both within gay liberation and in *Tales*' serial narrative, coming out could take numerous forms

beyond the single statement of being gay, including joining a queer social group, forging alternative kinship networks, making feminist and
queer art, and participating in political activism. This meant that coming out was a highly adaptable strategy for inhabiting queer ways of life
that could potentially respond to the particularities of queer-of-color
experience. In both Ordona's and Ramírez's accounts, the same Asian
American lesbian feminists who "remained closeted to their families,"
and queer Latinx activists who were "thrown out" by their *Raza*, still
came out to one another and were political activists in multiple radical movements. They responded to the needs of queer people of color
by organizing queer and feminist artists collectives in Berkeley and San
Francisco, holding queer-of-color dance parties, and opening Latinx-
run queer bars in the Mission District.[75] What is particularly vexing
about Maupin's constrained racial imagination, then, is that it flatly contradicts the overriding values *he* develops in *Tales*' larger arc, specifically
the ideal of queerness as an unpredictable social force that can produce
surprising affinities across difference. It is worth understanding this creative pitfall precisely to preserve the political promise of coming out as
it is articulated in *Tales* and make that promise attentive to differences
that Maupin himself struggled to grapple with.

Against this backdrop, Maupin's introduction of the only lead character of color in the story's first year of publication was a consequential
creative moment that promised to extend the logic of coming out, even
if partially, to a queer-of-color perspective. D'orothea is first introduced
as a mysterious beauty drinking alone at the bar where Brian Hawkins
works as a waiter. After a flirtatious first encounter, she agrees to meet
him for a drink following his shift, where she relates a story about returning to San Francisco to rekindle a passionate romance with her
former lover Mona Ramsey. The narrative initially stages the encounter
between Brian and D'orothea as an uncomfortable but necessary reckoning with white liberal guilt, in which a superficial white progressive
worldview is subjected to scrutiny by an actual person of color:

> D'orothea was a model . . . peddling her polished onyx features to Vogue
> and Harper's . . . and "everybody else who was hopping on the afro-
> bandwagon." She had made money . . . and lots of it. "Which ain't half bad
> for a girl who grew up in Oakland B.A." "B.A.?" asked Brian. . . . "Before

Apostrophe. I used to be Dorothy Wilson until Eileen Ford turned it into Dorothea and stuck an apostrophe between the D and the O. . . . It was either the apostrophe or one of those godawful African names like Simbu or Tamara or Bonzo, and I'd be goddamned if I'd go around town sounding like Ronald Reagan's chimpanzee!" "Was it tough growing up in Oakland?" She did a slow take, rolling her eyes at him. "Oh . . . I get it! A lib-ber-rull!" He reddened. "No, not exact . . ." "Gimme a hint then. A Vista Volunteer, maybe? A civil rights lawyer?" It annoyed him that she had guessed it so quickly. "I did some work for the Urban League in Chicago, but I don't see what . . ." "And all that guilt exhausted you so much, that you decided to-hell-with-it and chucked it all for a waiter's job. I hear you Brian. I hear you."[76]

Neither a misguided dupe nor a political purist, D'orothea is presented as a self-aware Black woman who understands, and has willfully exploited, the complex racial logics by which her skin tone and presumed cultural heritage have become fetishistic objects of desire within the racist fashion industry. The scene presents a woman of color negotiating her racial, gender, and sexual identities on multiple fronts both professionally and interpersonally: D'orothea's financial success signals her attempt to accrue monetary value to her Blackness after having grown up working class in Oakland, California, while that same success has also alienated her from her lesbian lover. In this instance, D'orothea promises to be a potentially productive, intersectional figure of critique within the narrative, even functioning as Maupin's attempt at self-criticism: if Brian represents Maupin's approach to race so far—modeled in the socially conscious but cynical "woke" white person's sarcastic humor—D'orothea is the racialized subject who speaks back to that cynicism, poking fun at the privilege required for Brian to summarily give up years of legal training and become a waiter on the basis of his white guilt.

Ironically, it is precisely Mona's frustrating form of white liberalism—captured in her self-righteous and ill-conceived judgment regarding D'orothea's "fierce reluctance to deal with her African heritage"—that ultimately exposes D'orothea's racial ruse. Obsessed with reuniting D'orothea with her estranged parents, Mona locates her lover's father, a working-class baker at a "Twinkie Factory," and invites the Wilsons to dinner; however, when days later, D'orothea's parents surprise their daughter by arriving for dinner unannounced, both we (the readers) and Mona are jolted by the discovery that both of them are white. In what is perhaps one of Maupin's most trenchant (if unwitting) critiques of white liberalism, it is, perversely, Mona's zealous need to assuage her white guilt over both her racial insensitivity and D'orothea's presumed internalized racism that literally leads to the reproduction of *more whiteness*, rather than greater cross-racial identification or cultural competence. In a tearful fit, D'orothea admits: "I never meant to make my life into a lie. . . . I just wanted to work. . . . Five years ago . . . nobody would hire me . . . so I did a couple jobs in dark makeup . . . and all of a sudden people started asking for the foxy black chick. . . . I'm a fraud Mona. . . . I'm nothing but a white girl from Oakland. . . . [I got] ultraviolet treatments . . . and I kept taking the pills. . . . Finally one day I decided . . . to move to San Francisco and go white."[77] In a matter of lines, D'orothea's previously trenchant critiques of white liberal platitudes become the ultimate ironic joke, an elaborate defensive posture intended to gain her cultural credibility against the threat of being discovered as a fraud, who by dint of her own superficial racism had stumbled upon a limited fame by inhabiting and capitalizing on brown skin. Moreover, the generalized association of Oakland with a working-class Black demographic (pitied and fetishized by white progressives) is now paired with the damning image of San Francisco as the place that fraudulent liberals move to "to go white," further obscuring both cities' actual racial diversity and immigrant histories.

Maupin has claimed that his decision to "out" D'orothea as white was based on a letter he received from a Black woman reader who accused him of creating a character who was a "white woman in a Black woman's skin."[78] This reader implied that Maupin had either failed to adequately capture Black women's experience or did not have the right to narrate a racial identity not original to his experience. In her work on racial and sexual passing, Amy Robinson has written about the complex procedures of internal policing that minoritized groups, particularly African Americans and gays and lesbians, deploy to identify putative members of their community who appear to (falsely) pass as white, straight, or both. This identity-based logic, grounded in the conceit "'It takes one to know one[,]' envisions identity politics as a boundary between inside and outside where identity itself breeds an intuitive apparatus of recognition."[79] In this framework, simply being "Black" or "gay" implies an infallible knowledge of these identities, their cultural meanings, and proper performance.

This logic wove its way through a range of social movements in the 1960s and 1970s, including those strands of radical feminism that held to a fixed notion of biological womanhood, the racial essentialism of Black and Asian American nationalisms, or the rigid sexual and gender identity politics of lesbian separatism. Yet this was an essentialist identity politics that both gay liberation and one of its most powerful cultural expressions, *Tales of the City*, were resolutely opposed to. Sociologist Elizabeth Armstrong explains that while "[o]ther movements understood identity politics as endorsing the creation of communities of similarity," the gay movement "[defined] the primary goal of gay politics as the expansion of the range of ways to express gay identity."[80] As a result, "Instead of extrapolating from 'what we share is that we are all different from straight people' to the notion 'we are all the same,' the gay identity movement acknowledged, 'yes, together we are different from straight people, but as individuals we are also different from one another.'"[81] Similarly, *Tales'* embrace of the endless surprise of identity, formally modeled in the unfolding of serial narrative, suggested that the only essential aspect of any given cultural or embodied identity was its perpetual openness to change.

With this in mind, Maupin could have taken a stand regarding the importance of having a Black lesbian as a central character, consequently taking time to find out more about what readers found inauthentically Black in his rendering of D'orothea and incorporating those critiques into his writing. We are left to wonder, for instance, if her lesbian sexuality or pretensions to bourgeois life rendered her not adequately "Black" to some readers, or if Maupin's writerly approach to the character seemed underdeveloped to others. Alternatively, Maupin could have outed D'orothea as white, but then told a story about her complex (if problematic) affinity to Black culture. This riskier approach might have allowed the narrative to productively "throw into crisis fixed understandings of race and question, generatively so, what constitutes blackness," just as it had done for gender and sexuality.[82] Sidestepping either of these possibilities, however, Maupin took his critic's interpretation of D'orothea at face value, revealing the character to be literally a white woman in a Black woman's skin.

This seemingly bizarre decision makes sense, however, if we consider Maupin's relationship to D'orothea allegorically. Maupin's lightning-speed ascendance to citywide acclaim as the writer of *Tales* (and by extension, the spokesperson for queer experience) looks not unlike D'orothea's rise to modeling fame, an unexpected outcome of her doing "a couple jobs in dark makeup," which rapidly escalated into a series of bookings. Similarly, Maupin initially passed off *Tales* as a straight story during its first weeks of publication, only later revealing that the serial was a decidedly queer narrative when he began to introduce more explicitly out gay characters like Michael. Both Maupin and D'orothea, then, gained cultural cachet and professional success by passing for something they were not. In Maupin's case, his most dramatic passing gesture was not as straight, but as the universal representative of queer experience, a role that his audience catapulted him into but that he also quickly embraced. In this light, the true problem posed by the introduction and subsequent cancelling out of a Black lesbian character in *Tales* is not fundamentally about the right of a gay male author to narrate Black lives, a right that Maupin certainly possessed and should have exercised with creative care. Rather, I want to suggest that the plot twist by which Maupin attempts to redress accusations of false racial representation capitulates to the letter writer's essentialized notion of Blackness in order to dispel a deeper authorial anxiety: that he, as a white gay man, cannot possibly represent all queer people. By conceding that he can't legitimately claim to represent a Black woman, Maupin implicitly defends his right to narrate the one thing he does presumably "know" or "own," gay and lesbian experience. But such a move allows for the reduction of gay and lesbian experience to the perspective of a singular (white) gay man, without having to directly address the ramifications of this universalization, much as D'orothea never ultimately reckons with her exploitative relationship to Blackness.

The irony of Maupin's decision is that it directly contravened the very ethos of his larger story: that coming out is a process, which can facilitate mutual understanding between radically different kinds of subjects. Maupin's "insider" knowledge of queer culture was not universal but rather a single meaningful perspective that captured the imagination of a mass audience. It was the specificity of *Tales of the City*'s characters that made them available for multiple, competing identifications among a vast demographic of readers. Recalling his relationship to *Tales*' cast of characters, former teacher David Goldman explained, "I'm not sure I identify with either Michael or Jon, his lover. Or Mary Ann. I just felt like I could have been in their group. . . . I would have been at one of Anna Madrigal's parties."[83] Goldman describes a relationship to character that is neither symmetrical identification nor disidentification, but what we might call a sense of *adjacency*, a feeling of recognizing particular kinds of people one might have "hung out" around, or evolved and explored new possibilities with, in the broader milieu of a queer San Francisco. Consequently, the specificity of various queer-of-color experiences of the world—which were historically adjacent to and frequently overlapped with the white-dominated gay social scenes of the Castro and Polk Street neighborhoods—would have been perfectly suited to articulation within Maupin's fictional universe had he held fast to the narrative's organizing values. D'orothea's coming out fails to produce meaningful transformation because, against the radical idea that coming out might allow us to *become* something else or inhabit the social world in new ways, her admission reveals she has always been, and can only be, *a white woman*.

I have lingered on *Tales of the City*'s awkward negotiation of race to show how its productively queer vision could also run up against stubborn understandings of essentialist identity politics in the 1970s, including rigid notions of gay white universalism and Black authenticity. Such moments bear study if we hope to dismantle the tendency in contemporary left political imaginaries to ultimately fix the proper boundaries of racial, gender, and sexual identities, rather than expand those boundaries with imaginative daring and historical nuance. But these representational failures do not mitigate the broader capacity of queer and feminist cultural texts like *Tales* to document and create space for the development of affinities across difference, which is why we would do well not to summarily discard those that fail to measure up to our contemporary norms of political progress. As reader Rima Kittner explained to me, "I didn't really identify with any of the characters—I wasn't single and looking for Mr. Right anymore; I wasn't a gay man . . . and I certainly wasn't cool enough to identify with Mrs. Madrigal. I think perhaps this was one of the reasons why I enjoyed reading it so much; it was a look into worlds I had little or no experience of."[84] Unsurprisingly, where Maupin's queer worldview succeeds most magnificently is in his rich elaboration of the lives of his singular characters, each of whom gave shape to various experiences of coming out, thereby rendering queerness an endless horizon of particularity. It is this very uniqueness of character, combined with our desire as readers to bridge the gap between ourselves and these idiosyncratic, infuriating, yet lovable imaginary beings, that would cement *Tales of the City*'s reputation as one of the most enduring cultural forms for the transmission and reproduction of queer life in the late twentieth century.

5

Stripped to the Bone

*Sequencing Sexual Pluralism in the Comic Strip Work of
Joe Brainard and David Wojnarowicz*

A visual spectacle: we see a full-color, six-panel panorama in what
appears to be a graphic narrative. At the center, in the largest panel,
an image of two men's bodies exploding together. Blood, organs, bone
shattering outward like a red and blue starburst. Surrounding the scene,
smaller panels depict moments of quiet intimacy: a man's hand on the
dead body of his friend; a shirtless man making dinner alone; a man's
face crying beneath the body of a lover: all presumably the same man,
the artist, writer, and AIDS activist David Wojnarowicz (figure 5.1/
plate 6). In this penultimate scene of Wojnarowicz's comic strip memoir, *7 Miles a Second* (1996)—respectively drawn and painted by artists
James Romberger and Marguerite Van Cook—Wojnarowicz describes a
desire to recuperate a queer bond, an impossible closeness, to a former
lover and friend who has died from AIDS. The text accompanying the
image reads, "If I could attach our blood vessels in order to anchor you
to the earth to this present time I would."[1] This attachment is rendered
visually as a literal, and violent, enmeshing of two bodies' blood and guts
that figuratively echoes comic strip form's often jarring visual collisions
between images and words.

The scene asserts one answer to the question, "What can comics do
for queer artists?" Yet it begs us to consider what other possibilities the
comic strip form offers for representing queerness as an erotic intimacy,
political vision, and way of life. Earlier in the narrative, Wojnarowicz
claims, "I'm a prisoner of language that doesn't have a letter or a sign or
gesture that approximates what I'm sensing."[2] Wojnarowicz's statement
speaks to the broader struggle of artists to marshal aesthetic tools for
the purpose of representing the sensate or felt intensities of gay sex. In
this scene, comic strip form allows an inarticulable affective intensity—

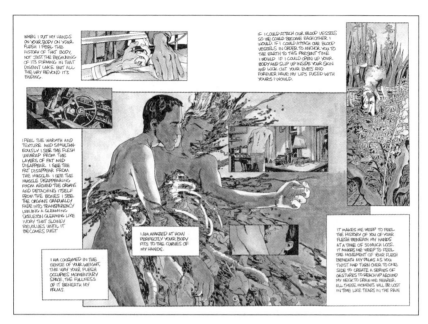

Figure 5.1. "If I could attach our blood vessels in order to anchor you to the earth to this present time I would." David Wojnarowicz, James Romberger, and Marguerite Van Cook, *7 Miles a Second* (Seattle: Fantagraphics Books, 2013 [1996]). Courtesy Estate of David Wojnarowicz; and James Romberger and Marguerite Van Cook.

Wojnarowicz's conflicting feelings of rage and desire amid the chaos of the HIV/AIDS epidemic—to be conveyed through representational density. The agglomeration of individual experiences captured in furiously overlapping panels visually invokes the shared magnitude of feeling that attends the loss of queer proximities in the face of AIDS. The most visible organ spilling out of the two men's bodies at the bottom of the page is a human heart, that vital muscle carrying the pulse of their shared avidity, hurtling beyond our perception. The framed image of two men's bodies physically rent in their attempt to "attach" to one another captures the frenzy of queer interpersonal and erotic ties when faced with the threat of imminent disappearance, while the flurry of accompanying panels and text index the constraints of medical institutions, homophobia, and a destructive disease, keeping that intimacy *squarely* in its place.

In this chapter, I develop a queer theory of comic strip form that can account for such inventive visual experiments in representing the felt experience of nonnormative or queer sexuality. I extend the previous chapter's arguments about gay serial fiction to the sequential movement of the comics medium, which relies on the indefinite production of drawn panels or images in succession. These series collectively produce unpredictable associational connections both within and across visual frames, while also creating opportunities for the infinitely varied combination or juxtaposition of bodies, objects, and meanings animated by the idiosyncratic, queer desires of any given viewer. This perspective considers not simply how gender and sexual dissidents of all stripes are represented in, help create, circulate, and consume modern comics—a worthwhile and necessary endeavor—but also how the formal codes of the comics medium are taken up in creative projects that seek to theorize, and give concrete shape to, multiplicious understandings of queer eroticism and affection at distinct historical moments. In my discussion of *Tales of the City*, I explored how the serial form of installment fiction provided a potent framework for articulating the gay liberationist political strategy of "coming out of the closet" to the surprising and pleasurable consequences of perpetual narrative disclosures about fictional characters' queer genders and sexualities. Here, I reapproach seriality, not as a characteristic of a consistently developing narrative, but as an open-ended sequence of expanding desiring possibilities. I consider how comics form has lent itself to visually rendering a key ideal of the movements for women's and gay liberation, the value of *sexual pluralism*.

I use the term sexual pluralism to describe the pursuit and celebration of an expanded erotic vocabulary or repertoire, which 1970s feminist and gay social movements centralized as one way to attain collective freedom for gender and sexual outlaws variously construed. The wide-reaching cultural impact of the early 1950s Kinsey Reports and the 1966 Masters and Johnson study—which respectively publicized the remarkable sexual diversity of US-Americans and revealed women's capacity for autonomous clitoral pleasure—alongside the growing influence of the sexual revolution, emboldened movements for women's and gay liberation to lay claim to sexual pluralism as a bedrock principle of an emergent feminist and queer ethics. This was a new conception of the sexual "good life," which involved redefining the erotic as encompassing a vast range of sensual contacts beyond heterosexual reproductive sex, valuing nonmonogamous relational forms like cruising, polyamory, and sexual friendships, and articulating previously denigrated sexual fantasies.[3]

To illuminate the link between sexual pluralism and sequential art, I ask how the specificities of nonnormative sex and sexuality at particular junctures in the development of contemporary US queer and feminist cultures collide with and are articulated to the abstract, transhistorical forms that make up the comic strip medium.[4] These include sequential organization, the visual framing (or squaring off) of disjointed panels, image-text combinations, and serialized narrative unfolding. I trace the formal elaboration of queer comics aesthetics by exploring two innovative uses of the comic strip medium by the queer mixed-media artists Joe Brainard and David Wojnarowicz. Both artists were New York residents of lower Manhattan at key moments in the development of US queer and feminist cultures—women's and gay liberation and the AIDS crisis, respectively—and each persistently showed artistic affinity with the comics medium throughout their short-lived but prodigious careers in the 1970s and 1980s.[5] Both artists made their own comic strips (whether hand drawn or produced out of mixed media); both used comic strips cut from newsprint and bound comic books in their collage and assemblages; and both deployed some of the central formal elements of sequential comics across the spectrum of their painting, sculpture, and installations. Despite their shared investment in the affordances of the comics medium, Brainard and Wojnarowicz deployed radically divergent visual styles and sensibilities. Brainard's art is whimsical, campy, and exuberantly optimistic, featuring radiantly colored palates and lavishing visual attention on his most cherished popular culture forms (comics paramount among them). Wojnarowicz's work is relentlessly confrontational, apocalyptic, and explosive, using highly charged ancient iconography (including Mayan and Indigenous American visual folklore), epic natural disaster scenes, and images of the human body decimated by disease and decay to "pile up swirling multiple layers of fragmented, monstrously toxic anthropomorphized cultural detritus."[6]

This contrast is vividly captured in two examples of the artists' most "traditional" comics work: Brainard's drawings for poet Jonathan Williams's chapbook *gAy BC's* in 1976, and Wojnarowicz's extra-large, six-panel abstract comic *Canal Street Piers: Krazy Kat Comic on Wall*, which he originally painted as a mural inside the eponymous New York City gay cruising site in 1983. Produced in a limited-edition print run, *gAy BC's* is a visual poem published as a slim seven-by-eleven-inch chapbook.[7] Every page features two large, four-inch-square comic strip panels, each corresponding to a letter of the alphabet. The panels depict close-ups of various gay sex scenes or eroticized male body parts sketched in graphite pencil: a flaccid cock and balls, a perked nipple being pinched, a man's mouth encircling the head of a penis, a man being fucked from behind (figure 5.2). The images are eminently playful, freely depicting sexual partners engaged in pleasurable acts, which entice us to imagine reaching out to touch or even participate. Williams's poem, printed at the beginning of the booklet, consists of the English alphabet rewritten so that each letter refers to a different man's name, followed by their sexual idiosyncrasies: "CHUCKS, of course, suck"; "EDS are also said to give head"; "MALCOLMS come miles!" Brainard's drawings, however, do not explicitly refer back to these imaginary men, since the figures in each panel go unnamed, or else are reduced to singular body parts. Brainard inhabits comics form to represent gay sex as an associational, freewheeling sequence defined by nothing other than the distinctive tendencies of plural CHUCKS, EDS, MALCOLMS, and WALTERS, who could correspond to any of the men depicted, and in infinite combinations. *gAy BC's* then literally outlines gay sex, not as a fixed taxonomy of "deviant" sexual practices, clear sexual identities, or political programs, but a *queer alphabet of desire*, an open-ended procession of sexual positions, pleasures, and "types" (the FRANKS and PAULS of the world who variously "suck," "fuck," "tease," and "please") that any reader can project themselves into.

Alternatively, in his mural *Canal Street Piers: Krazy Kat Comic on Wall*, Wojnarowicz reproduces a classic two-tiered, six-panel comic strip, but contorts the form and content of this traditional type of comedic or gag strip. Instead of six equivalent square panels ending in a punchline, we see a chaotic combination of unevenly shaped trapezoids pushing against each other in a crowded assemblage (figure 5.3). Each frame contains a disturbing image of comic book violence painted in varied artistic styles: a giant pterodactyl head terrorizes an urban skyline; a car careens down a highway about to be struck by lightning; a hand discharges a pistol with the stylized words "KRAK" underneath;

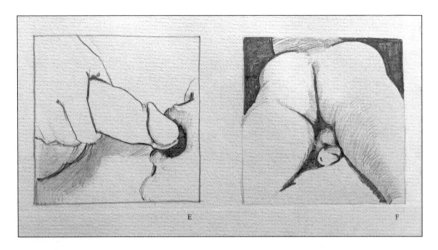

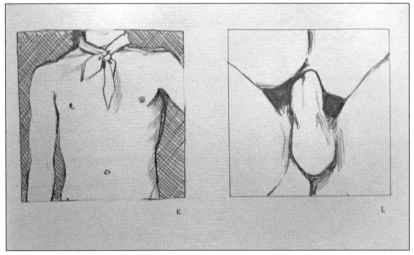

Figure 5.2. Jonathan Williams and Joe Brainard craft a visual alphabet of gay desire in *gAy BC's* (Champaign, IL: Finial Press, 1976).

a muscular man with a Siamese twin head bandages a bullet wound; and the classic comic strip characters Krazy Kat and Ignatz play out one of their most recognizable gags, Ignatz the mouse pummeling the oblivious Kat with a brick. In the eroticized context of the Canal Street piers, where gay men notoriously pursued anonymous sex, Wojnarowicz's crushing together of different icons of comic strip violence provides an abstract representation of the aggressive intensities of queer desire,

Figure 5.3. David Wojnarowicz, *Canal Street Piers: Krazy Kat Comic on Wall* (1983).

which frequently lead to the pleasurable interpenetration of gay men's bodies (obliquely gestured toward by the bloody bullet wound of the muscular he-man). Because the mural presents an abstract comic with no obvious linear narrative, its panels invite the viewer to read them in any sequence, formally replicating the spontaneous collision of gay sexual ambitions jostling in the charged cruising space of the piers. Finally, the seemingly out of place Krazy Kat gag, whose humor emerges from the irony that Ignatz is secretly (and queerly) in love with the Kat whom he regularly pummels, reminds us that beneath the anonymous, sexual energy of the piers may lie deeper affection, even love, between gay men, who symbolically speaking, "smash bricks" against each other night after night.[8]

Despite the dramatically different visual styles and affective registers Brainard and Wojnarowicz bring to their work, both *gAy BC's* and *Canal Street Piers* are forms of queer comics abstraction that exploit the medium's unrestricted sequentiality to represent gay sex as a plural, non-deterministic terrain of erotic potentialities. Consider that both comics inhabit highly standardized sequences—the English alphabet and the six-panel comic strip—but remake them into erotically charged, associational open sets, in which each letter or panel signifies in multiple ways. In fact, the aesthetic and conceptual form of Brainard and Williams's *gAy BC's* anticipated Dr. Charles Silverstein and Edmund White's bestselling 1978 book *The Joy of Gay Sex*. Modeled after its wildly successful heterosexual counterpart, the *Joy of Sex: A Gourmet Guide to Lovemaking* (1972), this popular primer on gay intimacy was organized as a series of alphabetical entries that affirmingly described distinct aspects of gay male sensual life (Blow Jobs, Clubs, Dirty Talk, Exhibitionism, etc.), accompanied by detailed, erotic pencil drawings of various sexual positions. Moreover, the specific affective feel and tone of Brainard's and Wojnarowicz's comics work—one languidly playful, the other aggressively ballistic—registers not only the unique aesthetic sensibilities of different creators, but alternate versions of sexual pluralism at distinct moments in the history of late twentieth-century women's and gay liberation. Brainard developed his art practice during the ebullient queer and feminist 1970s, while Wojnarowicz became an artist-activist under the apocalyptic shadow of the HIV/AIDS epidemic. This chapter then, also marks a shift from the 1970s into the 1980s, exploring how the central values of movements for women's and gay liberation conceptually mutated and took on different aesthetic expressions under the conditions of a renewed wave of murderous homophobia, a national backlash against feminism, and the emergent coalitional politics of AIDS activism.

Brainard's and Wojnarowicz's most prolific engagements with the comics medium occurred during a creative renaissance in countercultural and avant-garde comics production in the US, which was heavily inspired by the sexual revolution, the hippie counterculture, and the rise of women's and gay liberation. A number of scholars have shown how independent comics in the 1970s and 1980s, including underground anthologies and series such as *Wimmen's Comix* and *Gay Comix*, took advantage of the medium's social marginalization as trash culture to express radical political views and fantasies of sexual freedom that would have been censored in more "respectable" popular mediums.[9] In my analysis, however, I suggest that Brainard's and Wojnarowicz's very peripheralness to these countercultural and independent comics endeavors allows us to see something more broadly compelling about the comics medium than its mere social marginalization as an outsider artform predictably taken up by those who inhabit oppressed social identities.

That "something" is the comics medium's ability to give shape to, or visually construct, so-called deviant erotic fantasies and sexual practices by encouraging artists to keep drawing different versions of gay sex over and over in countless images. I say that comics "encourage" artists in this way because the medium's fundamental creative logic of handmade visual frames arranged in sequence is driven by an additive or proliferative impulse that produces *plurality* as its visual and conceptual sine qua non. Comics frequently require that a single body or object be drawn numerous times across many panels in a sequential strip, so every depiction of that figure will be slightly different, multiplying its representation across space. Moreover, there is nothing necessarily linear, teleological, or goal-oriented about traditional serial comic strip panels aside from the fact that they unfold one image after another.[10] Certainly, there exist artistic traditions in comics that have established particular organizations of comic strip panels as norms of narrative unfolding. This includes the six-panel sequence arranged in two or three tiers, a classic structure of the comedic gag strip that fits to one page and concludes with a visual punch line. Yet depending on how they are creatively produced and subsequently viewed by an individual reader, comic strip sequences can accrue numerous potential starting points, unfold in any visual or conceptual direction, expand to any length and size, and be perceived at multiple scales—from an individual panel to a complete strip to a full-length graphic narrative or series. The same is true, of course, of erotic desire, a widely shared, yet highly unpredictable affective force that can be activated by the simple training of one's eyes upon new objects of attention, which, like discreet comic strip panels, magnetize our libidinal energies, but only within a larger network of *other* bodies and objects that call to us in different ways. Seen from this vantage, the unpredictable procession of sequential panels that constitute any given comic strip is ripe for articulation with queerness as a description of the unpredictability of all forms of sexuality, encompassing erotic desire's inexhaustible potential to inaugurate new sexual sequences.

Rather than reconstruct the cultural history of LGBTQ comics production, I develop a local account of the queer formal architecture of

comics in the sequential art of Brainard and Wojnarowicz as two potent
sites where the erotic plurality of gender- and sexual-nonconforming
lives and desires were creatively yielded up to viewers in stylistically
divergent but conceptually resonant ways. I focus on two of the artists'
most sustained and imaginatively inventive uses of comic strip form:
Brainard's "If Nancy Was . . ." series, a serially and spontaneously produced collection of abstract portraits of the (very queer) comic strip
character Nancy, and Wonjarowicz's *7 Miles a Second*, an avant-garde
graphic autobiography of the late artist collaboratively produced with
James Romberger. In the early 1970s, Brainard adopted Nancy in a series
of over one hundred paper and canvas works collectively titled "If Nancy
Was . . ."[11] Using mixed-media including pen and ink, collage, colored
pencil, gouache, and everyday materials such as Kleenex and stamps,
Brainard depicted Nancy inhabiting numerous "deviant" sexual and social positions (as transgender, high on acid, having anal sex, acting in
a porno, and more). Entries in the series ranged from five-by-five-inch
squares to fifteen-by-twelve-inch rectangular frames, thus experiment-
ing with the visual scale of comic strip panels as much as Nancy's visual
form. Through these imaginative permutations, Brainard used the serialized character of sequential comics to depict sexuality as a seemingly
boundless chain of unanticipated whimsical installments. This practice
gave material form to early gay liberation's view of sexuality as a joy-
fully unrestrained performance of unfolding erotic possibilities that
worked against the consolidation of a unified gay identity. Little more
than a decade later, in David Wojnarowicz's graphic memoir, *7 Miles a
Second* (1988–93 [published 1996]), the artist and his collaborators James
Romberger and Marguerite Van Cook used the visual disjoint between
comic strip panels to formally dramatize the experience of social alienation and physical pain associated with being a queer person with AIDS.
Their techniques included extremely altering the traditional visual organization of comics panels (some diagonally bisecting, or stretching out
across, entire pages), and hugely expanding their size to symbolically
capture the monumental scale of grief and rage that accompanied the
loss of loved ones and the violence of government neglect in the face of
AIDS.[12]

Each of these works was respectively produced at a historical moment
when the meaning and performance of queer sexuality in the US was

in flux, and each roughly coincides with widespread acclaim for and critical reception of Brainard and Wojnarowicz's broader creative oeuvres as distinctly gay or queer artists. In both instances, encounters with Brainard and Wojnarowicz's dynamic, erotically charged sequences have the potential to disperse the direction of a viewers' most intensely held sexual attachments, desires, and values across an expanded field of intimate possibilities, so that the structure of comics enacts sexual pluralism as its psychic and affective outcome. As artists who never set out to be distinctly gay comics creators, Brainard and Wojnarowicz nonetheless engaged queerly with the medium as much through formal innovation in the comic strip as through actual visual representations of LGBTQ identity, sex, and sociality. Thus, I identify a shared investment across Brainard's and Wojnarowicz's art practice in using comics form to think through a central paradox of queer sexuality: its simultaneous specificity, or distinctness to individual embodied experiences, *and* its grand generality, attaching to many bodies that share similarly queer erotic and sensual experiences, affective states, and affectionate attachments at particular moments in late twentieth-century US culture. Because a comic strip is a visual assemblage composed of disjointed panels, comics provided Brainard and Wojnarowicz a ready-made formal structure for capturing the specificity of sexuality to any given body (depicted in each discreet panel), as well as its overarching sociality, or shared resonance between bodies (depicted in the multiple associations between panels).[13] We might call this quality the medium's *queer generosity*: for Brainard and Wojnarowicz, the comic strip was one place where the seemingly isolating experience of gay sexuality—its irreducible distinctness alongside its perceived stigma—could be made spectacularly visible, not once but over and over in endless permutations, so that it might become an aggregate experience hailing countless gender and sexual outlaws who together made up something like a culture and a social force. A queer sequence if there ever was one.

"If Nancy Was . . ."

> TIM DLUGOS: *Do you consider yourself a "gay artist"? Is there such a thing as a "gay art" outside of subject matter? Is there a "gay sensibility" that infuses your work? . . .*

JOE BRAINARD: I think it does . . . but I think it's sort of closing
    out. . . . I don't think it's that important to most kids now . . . while at
    one point, in my life, it was an issue . . .

TD: *Well, is it a matter of subject, or what's it a matter of?*

JB: It's a matter of being aware of it. . . . Sometimes it's a subject mat-
    ter, obviously; with a drawing of two guys fucking it's obviously
    subject matter. But I think it's more than that. Most artists are very
    straight . . . in their seriousness and in what they're trying to do. . . .
    I'm a lot more . . . ga-ga than that—but on purpose. No, not on
    purpose.

TD: *Sort of a ludic quality, playful?*

JB: Yes. (pause) I'm not really sure that has anything to do with being
    gay, though, 'cause I think my work is very sensual, very lush . . . but
    I'm not sure that has to do with being gay. If I was straight it might be
    that way too. I don't know.

—"The Joe Brainard Interview," *Little Caesar* (1977)

In a 1977 interview with poet Tim Dlugos for the arts journal *Little Caesar*, Joe Brainard gave a meandering and inconsistent answer to the question "Do you consider yourself a 'gay artist'?"[14] Brainard initially affirms the existence of a distinctly "gay sensibility" infusing his art, but then quickly denies that such a sensibility has any meaning for a new generation of youth, whom he believes now consider alternative sexuality a political non-issue. Seconds later, however, he reiterates that his art is indeed less "straight" than that of his contemporaries—"a lot more ga-ga" as he puts it. Then again, he follows up by stating that such a unique style may have nothing to do with being gay at all. In the brief space of this dialogue, Brainard manages to suggest that gayness—both the sexual orientation and its associated aesthetic "sensibility"—is, at once: a question of public, collective concern ("it was an issue"), but also less politically salient than in the past; something utterly obvious ("two guys fucking"), yet also murky and ineffable ("I'm not really sure that has anything to do with being gay"); an identifiable shared style ("very lush"), but also just an individual artist's idiosyncrasy ("If I was straight it might be that way too"). Brainard asserts different versions of what gayness might mean but subsequently undermines each of these characterizations as perhaps no more solid than "all that." Four questions in, he concedes: "I don't know."

Brainard's ambivalent response to the question of being a gay artist in the late 1970s might seem at odds with the spirit of his historical moment. As a gay man living in lower Manhattan during this period, Brainard would have witnessed the efflorescence of gay liberation with its attendant call to make queer sexuality public by "coming out," declaring that "gay is good," and politicizing alternative sexualities. Yet in the face of a growing investment in fixing same-sex eroticism as a gay *identity*, or transforming it into a political weapon, Brainard consistently celebrates the shapeshifting element of queer sexuality. This was the surprising ability of a seemingly neutral fact, same-sex desire, to collide with and radically reshape so many aspects of one's being—from aesthetic sensibility to interpersonal habits—sometimes a lot, sometimes a little or not at all. For Brainard, sexuality was something that unfolded in unpredictable sequence, a processional force that could take one form in a single instance ("fucking obviously") and become something else altogether the next. Throughout Brainard's artistic career, instead of attempting to categorically secure the definition of gayness, or else concede the impossibility of representing something so mutable as same-sex desire, he recurrently chose to give shape to queerness in the unrestricted structure of sequential artforms.

Brainard's whimsical and open-ended series—present in his poetic work as the euphonic inventory of memories from his queer adolescence in *I Remember*, and in his visual work as nonhierarchical sequential images like the alphabetical gay sex sketches in *gAy BC's*—formally produced the effect of sexual pluralism as a pleasurable disorientation of, or swerving away from, linear conceptions of sexuality and libidinal desire. Brainard, then, repeatedly expressed his gayness not through direct personal disclosure or political commitments, but through his careful choice of visual icons and his affinity to distinct objects of popular culture, specific color schemes, or wordplays. Among his favorites were the pansy flower and the comic strip character Nancy, whose names also indexed epithets for effeminate boys, and all of which could be considered gay by association more than by definition. Consequently, when Brainard replies to the question "Do you consider yourself a 'gay artist'?" with the statement "I don't know," he honestly admits that gay sexuality is, in the final instance, unknowable, but not for that reason *unrepresentable*: because it can appear in so many guises, mean so many things to different people, and take countless aesthetic forms. Brainard sought not to pin down the ultimate meaning of homosexuality, but to give it as many forms as one could imagine. Such an associational view of sexuality overlapped with those elements of women's and gay liberation that celebrated the unrestricted qualities of erotic desire, namely the remarkable heterogeneity of intimacies and attachments that were possible in a world where gender and sexuality were unhinged from their normative trajectories.

By the end of the 1960s, the US-American sexual revolution had shaken the foundation of the heterosexual nuclear family, granting women greater sexual autonomy through access to birth control, legitimizing men's desire to postpone marriage and pursue nonmonogamous relations (typified by the polyamorous communes of the hippie counterculture), and reclassifying free sexual expression as a variety of political freedom. The women's and gay liberation movements were, in part, a sustained critique of the masculine bias of the sexual revolution, which granted straight men greater latitude in exploring the entire gamut of their erotic interests without fundamentally undermining heteropatriarchy.[15] As Jane Gerhard has documented, in the early 1970s, radical feminists concentrated on clitoral pleasure as an embodied or experiential site of political possibility for women. Drawing upon the findings of the groundbreaking 1966 Masters and Johnson study *Human Sexual Response*, feminists argued that women's biological capacity for autonomous orgasm without penetration irrevocably undermined the presumed primacy of men to women's sexual life. Simultaneously, the mass migration of LGBTQ youth to major urban centers like New York City, San Francisco, and Los Angeles brought unprecedented numbers of queer people into new proximity, encouraging the growth of thriving gay erotic environments. These included the gay male cruising cultures of lower Manhattan's West Side piers, a growing national network of queer bars, dance halls, bathhouses, and sex clubs, and gay and lesbian collective living experiments.

The women's and gay liberation movements often, though not always, had different ideas about what counted as politically liberatory sex: on the whole, feminists were more invested in reducing the sexual objectification of women and making them willful agents of their own pleasure, while gay liberationists frequently fought for the freedom to express gay sexuality publicly and legitimize so-called deviant sexual practices like same-sex eroticism, promiscuity, sodomy, fisting, and BDSM. Yet by the early 1970s, a shared value of sexual pluralism had become an essential thread in the imaginative fabric of feminist and gay politics and social life. This included the capacity to explore the full range of one's bodily pleasures consensually with others, the pursuit of friendship and political allyship out of surprising sensual contacts, and the development of sex, romance, and companionship outside the limits of the heterosexual family life. This new sexual ethos was increasingly disseminated to mass audiences through innovative literary and cultural representations of feminist and gay sexual exploration, experimentation, and diversity in a range of popular genres and mediums.

In her bestselling 1973 feminist novel *Fear of Flying*, Erica Jong introduced the concept of the "zipless fuck" to describe the perfect one-night stand, an ideal passionate erotic encounter between strangers with no emotional attachment, usually initiated by a sexually empowered woman. Authors of 1970s lesbian and gay literature frequently described the complex affinities developed between sexual outlaws through serial erotic encounters that take place in queer social spaces and subcultures: from the drug-fueled sexual promiscuity of New York City's disco scene in Andrew Holleran's *Dancer from the Dance* (1978) to Larry Mitchell's description of free-loving faeries, queens, and "faggots" in his gay fable *The Faggots and Their Friends between Revolutions* (1977); from Rita Mae Brown's bold depiction of a sexually adventurous lesbian runaway in *Rubyfruit Jungle* (1973) to the sensual lesbian friendships described in Audre Lorde's *Zami: A New Spelling of My Name* (1982). In these texts, gay and lesbian camaraderie and community is forged through erotic vulnerability, where the porousness of sexual identities, including an openness to becoming out gays and lesbian or inhabiting queer ways of life, was materially enacted through bodily receptivity to others in a spirit of mutual pleasure. In all of these examples, sex between women and queers variously construed was remade not as sin or decadence, but as an unpredictable sequence of physical encounters with others—the experience of abutting other "frames" of reference through sensual communion that might include, in Lorde's words, "dancing hard," "playing," and even "fighting"—which had ethical, practical, and interpersonal consequences for the flourishing of feminist and queer lives.[16] Brainard's characteristically idiosyncratic entry into this emergent culture of sexual pluralism would be facilitated by his own years-long queer affinity to the classic US-American comic strip character Nancy, whose as-yet-to-be imagined erotic life Brainard chose to invent and elaborate in the context of late twentieth-century queer and feminist sexual revolution.

Between 1963 and 1978, Brainard visually adopted Nancy in a series of single-panel paper and canvas works that functioned as enlarged comic strip frames.[17] In these panels—most slightly larger than a letter-sized sheet of paper—Brainard depicts Nancy inhabiting myriad scenarios, taking on different shapes (as a ball, as an ashtray), formed from eclectic materials (made of Kleenex, drawn on stamps), and inhabiting distinct aesthetic styles (as if painted by Willem de Kooning, as if drawn by Larry Rivers). These formal variations compelled viewers to imagine a seemingly immutable comics icon as a potentially queer symbol performing multiple, nonsynchronous, embodied and erotic identities. Created by comics artist Ernie Bushmiller in 1933, Nancy headlined her own comic strip daily for more than five decades. In Bushmiller's world, she is a Bushmiller sly trickster figure who perpetually breaks rules, causes minor catastrophes, and pulls clever pranks on neighbors and friends. Drawn as a highly simplified caricature of a plump, homely young girl with a round, prickly mop of hair, a nondescript schoolgirl's uniform, and a flat nose and mouth, Nancy was at once eminently generic and utterly iconic.[18]

In his loving, and often perverse, appropriations, Brainard exploited certain generic qualities of Nancy's character—including her butch gender presentation, her mischievous pleasure in upsetting conventional gender roles, and even her name, which referenced a classic epithet for an effeminate man, the "nancy," "pansy," or "nelly" boy—to show how they surprisingly magnetized central elements of queer sexuality.[19] In Nancy, Brainard found a figure through whom he could express his own sense of gayness as a state of permanent childhood: playful, creative, "ludic," and non–goal-oriented.[20] Almost every image in the series is accompanied by a caption that begins "If Nancy Was . . . ," followed by a description of each permutation of Nancy's form. "If Nancy Was . . ." functions as a counterfactual conditional statement, or a phrase that invites one to conceive, even if only hypothetically, what Nancy would or could be under other circumstances. The sheer variety of contexts and materials into which Nancy's seemingly stable drawn form could be inserted, alongside the repeated, yet indefinitely open-ended phrase

"If Nancy Was . . . ," suggests the capacity of a serialized sequence of individual paper works to inhabit comic strip form for the purpose of articulating something queer not only about Nancy herself, but about the comics medium as one that invites the play of multiplicious desires, fantasies, and erotic identifications.

Each image in the series activates numerous desires—sexual, comedic, sensory, intellectual—and each produces a jolt of pleasure in seeing Nancy inhabit a new and unexpected identity, aesthetic style, or physical form. Yet each image also confuses the assumed location of any given attachment, that is, where desire emanates from (the creator, the viewer, the image itself) and what direction it is going. As a result, while any given entry in the series can initially be read as a distinctive instance of Brainard's queer misuse of Nancy, the countless affinities, erotic intensities, or simple fascinations each image can stimulate in the spectator makes the collected work itself a vehicle for spreading queer pleasures across the social field. The mobility of potential alternative satisfactions and desires is particularly apparent in those entries in the series that explicitly reference queer sexuality, including "If Nancy Was a Boy," "If Nancy Was a Sailor's Basket," and "If Nancy Knew What Wearing Green and Yellow on a Thursday Meant" (figures 5.4 and 5.5/plates 7 and 8). These three installments, all completed in 1972, produce a powerful and erotically charged associational sequence that links various forms of queerness (gender nonnormativity and gay desire) to Nancy's drawn figure. Together, they provide a lens for seeing all other images in the series as laden with sensual investments and possibilities, even when sex, gender, and sexuality are not explicitly referenced.

In "If Nancy Was a Boy," Nancy appears at the center of the page lifting her skirt to reveal male genitalia.[21] Brainard draws Nancy with her characteristic, generic smile as she playfully displays her body to the reader. Below her exposed figure are the words "If Nancy Was a Boy." A series of receding red lines connects this sentence to Nancy's feet, as though to indicate where our eyes should move, up from the statement toward its final materialization in Nancy's "male" form. The image surprises and titillates on multiple levels. First is the shocking bodily exposure of a mass-cultural figure traditionally thought of as lacking any identifying human physiology or sexuality. Brainard grants Nancy a gendered body, but one opposite to our expectations, thereby rendering

Figure 5.4a. Joe Brainard, "If Nancy Was a Boy" (1972). Courtesy
Tibor de Nagy Gallery, New York; Ron Padgett; and the Colby
College of Museum of Art.

her accessible to a range of possible erotic and bodily fantasies. These
might include the wish to be more than one gender, to present as female
despite having male genitalia, or to occlude one's femaleness altogether.
By lifting her skirt, Nancy covers over what might be her breasts, so that
any other physiological markers of gender are explicitly masked.

Second, Nancy's wistful smile, traditionally representing her generic
mischievous (even sadistic) gratification in one gag or another, now
comes to have specificity in relation to this surprising revelation: Nancy

Figure 5.4b. Joe Brainard, "If Nancy Was a Sailor's Basket" (1972). Courtesy Tibor de Nagy Gallery, New York; Ron Padgett; and the Colby College of Museum of Art.

seems eminently pleased with her exposure. Brainard suggests that Nancy could have queer impulses of her own, including being an exhibitionist, imbuing her not only with a gendered bodied but with a psychology of desire as well. Finally, the perspectival lines that recede toward Nancy's lower half almost demand that we look at her exposed penis, drawn as a simple icon with no adornment. Here, Brainard's own erotic preferences register on the page: his long history of drawing the male form, and of desiring men's bodies in his own sexual life, are present before us in the phallus. Brainard could have easily drawn Nancy with boy's clothing. The choice to render "boy" as an index of biologically male genitalia not only directly references potential gay male sexuality, but also figuratively plays on the idea that a "nancy" or effeminate man is really a boy in girl's clothing.

The image thus proliferates queer desire and pleasure across at least three locations: first, in the artist who imaginatively articulates Nancy to a range of nonnormative fantasies, scenarios, and imagery; second, in the viewer who takes pleasure in Nancy's various iterations and projects their own libidinal interests onto each of her queer performances; and

Figure 5.5. Joe Brainard, "If Nancy Knew What Wearing Green and Yellow on a Thursday Meant" (1972). Courtesy Tibor de Nagy Gallery, New York; Ron Padgett; and the Colby College of Museum of Art.

finally, in Nancy herself, an icon who is not only placed into a variety of deviant positions, but also seems to contain qualities that resonate with them, such as gender mutability and exhibitionism. Yet because the scene is presented with no context outside of the immediate frame, it is impossible to pin down any singular expression of queerness—as gay, lesbian, or transgender identity—in the creator, the spectator, or the icon. On the basis of this single image, we could not prove that the artist is unequivocally "gay." Similarly, we could not say that Nancy is necessarily (or only) transgender, since the mere fact of her having a penis could have countless meanings including, but not limited to, transgender embodiment. In each image Brainard unfolds, desire becomes a moving target both within any single panel, but also across multiple, serialized panels in a sequence.[22]

The work of "If Nancy Was a Boy" in expanding the locations of queer sexuality becomes more apparent as a broader conceptual project of the series when placed in relation to other entries that explicitly reference divergent sexualities and genders. In "If Nancy Was a Sailor's Basket," the central image is a cropped magazine photograph of a US sailor carrying his cap; a small drawing of Nancy smiling and waving is collaged over his crotch.[23] The image creates an association with "If Nancy Was a Boy" by visually and rhetorically referencing the phallus, but it appears as an alternative sequential possibility: in the first image, Nancy has a penis, while in the next, she stands in for one. The potential pleasures and meanings of the scene abound. The picture of the sailor may very well come from a generic periodical, yet it also references gay men's pornographic magazines and the gay fetishization of the sailor as sexual icon in the post-WWII period. And yet Nancy's smiling visage both points us to the sailor's penis while obfuscating our access to it. Such subtle play on the visibility and invisibility of the "basket" in question opens up numerous possible desiring positions for the observer. The image might suggest a yearning to be physically proximate to a sailor's basket (which could be both a gay or straight inclination). Alternatively, it could imply the wish to *be* a sailor's basket (either in the sense of taking the place of his penis or performing "the basket" sexual position, in which case *Nancy* would be the sailor's sexual object lowering herself onto his penis). Or perhaps, it merely pokes fun at the sailor's masculinity by suggesting that his basket is really just a fictional girl.

In these previous images, the phallus—in the form of an actual drawn penis or a euphemistic "basket"—magnetizes various queer erotic affinities without reducing them to a single gay male identity. Alternatively, in "If Nancy Knew What Wearing Green and Yellow on a Thursday Meant," queerness becomes unhinged from any given sexual organ and instead attaches to specific attire.[24] The image is based on the assumption that Nancy knows that wearing green and yellow on a Thursday means being gay—which was a 1950s bit of folklore used to identify potential "queers"—while her smile implies a sly satisfaction in that knowledge, which may or may not be shared with a given spectator. In using a seemingly anachronistic reference, Brainard makes queerness available to different generations of potential viewers in the 1970s and after. For some, the reference might resonate as a childhood memory of the ways that gayness was policed in the 1950s; for so-called "liberated youth," it might appear as a mysterious reference to something illicit about Nancy and her desires that is worth uncovering or inhabiting, since this insider knowledge clearly seems to gratify her. The specificity of one experience of gayness—Brainard's childhood memories of learning how others jokingly identified and stigmatized presumed homosexuality—becomes available for multiple meanings across sexualities, genders, *and* generations. Here, Nancy also appears dressed as a boy, in a way that she was denied in "If Nancy Was a Boy." The boyish quality of Nancy's ensemble, then, potentially associates her with butch lesbian identity (and female masculinity more broadly), even as the implication of her color scheme points to *any* gay identity.

In these preceding instances, the construction "If Nancy Was . . ." presents a nonessentialist view of gender and sexual identities, and their attendant desires or erotic aims, as something that can be "anything." In various images Nancy is both male and female (or neither), both subject and object, both desired and desiring. In her essay "Orientations: Toward a Queer Phenomenology," Sara Ahmed suggests how this multiplication of queer subject positions might elicit a generous or welcoming stance toward moments of gender and sexual disorientation: "For me, the important task is . . . asking what our orientation towards queer moments of deviation will be. If the object slips away, if its face becomes inverted, it looks odd, strange, out of place, what will we do? . . . A queer phenomenology would involve an orientation toward queer, a way to inhabit the world that gives support to those whose lives and loves make them appear oblique, strange, and out of place."[25] Every iteration of Nancy in Brainard's series represents an object—Nancy herself—that is "inverted, odd, strange, out of place." And every subsequent entry encourages us to respond to such moments by demanding more permutations so that sequential form, far from producing a linear movement to "straighten" or discipline "queer moments of deviation," fulfills a wish to extend them indefinitely. Brainard conceives of sequential panels, then, not as mere flat repetitions or attempts to reproduce a gendered, sexual, or formal ideal, but imaginative opportunities to perpetually shapeshift by performing, inhabiting, or depicting gender and sexuality differently, and nearly always with a smile.

Such shapeshifting similarly extends to the range of materials Brainard uses in various entries, both the physical substances he constructs Nancy out of (Kleenex, collaged paper, stamps) and the aesthetic tools he uses to render her (colored pencil, crayon, paint). In "If Nancy Was Just a Used Kleenex," Nancy's smiling face is burned into a dirty, crumpled Kleenex tissue.[26] Kleenex's multiple associations with bodily fluid—its use in absorbing tears and mucus as well as cleaning up ejaculate—transmutes Nancy into a porous surface for numerous physical emissions and sensations. By presenting Nancy as materializing out of this throwaway fiber, Brainard highlights how even ephemeral materials are laden with erotic and affective significance (that someone might need to reach for a Kleenex after viewing any of the images in "If Nancy Was . . ." also implies some of the possible physiological effects of its visual—and symbolically masturbatory—pleasures). In every iteration, Nancy simultaneously inhabits and deconstructs an identity, desire, or figuration without judgment or a demand that the viewer abandon their possible investment in it.

For instance, in "If Nancy Was an Underground Comic Character," Brainard draws a black-and-white, two-panel pornographic comic strip of Nancy frantically masturbating with a dildo in her mouth, which she then inserts inside her vagina (figure 5.6/plate 9).[27] The strip slyly pokes fun at the puerile visual imaginary of the male-dominated underground comix scene of the 1970s, which facilitated a new era of free sexual expression in sequential art, but did so from a predominantly straight male point of view. By using a rudimentary drawing style overflowing

Figure 5.6. Joe Brainard, "If Nancy Was an Underground Comic Character" (1972).
Courtesy Pavel Zoubok Gallery.

with frenetic movement lines, Brainard connects the dots between male underground artists' messy visual style and the aggressive intensity of straight male sexual fantasies. Rather than trash this hypermasculine "comix" style, Brainard (and by extension Nancy) tries it on for size. Nancy, then, is both subjected to this underground aesthetic, but in doing so, also becomes an agent of her own pleasure, unabashedly willing to "leak," shake, and expose herself regardless of who is watching. Ironically, Nancy boldly enacts the radical feminist value of women's autonomous clitoral pleasure, but within the very formal logic of a traditionally heterosexual male comix style. In Brainard's imagination, Nancy comes to offer an alternative affective history of queerness, not as oppositional identity but as mutable site of performance and play, one possible erotic expression or identity after another in an endless unfolding.

Sexuality doesn't figure immediately in all the images, and so it can appear fleeting or ephemeral, take on multiple meanings, or linger from one image to the next. In "If Nancy Was a Building in New York City," Brainard draws the skyline of Manhattan in a long horizontal frame that looks like a single comic strip panel (figure 5.7/plate 10).[28] Nancy's iconic pincushion hair appears as a physical interruption in urban space near the right end of the image. Easily mistakable for a rising sun, Nancy's hair emerges exactly where Brainard would draw the buildings of Manhattan's Lower West Side, which was coincidentally both his place of residence and the epicenter of gay liberation at the same moment of his serial experiment in 1971 (presciently, the flagship newsletter of gay liberation was called *Gay Sunshine*). In this context, Nancy becomes an ebullient expression of queer difference exploding from the rigidly phallic New York skyline, representing freedom not in any single political program or manifesto, but iconically, as a kind of queer Statue of Liberty.

This radiant possibility captured in "If Nancy Was a Building in New York City" is the signal characteristic of the series as a whole: namely, its understanding of the imagination as a distinctly queer force that drives the procession of sequential images, rather than any predetermined hierarchy, teleology, or governing order. The grammatical formulation "If Nancy Was . . ." functions as a seductive encouragement to fill in a presumably infinite number of erotic, aesthetic, affective, and conceptual possibilities that might complete the phrase, not merely in the present but also historically, or in the creative past. (In a number of the entries,

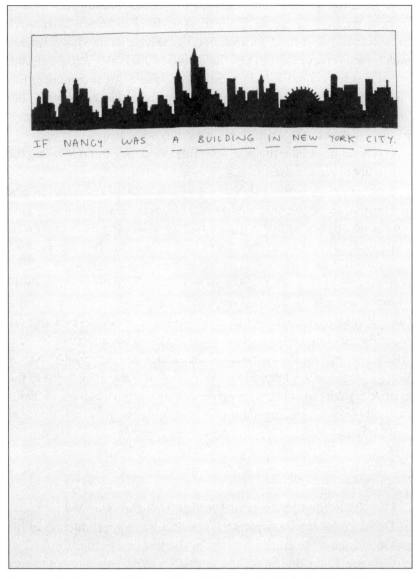

Figure 5.7. Joe Brainard, "If Nancy Was a Building in New York City" (1972). Courtesy Tibor de Nagy Gallery, New York; Ron Padgett; and the Colby College of Museum of Art.

Nancy infiltrates historically significant artworks, monuments, or aesthetic styles, from Leonardo da Vinci's sketchbook to Mount Rushmore). In "If Nancy Was a Boy," for instance, the revelation of what is hidden underneath Nancy's skirt can be understood doubly as a literal exposure of unexpected genitalia *and* a symbolic exposure of a secret queerness that was potentially always there from Nancy's creative inception. To believe this is the case requires a leap of the imagination, not only projecting ourselves into the seemingly simplistic comic strip world of *Nancy* (and presumably under the skirt of its title character), but embracing the mutability of gender itself as well.

To imagine scenarios such as these necessitates the invention of new or alternate sequences that might unfold from the reality of Nancy having always already been a boy, or a ball, or a drawing by Leonardo da Vinci, or a sexy blonde, or President Lincoln, or an interior decorator, or a building in New York City. Most telling about the series is the imagination it required for a white gay man from Tulsa, Oklahoma, to identify with and inhabit the creative world of a caricatured, sly, 1930s mass-cultural young girl, and then to make her queer potential available for countless possible viewers across genders, generations, sexualities, and artistic sensibilities. Taken together, the entries that compose "If Nancy Was . . ." represent a fabulous performance of queer imagination, the creative capacity to conceive of every identity category as a site of "trouble" and pleasure opening out into an indefinite but abundant future of possibilities.

Stripped to the Bone

In his 1990 framed photo print *Untitled (One Day This Kid . . .)*, artist David Wojnarowicz depicts a black-and-white reproduction of his childhood school portrait encircled by the text of a politically charged monologue. From one angle, the image is a hyperbolically crude version of a classic single-panel comic strip, starkly juxtaposing words and image. The monologue is composed of a series of declarative sentences in the form of an inexorable sequence that details the potential social destiny of this wide-eyed, smiling "kid": "One day this kid will come to know something that causes a sensation equivalent to the separation of the earth from its axis. . . . One day this kid will find something in his

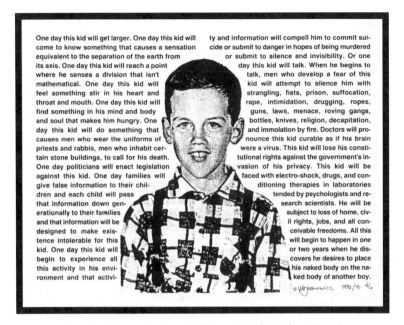

One day this kid will get larger. One day this kid will come to know something that causes a sensation equivalent to the separation of the earth from its axis. One day this kid will reach a point where he senses a division that isn't mathematical. One day this kid will feel something stir in his heart and throat and mouth. One day this kid will find something in his mind and body and soul that makes him hungry. One day this kid will do something that causes men who wear the uniforms of priests and rabbis, men who inhabit certain stone buildings, to call for his death. One day politicians will enact legislation against this kid. One day families will give false information to their children and each child will pass that information down generationally to their families and that information will be designed to make existence intolerable for this kid. One day this kid will begin to experience all this activity in his environment and that activity and information will compell him to commit suicide or submit to danger in hopes of being murdered or submit to silence and invisibility. Or one day this kid will talk. When he begins to talk, men who develop a fear of this kid will attempt to silence him with strangling, fists, prison, suffocation, rape, intimidation, drugging, ropes, guns, laws, menace, roving gangs, bottles, knives, religion, decapitation, and immolation by fire. Doctors will pronounce this kid curable as if his brain were a virus. This kid will lose his constitutional rights against the government's invasion of his privacy. This kid will be faced with electro-shock, drugs, and conditioning therapies in laboratories tended by psychologists and research scientists. He will be subject to loss of home, civil rights, jobs, and all conceivable freedoms. All this will begin to happen in one or two years when he discovers he desires to place his naked body on the naked body of another boy.

Figure 5.8. David Wojnarowicz, *Untitled (One Day This Kid . . .)* (1990).

mind and body and soul that makes him hungry. One day this kid will do something that causes men who wear the uniforms of priests and rabbis . . . to call for his death. One day politicians will enact legislation against this kid." Sentence by sentence, the text accumulates a series of violent, dehumanizing social consequences that will proceed from a young boy's developing knowledge about his desires. Presumably, the knowledge "that causes a sensation equivalent to the separation of the earth from its axis" refers to a boy's discovery of his own homosexual passions. Yet Wojnarowicz initially renders this longing conceptually abstract, referring to it as a cosmic "separation," a "feeling in one's throat," an intense "hunger." Like Brainard's description of a gay sensibility in his art as something "ga-ga" or "lush" or "sensual," Wojnarowicz homes in on the affective quality of gayness as an almost inexplicable felt intensity that radiates outward from the skin of an unnamed and "untitled" kid, presumably any kid who comes to intuit themselves as desiring queerly, rather than a clearly defined social or sexual identity.

Produced two years before Wojnarowicz died of AIDS, *Untitled (One Day This Kid . . .)* captured the artist's view of queerness as a visceral experience that places one at a disjoint from mainstream society, or what Wojnarowicz often called the "preinvented world." Wojnarowicz visually depicts this disjoint in the jarring contrast between the central photograph of a smiling boy (which could easily be the inaugural image in one of Brainard's many whimsical sequences) and the textual chain of murderous outcomes that literally hems the boy in, seemingly sealing his apocalyptic fate. The text reaches a crescendo with the lines: "One day this kid will [be compelled] to commit suicide or submit . . . to silence and invisibility. Or one day this kid will talk. When he begins to talk . . . this kid will be faced with electro-shock, drugs, and conditioning therapies [and the] loss of . . . all conceivable freedoms. All this will begin to happen in one or two years when he discovers he desires to place his naked body on the naked body of another boy." In a powerful twist to the boy's seemingly inevitable fate, Wojnarowicz inserts the possibility of a choice to speak about his desires rather than submit to "silence and invisibility." The choice is likely to bring about even more suffering, but it also offers a potential break in the unrelenting advance of homophobic repression. In the face of impending death, Wojnarowicz leaves his viewers, all those other "kids," a set of comic book instructions, a warning, and a guide for what might lie ahead "one day." But he also gives them a picture, in his own visage, of a radiant queer child as yet unchained by the logic of sexual conservatism, whose playful innocence might be an ever-regenerating force that could "one day" land in the hands of another kid whose life will unfold in an altogether different sequence.

By the mid-1980s, the sharing of intergenerational sexual knowledge among queers—as Wojnarowicz does in *Untitled (One Day This Kid . . .)*—came to have renewed urgency in the context of the HIV/AIDS epidemic, when a fatal sexually transmitted disease collided with the queer and feminist value of sexual pluralism. The sudden imminent danger surrounding once beloved sexual practices like vaginal and anal sex, along with the radical reduction of gay sex spaces, lead to the invention of "safe sex," not simply the use of condoms but also the revitalized interest in nonpenetrative forms of intimacy. Underscoring both the ethical and practical, life-saving ramifications of sexual pluralism, AIDS activist and cultural theorist Douglas Crimp bracingly argued, "We were able to invent safe sex because we have always known that sex is not . . . limited to penetrative sex. Our promiscuity taught us . . . the great multiplicity of those pleasures. It is that . . . conscious work on our own sexualities that has allowed many of us to change our sexual behaviors— something that brutal 'behavioral therapies' tried unsuccessfully. . . . Gay male promiscuity should be seen . . . as a positive model of how sexual pleasures might be pursued by and granted to everyone."[29] Crimp reframes the promiscuous, serial sexual encounters of gay male subcultures as dynamic erotic sequences that educate young queers through constructive experiences of bodily contact and exchange. In so doing, he models Wojnarowicz's description of the gay "kid" who chooses to "talk" about his queer desires, thereby exposing himself to the potential suppression of "behavioral therapies," but in this case inaugurating a new sequence of informed sexual exploration. Similarly, in his hybrid work of queer theory and sexual memoir, *Times Square Red, Times Square Blue* (1999), Samuel Delany underscores that spontaneous erotic liaisons between gay men in 1970s and 1980s New York City provided some of the most sustained cross-class and cross-generational interactions to be found in contemporary US culture.[30]

As these examples attest, the queer and feminist value of sexual pluralism that grew out of women's and gay liberation and became a bedrock ethos of HIV/AIDS activism was arguably one of the most incendiary ideas to emerge from projects for gender and sexual freedom in the late twentieth century. Sexual pluralism not only undermined heteropatriarchal norms, but imagined queer sex in public terms, as a collective practice that, like coming out, might encourage people to invent effective ways of negotiating their social and erotic differences, and hence function as another site for the production of left coalition building. Indeed, as Deborah Gould documents, the viscerally charged environment of AIDS activism, in which participants could actively fight for the lives of their friends and loved ones, while potentially meeting sexual partners who would become their political comrades, was a key incentive that kept participants coming back night after night, month after month.[31] As an active member of New York ACT UP (the AIDS Coalition to Unleash Power), Wojnarowicz lived out his most prolific artistic years in the politically and sexually energized milieu of AIDS activism, where the daily felt intensities of political rage and grief and lived experiences of queer sex became practically indistinguishable. Like Brainard before him, Wojnarowicz sought out the comics form to visually render the electric thrill of queer sexualities. He consequently produced a visual vocabulary that captured the AIDS epidemic's implosion of the borders between gay sex, friendship, politics, and existential being (boundaries that had steadily been eroding since the queer and feminist 1970s but which AIDS urgently collapsed).

In 1988, thirteen years after Brainard concluded "If Nancy Was . . . ," Wojnarowicz began a five-year collaboration with James Romberger and Marguerite Van Cook to produce a graphic memoir, *7 Miles a Second*. Completed sequentially in three parts between 1988 and 1993 (and published in 1996 by the Vertigo imprint of DC Comics), the text documents Wojnarowicz's years as a preadolescent hustler in Manhattan, a homeless teen runaway, and, finally, an AIDS activist and writer struggling to reconcile his failing health with his passionate desire to combat the murderous impulses of a homophobic culture. Like Brainard, Wojnarowicz and Romberger embraced the potential for associational sequences to link the specificities of individual queer desire to broader historical and cultural phenomena. Yet unlike him, these artists understood sequence as a rapidly accumulating series of images whose sheer volume could capture the affective intensity of queer desire subjected to the stresses of homophobia, AIDS, poverty, and political neglect. The opening lines of the texts explain that the "minimum speed required to break the earth's gravitational pull is seven miles a second. Since economic conditions prevent us from gaining access to rockets . . . we would have to learn to run awfully fast to achieve escape from where we are all heading."[32] Whereas Brainard's sequences figured queerness as a mischievous energy that magnetizes countless libidinal fantasies across serial images, Wojnarowicz's graphic memoir depicts queer sexuality as a ferocious velocity attempting to outpace its impending destruction by a biological disease and a politically "diseased" society. Throughout, the narrator consistently impresses upon the reader the necessity of cultivating physical and cognitive skills to make sense of and counteract the genocidal logics underwriting the HIV/AIDS epidemic. One such skill is the creative capacity to develop a lexicon of vivid textual and visual metaphors to describe sexual dissidents' experience of dislocation from societal norms and expectations.

This is dramatized in the opening spread of the third and longest section of the graphic memoir, eponymously titled "7 Miles a Second." This

Figure 5.9. "We are born into a preinvented existence within a tribal nation of zombies." David Wojnarowicz, James Romberger, and Marguerite Van Cook, *7 Miles a Second* (Seattle: Fantagraphics Books, 2013 [1996]). Courtesy Estate of David Wojnarowicz; and James Romberger and Marguerite Van Cook.

section narrates Wojnarowicz's adulthood as an activist artist in a series of disordered vignettes that function as explosive flashes of traumatic memory, nightmares, or hallucinations cumulatively reproducing the chaotic affective experience of living through the HIV/AIDS epidemic.[33] The inaugural sequence is composed of two extra-long rectangular panels layered atop one another that depict Wojnarowicz driving into a generic US Western landscape (figure 5.9/plate 11). In the second and largest panel, we see the back of Wojnarowicz's head to the left, while to the right a long, cluttered dashboard bisects the horizon line overflowing with cultural detritus including Mayan figurines, a Frankenstein doll, a snow globe with Lady Liberty inside, a Jesus figure, and a Mexican devil doll hanging from the rearview mirror. The dashboard displays the countless cultural and aesthetic sources Wojnarowicz finds himself drawn to throughout his artistic career—religious, mythological, and fantasy iconography—but it also functions as a screen that partly inhibits his view of the open road. A series of free-floating text boxes circulate around the image, proclaiming, "We are born into a preinvented existence within a tribal nation of zombies. / I was up until this moment a member of the industrialized . . . illusory tribe that catapults . . . this society, into something thick and hallucinogenic. / I feel something concrete slipping off the ledge back there behind my eyes. . . . / I'm looking with digital eyes past the windshield into the pre-invented world. . . . / I'm looking for a path out of the emptiness but all I see is the great wide earth in various formations." At the top right-hand corner of the page, a black-and-white image depicts a harrowing childhood memory of Wojnarowicz's father pointing a gun at his mother's head in their family living room.[34] The image extends past the borders of both long rectangular frames, as though it were a monstrous growth expanding outward from the present moment.

In this haunting sequence, Wojnarowicz's dashboard functions as a visual metaphor for a symbolic screen that society constructs between the self and a wider world. This includes the multitude of imaginary or "preinvented" icons deployed by institutions of power to keep us squarely in our place: Christ figures, devils, statues of liberty, and other fantasies of spiritual or national order that tether us to "the industrialized tribe." What Wojnarowicz calls "a preinvented existence" is the socially constructed package of goods, and the sense of entitled superiority, that comes with white, heterosexual, middle-class life. Through the shocking image of Wojnarowicz's father subjecting his own family to a fit of violent rage, the artist visually asserts how Wojnarowicz's childhood failed to accord with this "zombie-like" logic. The visual eruption of this jarring memory beyond the border of the two main panels suggests how, for the queer subject, such experiences of alienation from conventional family life repeatedly interrupt or spill over into the seemingly all-encompassing screen of a "diseased society." In this instance, comic strip form visually describes the kind of cognitive work queer people must engage to both figuratively widen their view of the social landscape that constitutes a heteronormative society—that is, to understand and strategically appropriate its ideologies and icons as a matter of survival—while managing their own memories of the numerous ways that same society fails them. Tellingly, this image of familial disorder appears directly beneath text that reads: "I feel something concrete slipping off the ledge back there behind my eyes." Wojnarowicz's traumatic memory is the kind of reality that forces a shift, or a "slipping off," of the pre-invented world. Consequently, his symbolic drive into an open field of possibilities grants him the opportunity to see more clearly, though not completely, past the "hallucinogenic" pall of normative society.

In Joe Brainard's *Nancy* series, language works as site of anticipatory possibility in the open-ended formulation "If Nancy Was . . ."; that potential is then rendered creatively in myriad whimsical or enchanting visual scenarios that unfold serially. By contrast, Wojnarowicz's and Romberger's graphic work hinges on visually invoking silenced or repressed felt experiences rather than serial possibilities. In *7 Miles a Second*, language functions to accumulate somatic intensities that are viscerally described yet inadequately captured by words alone; comics form, then, compensates for this lack with its amplified concatenation of multiple verbal and visual elements. For instance, many of the panoramas in the graphic memoir present elongated diagonal panels that cut through an entire page at odd angles like an X-Acto knife dissecting a scene into jagged segments. This formal strategy visually conjures the feeling of being fragmented, cut up, or disarticulated by the barbarism of government neglect, medical mistreatment, or sexual abuse at the hands of other queers. At the same time, the actual content of the panels frequently depicts violent types of bodily penetration.

In one three-page spread, Wojnarowicz recounts a hallucinatory experience of being drugged and raped by one of his clients while hustling as a teenage youth. The drugs lead Wojnarowicz into a terrifying dream state, which is illustrated using a rapid-fire series of diagonal panels cascading down each page: Wojnarowicz first imagines himself as a Black homeless man wandering aimlessly in a subway station; then transmutes into a stray dog pinned to the train tracks; and finally watches his canine avatar be eviscerated with a scalpel by police. With this last image, the narrative reads: "A quivering organ is bared / the cop delicately cuts it open / I can see the look of pain and terror in the dog's eyes change into some kind of sensual pleasure . . . / the life force in the living eye slowly extinguishing."[35] With these final words we see Wojnarowicz's own frail, youthful body laid out and tied to the bed with blood pouring from his anus (figure 5.10/plate 12). The knifelike, jagged cuts of the descending panels invoke the overlapping wounds of poverty, police brutality, and

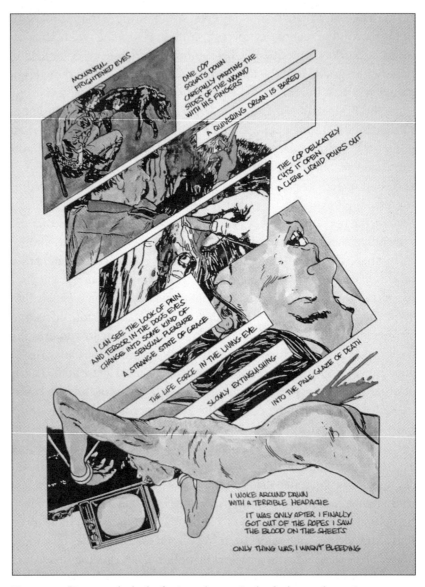

Figure 5.10. "I can see the look of pain and terror in the dog's eyes change into some kind of sensual pleasure . . ." David Wojnarowicz, James Romberger, and Marguerite Van Cook, *7 Miles a Second* (Seattle: Fantagraphics Books, 2013 [1996]). Courtesy Estate of David Wojnarowicz; and James Romberger and Marguerite Van Cook.

sexual violation. But they also create an erotically charged associational chain between multiple categories of social degradation or abjection shared by queer youth, Black men, and stray animals alike. As a gay teenager, Wojnarowicz has experienced homelessness like the African American man in his dream; as a hustler, he has been tied down like an animal by sexual predators; and as a homeless youth, he has been repeatedly assailed by police like so many out gay people before him. The erotically tinged description of the "delicate cutting" open of the dog's underbelly describes the ways that a brutally homophobic and racist society physically and sexually penetrates the hearts and bodies of racialized, sexualized, and animal others. Consequently, throughout the graphic narrative, the cutting counterforce of Wojnarowicz's visual images functions as the explosion of already existing but inarticulate somatic intensities, including visceral rage at the varieties of dehumanization, on the comic strip page.

This tension between descriptive language and ballistic visceral imagery is spectacularly displayed in a scene where Wojnarowicz imagines himself as a giant tearing down St. Patrick's Cathedral in protest of Cardinal Joseph O'Connor's murderous policies on AIDS (figure 5.11/plate 13).[36] This fantasy image appears in a massive square frame that takes up two-thirds of a double-page spread, while a long block of text lacking any punctuation is arranged along the left-hand side of the panel. The text reads: "And I'm carrying this rage like a blood-filled egg and there's a thin line between the inside and the outside a thin line between thought and action . . . and as each T-cell disappears from my body it's replaced by ten pounds of pressure ten pounds of rage . . . and at the moment I'm a three hundred seventy foot tall eleven hundred thousand pound man inside this six foot frame and all I can feel is the pressure and the need for release." At first glance, there appears to be symmetry between text and image. The text on the page describes the felt experience of being at odds with the limits of one's own body, which precipitates a fantasy of size and power enabling Wojnarowicz to fight the social forces working to oppress and murder people living with AIDS. Yet the radical disjoint between the text—which is set block left, completely unassimilated into the image—and the massive panel that accompanies it reminds us that words, no matter how powerfully crafted, cannot fully convey the immensity of queer feelings produced in response to

Figure 5.11. "And I'm carrying this rage like a blood-filled egg." David Wojnarowicz, James Romberger, and Marguerite Van Cook, *7 Miles a Second* (Seattle: Fantagraphics Books, 2013 [1996]). Courtesy Estate of David Wojnarowicz; and James Romberger and Marguerite Van Cook.

institutional homophobia. The words drawn on the page accumulate a level of tension so high they catapult the viewer into a visual spectacle of queer desire, figured as a kind of orgasmic velocity. Theorizing the concept of queer velocity, Jennifer Row claims, "In the realm of physics, velocity is . . . comprised of a magnitude (speed) and a direction. . . . I note the queerness of velocity when desires fail to conform to temporal norms, eliciting rushing or slowness that jars against prescriptive rhythms or deviates from hetero-reproductive ends."[37] In Wojnarowicz's jarring scene, the symbolic orgasmic release of queer fury is materialized in the physical destruction (and penetration) of an institution of violent normalization. In the frame we see police cars and pedestrians running from the scene, all made extraordinarily small in relation to Wojnarowicz as giant. The scene makes a gay man with AIDS physically and symbolically larger than both the Catholic Church and the police, suggesting that what is contained in the heart of one man could potentially out-scale those institutions of power that exist to discipline queer bodies. Wojnarowicz's gigantic size also invokes the collective social body of people with AIDS and their allies, who had in fact swarmed and infiltrated the same cathedral in one of the most daring and documented AIDS activist actions in 1989 (which Wojnarowicz had himself participated in): ACT UP's "Stop the Church" campaign.[38]

As its title indicates, *7 Miles a Second* repeatedly references the concept of velocity by visually linking technologies of motion (including cars, locomotives, and subway trains) with heightened interior states of emotional intensity. Three scenes after the destruction of St. Patrick's Cathedral, we see a double-page spread depicting a gigantic rectangular image of a locomotive hurtling across space carrying a chaotic assemblage of an ancient mammalian skeleton, intestines, thorny vines, television sets, gigantic pennies, and engine parts (figure 5.12/plate 14). At the helm is a mastodon skull, an emblem of the dead past moving

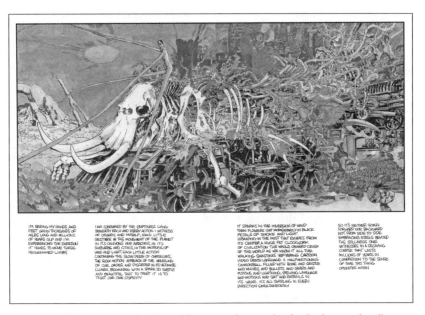

Figure 5.12. "I'm seeing my hands and feet grow thousands of miles long and millions of years old." David Wojnarowicz, James Romberger, and Marguerite Van Cook, *7 Miles a Second* (Seattle: Fantagraphics Books, 2013 [1996]). Courtesy Estate of David Wojnarowicz; and James Romberger and Marguerite Van Cook.

rapidly forward, while atop it sits Wojnarowicz himself, a naked figure with arms and legs stretched impossibly in all four directions. Below this surreal image, the narrative intones, "I'm seeing my hands and feet grow thousands of miles long and millions of years old and I'm experiencing the exertion it takes to move these programmed limbs . . . I am consumed by . . . the slow motion approach of the unveiling of our order and disorder in its ultimate climax . . . vibrating in the mist that exudes from its center a huge fat clockwork of civilization the whole onward crush of the world as we know it . . . spewing language and motion and shit and entrails in its wake."[39]

If the image of Wojnarowicz as a giant destroying St. Patrick's Cathedral seeks to visually capture the sheer extent and intensity of feeling that one man can contain in response to AIDS, this image scales up even farther to the movement of history itself, to account for the epidemic's place in the longer arc of human existence. The scene implicitly references German philosopher Walter Benjamin's "angel of history" from his classic 1940 essay "Theses on the Philosophy of History." Citing Paul Klee's 1920 monoprint *Angelus Novus* (which depicts a hovering angel, wings spread as though moving away from the viewer), Benjamin conceived of "human progress" as the experience of an angel flying backward while being buffeted into an unpredictable future by the force of the "wreckage of history."[40] Reversing this figuration, Romberger depicts Wojnarowicz riding the *literal* wreckage of history while looking forward and away from its carnage, echoing the earlier image of Wojnarowicz's frail teenage body forcibly tied to a bed, once again naked and vulnerable but held fast by the velocity of history.

The image stresses the desperate need to resist the pull of history's countless mind-numbing ideologies—whether figured as nostalgic reverie for the bones of the dead, the lure of financial greed, or the endless loop of mainstream media—even as one is "programmed" by these narratives in every fiber of one's being. The grand scale of the panorama, made possible by the representational expansiveness of the comic strip form, grants the viewer the perspective needed to steel themselves in the face of annihilation (symbolized by the long extinct mastodon and the atrophying limbs of Wojnarowicz's avatar). In scenes like these, including Wojnarowicz's drive into the Western sunset, the narrative emphatically underscores that every historical starting point is the inauguration of a sequence that will end with violent force—collision, destruction, and death—though simply at different rates of speed.

While the image of the ferocious locomotive might indicate the sense of rapid movement toward death experienced by countless people living with AIDS at the height of the epidemic, the narrative below describes the "slow motion approach of the unveiling of our order and disorder" as a universally shared experience from which there is no escape. This latter statement reminds us that gay sex is not to blame for AIDS, as the popular imagination might have it, for the disease is merely one highly dramatized and accelerated expression of a banal entropic process inherent to all existence. Rather than limiting possibilities for people living with AIDS, this view of sequence as a movement toward universal decay equalizes the social playing field by reminding us that everything, everybody, and every ideology, regardless of how dominant or repressed it might be, will ultimately come to ruin by the forces of time. Despite this seemingly apocalyptic reality, Romberger's and Wojnarowicz's frenzied proliferation of rebellious visual and verbal responses to the epidemic makes the impassionaed argument that the only appropriate response to "the onward crush of the world" is an incessant counterassault in the form of a tsunami of artistic production. This becomes one avenue for both dramatizing our shared vulnerability and materializing affective and sensual bonds between people regardless of their HIV status as they acknowledge, and consequently make collective meaning out of, the "slow death of ourselves."

Throughout *7 Miles a Second*, Wojnarowicz, Romberger, and Van Cook deploy what I call a technique of *deluge*, or the intentional flooding of readers' sensory experience by an onslaught of visceral language and imagery. In Brainard's "If Nancy Was . . ." series, each entry's minimalism leaves open interpretative possibilities by encouraging any potential viewer to fill in meanings, narratives, and desires that may be gestured toward in any given frame but never ultimately fixed by the manifest content. Alternatively, in *7 Miles*, the artists achieve a similar expansiveness of meaning-making potential, but through an additive approach of layering copious images, objects, scenes, words, and memories atop one another; this hypersaturation produces an overflow of connotation that formally corresponds to the lived experience of having to cognitively process or interpret more and more of a chaotic world in the face of impending death. Deluge also registers the body's permeability to the outside world, including its susceptibility to being overwhelmed by pathogens like HIV/AIDS transmitted through the liquid excretions of other bodies. The aesthetic technique of deluge apparent in the graphic text functions as both a description of the conditions of living in the historical moment of AIDS—swallowed up by a tidal wave of mass death and flooded with medical misinformation, competing political narratives, and emotional turmoil—as well as a critical defense against loss of self in the face of such historical atrocity.

Deluge appears in a variety of forms, including the frantic visual accumulation of images piling on one another; the display of massive panoramas exploding with visual detail; the insertion of long blocks of affectively charged text without punctuation; and the use of vibrant watercolors to depict bodies, objects, and scenes shown literally soaking into one another or else (in the formal idiom of comics panels) bleeding off the page. In an interview, painter Marguerite Van Cook corroborates this notion of "deluge aesthetics" in describing the conceptual vision behind her use of watercolors, which defies drawn borders and the "proper" coloring of objects: "On a very fundamental level, I wanted to break the rules. I felt this world of David's, of ours, which existed outside of the mainstream society, should not be represented with colors that reinforced traditional expectations and norms. I allowed this impulse to . . . [disrupt] traditional comic book colors . . . at times showing exactly how something looked and other times entering into the delirium of the narrative and images. . . . I colored in the state of heightened perception that had become our daily experience."[41] For example, in the detailed panorama of Wojnarowicz's dashboard as he drives into the Western horizon, Van Cook paints the entire scene, including Wojnarowicz's tchotchkes and figurines, in hues of yellow, blue, and green. The interior of the car comes to look and feel like the watery depths of a lake, eliciting the feeling of being dragged undertow while one is in the very process of trying to escape the constraints of one's society.

Arguably the most powerful of these techniques is the invocation of the sensation of drowning, which is depicted in a series of dreamlike images that show Wojnarowicz about to be swallowed up by a tsunami, sinking to the bottom of a lake, or overtaken by a trio of tornadoes.[42] In moments like these, the formal overflow of images, bodies, and concepts that characterizes the graphic memoir as a whole is made literal in representations of potentially fatal submersion. The slippage between formal and literal deluge—between a flood of imagery and the actual representation of drowning—makes the sequential unfolding of vignettes in *7 Miles a Second* materially felt on the body. These images reach their apex in a dazzling splash page near the conclusion of the graphic novel portraying Wojnarowicz in his apartment frantically completing an unfinished painting (figure 5.13/plate 15). He wears a gas mask to protect against the fumes of the spray paint he is using to fill the background of the canvas. The painting depicts a human figure looking into a microscope. The figure's body appears to contain the entire universe, including vividly colored planets, stars, and moons.[43] A string of text boxes cascade down from the top of the page, which read: "I'm acutely aware of myself alive and witnessing / All behind me are the friends that have died / I'm breathing this air that they can't breathe / Time is now compressed and every painting . . . I make with the sense that it may be the last thing I do and so I try to pull everything into the surface of that action / Cut straight to the heart of the senses and map it out as clearly as tools and growth allow." Around this central scene appear other examples of Wojnarowicz's painting, sculpture, and photography, including a faint tracing of a large-scale photograph of his former lover Peter Hujar on the wall above his workspace, one of the "friends that have died" keeping symbolic company with the artist. Echoing the tension between words and images displayed in the earlier scene of St. Patrick's Cathedral, here the figurative waterfall of text boxes visually gives way to a deluge of artistic production: these paintings, sculptures, and photographs materially index the frames (each a distinct work of art) that proliferate in comics form to capture affective intensities that would otherwise be underarticulated by words alone.

This gripping scene depicts Wojnarowicz's art practice as a survival tactic that keeps him afloat amid the avalanche of deaths left in the wake of AIDS. The fear of *losing* one's breath—indicated by the textual reference to breathing air that others can't breathe but also in the visual representation of Wojnarowicz wearing a gas mask—becomes an anxiety that motivates the necessity of learning how to *hold* one's breath long enough to leave a mark on history and to honor the deaths of loved ones. The desire to bring "everything into the surface" is a wish to recuperate

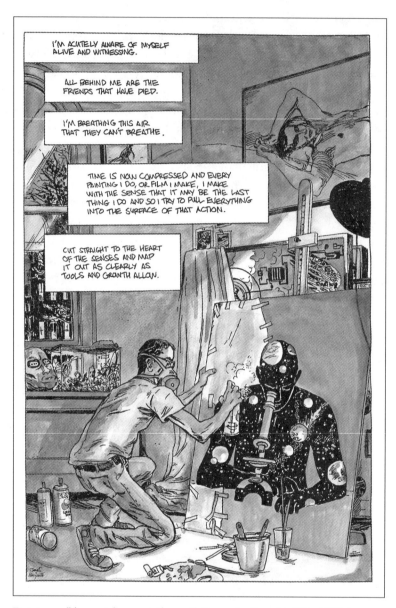

Figure 5.13. "I'm acutely aware of myself alive and witnessing." David Wojnarow-
icz, James Romberger, and Marguerite Van Cook, *7 Miles a Second* (Seattle:
Fantagraphics Books, 2013 [1996]). Courtesy Estate of David Wojnarowicz; and
James Romberger and Marguerite Van Cook.

queer forms of creativity, care, eroticism, and intimacy drowned out by homophobia, disease, and death. Yet the image of "surfacing" implies that one can counter one kind of deluge only with another, the flood of artistic production that is Wojnarowicz's oeuvre as well as the torrent of sequential images that make up *7 Miles a Second* itself. The painting Wojnarowicz is working on portrays a figure made up of the ultimate deluge: the very stuff of the universe itself filling the vessel that is the human body. According to Romberger, "it is an image of a scientist trying to understand the world, as [Wojnarowicz] did. . . . [I]t reflects his hope for a cure."[44] Seen from this perspective, the painting projects the idea that only a being porous enough to be flooded with the complexity of the cosmos can find such a cure. Of course, it was those very "friends who have died," the sexually active queers that welcomed the bodies of others into their own, who were virally deluged by a disease carrying a seemingly cosmic significance. Echoing Crimp's contention that "it is our promiscuity that will save us," here Wojnarowicz recuperates the "ghosts of queer sex" not as irresponsible sexual deviants but as enlightened guides whose permeable orientation to the world offers a spiritual cure to the virulent diseases of homophobia, racism, and sexism. In the context of the graphic narrative we hold in our hands, that figure can be recast as any potential reader of *7 Miles a Second* who keeps turning each page, taking in the persistent stream of visceral images that might become equipment for living beyond AIDS.

"Anything Can Happen in a Comic"

How do you draw what same-sex desire *feels like*? How do you visually render the experience of gender transitivity? How do you formally capture the emotional experience of seeing your friends die of AIDS? What shapes or forms adequately convey or translate what it means to be queer, to be trans*, to be non-binary in various contexts? In Joe Brainard and David Wojnarowicz, we see two gay artists responding to distinct personal and political understandings of queer sexuality through the formal possibilities of a specific medium, the comic strip. For Brainard, comic strip serialization allowed him to highlight the conceptual relationship between comics' unfolding sequential panels and sexuality itself as a form of repetition with a difference. Though Nancy traditionally appeared as a rigidly recurring icon in her original strips, Brainard maintains the use of traditional comic strip form while altering its figural content, so that Nancy becomes an emblem of sexual pluralism, shapeshifting to inhabit queer and feminist culture's proliferating social types, sexual positions, and deviant desires. Alternatively, for Wojnarowicz, Romberger, and Van Cook, comic strip forms' ceaseless sequential movement of text and image becomes an imperative to flood the world with scenes, icons, figures, and concepts that might collectively provide a lifeline for surviving the immanent reality of social and physical death in the face of AIDS. The two projects deploy radically different aesthetic styles. Yet in both, the comics medium remains flexible or generous enough to function as a vehicle for expressing the queer and feminist value of erotic diversity, which can be understood, in Eve Sedgwick's words, as "the open mesh of possibilities, gaps, overlaps, dissonances and resonances, lapses and excesses of meaning when the constituent elements of anyone's gender, of anyone's sexuality aren't made (or can't be made) to signify monolithically."[45] In the comics works of these two artists, the aggregate of sequential panels never add up to a single or monolithic sexual identity, but rather accumulate a potentially limitless "open mesh" of sensual and affective possibilities.

If US sexual conservatism has always aimed to make queer sexuality and eroticism invisible, and by extension inconceivable in the popular imagination (as when, in the 1986 *Bowers v. Hardwick* decision, the Supreme Court upheld anti-sodomy laws, thereby sanctioning legal abolishment of a sex act widely [mis]understood as an exclusively gay male practice), then comics provide one space for persistently and aggressively making visible nonnormative sex—not only directly representing alternative sexual practices but giving shape, contour, style, texture, color, and structure to multiplicious versions of gay, queer, or nonnormative sensuality, desire, bodies, and points of contact, in unbounded sequence. As Wojnarowicz once claimed: "[I]f I make a sexual image and put it on a wall, in a way, it's fighting against my need for anonymity—which I treasure to a certain extent. At the same time I'll make that image in order to put it on a wall so that I'm not alone."[46] As we see with his *Canal Street Piers* mural or his haunting print *Untitled (One Day This Kid . . .)*, making comics that displayed aspects of his own sexuality was one way of taking eroticized images and literally "putting them on the wall." Doing so allowed Wojnarowicz to communicate with a developing queer social world by making the specificity of his desires publicly accessible, and available for infinite sequences of response.

By placing these two artists together, I aim to inaugurate a conversation about the ways in which the comic strip form offers an alternative material and affective archive for the evolution of queerness in the late twentieth century. Such a conversation demands that we ask how comics might narrate the history of sexuality differently than other media by virtue of the medium's capacity to rethink sequence as a site of open-ended multiplicity, rather than a linear or teleological form. This question is especially important today, as the last decade has witnessed a renaissance in queer comics production unparalleled in the history of US visual culture: alongside the mainstream success of long-time lesbian and gay comics creators such as Alison Bechdel and Howard Cruse, we have seen the underground emergence of numerous transgender, bisexual, and genderqueer comics artists (including the surrealist fantasy comics of Edie Fake and the butch aesthetics of A. K. Summers), the spectacular introduction of out LGBTQ characters in mainstream superhero comics, the publication of anthologies of queer comics (including Justin Hall's LAMBDA Award–winning *No Straight Lines: Four Decades of Queer Comics* [2013], *Qu33r* [2014], and *Beyond: The Queer Sci-Fi/ Fantasy Comic Anthology* [2015]), and even the institution of a biannual international Queers & Comics Conference inaugurated by queer comics artist Jennifer Camper and Black studies scholar andré carrington. Despite the exponential growth of this archive, queer studies has only just begun to produce multiple theories attentive to how forms unique to the comics medium facilitate the articulation of divergent genders and sexualities, including how comics artists innovate visual metaphors and analogies for real-life erotic, sensual, or intimate experiences.[47]

In one his most self-conscious *Nancy* comic strips from 1947, Ernie Bushmiller depicted Nancy in four sequential panels (organized in a square) that begins with her strolling along a street and concludes with her walking upside down on the ceiling of her living room. The panels are held together by a single sentence whose individual components spread out across each frame: "Anything / can happen / in a comic strip." The surreal presentation of Nancy as capable of bending the rules of space to walk jauntily up the side of her living room wall reminds readers of the limitless imaginative potential of comics—a medium in which *anything that can be drawn can be believed.* This single strip can be seen as a conceptual template of Brainard's "If Nancy Was . . ." series, providing both an alibi and motivation for Brainard's imaginative exploration of all the things that Nancy could be (which, of course, is quite literally *anything*). Yet it also shrewdly points to another largely ignored capacity of the comics medium, namely its very queer ability to emerge from, or infiltrate, nearly every other visual form of the twentieth century.[48] Consider that a series of paintings when placed into a visual or narrative sequence can become a comic strip. A classic celluloid film reel composed of thousands of moving images is itself a comic strip. A series of photographs, with or without captions, can be organized so that they are transformed into a sequential comic. And television media appears as a serialized set of images combining verbal and visual elements.

The full conceptual and creative consequences of comics' extraordinary adaptiveness are still being studied, but queer artists have fundamentally understood this quality to be one of the most inventive aspects of the medium. Comics' mutability grants the medium a level of openendedness that approximates the shapeshifting qualities of erotic desire and embodiment in all its forms, perhaps most presciently in those queer expressions that swerve away from the normative sequence of "proper" gendered and heterosexual development. With its uncanny capacity to inhabit numerous mediums, bodies, materials, and figures, with its thrilling rush of visual and verbal information that overwhelms one's senses and sets the heart racing, the comic strip may be the closest creative form we have to sexuality itself. Like sexuality, that affective force capable of attaching itself to *any* body or object with unexpected results, in comics "anything can happen."

6

"I Cherish My Bile Duct as Much as Any Other Organ"

*Political Disgust and the Digestive Life of AIDS in
Tony Kushner's* Angels in America

I cherish my bile duct as much as any other organ. I take
good care of it. I make sure it gets its daily vitamins and
antioxidants and invigorating exposure to news of Antonin
Scalia and everyone else working for the Bush family.
—Tony Kushner, speech to the undergraduate class of Bard
College (2005)

In one of many verbally assaultive scenes in Tony Kushner's epic play *Angels in America* (1990–1992), the closeted, acerbic lawyer Roy Cohn rages at his naïve protégé Joe Pitt that politics is, in his words, "gastric juices churning, this is enzymes and acids, this is intestinal is what this is, bowel movement and blood-red meat—this stinks, this is *politics*, Joe, the game of being alive" (74).[1] Cohn's metaphor links politics to the gut, both as a state of being alive digestively *and* affectively. The metaphor is apt, for in the following scene Joe, also a closeted, Reaganite apostle, is chastised by the gay liberal Louis for downing hot dogs with Coca-Cola and Pepto Bismol, which leads to a bleeding ulcer. Roy also experiences violent convulsions of the gut brought on by complications of AIDS. Despite Roy's bravado and Joe's Pepto guzzling, their political conservatism and self-hating homophobia, the play suggests, are the worst kind of "gastric juices churning," causing painful gut feelings. What are we to make of this dizzying array of links between intestines, bowel movements, eating, and purging along distinct political lines and sexual identities? Not incidentally, these connections range across the entire play, depicted in the HIV-positive character Prior's repeated lamentations over his "chapped ass" from bouts of blood-filled diarrhea, as well as Harper, Joe's unhappy wife, who imagines being disemboweled by God on her journey of self-discovery.

This chapter explores what I call the "digestive politics and poetics of AIDS," or the proliferation of metaphors and figures linking the material experience of HIV/AIDS (including its pill popping and diarrhea and vomit-inducing pangs) to an intuitive or "gut feeling" of aversion to the state of US politics, particularly in its most racist and homophobic forms. I focus on *Angels in America* because it offered the most sustained examination of this link at the height of the AIDS epidemic by using the literal performance of digestive dysfunction in language and on stage to redirect public culture's disgust with the bodies of people with AIDS (and the syndrome's association with gay men) toward a disgust with the failure of liberal democracy to respond to the HIV/AIDS epidemic. This project expanded the social axes along which AIDS was understood. Simultaneously, it made those bodies most abject from US culture (people with AIDS, queers, women, racial minorities, and the homeless) the site of an alternative intuition based on the ability to perceive multiple, interlocking forms of oppression and the need to combat them. For instance, the character Belize, a Black, gay ex–drag queen turned nurse, responds to both Louis's left-wing humanism and Roy's racist conservatism with indignant disgust born of his knowledge of US racial history and his experience of AIDS among his patients. His name, "Belize," a drag moniker "that stuck," self-consciously references a Central American and Caribbean nation where the Atlantic slave trade once flourished. By maintaining this drag name in his everyday life, Belize deploys his former performance persona to signify both a personal history of queer cross-dressing as well as the broader history of North American racism. In Belize, Kushner depicts the intuitive or felt sense of a relationship between histories of racial violence, AIDS, and the state's simultaneous aversion to, and erotic courting of, the very abject (often queer) bodies it destroys. If the movements for women's and gay liberation in the 1970s frequently marshalled affects of ebullience, joy, pride, and righteous indignation against societal sexism and homophobia, under the nigh-genocidal conditions of the HIV/AIDS epidemic, these feeling states were honed into a fierce political disgust at the widespread, murderous disregard for the lives of women and queers everywhere.

I coin the phrase "the digestive politics and poetics of AIDS" to describe a dense rhetorical formation distinct to queer and feminist cultural production in the late 1980s and early 1990s. This emergent discourse developed metaphors, conceptual juxtapositions, and figures that linked the material forms of the gut (particularly as they were affected by AIDS)—the stomach, ingestion, digestion, and excretion—to the forms of US political life—democracy, the public sphere, the law, and liberal humanism. By employing viscerally charged representations of bodily and political forms that elicit affective responses, the digestive politics and poetics of AIDS worked to reroute the direction of a particular emotion—social and political disgust—but also to repurpose its content, that is, to transform a dehumanizing revulsion that enables public apathy toward people with AIDS into a galvanizing *antipathy* toward homophobic disregard that might incite political action in response to the AIDS crisis.[2] Following the work of Melissa Gregg and Gregory Seigworth, I use the terms "affect" or "affective" to indicate material or sensate intensities that "pass body to body" as well the body's physical response to external stimuli, including an array of encounters with human and nonhuman agents. Consequently, I use the term "visceral" (or the phrase "viscerally charged") to describe formal language and imagery that simultaneously invokes both the literal viscera (internal organs of the intestinal tract) as well as "gut-level responses" to impactful external forces.[3] Rather than separating the materiality of affect from "merely representational" discourse or language, then, I treat the visceral as a potent cultural site where the literal and the figurative aspects of embodiment are so tightly wound as to become coterminous, so that linguistic representations of the body figuratively invoke, and materially elicit, affective response.[4]

In previous chapters, I have explored how identifiable material and aesthetic forms like the human figure of the female replicant, the impenetrable dome containing a symbolic lesbian commune, or the circle composing a CR group session were respectively articulated to key feminist and queer concepts or values like equality, separatism, and consciousness-raising. In this final chapter, the material construct I explore is the vast physiological architecture of the digestive or alimentary tract, which is itself composed of, and generates, numerous discreet organic shapes and forms, from vital organs to liquid discharge. Consequently, the proper aesthetic form for this chapter is *metaphor*, namely the intentional yoking together of various apprehensible structures of the bowels to powerful feelings of revulsion. The shapeshifting quality of this particular queer form inheres in its intentionally disorienting slippage between physiological matter, metaphor or figuration, and "gut-level" feeling states, all of which come to overlap and mutually influence one another through the performative impact of language and rhetoric. To deploy gut metaphors in distinct ways can potentially trigger digestive processes like vomiting, stomach grumbling, and diarrhea, as well as visceral emotions, which in turn can themselves become sources for metaphorical play and experimentation in a perpetual (dare I say, *intestinal*) loop. This might be thought of as the aesthetic analogy to what scientists have called the "mind-gut" connection.

Beginning in the mid- to late 1980s, queer and feminist cultural producers working across an array of mediums and genres took up the digestive politics and poetics of AIDS by using viscerally charged language and imagery to imbue, or figuratively "infect," US political life with the material experience of living with HIV/AIDS. In the rageful, tactile mixed-media works of artists like David Wojnarowicz and Zoe Leonard; in the Guerilla Girls' public poster art declaring feminist disgust for the sexist and homophobic art world; in the performance of "gut feelings" on stage in productions like Kushner's *Angels in America* and public displays of the bleeding body in the solo performances of Ron Vawter (1992–1993) and Ron Athey (1994); in the humorous "assplay" of films like John Greyson's *Zero Patience* (1993); in images of the body's painful and messy excretions under stress from AIDS in the documentary work of Peter Friedman and Tom Joslin (1993); and in the impassioned descriptions of piss drinking and cum eating in the journals of Gary Fisher (1996), queer artists, filmmakers, and writers deployed the digestive politics and poetics of AIDS to explore what kinds of rhetorical moves could elicit the same gut-wrenching symptoms of HIV/AIDS, but as a physical response to the abhorrent political realities that enabled the dehumanization of people living with the disease. These creators' representations of the disease came to carry a figural weight capable of arousing and repurposing what Deborah Gould has called *political feelings*. Writing about the political uses of rage in AIDS activism in this same time period, Gould uses the term "political feelings" to describe instances in which seemingly individualized "bodily, felt experience" becomes the ground for articulating matters of collective concern, allowing such sensations to be named (as rage or disgust, for instance), transmitted between bodies, and deployed to motivate public action.[5]

The rerouting and repurposing of political feelings undertaken by the digestive politics and poetics of AIDS was spectacularly displayed in the genre of drama, where embodied performances of viscerally charged language model new ways of inhabiting specific affects and relating them to other bodies and objects in public. How any given actor might publicly perform an emotion or enact a physical expression of "gut feelings" indicated by a stage direction is always open to interpretation. The choice to perform one way or another requires an intuitive *affective* embodiment of that direction that can impact an audience and other actors on stage in a variety of ways. *Angels in America* is an exceptional case for this process because it organizes the logic of its characters around distinctly digestive language, while requiring its actors to perform that language with extremely heightened levels of emotional and corporeal intensity.

Angels in America is a repository of alimentary metaphors, figures, and puns. From quotidian insults—"Your problem is that you are . . . full of piping hot crap"—to grand political comparisons—"the Law's a pliable, breathing, sweating . . . organ"—the play relentlessly deploys visceral language to describe abject or dysfunctional forms of embodiment (227, 72). Characters are also directed to perform vomiting and diarrhea, bleeding, gagging, (painful) fucking, and swallowing (both pills and cock), often in conjunction with these metaphors, at other times independent of them. At a historical moment when the question of viral transmission remained a hotly contested one in both medical discourse and public superstition, for a play like *Angels* to stage HIV-positive, and *possibly* positive, characters expelling blood, spit, and shit in proximity to one another and the audience had the potential to invoke serious discomfort, fear, or aversion in viewers.[6] When at one point the character Prior claims, "My heart is pumping polluted blood. I feel dirty," he captures the affective project of the play: *Angels* makes its audience "feel dirty" by reminding viewers through its visceral language that the "petrified little fetishes" of liberal thought—humanism, democracy, tolerance, and individualism—are "full of piping hot crap" (40). *Angels* both discursively and performatively elicits such affective responses from its actors, and potentially its audience, so that these responses might be worked upon, and transformed, in the course of the play. To articulate the stakes of this project, I begin by placing the digestive politics and poetics of AIDS within its cultural context, as well as its broader affective investments. I then offer a sustained reading of *Angels* that systematically works through (or metabolizes) the digestive dysfunctions of its various characters. By mapping the play's characterological universe in alimentary terms, I provide a blueprint for how Kushner ultimately theorizes a queer and feminist politics attentive to "the gut as much as the mind."

Feeling Vomitey: Invoking Bodily Intensities in the Digestive Politics and Poetics of AIDS

In his introduction to the special issue of *October* on "AIDS: Cultural Activism/Cultural Analysis" in 1987, Douglas Crimp claimed, "If we recognize that AIDS exists only in and through its representations, culture, and politics, then the hope is that we can also recognize the imperative to . . . analyze . . . and wrest control of them. . . . We need cultural practices actively participating in the struggle against AIDS."[7] The digestive politics and poetics of AIDS was just such a "cultural [practice] participating in the struggle against AIDS," one that intentionally blurred the lines between the material and the representational in order to make visible the ways that bodies are literally affected by discursive productions or cultural forms, particularly metaphors. This was a point that cultural theorists of AIDS like Crimp, Paula Treichler, Leo Bersani, and Simon Watney, among others, vehemently argued in their critique of attempts to bracket cultural representations of AIDS from the corporeal realities of the disease.[8] These scholar-activists illuminated how popular assumptions and socially constructed meanings that came to attach to the syndrome—including erroneous medical suppositions about sites of genital transmission of HIV that equated the vagina with "rugged" elasticity and framed the anus as a "vulnerable" membrane more susceptible to the disease—affected medical and political responses to AIDS, resulted in the uneven distribution of treatment, and explicitly influenced the direction of epidemiological research on the virus.[9] As Paula Treichler famously claimed, "AIDS is a real disease syndrome, damaging and killing real human beings . . . yet [it] . . . is simultaneously . . . an epidemic of meanings or signification."[10] Perhaps the most pernicious meaning-making around the virus was the popular association of the disease with the "perverted" or "disgusting" sex acts of gay men, namely anal penetration, and the similarly stigmatized lifeways of drugs addicts and female sex workers. Such stigmas lead to the widespread focus on these "high-risk" groups as the supposed progenitors of the disease, producing a negative chain of signification between sexually "deviant" gay men, straight women, and a multiracial economic underclass. The popular conception of a coalition of "bad actors" ideologically supported the US government's neglect of those who were perceived as willfully courting the virus through illicit behaviors.

The digestive politics and poetics of AIDS emerged in the late 1980s as a nuanced attempt to "wrest control" over a specific emotion, disgust, to offer alternative outlets for expressing feelings of revulsion, contempt, and general dis-ease at different targets than people with AIDS (PWAs), the queer community, and the variously identified high-risk groups of early HIV epidemiology. This is captured in a hilarious number, "The Butthole Duet," in the AIDS musical comedy *Zero Patience* (dir. John Greyson, 1993), which narrates the adventurer Sir Richard Burton's attempt to locate the origin of AIDS in a "patient zero." Having discovered and brought back the promiscuous "Zero" (purportedly the progenitor of North American AIDS) to his home, Burton and Zero fall asleep together. In their slumber, the two men's buttholes (puppets made of pink silk with gaping black holes for mouths) melodically debate the merits of anal sex. Representing the uptight British patriarchy, Burton's butthole claims, "Freud said we have a death wish, getting buggered's getting killed. This ghastly epidemic is something our subconscious willed." To which Zero's talented rear retorts, "An asshole's just an asshole, skip the analytic crit. The meanings are straightforward, cocks go in and out comes shit." Zero debases Burton's judgment-laden assessment of anal sex as the embodiment of a "death wish" with his reference to the asshole's primary physical functions—taking cock and shitting. He not only deflates the negative meanings associated with anal penetration, but also affectively performs disgust for Burton's sex-phobia: "Your asshole's such an asshole. You'll regret being so uptight," Zero sings with disdain. By deploying the digestive politics and poetics of AIDS, the very queer form of Zero's "literal" ass makes a figurative ass out of both Burton's bum and his conservatism around sex, rerouting aversion to so-called deviant sex acts toward those who misunderstand its pleasures.

The cultural work of the digestive politics and poetics of AIDS was aligned with, and made possible by, both radical AIDS activism and AIDS cultural theory in the late 1980s and early 1990s. As Deborah Gould has shown, the inception of the radical AIDS activist organization ACT UP in 1987 was driven by a collective rerouting of grief among members of the gay community into political rage. This rage was expressed through forms of direct-action activism—including civil disobedience and visual culture—that materially embodied, and ideologically supported, feelings of righteous indignation at the medical and political stigmatization of people with HIV/AIDS.[11] As Douglas Crimp has thoughtfully noted, the activist drive to mobilize militant political energies toward the movement often led to the diminishment of less politically effective emotions—depression, malaise, apathy, confusion—and a refusal to portray people with AIDS as suffering in the movement's visual media.[12] Against "dominant media" images of PWAs as "wasting deathbed images," Crimp declared, "We must continue to demand and create our own counter-images . . . of PWA self-empowerment, of the organized PWA movement and of the larger AIDS activist movement. . . . [W]e must therefore wage a war of representation, too."[13] Heavily influenced by the gay cultural politics of the feminist and queer 1970s, the various arms of the AIDS activist movement—including direct-action and mutual aid organizations like ACT UP, the Gay Men's Health Crisis, and the PWA Coalition, as well as "art-theoretical activism," typified by artist collectives like Gran Fury, Diva-TV, Testing the Limits, and the AIDS Memorial Quilt Project—fundamentally understood that political freedom for gender and sexual dissidents under life-threatening conditions was as much a formal or aesthetic problem as a political and social one. This meant that activists had to work toward a radical transformation of the ways in which a mass public could cognize or figure HIV/AIDS, and its associated high-risk populations, in the mind's eye as something other than faceless, disposable demographics.[14]

The digestive politics and poetics of AIDS was just such a "war of representation," and it shared with AIDS activism a commitment to the rerouting of emotion through attention to the somatic and fleshy experiences of actual bodies. Yet unlike AIDS activism, the digestive politics and poetics of AIDS risked representing the most medically devastating aspects of the illness and its various treatments, to make the physical symptoms of the disease politically and affectively productive *for* PWAs and their allies. As I discuss below, in stage dramas like *Angels in America*, this rhetorical productivity was literalized in the physical performance of viscerally charged language around the AIDS epidemic that actors affectively embodied on stage. Affect theorists like Sara Ahmed, Lauren Berlant, and Sianne Ngai have compellingly shown the ways that different feeling states come to attach (or "stick") to particular objects through powerful cultural imperatives and ideological mechanisms.[15] Yet there remains a dearth of theoretical tools for analyzing how feelings are modified, rerouted, or forced to become *unstuck* from dominant meanings by formal strategies that set themselves to the task of altering people's emotional landscapes. My analysis of the digestive politics and poetics of AIDS is an attempt to clear a space for understanding how transformations in the affective register of subjectivity can be enabled when viscerally charged discourse sidles up to, prods, and provokes emotional response, as when an interlocutor pushes an interviewee to a level of intensity they cannot physically contain, inciting an immediate bodily reaction.

One response that people have to such situations of heightened emotional impact or shock is to vomit. Indeed, the verbal delivery of an HIV-positive test result itself can produce an intensity of feeling powerful enough to induce vomiting (in Gregg Araki's 1992 film *The Living End*, the protagonist is shown throwing up into a toilet immediately after receiving positive test results from a doctor). Yet the desire to throw up, whether acted upon or merely felt, is also a gut-level sensation that AIDS activists and cultural producers have used to express the affective intensities provoked in them by government neglect, racism, and homophobia.[16] As mixed media artist and AIDS activist David Wojnarowicz searingly expressed in his 1991 memoir, *Close to the Knives*: "I want to throw up because we're supposed to quietly and politely make house in this killing machine called America and pay taxes to support our own slow murder."[17] Wojnarowicz links an overwhelming sensation —"feeling vomitey"—to a political reality so horrific it provokes violent physical reactions.

Of course, both the virus's myriad degenerative effects on the digestive system and the consequence of swallowing countless pills to combat it often cause/d people with HIV/AIDS to experience literal bouts of vomiting and diarrhea. In a 1999 interview with *Poz* magazine about his digestively inspired mixed-media show *Space Oddity (lesson in survival)*, artist Chuck Nanney explained, "I started my [HIV drug] regimen three years ago. . . . My body went berserk. I'd take the Viracept, throw up this gray nuclear bile and cry. Then things got better. But the emotional impact of 'I'm taking these pills to save my life but the way they make me feel is worse than death' is still with me. And I've stayed very tuned in to all the internal functions of my body. For example, I'm obsessed with my bowel movements."[18] Shuttling back and forth between literal and figurative digestive rhetoric allowed cultural producers like Wojnarowicz, Araki, Nanney, Kushner, and others to represent the material fact of HIV/AIDS as a conceptual figure that could magnetize political feelings imbued with force through their articulation to the somatic experience of illness.

Before moving to my reading of *Angels in America*, let me offer an example of this operation from a related cultural text. In one of the most disturbing scenes of his memoir, *Close to the Knives*, Wojnarowicz recounts the following story about a quack physician that many people with HIV/AIDS, including his former lover and friend Peter Hujar, flocked to in New York City when this doctor claimed to have found a cure for the disease in the late 1980s:

> The deciding factor for many people to leave this doctor was a vaccine he'd developed from human shit which each person was eventually injected with. When Peter told me about this treatment I figured that because shit was one of the most dangerous corporeal substances in terms of passing disease . . . maybe this guy figured out something in the properties of shit to develop a vaccine. After all, the bite of a rattlesnake is treated with a vaccine made of venom. But I also assumed that the doctor had at least made a vaccine for each patient out of their own shit. Later we found that one person's shit served as a base for all treatments.[19]

This brief recollection is stunning both in its calm delivery (unusual in a text where most of the language is conveyed with ferocious rage) but also in the visceral reality it presents. Wojnarowicz describes an act of medical barbarism. Hence, one might expect him to deliver a direct condemnation of the kind he repeatedly lobs against politicians and religious leaders like Jesse Helms and Cardinal Joseph O'Connor. What appears to be the absence of direct opposition here, however, is in fact a critique delivered at the level of affect. The linguistic invocation of a material digestive form, literal human feces, combined with a blistering description of its brazen misuse to medically exploit vulnerable patients has the potential to invoke extremely negative emotions or sensations around this scenario (it is difficult to read this scene without feeling your skin crawl). This possibility is materialized through Wojnarowicz's canny reorganization of the popular logic surrounding HIV transmission. In the public imagination, people with AIDS were repeatedly framed as social lowlifes who, by allowing themselves to be exposed to "tainted" blood and body fluids, had been infected with a life-threatening disease that merely confirmed the popular presumption of them as "human shit."[20] Here, however, Wojnarowicz presents us with a situation in which people who are already sick allow themselves to be injected *with* shit by supposedly trustworthy medical practitioners because they have no other treatment options. Wojnarowicz replaces the AIDS virus with US medicine itself, the latter framed as the lethal agent of an inhuman treatment that "bites" or infects its victim with the force of a viper. By juxtaposing some of the most viscerally discomforting elements of the disease—tainted injections, "polluted" bodily excrement—with the practices of US medicine, this scene makes possible the rerouting of disgust from bodies themselves to the larger systemic dehumanization of people with AIDS.

This is a point Wojnarowicz underscores in one of his most cited statements: "When I was told that I'd contracted the virus, it didn't take me long to realize that I'd contracted a diseased society as well."[21] Wojnarowicz's claim resonates with the character Prior's previously quoted statement from *Angels in America*: "My heart is pumping polluted blood. I feel dirty." In Kushner's digestive imaginary, and Wojnarowicz's visceral language, such "dirty" feelings are the direct result of government inaction, social stigma, and medical malpractice. Consequently, for those artists working within the rhetorical practices of the digestive politics and poetics of AIDS, the solution to "dirty feelings" was not to wash them away beneath pride or dignity, but to multiply them in all those who imagine themselves as "unpolluted" by the stigma of AIDS.

No cultural production of the late 1980s and early 1990s took up this project more boldly or effectively than *Angels in America*, which was being written and performed at the same time that AIDS cultural theory and radical AIDS activism reached their zenith between 1987 and 1993. The play renders the realm of politics itself as an affective intensity experienced on the body both in the visceral metaphors used to describe it and in the possible performance of those metaphors elicited by stage directions that demand "fury," "distaste," "terror," and "despair." Simultaneously, it links its characters' seemingly individual experiences of AIDS, racism, homophobia, and sexism—in particular, their digestive responses to the disease and its corollary social stigmas—to wider orders of experience including the nation, the globe, even the category of the human.

Composed of two distinct dramatic works performed over seven hours, and ranging over countless political issues including AIDS, religion, Reaganism, environmental catastrophe, and race relations, *Angels in America* has earned its reputation as one of the most logistically and politically ambitious plays in the history of US-American theater. At the center of the production are two couples at a moment of crisis. Living together for four years, the gay couple Louis and Prior are shaken by news of Prior's HIV diagnosis, while Harper and Joe Pitt, Mormon migrants to New York, reach a breaking point in their marriage when Harper begins to suspect that her husband is gay. In Part One, Louis leaves Prior, unable to deal with his lover's illness, and starts an affair with Joe. Joe considers leaving his wife and seeks professional advice from Roy Cohn, a successful lawyer and famed McCarthyite who, unbeknownst to Joe, is dying of AIDS. Confined to bed rest, and visited by his best friend Belize, Prior experiences a series of dreams that foreshadow the arrival of an otherworldly presence. In Part Two, we learn that this is an angel, sent from Heaven on a mission to ordain Prior as a prophet who will halt the spread of AIDS by convincing the world to "stop moving." Part Two narrates Prior's struggle to decide how to respond to this mandate, Louis's attempts to make amends for his abandonment, and Harper's soul-searching to imagine a life beyond her marriage. Concurrently, Roy is forced to come to terms with his political past as he dies of AIDS in a hospital ward while being nursed by Belize. At the play's conclusion, Prior rejects his mission in order to seek "more life" among a newly formed community of queer friends and loved ones, rather than the comforts of stasis or death.

In his foundational analysis of *Angels in America*, David Román locates the play's transformative potential in its ability to instill hope among its audience members, especially gay men, who, in the face of homophobia, illness, and death, witnessed in the play a reconfiguration of alliances between characters who become unlikely friends and companions in the struggle against AIDS.[22] Texturing this reading, I argue that the production of hope in the play that Román associates with its queer relational politics is paradoxically predicated on *Angels'* engagement with the seemingly *antisocial* sensation of disgust. If we feel hope at the play's conclusion, it is not merely because of the visibility of a longed-for queer community in the face of AIDS (though that is certainly available), but because we have also affectively internalized a proper abhorrence for the systems of power that prevent people from seeing those kinships as viable in the first place. This is a distinctly queer and feminist political feeling articulated from the subordinated position of sexual and gender outlaws of many stripes, among them an effeminate gay white man with HIV, a Black queer nurse managing a hospital's AIDS ward, a staunch Mormon mother turned AIDS caregiver, and a once devoted Mormon wife now a feminist apostate. Moreover, this affective orientation is cultivated not at the level of the plot but rather *at the level of the text*, namely in the visceral language, including rich gut metaphors, used to organize the logic of each character. For this reason, my analysis will work through the digestive rhetorical forms that coalesce around the play's central characters, as a shapeshifting conceit that links alimentary functions and dysfunctions to queer and feminist political feelings.

Ill Liberalism

LOUIS: I'm trying to be responsible. Prior. There are limits. Boundaries. And you have to be reasonable.

PRIOR (*furious*): Reasonable? Limits? Tell it to my lungs, stupid, tell it to my lesions, tell it to the cotton-wooly patches in my eyes! . . . You

cry, but you endanger nothing in yourself. It's like the idea of crying
when you do it. Or the idea of love.
—*Angels in America, Part Two: Perestroika*, act 4, scene 1

Midway through the second half of *Angels in America*, Louis Iron-
son, wracked with guilt, attempts to make amends for abandoning his
ex-lover Prior while he laid in a hospital bed sick from AIDS. Falter-
ingly, Louis justifies his leaving as a rational choice based on the desire
to protect himself from emotional pain and potential physical infection.
His language is that of boundaries, rational judgment, and clear moral
distinctions. Except as an object to be safeguarded, Louis's body remains
outside the calculus of his reasoning. Prior's "furious" return makes a
mockery of Louis's rhetorical attempts at setting limits by invoking
the messy materiality of his own HIV positive body, a fleshy substance
whose biological boundaries have been broken down by the disease's
myriad symptoms. His visceral language—given affective charge by the
direction to perform these lines with "fury"—issues a scathing critique,
not of Louis's abandonment as such, but his unwillingness to "endanger"
anything in himself either physically or emotionally, in his engagements
with the world.

This moment underscores *Angels in America*'s most fundamental
source of conflict: the inability of liberal democracy to account for and
respond to the embodied or corporeal experience of its subjects. Louis
articulates this dilemma early in the play. After learning of Prior's HIV
diagnosis, Louis asks the rabbi who presided over his grandmother's funeral what "the Holy Writ says about someone who abandons someone
he loves in a time of need." When the rabbi responds, "Why would a
person do such a thing?" Louis explains, "Maybe because . . . a person
who has this neo-Hegelian positivist sense of constant historical progress towards happiness or perfection or something . . . can't . . . incorporate sickness into his sense of how things are supposed to go. Maybe
vomit . . . and sores and disease . . . really frighten him, maybe . . . he isn't
so good with death" (31). As the play's representative liberal (both a humanist and a good Democrat) Louis is not only presaging his abandonment of Prior but also articulating, under the sign of a "neo-Hegelian
positivism," a broader political subjectivity so invested in notions of pure
historical progress that it must deny human mortality. *Angels* frames

US liberalism as a worldview that assumes the existence of a rational, rights-bearing subject and holds fast to a conviction that human progress and "happiness" are contingent upon an ever-expanding horizon of individual freedom. Yet the play also associates this worldview with an idealized political subject that is disembodied, transhistorical, and immortal. *Angels* counters this vision by presenting audiences with an alternative political subjectivity that I call "ill liberalism," a viscerally attuned worldview most powerfully enacted by the play's central HIV-positive character, Prior Walter, but that also gets variously taken up by a network of feminist and queer friends, caregivers, and empathic strangers across the span of the epic narrative.

In the logic of the play, ill liberalism retains the liberal commitment to democratic freedom and political recognition, while also recasting the subject of any democracy as materially contingent and affectively impacted by external forces that attenuate its attachment to humanist notions of universal progress. In the sense, the ill liberal subject profoundly embodies the visceral project of the digestive politics and poetics of AIDS by both literally inhabiting a sick or dysfunctional body (as all bodies inherently are or will one day be) and figuratively being "*sick of*" the false ideology of liberal progress. As an expression of this ill liberal politics, Louis's and Prior's respective political orientations to liberalism are characterized throughout the play by the dual digestive dysfunctions of constipation and diarrhea, both common symptoms of illness, but especially of HIV/AIDS. By articulating a critique of liberalism to the physical forms of defecation, the play creates a series of formal equivalences between dysfunctional alimentary processes and political rhetoric that confront the abstraction inherent to the liberal framework with the messy experience of carnal life. Thus, *Angels* encourages audiences to see corporeality and political subjectivity as intimately interwoven categories that co-create or give shape to one another.[23]

As his dialogue with the rabbi indicates, Louis is defined by a phobia of sick and dying bodies. Following his grandmother's funeral, he admits that his discomfort with her aging lead him to "[pretend] for years that she was already dead" (30). His revulsion at bodies is repeatedly commented upon by friends and loved ones and catalyzes some of the play's central events, including his abandonment of Prior. When Prior meets

Hannah, Joe Pitt's mother, in Part Two of the play, he jokes, "I wanted to warn your son about *later*, when his hair goes and there's hips and jowls . . . human stuff, that poor slob there's just gonna wind up . . . frightened and alone because Louis, he can't handle bodies" (231). Louis's inability to "handle bodies" is framed as an expression of a constipated orientation to the world that is both literal and figurative. Not long after this scene, Prior becomes ill and is rushed to the hospital, where Louis abandons him. Louis retreats to Central Park, where he begs a male hustler to "fuck me, hurt me, make me bleed" as a self-imposed punishment for his liberal intolerance in the face of his dying lover. Unsurprisingly, his ass is so tight the hustler asks him to relax, to which he characteristically responds "not a chance" (60, 63). His clenched sphincter muscles cause the condom to break, and Louis's guilt-induced wish to be infected with AIDS disgusts the hustler enough that he leaves the scene.[24] Even when he willfully seeks infection, Louis's physical tightness refuses to "endanger anything in himself" by disallowing the entry of foreign fluid (or dick) into his body. We soon learn that Louis suffers from hemorrhoids, a classic symptom of constipation, and throughout the rest of the play, both Prior and his friend Belize hurl defecatory insults at Louis—claiming he is "full of piping hot crap" and characterizing him as a "shitbag"—intimating the stored-up material he badly needs to release. The very shape of Louis's asshole, then, including its hemorrhoidal growths, is an allegory for his entire emotional landscape and ideological worldview.

Belize and Prior's canny insults conceptually link Louis's digestive dysfunction and his questionable ethics, pointing to a larger relationship between embodied realities—in this case, a tight sphincter—and distinct political orientations that Louis himself vehemently denies. This symbolic equivalence then becomes formally constituted in the mind of any viewer through repeated references to the physical structure of the digestive tract. When Belize first visits Prior after Louis abandons him, Prior claims, "Well, at least I have the satisfaction of knowing he's in anguish somewhere. I loved . . . [w]atching him stick his head up his asshole and eat his guts out over some relatively minor moral conundrum" (67). The metaphorical rewriting of Louis's "anguish" as the act of "sticking his head up his asshole and eat[ing] his guts out" materializes liberal guilt—which is often characterized as a stalled political emotion—as an embodied tautology. To eat your own guts results in constipation, or the incapacity to release a bowel movement, since the material one eats *is* your digestive tract, which is the conduit for working through food and expelling shit.

Ironically, when Louis expresses his own frustrations with liberal politics to Belize, he uses strikingly scatological language that suggestively links the forms of the bowels to the political logic of democracy. He defines democracy as the "[inexorable] shifting downwards and outwards of political power to the people" and claims: "The American Left can't help but trip over all these petrified little fetishes: freedom; that's the worst. . . . The worst kind of liberalism, really, bourgeois tolerance, and what I think is that what AIDS shows us is that it's not enough to be tolerated, because when the shit hits the fan you find out [that] underneath all the tolerance is intense, passionate hatred" (98, 96). In a play where malfunctioning digestion is a hallmark of HIV/AIDS, Louis's description of the "downward and outward" movement of democracy can be read as parallel to a bowel movement, while the "petrified little fetishes" of liberalism are so much hardened stool. If democracy is a "good shit," Louis unwittingly indicts himself when he rails against the constipated ideologies of liberalism. Indeed when in Louis's life "the shit hit the fan" (literally the moment when Prior's shit hit the floor only a few scenes earlier), his tolerance for the bodies of people with AIDS reached its limit. Louis may not notice that his literal constipation is an embodied metaphor for the uptight liberal tolerance he disparages, but the play's digestive language has prepared audiences to do so and to feel proper disgust for Louis's lack of self-awareness.

Belize legitimizes this potential reaction by responding to Louis's political hypocrisy with palpable revulsion. Moments after his critique of liberal tolerance, Louis shockingly suggests that despite a history of white supremacy, US democracy has never reflected a genuine belief in racial hierarchy, but that some white US-Americans have leveraged the *idea* of racial supremacy in their various bids for social, economic, and political power. Thus, the constitution's underlying egalitarian spirit has allowed the nation's citizens to overcome their "racial past" (95–96). Once again, Louis purifies liberal politics of actual bodies, specifically racialized ones, and their distinct material histories. Belize responds by radically reducing Louis to his own body: "I know the guilt fueling this peculiar tirade is obviously already swollen bigger than your hemor-rhoids."[25] Louis denies the claim until finally admitting:

> LOUIS: Prior told you, he's an asshole, he shouldn't have . . .
> BELIZE: You promised, Louis. Prior is not a subject.
> LOUIS: So it's indirect. Passive-aggressive.
> BELIZE: Unlike, I suppose, banging me over the head with your theory
> that America doesn't have a race problem. (98–99)

This exchange exemplifies the rhetorical and affective work of the digestive politics and poetics of AIDS. Belize uses a visceral metaphor to link Louis's liberal politics to an anal bodily form (Louis's "tirade" is "swollen bigger than [a] hemorrhoid"). This metaphor reroutes an-tipathy for dysfunctional bodies toward the hypocrisies of a constipated liberalism. Belize's comments reveal that Louis equates race itself with something as medically undesirable as hemorrhoids, an issue suppos-edly cured by "the shifting downward and outward of political power to the people" (92). Pointing out this parallel, Belize writes race back onto Louis's body by materially marking his digestive dysfunction, and its at-tendant anal symptoms, as something that identifies him with a distinct political position, namely a racist liberalism.

Belize's critique of Louis echoes the rhetoric of contemporaneous AIDS activist organizations that described government inaction in the face of the AIDS in constipated terms. In a handbook accompany-ing their action against the Federal Drug Administration in October 1988, ACT UP characterized the FDA as "actively *blocking* the delivery of promising drugs to PWAs" and explained that the FDA's job is "to compel reluctant drug sponsors to *release* experimental treatments" (my italics).[26] Organizations like ACT UP saw themselves as helping "un-block" the machinery of government by opening up access to treatment and galvanizing humane health policies. This excremental language in activist discourse, as well as cultural productions that used anality as a touchstone for discussions of HIV/AIDS, was particularly prescient at a moment when the anus had become one of the most contested sites of meaning-making in US culture. In his field-defining 1988 essay "Is the Rectum a Grave?" Leo Bersani argued that the predominance of

HIV transmission by anal intercourse not only produced the asshole as a site of deadly, "perverse" pleasures in the public imagination, but also elicited a murderous rage against the actual or perceived practitioners of anal sex, who were ignorantly assumed to be almost exclusively gay men.[27] Bersani shows how the widespread disgust for gay men relied on a cruel and sexist chain of signification where a gay male with HIV/AIDS was understood as someone who, by choosing to be sexually penetrated by another man, had abdicated his manhood to become, at least symbolically, a women (and a diseased one at that). As a result, "The public discourse about homosexuals since the AIDS crisis began has a startling resemblance . . . to the representation of female prostitutes in the nineteenth century 'as contaminated vessels, conveyancing "female" venereal diseases to "innocent" men.'"[28] Bersani suggests that sexually active gay men and straight women came to occupy the same ideological location in a sex-phobic culture, with gay men seen not only as "contaminated vessels" but people who were biological killers of innocent heterosexuals by virtue of having figuratively murdered their own claim to normative masculinity.[29]

Despite the conceptual power of his argument, Bersani's essay ironically avoids discussing the actual physical trials of getting fucked. As anyone who enjoys anal sex knows, taking it up the ass takes practice, can be messy and painful, *as well as* pleasurable and orgasmic. *Angels in America* ventures into this territory by depicting the discomforts of "opening up" (including Louis's encounter with the hustler) and the asshole's variety of physical ailments. The play's central protagonist, Prior Walter, is the character whose asshole is made most vulnerable in the narrative, both as the putative site where he contracted HIV and as the orifice most affected by the disease through cycles of diarrhea. It is this anally dysfunctional queer, effeminized figure, the very object of US-Americans' vicious calumny according to Bersani, upon which *Angels* hitches its political vision.

If Louis exhibits a constipated liberalism, Prior inhabits a diarrheal (or excremental) political imaginary. Where Louis fervently denies rhetorical practices that point back at his own embodiment, Prior is relentlessly embodied, both in the spectacular symptoms of his illness and in his emotionally excessive relationship to the world. He is by turns melodramatic, histrionic, flamboyant, and fabulous in his emotive responses to his illness and Louis's abandonment. Prior literally ingests countless pills, vomits, and diarrheas on stage, and repeatedly verbalizes his physical symptoms to loved ones, friends, and medical professionals, almost always women and other (feminized) gay men, who come to represent his interpersonal and ideological allies in performing an ill liberal politics attuned to "the gut as much as the mind."[30] Prior represents the constitutive limit of liberal thought in the mid-1980s, a man whose HIV status renders him already "dead" in the eyes of the general public, but whose loud, angry, and bombastic refusal of death contradicts this assessment, presenting someone who "lives past" their physical deterioration (267). If Louis's (and by extension, liberalism's) disgust for bodies polices the boundary between healthy liberal subjects and the deathly ill, Prior's hyperbolic performance of counter-disgust at Louis's unwillingness to "endanger anything in himself" becomes an affective force that underwrites a new political subjectivity at the margins of US democracy that I call "ill liberalism." As expressed in the figure of Prior, ill liberalism is defined by three qualities.

It is, first and foremost, a form of liberal politics that takes at its starting point the common phenomenological reality of inhabiting a body (with its capacity to register sensation) and an awareness of the uneven distribution of bodily privileges. Ill liberalism recognizes that political subjects are inherently heterogeneous despite any common conception of rights or privileges they may share because of their distinct corporeal or somatic experiences of the world. Yet because politics is so often enacted in discourse (namely language and representation), ill liberalism performs radical acts of resignification that link felt and discursive registers of experience to make political language more amenable to responding to fleshy realities. When, near the conclusion of *Angels in America*, Louis tries to make amends to Prior by claiming that he is emotionally bruised "inside" from the choices he's made, Prior demands that he "come back when they're visible. I want to see black and blue, Louis. . . . Because I can't believe you even have blood in your veins till you show it to me" (226). Prior seeks material accountability from Louis for the psychic pain he has inflicted by bearing physical marks on his own body as an outward expression of his atonement and empathy for others. In this case, those marks are "black and blue" bruises that echo the "wine-dark" mark of Kaposi sarcoma lesions that so many people with HIV/AIDS physically exhibited.

Second, ill liberalism functions as a critical political orientation that speaks truth to power from the position of the sick, the infirm, and the disabled. It takes up what Robert McRuer has termed a "severely disabled" vantage point on political engagement by "revers[ing] the able-bodied understanding of severely disabled bodies as the most marginalized . . . instead suggest[ing] that it is precisely those bodies that are best positioned to refuse 'mere toleration' and to call out the inadequacies of compulsory able-bodiedness."[31] In doing so, ill liberalism recodes illness as a source of political power that is not reducible to the will or fantasies of overcoming. This ill liberal posture toward traditional liberal notions of health is evident in Prior's response to Belize's gift of AZT pills at the play's conclusion. Louis says, "These pills, they . . . make you better," to which Prior replies, "They're poison . . . This is my life, from now on, Louis. I'm not getting 'better.'" (272). Prior's judicious response to the supposedly lifesaving properties of modern medicine acknowledges that the attempt to cling to a progressive view of history—to imagine that the goal of life is to always "get better"—can itself be poisonous, or at least lead one to choose poison above one's own gut sense of what is right for one's body. Prior's "life, from now on" is not about "getting better," which might mean inhabiting the world in new and unforeseen ways.

Finally, ill liberalism is a promiscuous political outlook that actively seeks engagement with the messiness of everyday life. It is, like Prior's diarrhea, an excremental political imaginary that functions through contamination, diffusion, and proliferation. We can see one example of this in the Angel's poetic description of Prior as a "battered heart; Bleeding life in the Universe of Wounds" (180). The image of Prior as a "battered heart" resignifies the figure of the "bleeding heart liberal," not as an epithet, but as a messy and productive outpouring of political energies that injects (polluted) blood into a social world understood as a porous "Universe of Wounds." In Ben Highmore's words, this rhetorical gesture—which yokes the material form of the beating human heart to the figure of the vulnerable, symbolically "bleeding" political subject—recasts politics as "a form of experiential pedagogy, of constantly submitting your sensorium to new sensual worlds that sit uncomfortably within your ethos. . . . [I]f this politics was dedicated to opening up the affective, sensorial tuning and retuning of the social body—then it would need to be exorbitant . . . a politics of the gut as much as the mind."³² As an "exorbitant" politics of "the gut as much as the mind," ill liberalism retools liberal thought to value the body's potentially transformative encounters with a "sensual world" of other bodies, fleshy agents, objects, even ideas, and to recognize that such encounters might alter what counts as "human" or worthy of political recognition.

At once aggressively embodied, attuned to mutual care, and materially and psychically permeable to a wider world, Prior's ill liberalism is also a distinctly *feminized* political subjectivity. Throughout *Angels in America*, Prior explicitly inhabits so-called traditional feminine roles—as Louis's abandoned "wife," an emotional hysteric, a sexually "penetrated" bottom, and a spiritual vessel for the Angel—while also experiencing his most sustained and meaningful on-stage interactions with women and queer femmes. Among these are his best friend, Belize; his "smart-mouthed" nurse, Emily; Joe Pitt's austere but loyal mother, Hannah; the rebellious Mormon wife, Harper; and the Angel, who despite being an androgyne, appears in a divine female form. In this extended relational network, Kushner recalls the variety of roles straight and lesbian women inhabited in the context of coalitional AIDS activism: the women nurses who showed humanity toward AIDS patients, the lesbian best friends who became direct-action activists, the mothers and sisters who took on unexpected roles as caregivers. The play then materializes Bersani's trenchant arguments about the shared social and ideological positioning of women and gay men in the AIDS crisis.

By the mid-1980s, in the face of a national backlash against feminism, the internal fracturing of the women's movement along axes of race, class, and pro- or anti-sex stances, and the dissolution of gay liberationist energies into a strategy of assimilation, the urgency of the AIDS epidemic provided an opportunity for women and queers to discover renewed common cause. Just as the movements for women's and gay liberation in the 1970s found shared ground in their mutual refusal of heteropatriarchy and arbitrary sex-class division, AIDS activism wedded feminist critiques of the medical establishment's control over women's bodies with a uniquely queer approach to coalitional politics aimed at drawing together women and queers, racial minorities, drug users, and the homeless. As Ann Cvetkovich and Deborah Gould have documented, lesbians who had participated in 1970s feminist political projects brought the wealth of their strategic knowledge, including consciousness-raising, zap actions, and movement organizing, to bear on AIDS activist mobilization efforts.[33] In their support of causes like the Women's Health Movement, including access to abortion and contraception, and the fight for an Equal Rights Amendment, these women had been enacting a distinctly *ill liberal* politics by publicly articulating a visceral disgust for patriarchal domination over women's bodies. Now, like women before them, gay men were being aggressively manipulated and abused by a sexist and homophobic medical establishment, and treated as second-class citizens by a government that policed their sexual conduct. This demanded a return to an earlier gay liberation view that gay men's political destinies were bound to the freedom of all women since both groups were perceived as the constitutive outside of normative masculinity, and hence experienced similar limitations on their right to health care, free sexual expression, and basic bodily autonomy due to arbitrary forms of social control. In this way, Kushner's conception of ill liberalism, based in a healthy political aversion to virulent forms of institutional homophobia and sexism, not only acknowledged the cross-gender coalitional contexts of AIDS activism, but underscored the gut-level resonance between the movements for women's and gay liberation in the 1970s, whose shared vision of gender and sexual freedom remained inextricably, and viscerally, bound together.

Kushner registers this shared vision by not only repeatedly bringing women and queers into each other's orbit but imbuing them with the ability to intuit or viscerally sense shared "truths" about their relative social positions. Consistently throughout the narrative, Prior suddenly and surprisingly encounters Harper and Hannah Pitt, nearly always during his greatest moments of bodily vulnerability while enduring night sweats, diarrhea, and coughing fits. Both women share with Prior the experience of being abandoned by the central man in their lives, in their case Joe Pitt. And all three appear to share a kind of second sight or ability to perceive the injustice leveled against their psyches and bodies by selfish men as much as vast institutional structures like the medical system, the Mormon and Catholic churches, and the US government.

Early on in the play, Prior encounters Harper in a vivid, sweat-soaked dream brought on by the side effects of AZT medication. Harper experiences the same encounter as a valium-induced hallucination (the drug of choice for the depressed 1950s housewives profiled in Betty Friedan's *The Feminine Mystique*). Both characters intuitively understand that the dreamworld they find themselves in is "the threshold of revelation," a liminal space where one can "see things" as they really are. A gay man and a straight woman literally interpenetrate one another's imaginations in and through their shared bodily permeability to unpredictable chemical substances and diseases of the blood (AIDS) as much as the mind (chronic depression). Harper sees in Prior his sickness, but she also instinctively apprehends that "[d]eep inside" of him "the most inner part [is] entirely free of disease." In turn, Prior sees that Harper is "amazingly unhappy," because her "husband is really gay" (39). Initially flummoxed by one another's seemingly divine awareness, Prior explains, "I just looked at you, and there was . . ." Harper finishes his sentence: "A sort of blue stream of recognition . . . like you knew me incredibly well" (40).

The threshold of revelation is a space of queer and feminist political imagination, where the recognition of mutual experiences of gender and sexual oppression—AIDS stigma, marital dissatisfaction, and abandonment by men all resonating as comparable forms of societal and interpersonal betrayal—is offset by a sense of shared (feminist) insight, that women and queers might make up for their denigration in the wider society by turning toward one another, speaking radical truths, and building a politics born of their shared embodied experiences. It is perhaps no surprise that throughout the scene Prior is dressed in drag, indicated women and gay men's overlapping performances of gender. When Prior sees how despondent Harper becomes at news that her marriage is a lie, he says: "I'm sorry. I usually say 'fuck the truth,' but mostly the truth fucks you" (40). And indeed, both characters have been "fucked over" by shared realities—illness, depression, neglect—that their former partners have chosen to ignore. But both are also willing to fuck the truth, even risk getting "sick" from it, if it means reclaiming their humanity and health from the forces that deny their material existence. Near the end of the play, emboldened by Prior's earlier recognition and his unflinching "read" of Louis and Joe, Harper will confront her husband naked and fully exposed in their shabby Brooklyn apartment: "What do you see?" to which he replies emphatically: "*Nothing.*" "Thank you," she responds, "Finally. The Truth. . . . It sets you free. Goodbye." (239). If Harper was once literally "fucked" by a husband who sees her as "nothing," she now willfully chooses to expose herself to his callous disregard, to be "promiscuous" with the truth, which in turn unmasks his virulent misogyny, making it a palpable form of inhumanity she can finally free herself from, much as Prior had freed himself from Louis's liberal guilt.

Similarly, in Hannah Pitt, Joe's mother, Kushner presents a highly unexpected proxy for the lesbian AIDS activist and caregiver. Having sold all her possessions and moved to New York City to attend to her son's failing marriage, Hannah finds herself isolated in an unfamiliar urban environment, forced to work at the NYC Mormon Visitors' Center to make ends meet. When in a jealous rage, Prior follows Joe to the Center one rainy night, he watches from afar as Joe berates Hannah for coming to Manhattan before disavowing her and storming off. After Joe exits, Prior, now wracked with cough, enters the Center looking for help, where he promptly collapses in front of Hannah and is rushed to the hospital. In an odd symmetry, Prior and Hannah are both made sick, one physically, the other emotionally, by callous men. Both also come to reinhabit their previous social positions, ailing son and concerned mother, in new ways: Prior becomes Hannah's figurative gay son with AIDS while Hannah becomes Prior's accidental friend and caregiver. At one point, Hannah catches a glimpse of Prior's Kaposi sarcoma lesions: "Look at this . . . horror," he exclaims, "That's not human." Without hesitating she replies: "It's a cancer. Nothing more. Nothing more human than that." Just as it took Harper, a woman struggling to define an inner self free from her husband's pathologizing, to remind Prior that "the most inner part [of you is] entirely free of disease," so it takes a Mormon mother, a woman spiritually attuned to worldly suffering, to remind Prior that his illness is nothing more than an index of his fundamental, material belonging to the vulnerable category of the human.

When Prior voices his assumption that a Mormon like Hannah must be "repulsed" by a "homosexual . . . with AIDS," she rebuts, "No you can't. Imagine. The things in my head. You don't make assumptions about me mister; I won't make them about you" (235). Hannah surprises not only because her Mormonism sits comfortably with her empathy for

Prior, but because she views his disease dispassionately—she is a woman
who has seen true unfairness, the muck of the world, which is not sick
and dying people but the injustices of selfish, "stupid," and self-serving
men. Shortly after, when Prior asks how she responded to her son's coming out:

> HANNAH: I flew into a rage when he told me, mad as hornets. At first I
> assumed it was about his . . . (*She shrugs*)
> PRIOR: Homosexuality.
> HANNAH: But that wasn't it. Homosexuality. It just seems . . . ungainly.
> Two men together.
> It isn't an appetizing notion but then, for me, men in any configura-
> tion . . . well they're so lumpish and stupid. And stupidity gets me
> cross.
> PRIOR: I wish you would be more true to your demographic profile.
> Life is confusing enough. (236)

Hannah's staunch attitude in the face of seeming catastrophe (captured in Prior's claim that her presence "stiffens his spine"), her refusal
to moralize about bodies or attach negative political meaning to illness,
and her humorous distaste for the "ungainly" and "unappetizing" image
of "two men together" (which is really an animus toward male "stupidity" rather than genuine homophobia) associate her with the iconic figure of the 1970s lesbian feminist and women's health advocate. This was
a political figure who combined a healthy distrust of men with a commitment to mutual aid across identities, a critique of traditional mothering with a devotion to caregiving, and a view of women's bodies as
sacred alongside a realistic understanding of universal human frailty.
Hannah's failure to live up to her "demographic profile" similarly registers the difficulty of pinning down the assumed political or identitarian
allegiances of the feminist lesbian, whose seemingly essentialist politics in the 1970s gave way to cross-gender, cross-racial, and cross-class
affinities in the context of 1980s AIDS activism. This lesbian feminist
vociferously advocated for both gay men's access to non-homophobic
medical care as well as women's right to be counted as a legitimate HIV
risk group requiring treatment and care. And like her activist counterpart, Hannah cares for Prior not simply by soothing him but through

radical candor, seeing through Prior's self-deprecation and pushing back against his narrow liberal assumptions about a Mormon woman's potential political values. It is fitting that, in the play's final moments, Hannah becomes an integral part of Prior's queer community, sitting with Black, white, and Jewish gay men debating the future of democracy in a post–Soviet Union world: in this gay and feminist friendship circle, we see a multiracial, cross-gender, cross-class version of the liberal democratic promise enacted by practitioners of a rigorous ill liberalism.

The various components of ill liberalism I have enumerated above—including its embodied politics and commitment to mutual aid, its physical and affective permeability to others and staunch feminist sensibility—are captured in Prior's final statement to the Angels when he refuses their prophetic injunction to "stop moving" at the play's conclusion:

> Even sick, I want to be alive. . . . I can't help myself. . . . I've lived through such terrible times, and there are people who live through much much worse, but . . . you see them living anyway. When they're more spirit than body, more sores than skin. . . . When flies lay eggs in the corners of the eyes of their children, they live. . . . I don't know if that's just the animal . . . if it's not braver to die. But I recognize the habit. The addiction to being alive. We live past hope. . . . [It's] so inadequate but . . . Bless me anyway. I want more life. (265–267)

Prior's invocation of the array of human infirmities acknowledges the many physical forms that the human takes, while recognizing the corporeal registers of human existence, including potentially "animal" forces that drive us. His ill liberal interpretation of life itself as an "addiction" blurs the lines between a pure humanist category and a disease. It makes life fleshier, and less abstract, as a biochemical longing for existence *and* a potential spiritual or ethical ideal oriented toward practices of "living anyway." In conjuring the image of the unmarked parent whose child appears ill beyond saving or near death, he gestures toward the political necessity of mothering, not as a woman's natural job, but as the innate human impulse to guard and stand by even the most devastated of human lives. This is a uniquely feminist outlook that sees every child as a ward of the human race. As the iconic ill liberal subject, Prior enacts the visceral as a political stance, but is also a character who is textually produced through relentlessly visceral language—in one moment taking the form of a bleeding heart, in another a messy shit, and yet another a "wine-dark" bruise—that enables him to be seen as literally and figuratively alive *because* of his experience of illness. It is this discursive work of Prior's ill liberal orientation to the world that enables one of the most ambitious resignifying projects in the history of AIDS cultural production: the disarticulation of AIDS and DEATH, and the rearticulation of AIDS with *MORE LIFE.*

Certainly, this ill liberal perspective maintains the teleological thrust of liberal thought. It looks forward to a democratic future yet to come and it demands accountability from the very social forces and political institutions—medicine, the legal system, the Council of Angels, even God ("Sue the bastard for walking out," as Prior puts it [264])—that "interfere with progress for people with AIDS."[34] Yet the play's teleology reorients liberalism's commitment to an idealized political horizon, toward immediate egalitarian projects to abolish real-world suffering. When, in his meeting with the Angels, Prior declares, "this plague, it should stop. In me and everywhere" (264), he echoes Douglas Crimp's assertion, "We don't need to transcend the epidemic; we need to end it." An ill liberal worldview allows Prior to hold two seemingly contradictory ideas at once: that living things are "animate" desiring beings that move forward in time and space (who don't "need to transcend" the epidemic through angelic intervention), but that certain atrocities and forms of suffering should simply *stop.* This was also the orientation of radical AIDS activism, which highlighted the vibrant lives of people with AIDS and their allies, while also fighting to bring an end to the epidemic.

"A Stomach Grumble That Wakes You in the Night": Disgust, Contempt, and Other Gut Feelings

In the preceding section, I mapped a formal dualism between the material structures of the digestive tract and the political orientations that attach to them in the characters of Louis and Prior. Yet even as it stages this dualism the play does not ultimately seek a middle ground or dialectical reconciliation in the figure of a "healthy bowel movement." Rather, in the spirit of ill liberalism, the narrative multiplies forms of messy excretion and comingling that might allow for a greater attentiveness to actual bodies and their humane treatment within US-American democracy.[35] To demonstrate this, in this section I extend my analysis of Louis and Prior to three supporting characters—Roy Cohn, Belize (Norman Arriaga), and Harper Pitt—around whom the play constructs a variety of metaphors and tropes of "the gut" that slide from the literal to the figurative. This includes the catalog of alimentary functions (chewing, swallowing, and spitting up) and the stomach's appetitive demands, as well as gut feelings (disgust, contempt, rage, anxiety, even hope). The play's proliferation of meanings and uses of the gut—as literal digestive system made up of numerous physiological forms, as intuitive sense of dynamic social relations, as politics itself—maps a network of political relationships across race, class, and gender, shifts emotional investments, and links alimentary sensations like the churning of the stomach to "gut" feelings of aversion to US racism, sexism, and homophobia.

No character in *Angels in America* is more richly drawn in digestive terms than the play's putative villain, Roy Cohn, the successful but reviled attorney who first made his name as Joseph McCarthy's right-hand man. Throughout the play, Roy's closeted homosexuality and AIDS diagnosis are emblems of his despicable political hypocrisy, while his unfettered pursuit of political power is characterized by a voracious appetite for food and sex. The first stage direction introducing Roy links his personality to a prodigious excess of embodiment: "Roy conducts business with . . . sensual abandon: gesticulating, shouting, cajoling, crooning, playing the phone . . . with virtuosity and love" (17). Both his endearments and epithets are gastronomic in character. In his first scene he encourages Joe Pitt to "live a little . . . eat something for Christ sake," screams at a former client to "eat me," and responds to Joe admitting he is a Mormon with the word "delectable" (19, 21).

Roy's promiscuous engagement with gustatory pleasures would initially appear to make him an ideal figure of ill liberalism. Yet it is immediately clear that his ravenous appetite is a material symptom of his self-image as a shark at the top of the political "food chain." When he is first diagnosed with AIDS, he tells his doctor:

AIDS. Your problem, Henry, is that you are hung up on words, on labels. . . . AIDS. Homosexual. Gay. Lesbian. You think these are names that tell you who someone sleeps with, but they don't tell you that. . . . Like all labels they tell you one thing and one thing only: where does an individual so identified fit in the food chain. . . . This is what a label refers to. Not ideology, or sexual taste, but something much simpler: clout. . . . Homosexuals are men who . . . cannot get a pissant anti-discrimination bill through City Council . . . who have zero clout. Does this sound like me, Henry? . . . AIDS is what homosexuals have. I have liver cancer. (51–52)

In this remarkable speech, Roy deconstructs how identity categories, rather than reflecting objective truths about a person, are ideological inventions that attach to bodies for the purpose of instituting and maintaining social and political pecking orders. Yet even as he deconstructs one set of hierarchies around AIDS and sexual identity, he reinstates another through the metaphor of the "food chain," placing himself at the top of a complex organization of power based on sexual and class privilege by exhibiting contempt for the identities that compose its lowest rungs, gay men and PWAs. As his storyline unfolds however, the play makes clear that Roy's downfall is not due to his conservatism alone, but rather his inability to see his own compromised position *within* the very hierarchies of race, class, and sex that he so admires.

This irony is performatively expressed through Roy's most visible AIDS symptom: excruciating stomach cramps. Roy's onstage performance is organized around a series of verbally acerbic expressions of disdain for those he deems beneath him, followed by (or concurrent with) debilitating belly spasms that undermine his attempts to get distance from politically "spoiled" bodies. By suturing a violently painful gut feeling to Roy's corrupt politics, the play performs an ill liberal reading of Cohn to suggest that he has no intuition, or "gut feeling," for his own precarious position in the pecking order. When Roy dies, having been summarily disbarred for laundering money from a client, it is with the knowledge that his colleagues gleefully brought down a judgment against him, both professional and social, one of them confessing, "Finally. I've hated that little faggot for thirty-six years" (245). It is telling that the only other person in the play who calls Roy a "faggot" is his nurse Belize, a Black ex–drag queen who brilliantly uses the term to signal the unexpected commonalities between them as abject bodies in the US-American political "food chain."

At the conclusion of the third act of *Angels in America*, Part Two, Roy Cohn, in a morphine-induced stupor, asks his nurse Belize to describe the afterlife. Belize humors Roy, who has up to this point treated him with racist scorn: "[A] big city . . . like San Francisco . . . on every corner a wrecking crew and something new and crooked going up catty-corner to that . . . piles of trash, but lapidary like rubies . . . and voting booths . . . and everyone in Balenciaga gowns with red corsages, and big dance palaces full of music and lights and racial impurity and gender confusion. And all the deities are creole, mulatto, brown as the mouths of rivers. Race, taste and history finally overcome" (209–210). Belize describes an urban fantasy-space where the uneven geography reflects the breakdown of traditional social status, the figurative and literal intermixing of racial and gendered differences, and the emergence of sites of collective expression and political participation for formerly disenfranchised people. This is a queer afterlife indeed, where the lowliest citizens appear in exquisite fashion ready to vote, where trash hides gems, where gods look like the people they represent . . . a lot like "San Francisco." This is the antithesis of the world as Roy understands it. Roy responds to Belize "*Who are you?* . . . I know you. A stomach grumble that wakes you in the night" (210). The act in which Belize describes his version of Heaven is aptly titled "Borborygmi"—the rumbling noise made by gas moving through the intestine. Belize, then, is the figurative borborygmi of the play, someone who performs political indigestion in response to the "hot air" of racist, homophobic conservatism and self-interested liberalism.[36]

Belize is the only explicitly racialized figure in *Angels in America*, and he articulates the most nuanced critique of race in the play by repeatedly forcing into view those bodies and social worlds occluded by Louis's constipated liberalism and Roy's conservatism. Though he appears to identify as African American, both his drag name and surname (Norman Arriaga) link him to Central America, while his anti-imperialist critique of US racism expresses an affinity with diasporic cultures across the Americas. When Prior first relates to Belize the Angel's prophecy, Belize immediately points out the colonial implications of the heavenly injunction to "Stop Moving!": "This is worse than nuts . . . don't migrate, don't mingle, that's malevolent, some of us didn't exactly choose to migrate, know what I'm saying?" (180). Where the Angel conceives of "the virus of time" as transhistorical, Belize reminds us that all kinds of movement—voluntary or coerced—have a history grounded in real flesh-and-blood lives, including the enforced diasporas of colonized peoples and the global movement of AIDS across continents *and* bodies.

Throughout the play, Belize's performs what William Ian Miller calls "upward contempt" for those at the top of US social hierarchies.[37] In one particularly direct expression of upward contempt, Belize exclaims to Louis, "I hate America. The white cracker who wrote the national anthem . . . set the word 'free' to a note so high nobody can reach it." For Belize, neither the soaring heights of Heaven nor the lofty ideals of democracy are beyond critical scrutiny (228). When Roy asks him to stay and talk in his hospital room, Belize responds, "Mr. Cohn. I'd rather suck the pus out of an abscess. I'd rather drink a subway toilet. I'd rather chew off my tongue and spit it in your leathery face" (158). Belize's willingness to endanger his bodily boundaries to consume such vile ingestibles *above* conversing with Roy dramatically reverses their positions of power, placing Cohn and his ideology beneath pus and toilet water. Belize raises himself to the level of a saint in his reference to sucking pus from an abscess, an act attributed to Catherine of Sienna. One might assume that Belize should be afraid of Roy's bodily fluid (spit and blood) as a potential site of HIV transmission. But Belize is far more wary of the dishonored lawyer's words, which transmit his conservative politics. Belize inoculates himself against the possibility of being *affected* by Cohn's base politics by threatening to soil Roy with his tongue, itself a powerful vehicle for caustic language but also visceral revulsion for Roy's worldview. At one point, when Belize asks Roy why he won't share his stash of AZT pills with those in need, Roy claims, "Because I hate your guts, and your friends' guts" (190). Roy hates Belize and his friends' guts because he sees in them the kind of labels (AIDS, gay and lesbian, Black) that signal the loss of his standing in the political "food chain."[38] Belize's counterclaim that he "hates America," rather than people with AIDS, rewrites those very identities as a gut feeling for how the food chain is organized unevenly. He innovates a political language that acts as counterknowledge to a whitewashed liberal imaginary (228).

At the same time, Belize's understanding of multiple axes of oppression makes him the play's most intersectional character. This is evidenced in his first encounter with Roy, who is admitted to Belize's AIDS ward with the diagnosis of "liver cancer":

> BELIZE: (*with . . . distaste*) This didn't come from me and I don't like you but . . . They have you down for radiation tomorrow for the sarcoma lesions, and you don't want to let them do that, because radiation will kill the T-cells and you don't have any you can afford to lose. So tell the doctor no thanks for the radiation . . . Persuade him. Or he'll kill you.
>
> ROY: You're just a fucking nurse. Why should I listen to you over my very . . . expensive WASP doctor?
>
> BELIZE: He's not queer. I am . . . consider it solidarity. . . . One faggot to another. (*Belize snaps, turns, exits*). (159–160)

Belize is directed to deliver his advice with "distaste," performing an emotional gag reflex before Cohn's vile conservatism. His political orientation is linked to a visceral or affective performance that carries with it both an impatience for Roy's naïveté about homophobic medical practice, but also a frustration that he must be the purveyor of this information. Belize first disabuses Roy of his attachment to the "respectable" designation of liver cancer, which ultimately benefits the powers Roy thinks he is fooling by leaving him susceptible to a fatal medical treatment. In deploying the term "queer," however, Belize also reminds Roy of their shared precariousness within the institutional power structure Roy so admires. Lines of race and class may separate the two men, but they are both queered by their ethno-racial backgrounds (including Roy's disavowed Jewish heritage) and sexual practices. By snapping his finger in the style of a gay Black "snap queen," Belize flamboyantly performs his relative superiority to Roy as someone who can see through his patient's attempts to mask his queerness. Yet his gesture also retroactively queers Roy, since we can now imagine the lawyer performing just such a "gay snap" after telling off his doctor about his treatment plan.

Belize's capacity to reveal gut-level affinities between disparate racial and sexual identities finds one of its most breathtaking expressions when he links HIV/AIDS to the history of US slavery. When Louis affirms his emotional commitment to Prior, claiming that his "love isn't ambivalent," Belize responds, "I'd swear that's a line from my favorite bestselling paperback novel, *In Love with the Night Mysterious*, except I don't think you ever read it":

> You ought to. Instead of spending the rest of your life trying to get through *Democracy in America*. It's about this white woman whose Daddy owns a plantation in the Deep South in the years before the Civil War—the American one—and her name is Margaret, and she's in love with her Daddy's number-one slave . . . Thaddeus. . . . [S]he's married but her white slave-owner husband has AIDS: Antebellum Insufficiently Developed Sexorgans. . . . [T]he Yankees come, and they set the slaves free. . . . Somewhere in there . . . Margaret and Thaddeus find the time to discuss the nature of love. . . . She says to him, "Thaddeus, real love isn't ever ambivalent." . . . Thaddeus looks at her . . . he isn't sure he agrees. (102–103)[39]

In full Belize form, this narration undercuts a variety of traditional hierarchies of "race, taste, and history." Belize simultaneously, and deftly, elevates the "low" cultural form of the romance novel above classic political theory like Alexis de Tocqueville's *Democracy in America*; unhinges the Civil War's distinctly US attribution by indicating the existence of other civil wars outside North America; debases white masculinity; and puts into question the sincerity of the white liberal "romance" with, or "love" for, Black bodies, which Thaddeus recognizes as mere fetishism. Most importantly, these reversals materially and conceptually link HIV/ AIDS and US slavery: if modern liberal democracy is ambivalent about the bodies of people with AIDS, Belize's story implies that the historical antecedent to this is the country's foundational ambivalence about the humanity of Black and brown bodies.[40] Belize's neologism, "Antebellum Insufficiently Developed Sexorgans," rewrites AIDS as an affliction of white male insecurity about the purported hypersexuality of Black men, mythicized in their supposedly huge genitals; yet it similarly reminds us that the national panic over AIDS rest largely in white straight patriarchal anxieties about the hypersexuality of gay men who were primarily blamed for spreading the disease. Through Belize's visceral responses to an array of racisms and homophobias, we become attuned to the ways that anti-Blackness and AIDS function as historical and conceptual switch points: the one drop rule of racial miscegenation anxieties has merely transmuted into the fear of a gay man's infected blood. Belize, then, represents the play's most "activist" quality, namely, its critical project of shifting affective flows, especially those of murderous feelings of disgust against human bodies—Black, brown, and queer ones—back toward the institutional structures that enabled such lethal contempt in the first place.

Like Belize, Harper Pitt, Joe Pitt's alienated and spiritually lost wife, is one of the play's producers of counterknowledge born out of intuitive feelings grounded in her distinct social location as a woman, housewife, and (failed) Mormon. If Roy's locus of vision is limited to his own narcissistic social and political interests, and Belize's worldview is shaped by larger networks of unevenly distributed power and privilege, Harper's intuition is planetary in scope, taking in the immense web of relations between human beings, nonhuman life, and the globe. In her opening monologue, Harper voices her gut sense that "things [in the world] are collapsing, lies surfacing, systems of defense giving way." She asserts: "People are like planets, you need a thick skin. Things get to me" (23–24). In referencing "systems of defense giving way," Harper is describing the dissolving of the ozone layer (*Earth's* immune system), a phenomenon that fascinates and horrifies her. She then unwittingly identifies the central consequence of AIDS, the "giving way" of the body's immune defenses to a deadly virus, as a grander planetary event of species-wide significance. If, as Gregg and Seigworth suggest, "the political dimensions of affect generally proceed through . . . the body's capacity for becoming sensitive to the 'manner' of a world," then Harper is arguably the most politically attuned character in the play.[41] As someone without a "thick skin" who lets things "get to her," Harper is vulnerable to the world and hence able to affectively register the consequences of vast social, political, even cosmic upheavals.

Harper's idiosyncratic diet is associated with her openness to broader scales of existence. She pops valium pills, eats Jell-O, M&Ms, and frozen dinners, and binges on soda and potato chips, all "bad objects" antithetical to healthy eating. Each act of ingestion facilitates hallucinations in which Harper's imagination allows her to give structure and meaning to her premonitions through dream narratives. When Harper transports herself to the North Pole in a valium-induced vision, she marvels at being so close to the ozone layer, exclaiming, "There are ice crystals in my lungs, wonderful and sharp. And the snow smells like cold, crushed peaches. And there's . . . some current of blood in the wind . . . it has that iron taste" (107). If the Earth is sick, Harper is unafraid to contract whatever virus it has, relishing the taste of the world's lifeblood in her lungs.

Echoing Prior and Belize's ill liberal worldviews, Harper resists traditional notions of human progress, both Louis's narrative of historical evolution toward "perfection" and her husband's vision of moral regeneration through a conservative political revolution. Her sense that "lies are starting to surface" references not only her husband's dishonesty about his sexuality, but the broader deception of a Reaganite revolution whose image of a bright US-American future criminally neglects the realities of environmental collapse, the AIDS epidemic, racism and homophobia, and political corruption. At one point, Harper goes to the Mormon Visitors' Center in Manhattan, where she fantasizes that the female puppet representing Joseph Smith's wife comes to life. Harper asks her, "In your experience, how do people change?" The Mormon Mother replies: "God splits the skin with a jagged thumbnail from throat to belly and then . . . grabs hold of your bloody tubes and . . . pulls and pulls till all your innards are yanked out and the pain! . . . And then he stuffs them back, dirty, tangled and torn. It's up to you to do the stitching. Just mangled guts pretending" (211). Figuratively torn apart by her husband's deceit and her own fear of change, Harper finds comfort in the Mormon Mother's description of change as the excruciating feeling of literally having one's guts torn out. Where once Harper felt out of joint with the movement of human progress as a woman without a husband and a Mormon without a calling, this visceral description of humans grappling with their mangled insides describes a form of "painful progress" that accords with her sense that real change is enabled when people acknowledge their self-deceptions. In the personification of "mangled guts pretending," the play proposes a potent, gastric metaphor for unraveling the ideological fantasies that humans produce to imagine themselves as whole or uncontaminated, fantasies deployed to murderous effect in the AIDS epidemic. These modes of being in the world, like Louis's myopic liberalism, are forms of "pretending" that mask both the messiness of the body and its psychic and social wounds. Unlike Roy and Louis, Harper listens to the grumbling in her stomach. It ultimately leads her to leave her husband and take off on a night flight to San Francisco, the very city that Belize described as a homeland of misfits, queers, and all those willing to let their "mangled guts" show.

If Prior provides audiences with an alternative conception of human progress through his demand for "MORE LIFE," so too Harper transmits to us an original view of collective growth and evolution in the image of "mending." She sees both human immune systems and the Earth's defense system (the ozone layer) as injured structures capable of healing in concert with other bodies. As her airplane ascends at the play's conclusion, Harper leaves us with a final vision:

> The plane leapt the tropopause, the safe air, and attained . . . the ozone, which was ragged and torn. . . . But I saw something only I could see. . . . Souls were rising, from the earth . . . of people who had perished, from famine, from war, from the plague . . . they floated up, like skydivers in reverse, limbs all akimbo, wheeling and spinning. And the souls of these departed joined hands, clasped ankles and formed a web, a great net of souls . . . three-atom oxygen molecules, of the stuff of ozone, and the outer rim absorbed them, and was repaired. Nothing's lost forever. In this world, there is a kind of painful progress. Longing for what we've left behind, and dreaming ahead. At least I think that's so (275).

Harper's "painful progress" implies a difficult but beneficial digestive process, the peristaltic movement of human bodies through the gut of the universe. It is the space where once solid forms are transmuted in an endless process of change: vulnerable bodies ceaselessly become sick and dying ones, "people who had perished" become freewheeling souls, and those souls become "three-atom oxygen molecules" capable of repairing a "universe of wounds." From where she stands—as a newly minted feminist, queer, heretic—she can take in the extraordinary idea that the material form of a deadly viral molecule attacking flesh-and-blood bodies might paradoxically facilitate the creation of an altogether different and generative molecular structure of people linked in a practice of mending. This image is not unlike the coalition of AIDS activists, who in the tradition of women's and gay liberation before them, "dreamed ahead" by literally and figuratively linking arms—on the street, in activist meetings, on dancefloors, in bedrooms—to create space to breathe for gender and sexual dissidents. In the process, they formed a "web" of friendships that could outlive the destructive forces of sexism and homophobia, a great "wheeling and spinning . . . net of souls" rising together.

Spit or Swallow?

Through a close reading of the viscerally charged discursive work of *Angels in America*, I have identified the digestive politics and poetics of AIDS as a historically situated rhetorical complex that linked the physiological forms of the gut to rebellious feelings of political disgust as a matter of survival in the AIDS epidemic. If, as Roy Cohn claims, politics is "enzymes and gastric juices churning," then the digestive politics and poetics of AIDS suggests we should know something about the stomachs of those who participate in it. At the conclusion of *Angels*, Louis is redeemed because of his willingness to see Joe Pitt's abysmal diet (of hot dogs, Pepto Bismol, and Coca-Cola) as an allegory for his racist and homophobic legal decisions. When Louis confronts Joe about his unethical politics, including his professional (and potential sexual) attachments to Cohn, Louis screams, "How many times has the latex-sheathed cock I put in my mouth been previously in the mouth of the most evil twisted, vicious, bastard ever to snort coke at Studio 54, because lips that kissed those lips will never kiss mine" (243). In the classic structure of the digestive politics and poetics of AIDS, Louis's redemption is confirmed when he reroutes his inability to stomach the reality of AIDS toward a refusal to stomach a cock attached to a man with bankrupt civic ideals.

Despite his evolution, Louis's admission that he only ever sucked Joe's cock with a condom on reminds us that even after shedding his liberal intolerance of AIDS, his stomach remains free of the potentially polluted fluids of other men's bodies, including semen, blood, and urine. While *Angels in America*'s deployment of the digestive politics and poetics of AIDS makes people and politics dirty for the purpose of developing a richly embodied political language in response to the AIDS epidemic, it paradoxically sidesteps some of the most viscerally charged aspects of bodily pleasure and potential HIV exposure, including those of cum eating, piss drinking, and barebacking. In other words, if the play's use of digestive rhetoric often produces the gut reaction to spit, it leaves open the critical question of what it would mean to articulate the digestive politics and poetics of AIDS from the position of someone who chooses to swallow. At the same time that *Angels* was being written and staged, numerous independent queer cultural producers working and living with AIDS were deploying the digestive politics and poetics of AIDS to ask just this question. I conclude by briefly glossing three contemporaneous cultural producers who pursued this latter approach to the digestive politics and poetics of AIDS to show how generative this discursive formation was for articulating multiple positionalities within the epidemic.

For Gary Fisher, an African American poet and journalist, the alimentary tract functioned as both a site of radical pleasure and a figurative zone where competing, and sometimes incommensurate, desires clashed. In his autobiographical writings of the late 1980s, Fisher lovingly describes his oral fixations with men's semen and piss: "I have no words for it, just an image, at once holy and profane, of the nigger on his knees taking cock juices in his body, particularly piss as a kind of spiritual cleanser."[42] Fisher's near ecstatic pleasure in receiving the gift of cum and piss, particularly from white masters who racially debase him, comes into conflict with his loathing of US racism. Fisher is aware of the contradictions in his thinking, yet as his actual digestive system deteriorates with the advancement of his disease, he astutely comments on the structural similarities between his subjection to white men as sex slave and his subjection to medical doctors as patient: "Right now, I hate my doctor for my crazy symptoms. . . . And yet I've accumulated so much love and respect (maybe a little lust too) that I will take his prescription unquestioned—that same way I used to have sex."[43] In each case, Fisher reveals how ingestion—whether of men's bodily fluids or medicine—is a site where hierarchies of race and sexuality are powerfully displayed. As a gay Black man with AIDS and no health insurance, Fisher feels compelled to say "yes," a response that subjects him to white power but also reveals a limited form of agency in willingly accepting, even taking sexual pleasure, in one's own abjection.[44]

Similarly, in their acclaimed documentary *Silverlake Life: The View from Here* (1993), filmmakers Tom Joslin and Peter Friedman offer viewers some of queer cinema's most visceral images of the embodied experience of AIDS. The film documents a year in the couple's life as they both struggle with AIDS, culminating with Tom's death, which Peter films. In this penultimate scene, we see a close-up of Tom's emaciated body inert in bed, while Peter implores the viewer between sobs, "Isn't he beautiful? He's so beautiful." The question is jarring, for it demands any spectator to the scene to confront their own gut-level discomfort with the idea that sickness and death can be anything but revolting. Because of the visual conventions of documentary film, viewers are made to inhabit Peter's subject position both literally and figuratively as someone who values the body of a loved one who has suffered the physical effects of a terrible disease. Later, when Peter receives Tom's ashes in the mail, he clumsily cuts himself while trying to open the metal container. He then spills bits of bone and ash on the floor while pouring them into an urn. Like the shot of Tom's corpse, the scene has the potential to elicit intense discomfort because of its messy breakdown of bodily and symbolic boundaries, including Peter's bleeding finger mingling with Tom's remains. Just at the moment that one is tempted to cringe, Peter offhandedly jokes, "You're all over the place, Tom." The campy quality of the joke cuts through the viewer's potential distaste by making us aware that any disgust we might feel is based on a need to assert boundaries between our own bodies and that of two people with AIDS. Through its unflinching visual depictions of the lived experience of the virus, *Silverlake Life* facilitates a reconsideration of the ethics of disgust by encouraging us to ask ourselves who or what we might be protecting when we deploy aversive emotions to defend against the perceived threat of those bodies we deem beneath us.

Finally, in his 1999 exhibit *Space Oddity (lesson in survival)*, mixed-media artist Chuck Nanney expresses the material and psychic anxieties surrounding the daily practice of taking AIDS medication through a series of found-object works that transform discomforting digestive dysfunctions into deceptively simple visual abstractions made of acrylic, latex, thumbtacks, paper clips, book rings, and basic office supplies.[45] In one piece titled *fiery turd* (1998), a bright-red latex cutout in the shape of a clown's irregular smile is pinned to a wall by a curved piece of wire, presumably an abstraction of a painful shit. The seemingly playful quality of the pieces, indicated by their larger-than-life size and colorful textures, is undercut by their frequently distressing titles (including *colostomy*, 1998; *sideways stool*, 1998; and *stomach lining*, 1999), many referring to painful bowel movements or fleshy parts of the alimentary tract. Similarly, the sharp edges of the wires and thumbtacks that prop the pieces up, puncture materials representing sensitive stomach linings, bellies, and throats. The colorful impact of a bright-red shit in *fiery turd*, for example, invokes the searing hot pain of a bad bowel movement (as does the sharp wire running through the red latex). Nanney's displays abstract and visually expand digestive complications specific to taking HIV medication in order to generalize feelings of bodily precariousness to his viewers, who are encouraged to meditate on the vulnerability of their own bellies, stomach linings, and stool.

A brief look at these creators' works reveals that the forms of digestive tracts and their corporeal processes were a common reference point for a variety of queer cultural producers both at the height of the AIDS epidemic and after. Like Kushner, each of these artists linguistically and visually invoke digestion, and its breakdown, to route different affects—pleasure, abjection, discomfort, rage, empathy—toward a multiplicity of alternative bodies, objects, and political commitments. If Kushner and Wojnarowicz direct their projects at a critique of the grander operations of political power, Fisher, Joslin, Friedman, and Nanney elicit empathetic responses to the quotidian aspects of illness. All do so, however, through the gut. Considering the centrality of the digestive system to the AIDS epidemic, it is clear why it became a touchstone for queer activists and artists: struggles over getting "drugs into bodies," the deterioration of digestive functions caused by AIDS and its treatments, and the gut-level vitriol issued from both sides of the political divide (toward people with AIDS and toward political inaction) all marked the digestive as a contested site of political and affective meaning-making.

In her now classic essay "An Epidemic of Signification," Paula Treichler called for "an epidemiology of signification—a comprehensive mapping and analysis of [AIDS's] multiple meanings—to form the basis for an official definition that will in turn constitute the policies, regulations, rules, and practices that will govern our behavior for some time to come."[46] The digestive politics and poetics of AIDS was just such an "epidemiology of signification," at once a diagnostic rhetorical tool that used formal equivalences between alimentary organs and political ideologies to uncover the varied types of discursive violence being done to people with AIDS, *and* a formal practice that proliferated alternatives to the negative metaphors that surrounded the disease. The digestive politics and poetics of AIDS thus provided the imaginative basis for AIDS activists' direct actions to alter policies and regulations, and galvanize more humane scientific research; it functioned at the level of affect, to vitalize new ways of feeling in the world by resignifying the meanings of HIV/AIDS so as to cultivate ethical orientations toward those struggling with the disease.

The fact that *Angels in America* begins with Roy Cohn rhetorically linking AIDS and gay men with political impotence, and ends with Prior Walter articulating AIDS with "*more life*" and queer citizenship; the fact that Peter Friedman could film his lover Tom Joslin's body following his death from AIDS and claim "he's so beautiful"; the fact that David Wojnarowicz could speak of the disease that tormented his insides as an incitement to develop his most potent creative work and express his political rage more sharply than ever before—these and countless other examples from queer and feminist cultural productions of the late twentieth century suggest the powerful capacity of the visceral to resignify HIV/AIDS, a disease that evoked ferocious disgust not only because of its association with gay men, drug use, and moral degeneracy, but because it made visible the universal vulnerability of the body, an existential fact that no liberal imaginary could will away. It is in the digestive politics and poetics of AIDS that a new generation of queer and feminist cultural producers found a formal language with which to show a wider public a reality they themselves had long understood as social pariahs: that beneath the facades of liberal progress, happiness, and freedom, we are all "just mangled guts pretending."

Conclusion

"Something Else to Be": On Friendship's Queer Forms

Because friendship has been so idealized in the Western philosophical canon—forming the bedrock of Aristotle's *polis*, surpassing romantic love for Montaigne—it is no surprise that gays and lesbians have likewise valorized it as a respite from social ostracism as well as an alternative to compulsory heterosexuality. . . . If one's very being and its attendant relations are deemed inferior . . . why not align that self and its community with a superior relational form? Foucault's concept of friendship, however, is anything but utopian: betrayal, distance, brutal honesty, indeed an impersonal intimacy founded in estrangement are its makings. This is, to be blunt, the shit of friendship. When the most troubling aspects of relationships become the very foundation of a friendship . . . new subjective, communal, and political forms can be imagined.
—Tom Roach, *Friendship as a Way of Life: Foucault, AIDS, and the Politics of Shared Estrangement* (2012)

So when they met . . . they felt the ease and comfort of old friends. Because each had discovered years before that they were neither white nor male, and that all freedom and triumph was forbidden to them, they had set about creating something else to be. Their meeting was fortunate, for it let them use each other to grow on.
—Toni Morrison, *Sula* (1973)

In the penultimate sequence of *Thelma & Louise*, before our heroines fly headlong into the Grand Canyon, the pair outwit a phalanx of police cars in a harrowing chase across the Arizona desert. Suddenly alone along a barren stretch of highway, the women share a final quiet moment in Louise's Thunderbird. With a mix of breathless terror and exhilaration at their bare escape, Thelma looks to her companion and says: "You're a good friend." Without hesitation, Louise replies: "You too, sweetie, the best." Seconds later, Thelma adds: "Good drivin'." In this electric exchange, Thelma and Louise spontaneously recognize that something in each has irrevocably been altered as a result of their journey (what Thelma at one point calls having "crossed over" into a new state of being), and they mark that transformation by performatively declaring each other "good friends" and "good drivers." What the pair acknowledge in one another are not established identities, ideals, or social types, as though they had achieved true "womanhood" or become self-proclaimed feminists, but rather their shared capacity to be genuine interlocutors and decisive agents of freedom. In the light of their mutual recognition, the two women quite literally *form* into new kinds of subjects: they exchange wardrobes, adopt each other's mannerisms, appropriate the accoutrements of cowboys and outlaws, and inhabit new structures like the driver's seat of a Ford Thunderbird convertible. That either or both women would, in the face of extraordinary danger, the threat of incarceration and even death, end up evolving into "good friends" and "good drivers" was never guaranteed, but rather the unpredictable outcome of countless instances of acting together for their mutual survival and flourishing. In shooting Harlan, Louise's impulsive act of feminist rage sets off a chain of unforeseeable events that endanger the friends' lives while also creating expansive possibilities for their shared evolution—on the road, the two discover what they are capable of in terms of sheer ingenuity, resolve conflicts of temperament and judgment, speak truthfully about their dreams, and make and keep promises.

This was in microcosm the structural logic of women's and gay liberation, social movements that could trace their origins to multiple spontaneous acts of public, sometimes even violent, rebellion against male domination, homophobia, sexism, and transphobia (as in the explosive episodes of the Compton's Cafeteria and Stonewall riots). These events inspired a cascade of individual and collective responses—from interpersonal acts of coming out to the formation of radical political organizations—drawing women and queers of all stripes into their radiant horizon of change. When, near the end of their journey, Thelma fears that Louise might make a pact with the sympathetic detective Hal Slocumb, Louise laughs at the thought: "Thelma, I'm not making *any* deals." Louise's promises, she reconfirms, are already sealed to her friend. And so too, the women and queers who animated projects for gender and sexual freedom in the 1970s turned away from the seductive lure of a "normal" life toward making mutual promises to one another. In the figure of two women repeatedly "taking the wheel" of their shared fate into their own hands, *Thelma & Louise* offered a potent visual metaphor for feminist and queer freedom as a process of *indefinitely taking shape in the company of one's friends*.

The bold depiction of feminist and queer friendship in *Thelma & Louise* was no minor representational achievement in an era that saw a national backlash against feminism, a catastrophic HIV/AIDS epidemic, and a vicious internecine conflict between women over pornography and censorship dubbed the feminist sex wars. Amid these accumulating shared traumas, friendship remained the most local and intimate "island of certainty in an ocean of uncertainty"[1] for women and queers everywhere. This was a relation founded in mutual dialogue, the ability to negotiate differences, and the possibility of being seen and heard, not simply as you are but as what you might be or become. Such a bond could provide resources for thriving amid the natural evolution and dissolution of once-thought-permanent social and political identities, ideals, communities, and shared contexts for action. In their final decision to "keep going," Thelma and Louise register how friendship remained the most enduring social relation of the movements for women's and gay liberation, a bond that could withstand the contingent fate of projects for gender and sexual freedom, which inspired hopes for a better future but alone could not shield their participants from the ongoing harms of a sexist and homophobic world.

Across the arc of this book, I have tracked the imaginative lives of queer and feminist cultural forms as they gave shape to, clarified, and invigorated key concepts for gender and sexual freedom, while transmitting powerful affective experiences of queer rebellion, heartache, ecstasy, ebullience, eroticism, and wonder. In each chapter, I began with a material shape and traced its articulation to diverse expressions of gender and sexual nonconformity across manifold cultural objects, materials, mediums, and genres. In this conclusion, I reverse my order of priority by beginning with an enduring concept, feminist and queer *friendship*, which came to inhabit countless cultural forms in the 1970s and after. I suggest that friendship is a wild or anarchic social relation that discloses new aspects of the gendered and sexual self through continual dialogue with an impassioned interlocutor. The friend is one version of the female replicant in feminist speculative literatures, which, as we saw in chapter 1, posited an unfamiliar doppelgänger, android, or clone who, by demanding to be accounted for in some significant way by other women, facilitates continual discourse with her peers to negotiate their many differences. Friendship can offer a potent model for better understanding, relating to, and studying queer forms in all their variety—both those transmitted to us from the feminist and queer past and those still being invented—while helping to enrich and refine our commitments to contemporary gender and sexual freedom movements.

Today, feminist and queer cultural representations proliferate in global media. Feminist, queer, and trans* social movements continue to make headway in generating, naming, and validating a seemingly boundless list of new gendered, erotic, and relational forms and identities. Feminisms past and present splinter, multiply, and evolve at a "breathless pace" as trans*, women-of-color, radical, socialist, queer, and "crip" feminist theories and social movements continue to be elaborated and enacted. And previously marginal or fringe LGBTQ subcultures, from the queer-of-color ballroom scene to drag performance to numerous kink and fetish communities, are increasingly recognized as meaningful social formations and distinct art forms. In the midst of this vertiginous expansion of feminist and queer possibility, the temptation to identify a singular or all-encompassing ideological system, social movement, fluid identity category, or relational form that could account for, adjudicate, and resolve all the potential conflicts and disagreements of gender and sexual existence is everywhere around us. This totalizing impulse can be seen in the ideological policing mechanisms of so-called cancel culture, which functions as a scathing system of accountability for those who fail to uphold or properly perform the dictates of progressive gender and sexual political programs. It is apparent in the extraordinary attention paid to ameliorating structural and interpersonal harm and the mind-numbingly predictable ideological critiques of "failed" or "negative" representations of queer and gender-nonconforming lives. And it is glaringly present in the transformation of once flexible conceptions of gender and sexual identity, or supple analytical concepts like intersectionality, into ironclad shibboleths. These trends evidence a shared queer and feminist fantasy for a comprehensive set of rules or ethical instructions that could finally secure us against the contingency of all categories of gender and sexual being. The tenacity of this desire reveals that even for those gender and sexual warriors who declare a staunch commitment to rejecting all gender and sexual regulations, there exists a will to produce *new* norms of conduct, both salubrious ones that enable the flourishing of feminist and queer life, but also prohibitive ones that seek to abolish or forestall potential missteps on the road to liberation.

As we have seen throughout this book, however, queer forms can never function as a rule, essential identity, norm, or dictum that would "subsume the particulars" of gender and sexual existence, explain what gender and sexuality are or should be, or provide a blueprint for universal belonging, social uplift, and collective freedom. Rather the power of queer forms lies in their incitement to produce multiple, competing interpretations of the same phenomena, thereby pooling perspectives on different aspects of gender and sexuality as lived experiences, categories of self, social relationships, or clusters of desire. The great gift of forms is their potential to teach us how to receive, negotiate, and meaningfully respond to, rather than control or finally resolve, the world's fundamental heterogeneity, *if only we would let them*. And so too, friendship is the kind of social relation that comes closest to modeling the world-opening aspect of forms, for its unique brand of affinity is the most local, intimate, and intense site for the negotiation of differences between two people.

Across all the cultural forms discussed in this book, what persists is the presence of friendships between women and queers variously construed, their unexpected constitution and growth, daily joys and betrayals, shared triumphs and losses. In Ira Levin's *The Stepford Wives*, the friendship that blossoms between Joanna Eberhart and Bobbie Markowe anchors their common struggle to resist the soul-crushing conformity of a suburban neighborhood. Indeed, the twin tragedies of the novella lie first in the rending of Joanna and Bobbie's friendship by the overpowering force of patriarchy, and second, in Joanna's failure to befriend

Ruthanne Hendry as a result of her own political myopia toward cross-racial solidarity between women. In *Zardoz*, the Vortex, a stultifying commune whose telepathically enforced togetherness makes voluntary friendships impossible, is undermined by a member who goes by the very name of "Friend." Friend counts his long-standing affinity with Arthur Frayne—an anarchist Vortex member who sabotages their idyllic collective—as one of the reasons he consents to the destruction of the only community he has ever known. In *Born in Flames*, Adelaide Norris, the leader of a radical "Women's Army," recruits women from varied class backgrounds, races, and ideological leanings by engaging them in sustained conversations about their political values and forming mutual aid networks across underserved communities. Her untimely death by assassination is widely experienced as the loss of a beloved friend, a tragedy that knits together her vast network of feminist companions into a united front against a patriarchal socialist government. Both *The Boys in the Band* and *Tales of the City* are stories about chosen or "logical" families formed among strangers struggling to balance the newfound erotic and social freedoms of queer urban life with the project of dismantling their own internalized homophobia and sexism. And in Tony Kushner's *Angels in America*, the dissolution of bonds among two couples through betrayal and abandonment clears the way for the constitution of a community of fellow travelers across genders, generations, sexualities, and political beliefs. In each of these stories, feminist and queer friendship takes a concrete social form, a bond of trust between sexual and gender dissidents, represented in specific characters' interactions and unfolding plots. And yet in every instance, friendship is potentially anarchic, an unexpected eruption of affective energy that underwrites connections which exceed the bounds of existing ideologies, identities, and familial obligations.

Friendship is always that which is "out of order," to borrow Linda Zerilli's phrase, because it establishes completely new orders of ethical belonging based not on preexisting rule, law, or moral commandment but on mutually negotiated, contingent criteria between two equal participants.[2] This is true of all the political concepts explored in this book—from consciousness-raising to coming out of the closet to sexual pluralism and more—which facilitated unexpected friendships even when their stated aims were to seek political justice for the oppressed, conceive strategies to dismantle patriarchy, cultivate self-worth, or any other expedient goal. By bringing gender and sexual outlaws together in mutual dialogue, CR sessions produced opportunities for participants to experience spontaneous affinities that might grow into a lifelong rapport. By making queer genders and sexualities public, coming out promised to call forth fellow travelers who might turn on to another person's visible performances of gender and sexual transformation. And simply by valuing multiple expressions of erotic desire, sexual pluralism encouraged physical and emotional proximities between former strangers that could inaugurate sustaining friendships.

As these examples attest, friendship is a critical object of study necessary for grasping the long-term cultural impact of women's and gay liberation on our present-day political imagination. To illuminate this fact, I draw on the work of political theorist Hannah Arendt, who movingly described democratic public life as an extension of the bonds of friendship, both being "institutional and associative affiliation[s] based not on family, tribe, or religion but on equality."[3] Against the extraordinary contingency of "human affairs," Arendt tells us, democratic politics places its faith not in or preexisting codes of conduct, but in the faculty of making and keeping promises—which inaugurates new social and civic relationships among men—and the capacity to forgive—which allows each person to act in an unpredictable world knowing they can never control the outcome of every action. Promising and forgiving, provided that they are enacted continuously between interlocutors who appear to one another in speech and action, briefly free men from the seeming arbitrariness of life by providing "islands of certainty in an ocean of uncertainty." Similarly, friendship as a cultivated relationship built on the mutual exchange of words and deeds allows each participant to "understand the world from the other person's point of view."[4] The trust that evolves out of friendship is based not on presupposed group belonging, ideological commitments, or shared interests, but in making and keeping promises in relation to immediate, contingent circumstances, as well as "forgiving, dismissing, in order to make it possible for life to go on by constantly releasing men from what they had done unknowingly." When friends follow through on their promises, the trust between them creates the conditions for "truthful dialogue," opening up the space for friends to disagree or even betray one another, and still be forgiven—it is in this sense that friendship, like democratic thought and action, is attuned to human plurality and amenable to contingency. At the same time, I would submit that this description of friendship as providing "islands of certainty in a world of uncertainty" offers one potent definition of the work of queer cultural forms.

As I have argued throughout this book, in a world where gender and sexuality are highly variable and idiosyncratic categories of lived experience—that therefore cannot easily be disciplined to conform to our political values—queer forms provide provisional outlines that allow us to conceive one or another version of gender and sexuality in the mind's eye. These figures become launching pads for flights of the imagination about gender expression, desire, intimacy, or kinship that can work on, and substantively alter, people's affective relationship to these terms. Everyday experience readily confirms that cultural representations of difference—even the most nuanced fictional stories about women and queers of color for instance—rarely disabuse people of pernicious logics like racism, sexism, homophobia, or transphobia all on their own. Yet aesthetic forms do enter people's lives in startling and unforeseen ways, sometimes eliciting meaningful dialogue between friends about their distinct interpretations of various works of art, literature, and media that can reorganize or subvert entrenched assumptions and values. We saw in chapter 4 how *Tales of the City* successfully promoted a positive conception of queer and transgender existence that had tangible psychic and behavioral effects on its audience. This was possible because of the combination of *Tales'* depiction of queerness, as a pleasurable and desirable form of serial public disclosure, and the unique contexts of its reception, which encouraged recurrent dialogue between local readers. Over time, these conversations influenced many to alter their views about homosexuality, expand their definitions of family, learn to support queer friends, or else come out themselves.

If queer forms allow us to conceive categories like gender and sexuality as something different than we have ever understood before, it is in the dialogic context of friendship, where competing interpretations of these same categories can be freely shared, that we have the opportunity to cultivate novel ways of responding to our newfound imagination in daily life. This can encompass the deliberate construction of ethical practices or commitments to facilitating an anti-homophobic and anti-sexist world. The question for radical social movements today is how to maximize the possibilities for such free exchange in the manner of friendship. That is, how to produce culture under conditions that facilitate sustained, mutually transformative public dialogue, rather than merely attempting to educate populations in politically correct language and behavior.

Consider that although the original historical conditions of *Tales of the City*'s production and circulation can never be replicated exactly, the general principles that enabled its cultural and interpersonal effects are completely transferable to other aesthetic projects. This included the idea of a locally distributed literary production; printed in a medium made for public circulation and consumption; written in a worldly yet accessible and entertaining idiom legible to a specific but wide-reaching community; while offering readers alternative ways of understanding their own lives. It was precisely because of Armistead Maupin's ability to become, even provisionally, like one of his readers' close friends, that his unfolding story reached them in the spirit of loving exchange. Instead of condescendingly instructing his audience on the correct way to be gay, the proper language to use around all LGBTQ people, or the most progressive view to hold on queer life, he generously shared his own version of that life with them, over and over. By choosing to give shape to 1970s gay urban cultures one way, then another, then another, on a daily basis, Maupin continually took a position on the nature and meaning of modern-day queerness that could then be embraced, adapted, dismissed, or argued against by any member of his readership. Without artists' willingness to publicly give shape to their own fantasies of contemporary feminist and queer life, and consequently solicit the views of others, no sense of a shared reality between gender and sexual outlaws and their allies could possibly have emerged in the radical 1970s.

In what follows I suggest that friendship might provide one important, but underutilized, framework for studying social movements as political cultures that coalesce around everyday personal affinities and intimacies as much, if not more so, as shared categories of identity or ideological commitments. Friendship might allow us to see social movements for what they really are—ideologically and interpersonally messy laboratories of collective action and cross-identification—without fetishizing their political demands, assuming they can explain or ameliorate all forms of oppression, or expecting any movement to eternally live on intact from its inception. This in turn can facilitate an understanding of forms as cultural or aesthetic "friends" to our present-day visions for queer and feminist freedom, provisional and adaptable tools for "getting the shared world in view" between gender and sexual outlaws of all stripes.

I begin by offering a gloss on the role of friendship in the political imagination of 1970s women's and gay liberation, particularly as it was theorized as a practice of *forming* new feminist and queer subjectivities. I then distinguish friendship from the concept of "care," which has become a dominant keyword in contemporary queer, feminist, and disability justice–focused theory and practice. Because of its localness, idiosyncrasy, and variability, friendship, I suggest, is far less concerned with redressing structural harm (as care work aims to do) than it is with producing spontaneous and energetic mutual exchanges of perspectives. Friends show "care" not by ministering to the wounds of marginalization or oppression but by illuminating different versions of yourself you never thought possible. Finally, I show how cultural representations of queer and feminist friendship creatively capture this distinction by relentlessly presenting figures, icons, or forms of impassioned dialogue between women and queers variously construed that irrevocably transform all parties involved.

Consequently, while recognizing that friendships between people are not identical to the work of cultural interpretation conducted between a viewer and an aesthetic form, nevertheless, I ask what might happen if we treated cultural representations *as if* they were our friends—not in a sentimental mode, but in the sense of someone with whom we engage in meaningful dialogue and action. This is the kind of exchange that changes us, clears space for growth, and refuses the comforts of recognition for the thrill of "becoming other" to ourselves and the world. We might see these queer forms as arriving to us, like friendships, in the form of promises to expand our wild imaginations about gender and sexual freedom. And we might learn to forgive these forms when they fail us, acquitting them of their pitfalls as easily, and tenderly, as we would forgive the ordinary trespasses of any good friend who will invariably at times "know not what they do." One outcome might be a revivification of contemporary gay cultural politics that sees queer forms as ways to inaugurate new social relations that are durable but flexible enough to shapeshift along with us, rather than liquifying beneath fantasies of formless being or rigidly embodying our favored political categories. The extraordinary proliferation of queer and feminist friendships in popular media since the 1970s discloses the continued desire among women and queers for a mode of relationality that can provide equipment for living past the moment when our most cherished movements for gender and sexual freedom evolve, decline, disperse, or altogether disappear. Thus, another outcome of treating queer forms with the open-heartedness and energetic engagement intrinsic to friendship might simply be that our cultural forms would become one place we practice and learn to be better friends to each other.

The Faggots and Their Friends between Revolutions

As Tom Roach underscores in the first epigraph to this conclusion, it should come as no surprise that friendship was a pivotal form of sociality for women and queers in the 1970s. Because these groups rejected and sought to dismantle conventional models of kinship, intimacy, and reproductive sexuality they, perhaps more than any other social and political dissidents of the 1960s and 1970s, experienced severe familial and social shunning. Gender and sexual outlaws of all stripes turned toward one another to knit together previously unthinkable communal and interpersonal bonds that thrived in the public light of social movement activism. What made these friendships uniquely feminist and queer was their attentiveness to gender and sexuality as sites of transformational change, which included granting others the space to explore new gender expressions, erotic desires, collective living forms, and the emergent political values associated with all three. Yet while social movement politics often facilitated the evolution of meaningful friendships—including the bonds forged while engaging in practices like consciousness-raising or zap actions—those same affinities quickly exceeded the limits of every category of political belonging put forth by both movements, which often went by the names of "woman," "sisterhood," "liberal," "radical," "woman of color," "separatist," "gay," or "lesbian." As Ann Snitow movingly relates, "The particular rush I experienced in those first months [of women's liberation] couldn't maintain itself for two breaths. Sisterhood crumbled at a touch, weakened by differences of race, class, and political traditions. . . . Our astonishing and bracing rage at patriarchy was necessary but insufficient for the long haul."[5]

Categories like those listed above have regularly been used to silo the heterogeneous participants of women's and gay liberation into competing identitarian camps. Yet on-the-ground friendships between those participants were forged in the heady brew of the radical 1970s—where sexual revolution, psychedelics, a political civil war over Vietnam, student protest, and the light-speed formation and dissolution of new political groups ceaselessly undermined such easy classifications. One could be a hardcore lesbian separatist who surprisingly forges a sustaining friendship with a non-feminist straight woman. One could be a Chicana lesbian poet invested in women-of-color feminism whose friend turns out to be a gay man afraid of acknowledging his femininity. One could be a Black feminist literary scholar who claims a white feminist colleague as her confidante. One could be a gay white man who develops a lifelong friendship with a Black trans* woman community organizer.[6] These friendships brimmed with practices of cross-identification, mutual dialogue, code switching, irreverence, and play born out of exhilarating and often bewildering historical circumstances. In turn, they revealed how temperament, taste, spiritual worldview, a sense of humor, or basic chemistry could play a far more powerful role in binding people together than any presumed group allegiance or ideological program. Because movement politics can be exhausting and disappointing, enforce group unity for the achievement of focused goals, and easily unravel under shifting contexts, friendships have always provided women and queers with the emotional resilience needed to sustain participation in projects for gender and sexual freedom, without necessarily being a conflict-free or therapeutic space.

Across the 1970s, artists, intellectuals, and cultural critics invoked different concepts for describing the passionate affections that sprung up between women and queers in the context of evolving women's and gay liberation movements. In his exuberant gay fable *The Faggots and Their Friends between Revolutions* (1978), author Larry Mitchell imagined "the faggots" as a rebel tribe of sexual dissidents who refused to be "men" throughout history, engaged in countless acts of sedition against a patriarchal order, and found common cause with a vast assortment of "friends" that included "women," "queers," "queens," and "faeries" (all distinct kinds of gender and sexual outlaws).[7] Throughout the text, Mitchell nearly always rhetorically yokes "the faggots" to the phrase "and their friends," while continually expanding who counts as a potential friend. He goes on to suggest that lovers and confidants necessarily evolve *into* friends, a social relation that endures past the waning of erotic desire. In this way, Mitchell concludes that romantic love is "the last illusion," a regressive fantasy of ideal union, that "keeps us alive" in the midst of male domination but is necessary only "until the revolutions come" and institute polymorphous friendship as a primary way of life.[8]

In her widely cited lecture "The Uses of the Erotic: The Erotic as Power" (1978), Black lesbian poet and theorist Audre Lorde redefined the "erotic" outside the terms of traditional genital sexuality as a creative energy or life force exchanged between women through reciprocal, nonexploitative relations of pleasure.[9] While Lorde retains the idea of the erotic as an inchoate and unrestrained energy capable of near-infinite expressions, throughout her speech, she argues that the erotic is best apprehended when it is actively molded into a range of experiential forms, usually those that involve the stuff of friendship, from "dancing hard" to "building a bookcase" to arguing over issues of common concern. The erotic, then, is sensual or affectional energy channeled through passionate human interaction.[10] In her 1980 essay "Compulsory Heterosexuality and Lesbian Existence," lesbian feminist and poet Adrienne Rich built on Lorde's expansive understanding of the erotic as an affective force that exceeds the sphere of sexuality by introducing the concept of "the lesbian continuum," which she used to describe the gamut of overlooked or "hidden" intimacies that have existed between women alongside same-sex erotic desire.[11] This includes "the sharing of a rich inner life, the bonding against male tyranny, [and] the giving and receiving of practical and political support."[12] In this frame every lesbian-oriented practice was a fundamentally creative act, for it required women to invent previously unimaginable forms of relating to one another, most notably female friendship, while conceiving novel strategies for mitigating the effects of patriarchal domination.

Finally, in Michel Foucault's last published interview, the celebrated French philosopher identified friendship as the raison d'être of "homosexuality": "[Homosexuals] have to invent, from A to Z, a relationship that is still formless, which is friendship: that is to say, the sum of everything through which they can give each other pleasure. . . . Homosexuality is a historical occasion to reopen affective and relational virtualities, not so much through the intrinsic qualities of the homosexual but because the 'slantwise' position of the latter, . . . the diagonal lines he can lay out in the social fabric allow these virtualities to come to light."[13] In this view, friendship is a multidimensional social container or mold that gives shape to a previously "formless" felt experience of living "slantwise" to dominant sexual norms. Like Lorde before him, Foucault identified the sharing of "pleasure" between sexual dissidents as a practice that constitutes new orders of collective life, new friendships. Friendship in this frame is fundamentally nonideological, not operating under a rule or program, but a creative practice of freedom.

Despite their different terms for friendship—from "friends between revolutions," to "the lesbian continuum," to "the erotic," to a "way of life"—all four of these thinkers identify friendship as a powerful affective energy that responds to human plurality by extending outward from the self to others. It manifests in concrete associational bonds that make women and queers more proximate and hence more capable of forging unpredictable social and political coalitions. Roach captures the sensibility inherent to all these perspectives when he states: "The friend is neither possessive nor possessed, neither owner nor owned. . . . The friend is the fleeting placeholder of a subjective affectivity moving through ontologically variegated singularities; it is the figure that intuits and enacts the common, that which seethes beneath and is excessive of relations and communities founded on identitarian difference."[14] In other words, the category of the "friend" stands in for no predetermined subject position, ideology, or community that would subsume our differences by providing an essential basis for our bond. Rather the friend is merely a figure for *what we hold in common across our differences*, a shapeshifting form that both binds and separates us, and through which we exchange our points of view.[15]

The power and necessity of feminist and queer friendships since the 1970s is registered not only in their countless successful expressions, but also in the catastrophic consequences of their breakdown. In recent years, numerous commentators have explored the destructive outcomes of friendships' failure in the wake of social movement decline. In her devastating portrait of Shulamith Firestone following the feminist revolutionary's untimely passing in 2013, journalist Susan Faludi documented how Firestone lived much of her adult life after the 1970s isolated, struggling with severe mental illness and poverty, and largely abandoned by her former activist companions.[16] Winifred Breines's richly researched study of conflict between Black and white women in second-wave feminism, *The Trouble between Us*, suggests that much of the cross-racial tension among 1970s feminists was based less on intractable ideological differences and more on widespread despair at the social divisions that US racism had created between women.[17] And in her clear-eyed reappraisal of the promises and pitfalls of lesbian separatism, Charlotte Bunch suggested that the philosophy would never have taken root had straight women simply befriended lesbians within the feminist movement. She explained: "Separatism . . . happened because straight feminists were unable to allow lesbians space to grow—to develop our personal lives and our political insights. And unless lesbian-feminist politics is incorporated into feminist analysis and action, we will reexperience the old and destructive gay-straight split."[18] These accounts are particularly resonant today, when vibrant feminist, queer, trans* freedom movements struggle to balance collective unity against systemic oppression with an openness toward interpersonal differences and disagreements that are the bedrock of both friendship and democratic public life.

From the Duty to Care to the Freedom of Friendship

Anyone invested in gender and sexual freedom today knows that feminist, queer, and trans* social justice projects, and the organizing spaces they create, can be extraordinary sites of community building and care, while also paradoxically being deeply *unfriendly* places. Despite a stated commitment to values like universal inclusion, collective uplift, mutual recognition, and the dismantling of systemic oppression, the social justice discourse that infuses these projects can also be rife with moralizing, political purity tests, surveillance and policing of behavior and speech, backbiting, and group cliquishness. As we saw in chapters 2 and 3, such interpersonal hostility was a prevalent and widely commented upon phenomenon within the cultures of 1970s women's and gay liberation. It was often born out of the intense psychological pain of homophobia and sexism, combined with the frequently disappointed hope that liberation movements could provide ideological frameworks and social environments capable of ameliorating harm, both systemically and interpersonally.

Counterintuitively, then, as writers like Sarah Schulman, Jennifer Nash, and Adrienne Maree Brown have shown, it is frequently at the heart of present-day social movements that theorize and uphold the value of collective care that a "punitive," "defensive," or recriminatory tendency has emerged. This is most potently captured in the rise of what is commonly named "cancel culture."[19] Though a vague and politically loaded term that should be used with caution, cancel culture nevertheless potently captures a widely recognizable argumentative style deployed by people across the political spectrum, but especially prevalent in left-wing social justice circles. This discourse is commonly characterized by oppressed subjects' collective "upward contempt" toward individuals, objects, and cultural phenomena that are seen to reproduce systemic harms like racism, sexism, and homophobia. Cancel culture's favored tactic is what might be called the "canceling gesture," a performatively combative, interpersonal behavior pattern that combines the public calling out of injustice perpetrated by a particular person or cultural product (aimed at disgracing or delegitimizing them) with a strategic, often aggressive, cutting off of communication with the object of one's critique.[20]

Like the 1970s separatist revenge narrative, which legitimized lesbian feminist rage at men and so-called "male-identified" women on the basis of lesbians' perceived injured identity, the canceling gesture provides a thrilling form of takedown based on the public exposure of both enemies and supposed allies as corrupt or injurious to others. Such takedowns are always justified on the basis of one's sense of having been the victim of such harm. While Brown attempts to encourage a more self-reflective and measured approach to canceling that does not reproduce the kinds of surveillance and policing abolitionist movements seek to dismantle, she still assumes that the punitiveness of the canceling gesture is not intrinsic to social justice projects but an unfortunate outcome of the continued internalization of oppressive ideologies like racism, sexism, homophobia, and colonialism.[21] This logic echoes the 1970s separatist claim that punitive behavior among lesbian feminists could always be explained away as a failure to decolonize one's mind of patriarchal ideologies, rather than malicious intent on the part of the women involved. Yet what if part of the problem here is the very presumption that social movements can and must eliminate trauma, negativity, or psychic pain from the lives of their participants? Is it possible that the internecine punishing tendency of contemporary social justice projects is an effect not of internalized oppression, but of the very expectation that one must be cared for and by "the movement," an expectation that breeds bad blood, disappointment, and blame every time it isn't met? Moreover, must all aspects of one's life, from social relationships to the art and culture one produces and consumes, be an extension of some kind of movement ideology? Is there life after or beyond "a movement," whichever one it may be?

If it is difficult to critique notions of care or mutual aid, it is not least because they appear as an innate social good. But precisely because care is so self-evidently necessary in a systemically unjust world, it can also function hegemonically as a framework that cannibalizes all other forms of relating within and without social justice movements. For instance, the writers of "The Care Manifesto" describe care as an ethically necessary model for political action to combat the unequal distribution of resources at every scale of human existence, from global to national, local to interpersonal. In this logic, care is about the interconnected weave of various scales of community, so that the failure to address systemic suffering in one is to exacerbate existing vulnerabilities in others.[22] Similarly, legal scholar Dean Spade suggests that the concept of "mutual aid" is about the development of alternative networks of support "to meet survival needs and build shared understanding about why people do not have what they need."[23] These are undoubtedly legitimate goals, but they frequently conflate the concept of political freedom with "social justice, which [is] really an argument about expediency," or a view of politics merely "as a means to an end," namely "solving certain social problems."[24] Whether intended or not, this approach implies that the purpose of every public or interpersonal act (from civic engagement to a conversation over coffee) should be to uplift a constituency of marginalized people, provide alternative care networks in the absence of institutional support, and validate others' injured identities so that our "wounded attachments," to borrow Wendy Brown's well-known phrase, might themselves become a source of meaning and value.

One outcome of this worldview is that it can encourage individuals to reframe all their intimate relationships, including interpersonal bonds with friends and family, as mere local expressions of wide-reaching systemic inequalities. Consequently, the insult of one person's microaggression, misstatement, or failure to attend to another's needs always comes to be felt as the crushing weight of a system. That feeling, of course, then requires collective response to mitigate harm, trapping us in an endless loop of pain and redress. Zerilli cautions us that "[t]his logic keeps [the] radical demand for freedom, for unqualified participation in common affairs, bound to an economy of use that deeply restricts [the] emergence [of] political collectivity."[25] Moreover, "if we value . . . freedom because it is useful in solving certain social problems, we may not value freedom when it interferes with social utility."[26] Thriving beyond necessity involves an attunement to public life as a space for debating issues of common concern, including the very question of what will count as "the good," and the possibility that values other than care, like deliberative judgment and speech, might matter, perhaps even more, to the public square. As we have seen throughout this book, the signal power of movements for women's and gay liberation lay not in their ability to stop harm, which they accomplished only occasionally and provisionally, but in their imaginative capacity to project the categories of gender and sexuality into entirely new contexts for thought and action.

My discomfort with the discourse of care lies with its twofold assumption that (a) the subject of care is always someone starting from a place of lack or who does "not have what they need"; and (b) that the primary purpose of politics is to make up for that lack at all levels of human experience. As I understand it here, the social relation of friendship is not predicated on a lack that must be redressed, but rather begins with the plenitude or creative capacity of two people to engage in mutually transformative exchange. Feminist and queer friendships are one place where two (or more) people clear space for each other to inhabit and perform desire, intimacy, affect, kinship, and attachment in countless new ways. Friendship, then, is a deeply unpredictable space of experimentation precisely because one reveals oneself to another, only to have one's self-perception reworked and potentially dismantled through their eyes. As Roach underscores: "The friend's role is actively to enhance the other's potential, to push the friend to become-other.

Betrayal is one practice through which this occurs; it instigates an ethical relation that cares little for historically determined identity."[27] In
this sense, queer and feminist friendship is corrosive to the traditional
concept of care, altering the very definition of caring for something
or someone from a practice aimed at remediating systemic harm to a
form of *radical honesty* based in intense dialogic back-and-forth, one of
whose outcomes is the cultivation of resilience and skill at coping with
change.[28] This is a type of mutual forming or taking shape in concert
with others. Thus, the greatest betrayal to feminist and queer friendship
is not the enactment of social injury, but the refusal to engage or talk
out conflict.

This kind of cutting off has recurrently undermined movements for
gender and sexual freedom since the 1970s. It is evidenced in some separatists' unilateral refusal to communicate with men and straight women;
some feminists of color's choice to cut ties with white women; many
gay men's willful neglect of lesbians who had been their caregivers and
political allies at the height of the HIV/AIDS epidemic; and today, in
queer, feminist, and trans* social justice warriors' use of canceling as a
tool of ideological policing. Each of these examples describe moments in
the history of gender and sexual liberation when people began to see the
contingent promises of feminist and queer social movements as ironclad
agreements that could or should secure a future free of hurt, trauma, or
violation. Snitow explains that such demands fundamentally misunderstand what feminist and queer politics are meant to accomplish, neither
providing a stable future beyond sexism, homophobia, and transphobia nor unmitigated happiness in a community of fellow travelers, but
productive uncertainty, a capacity to live with contingency: "Feminist
narratives are internally contradictory, diverse, reactive, unsettling, unclear. . . . In contrast to traditionalist movements, which promised so
much depth of feeling, does feminism keep you warm at night, provide
you company in old age, offer a sustaining sense of meaning and purpose? Not only does feminism fail on all these counts, but it fails by design. Only in brief periods among a few groups was feminism meant to
be an all-encompassing ideology . . . a panacea for all ills, or a comfort-
able, permanent home."[29] And indeed, contemporary feminist, queer,
and trans* activists' smug dismissal of 1970s women's and gay liberation
often stems from an assumption that these movements failed to make

good on their promise to universally provide a "permanent home" for *all* gender and sexual dissidents.

Friendship's promises, on the other hand, are local, intimate, and open to revision, rather than cosmic commitments to ensure a utopian future for a vague political collective (oppressed people everywhere). It is for that reason that they frequently withstand the sheer unpredictability of social movement politics, living past the last consciousness-raising meeting, zap action, or march. Indeed, anyone who has cultivated sustained friendships, especially feminist and queer ones, knows that the trust forged between friends through their dialogue creates extreme latitude for harms done, a space for humor, irreverence, and offensiveness coupled with an equal measure of accountability *and* letting go. Recall that at the end of a long night of emotional abuse at the hands of his friend Michael, Harold casts a searing judgment against Michael's behavior, but ultimately says, "I'll call you tomorrow." Despite Mary Ann Singleton's residual homophobia and terrible choices in men, Michael Tolliver never abandons her, maintaining a loving dialogue that ultimately allows both to become more ethical with one another and their "logical family" at Barbary Lane. And because of Mother Pitt's brutal honesty and unwillingness to look away from Prior's ailing body, a "bleeding heart" faggot and a Mormon mother become lifelong friends.

Friendships of the kind I am describing, then, ones that carry the spirit of inventiveness and experimentation described by Lorde and Foucault, are exceptionally capable of handling conflict, because a genuine equality between the parties (that is nothing like sameness but has to do with two people equally valuing one another) means that both are actively engaged in the construction of the bond. This is why friendship can never function as the application of a rule (you must care for me in this predetermined way as a condition of our speaking) but rather takes shape *in the doing of it*, as the mutual creation, and continual renegotiation, of shared criteria for dialogue (we will speak, again and again, in order to figure out what conditions best enable our mutual growth).[30] This model of sociality leaves far less space for victims and perpetrators, accusers and accused, because of a sense of mutual involvement, a complicity of the best kind not unlike Lorde's conception of "the erotic" as a force that animates a shared creation or "invention" of new social forms between two people. It is also a description of the kind of interaction that incites people to change, to release destructive or oppressive logics like homophobia, sexism, transphobia, and racism, not under ideological duress, shame, or demand, but in the surprising encounter with others who shift the ground beneath one's feet.

This perhaps explains why queer and feminist friendship has endured not only as a lived relation between women and queers of all stripes, but as a proliferative cultural form in so much popular media—from the sisterhood forged between four sexually adventurous, fifty-something roommates in *The Golden Girls* to the lovingly caustic banter between straight and gay best friends in *Will & Grace*; from the erotically charged friendship circle of *Queer as Folk* to the unconditionally loving ballroom family in *Pose*; from the lesbian feminist chosen kinship of Allison Bechdel's *Dykes to Watch Out For* to the fierce network of lesbian lovers and friends in *The L Word*. These and countless other cultural representations of feminist and queer friendship capture the popular imagination not only because they entertain, titillate, or delight us with images of "ourselves" (though they certainly at times do all three). Rather, our enduring investment in these queer forms registers simply this fact: the inevitable failure of feminist and queer movement ideologies to make good on their utopian aspirations, and the impossibility of binding categories like sisterhood, queerness, Blackness, or transness to provide a safe place of indefinite belonging, leaves us with the need to figure, over and over in the mind's eye, the types of relationships that might endure beyond all ideologies, identities, and categories. This is crystalized in Kathie Sarachild's claim that the original fantasy of feminist "unity" gave way to an idea of *persisting* with one's companions in the struggle.[31] The need for friendships to model ideological structures of unity often signals their death, substituting political purity for productive interpersonal discord, blind loyalty for loving honesty, recognition for mutual transformation, and frankly, mind-numbing dullness in place of friendship's special brand of hilarious, ribald, juicy surprise. And indeed, when this same logic of care is extended to the realm of cultural production, it destroys the ability of queer forms to function as agents of perceptual or imaginative expansion that surprise our senses with new views of the world, by measuring each and every one against an unshakable calculus of political utility.

"A Constant Sharing of Perceptions"

During the years I have worked on *Queer Forms*, this project has taken on increasing urgency in relation to my students, who comprise a new generation of queer, feminist, and trans* activists and their allies. Members of this cohort more forcefully and courageously articulate their political commitments to contemporary radical and progressive social movements than any group of students I have encountered before—from Black Lives Matter to climate justice, from transgender liberation to the Me Too movement. Yet paradoxically, they are also more creatively constrained, moralizing, and ideologically rigid in their conception of what counts as proper political progress. This conjoining of inspiring political intensity with dogmatic narrowmindedness limits my students' capacity to see the value of multiple, competing, even contradictory visions of gender and sexual freedom in the creation of a more just world. While many pundits call this phenomenon "political correctness," I prefer to identify it as a narrative of radical left-wing *alignment*, whereby all the political, social, and cultural variables of one's life must perfectly line up to produce a seamlessly progressive ideological structure. Even as this stance is intended to reflect a deep commitment to radical liberation projects, it ironically makes my students far less generous toward the messy lived realities of left-wing movement politics. This includes the basic fact that any collective endeavor to transform shared conditions of existence will always include flawed participants who make interpersonal and political mistakes, as well as produce and consume cultural products that can be ideologically incoherent or impure, without disqualifying either as pivotal to the history of social change.

Let me illustrate this point by returning to where I began: I have been teaching *Thelma & Louise* in a variety of US cultural studies courses for more than a decade. My students are always awestruck by the film's boldness and its protagonists' radical, even anarchist, refusal of the social order as it stands. But in recent years when I teach the film in more explicitly queer and feminist theory seminars, my students invariably ask some version of the following questions: "Why don't they admit to being lesbians at the end of the movie?"; "Why wasn't the movie about two Black women?"; or "Why do they have to die at the end?" These wonderfully curious youth, who espouse the value of gender and sexual fluidity; who repeatedly scoff at the notion of fixed identities; who want to be recognized as multidimensional, "intersectional" beings, surprisingly almost always uphold a demand that the movie provide them with definitive sexual or racial identities to attach to or a clear narrative of social uplift. Such demands are representative of a broader trend I frequently encounter from highly politicized, ethically committed queer and feminist students who expect that popular culture forms should reproduce their *perceived* idea of positive, inclusive, and intersectional representation. In other words, rather than attend to a cultural text's imaginative content, how a work of art or literature allows them to conceive gender and sexuality in new ways, my students' initial impulse is to measure it against a predetermined idea of social justice—which is really a moving target based on whichever group identity they have decided is the most oppressed or subjected at any given moment—a measure nearly every cultural representation fails to meet. As a result, when we discuss a film like *Thelma & Louise*, they initially overlook the movie's proliferation of unexpected feminist and queer forms and reduce its conceptual possibilities—including the idea that the women never actually "die" at the end but take an epic leap into the sky meant to inspire us to symbolically do the same—to a singular political metric of presumed liberal progress.

This knee-jerk reaction is not intentionally obtuse. Rather my students genuinely feel they are asking ethically appropriate questions of the film and doing their part to promote feminist and queer political advancement. Lovingly pushing back against this logic, I point out that the film's refusal to identify the women as lesbians leaves open the possibility that friendship between women of any sexuality can be a sustaining social bond that exceeds the limits of romantic or erotic desire. While the film does not provide a robust critique of race, in representing two white women as outlaws, it associates the feminist flight from patriarchal law with other racially inflected anarchist projects like Black fugitivity. And by refusing to see the women killed by police or taken away in chains, the movie celebrates feminist freedom above mere survival. The friends do not die on screen, but *fly*. I remind them too that a rich archive of Black, queer, and trans* outlaw movies does exist—including the Black women bank robbers of F. Gary Gray's *Set It Off* (1996) and the anarchist gay lovers of Gregg Araki's *The Living End* (1992)—and that no single cultural text can, or necessarily should, carry the weight of all their political aspirations at once. This shift in conceptual frame always comes as a revelation because it interrupts my students' need for the film to transparently recognize their identities, mirror their political values, or actively mitigate or combat social ills to have meaning and value. Instead, it opens up the possibility that the purpose of any cultural form is to render one's most cherished ideas, attachments, or fantasies— about gender, sexuality, the law, norms, or desire—unrecognizable. And moreover, that the task of the reader or viewer is, in the words of Barbara Johnson, to "set [themselves] up to . . . encounter and propagate the surprise of otherness," that is, to see the text and the assumptions they bring to it from a fresh and unexpected angle.[32] This is of course, what both friends *and* forms do at their best, continually disclosing surprising new aspects of reality to us and soliciting our response.

My students' astonishment at this change in perspective is redoubled when I explain that such expansive understandings of gender and sexual nonconformity claim a significant part of their origin in the women's and gay liberation movements of the 1970s. Armed with an arsenal of self-righteous critiques of the perceived whiteness, transphobia, and classism of radical feminist and gay freedom projects, my students are shocked to discover that, a half-century ago, the movements for women's and gay liberation refused traditional notions of gender, racial, and sexual identity; projected categories like woman, gay, Black, lesbian, transsexual, dyke, and Third World into completely new political and imaginative contexts; and produced forms of sociality, collectivity, and intimacy that provided alternative models to normative conceptions of the heterosexual couple form, the nuclear family, and the nation. When I reframe a text like *Thelma & Louise* as a contemporary extension of these projects, the world opens up anew: suddenly the loss of ground beneath Thelma and Louise's feet (or wheels, as it were) becomes not an expression of failed representation, but the necessary precondition for arriving at a realm of open-ended possibilities for gender and sexual freedom. And yet if in contemporary social justice circles a widespread logic of care has had the tendency of subjecting the unpredictability of both friendship and cultural forms to a rigorous standard of harm reduction, the same cannot be said of feminist and queer art and culture from the 1970s onward, where friendship was and remains a wild, unpredictable, and desirable form of freedom between two impassioned correspondents.

Take, for example, Toni Morrison's *Sula* (1973), arguably the greatest meditation on female friendship in US literature and a novel that represents the author's most sustained conversation with the feminist 1970s. Midway through the narrative, the eponymous title character returns to her hometown of Medallion, Ohio, after a decade of travel, where she promptly sleeps with her best friend Nel's husband, Jude.[33] Enraged by Sula's betrayal, Nel summarily cuts off her chosen sister, the woman that was her most "authoritative interlocutor," her right hand since childhood, "with whom the present was a constant sharing of perceptions."[34] Following years of estrangement, Nel visits Sula while she lies on her deathbed wracked with a mysterious illness. In the novel's lengthiest dialogue, Sula confronts Nel's long-standing grudge by declaring her retreat from their friendship as the greater betrayal: "I didn't kill him, I just fucked him. If we were such good friends, how come you couldn't get over it?"[35] By valuing the fidelity of marriage above that of lifelong friendship; by choosing a man (a boring, selfish one at that) above her soulmate; by refusing to understand what Sula meant by her seeming act of betrayal, Nel had voided their trust. Blinded by hurt, Nel could not fathom that Sula slept with Jude to feel closer to her best friend, to know viscerally an experience Nel had so often enjoyed, and to figure out what exactly Nel saw in this rather middling lover. And in fact, the affair revealed Jude's unworthiness of Nel, whom Sula held in such high esteem. To borrow Roach's formulation, Sula betrayed Nel not to spite her but to "actively enhance her potential," to help Nel see that her role as Jude's doting wife—the form she had chosen to shape her life into—was inhibiting her potential for greatness. In her final parting words, Sula says, "How you know it was you [that was good]? . . . [M]aybe it wasn't you. Maybe it was me."[36] It is not until years later that Nel absorbs the full import of her mistake—that her "canceling" of Sula was only a harm she inflicted upon herself, and that the great loss of her life was not her husband but her best friend. In the novel's famous last lines, Nel whispers to the wind, "All that time . . . I thought I was missing Jude. . . . 'O Lord, Sula.' . . . It was a fine cry . . . but it had no bottom and no top, just circles and circles of sorrow."[37] Sula had always been Nel's closest and most significant queer form, a figure she used to "grow on." In the absence of her greatest correspondent, Nel can now only trace a circle of sorrow around herself.

What we see in *Sula* is not only a powerful depiction of two Black women's friendship, but two feminist and queer forms in the shape of engaged interlocutors, female replicants, or repliers involved in continual discourse. The effect of that correspondence is twofold, for it radically shifts the ground beneath Nel's feet, compelling her to see from Sula's perspective and hence question the limits of her own, but *it does the same for us as readers*, by forcing us to recognize our complicity with Nel's heteronormative attachments, and perhaps opening up our mind to a new way of seeing what friendship between women can be. This is a model of "care" based not on social utility, or attending to needs, but on the "constant sharing of perceptions." And what is a feminist and queer form but a figure, an outline, a picture in the imagination that shifts our place in the world as we know it by expanding what we can think and feel of gender and sexual existence? Could a cultural representation of feminist and queer friendship like that offered in *Sula* reconfigure how we relate, to one another and to our most cherished queer cultural forms? Could the formal depiction of engaged discourse, the rigorous back-and-forth required to see, hear, and feel from another's perspective, provide us a model for how to create "something else to be" for women and queers of all stripes? Could we, like Sula and Nel, "use each other to grow on"? If so, then queer forms are objects that can speak back to us like friends, if only we would listen, and respond, without end.

By their continual movement into new contexts; by their flight into different people's imaginations; by their travels through diverse interpretative frames, queer forms are always on the move, giving structure to even the most seemingly fluid, formless, open-ended aspects of gender and sexual being, including the boundless correspondence between women and queers everywhere. In their sheer variety, ordinariness, and creative possibilities, queer cultural forms remind us that social movements alone do not make, nor completely contain, the full range of feminist and queer lives or experiences. But they can clear space for diverse expressions of gender and sexual being to develop, evolve, and cohere in countless ways. That persistence, the ability of gender and sexual dissidents to keep taking shape across time and against all odds, approximates the fantasized, fluid state that so many contemporary queer, feminist, and trans* discourses conceptually aspire to, but without losing the solidity of friendship as a social form that enables meaningful and measured change across time.

Let me end, then, with a final image of a queer form taking shape in the liquid expanse of the Atlantic Ocean, one that might provide a different sustaining metaphor for our own relationship to the feminist and queer past. In director Barry Jenkins's film masterpiece *Moonlight*, Juan, an adult, Black male drug dealer, develops an unlikely friendship with a shy, twelve-year-old queer boy named Chiron. Early in the film, a vividly arresting scene depicts Juan teaching Chiron how to swim in the waters off a Florida beach. Holding Chiron's body afloat with his hands, Juan reassures his young friend: "Let your head rest in my hand, relax. I got you, I promise. I'm not gon' let you go . . . Feel that right there? You're in the middle of the world" (figure C.1/plate 16). As the scene unfolds, the camera floats alongside them at the surface of the water, reproducing the embodied sensation of floating up and down in the current. Shortly after, as the pair sits on a picnic table looking out at the water, Juan tells Chiron: "Let me tell you something man, there are Black people everywhere. No place you can go in the world ain't got no Black people. . . . I've been here a long time, but I'm from Cuba. . . . I was a wild li'l shorty, just like you, man. Runnin' around with no shoes on when the moon was out. This one time I run by this old lady. She stopped me, she said: 'Running around, catching up all that light. In moonlight black boys look blue.'" Against the barbaric history of Black bodies liquidated in the slaveholding Atlantic, against cruel stereotypes of absent Black fathers, and violent, criminal, or emotionally distant Black men, *Moonlight* presents Black masculinity itself as vast and oceanic, fluid *in spirit*, but always taking form: the form of an embrace. In Juan's tender cross-generational hold, it becomes possible to conceive that a Black queer boy can inhabit "the middle of the world" rather than its periphery. That "Black people are everywhere." That Black boys can look "blue in the moonlight." That a Black straight man can support a Black queer boy, as gently and lovingly as the liquid touch of water.

And indeed, we learn too what this embrace might feel like. By choosing to carry us afloat in the pulsating current, Jenkins formally extends to his viewers the visceral sensation of being buoyed in water by the creative hand of a Black male film director. In this way, both moonlight and

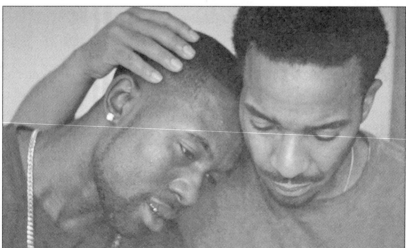

Figure C.1. Top to bottom: Juan carries Chiron aloft in the waters of the Atlantic Ocean; Kevin cradles Chiron's head against his shoulder in *Moonlight's* final scene. *Moonlight*, dir. Barry Jenkins (A24, 2016).

Moonlight shine a Black feminist *and* queer light on the surface of Black masculinity, drawing out its most affectionate, nurturing depths, which include the capacity to feel sadness and longing but also beauty and tenderness. As the film progresses, Juan's gentle but firm hold on Chiron, his promise to "not to let go," becomes an enchanting and affectively abundant form for describing a vast range of Black queer intimacies: the symbolically queer chosen kinship between adult and child, as well as the sensual affection between Chiron and his friend and one-time lover Kevin, who cradles Chiron's head against his shoulder in the film's final scene as an act of loving kindness (figure C.1/plate 16). Each embrace traces the outline of a single Black boy struggling to cope with the upswell of queer feelings that reside in the ocean of his heart, giving him a container, a solid form against which to take shape. Like the unmarried woman, like the female man, like the woman warrior, like Zed, like the boys in the band, like Barbary Lane, like Nancy, like a Ford Thunderbird, the "blue-Black boy" is a figure of the newly thinkable that participates in a long cultural history of feminist and queer forms that model the longings, aspirations, desires, and intensities of gender and sexual dissidents everywhere.

What would it mean for us to hold feminist and queer forms with the tenderness of a man holding a boy afloat in water? What if we recognized the world as an unpredictable, liquid medium within which gender and sexual existence deliberately coheres and shapeshifts in countless ways? Rather than aspire to an impossible fluid state, could we imbue our material and symbolic forms with an *ethos* of flexibility and openness that might also provide a model for a feminist and queer ethics? If the world unfolds before us as a seemingly boundless expanse of sensory data and appearances, forms allow us to differentiate what will come to matter to us in this infinitely multiplicious landscape—this includes all the distinct molds, identities, or appearances we take in the course of a life, but also all the figures, icons, images, and constructs we craft to share our worldly reality, our sense of things, to others. When we choose to give apprehensible shape to our highly particular, idiosyncratic, yet meaningful experiences of gender and sexuality, we make a judgment about, or develop our own interpretation of, some aspect of embodied, erotic, intimate life. And we make our viewpoint public. This is what David Wojnarowicz once described as the act of creating an image based on his most private queer desires and "putting it on the wall," in the hopes of soliciting the reaction of countless potential viewers whose perspectives might make life less lonely. That is the meaning of *queer form*.

It is the continual practice of *forming* that leads to the constitution of new kinds of collectivity, the inhabitation of novel styles of self-expression, the adoption of unexpected political views, or perhaps simply finding out that "maybe it wasn't you" who was always right, or morally superior, or the most politically progressive, or the queerest of them all. But how would you know, if you didn't risk taking shape? When we seek a false freedom in the fantasized ideal of fluid being or revert back to our most rigid predetermined categories of identitarian belonging, we abdicate the responsibility to articulate and share our distinct perspective about what it means to be queer, femme, gay, trans*, non-binary, feminist, bisexual, or something else entirely.

People *do* change from one form to another. People *do* inhabit their skin in new and unexpected ways across time. People can and do become *less* or altogether *anti*-racist, sexist, homophobic, and transphobic. Yet these transformations are not effortlessly achieved by approximating an idealized mellifluous state or waiting for an absolute and unimpeachable set of rules on how to properly pursue a progressive life. Rather they commonly take place through clumsy, laborious social and affective processes of testing out new identities and desires, incorporating foreign experiences, and creatively conceiving other ways of inhabiting the world. Such transformations require the presence of multitudinous queer forms to provide formerly unimaginable possibilities for what we could be or become, but always our own version of it. Across the preceding chapters, I have collated an archive of feminist and queer forms, perceptible aesthetic shapes that help us describe, render, or coalesce the manifold faces of gender and sexual existence, "which are, until the [artwork], nameless and formless-about to be birthed, but already felt."[38] And throughout, I have modeled a rigorous queer formalism, a method of interpretation that holds out the possibility of recognizing such figures, making meaning of them, and testing out their capacity to speak in the name of different feminist and queer experiences and lives without forever standing in for them.

Like Juan to Chiron, the movements for women's and gay liberation were imperfect mentors, but they taught us to imagine gender and sexuality differently, to conceive of more felicitous and adaptable forms that might give solid shape, even provisionally, to our most audacious dreams of alternative erotic and intimate bonds, gender expressions, and chosen kinships. The ease with which we disavow a feminist and queer past, the withering condescension that accompanies our dismissal of women's and gay liberation as a shared history of misguided failures, tells us nothing about those social movements and everything about the impoverishment of our contemporary political imaginations. No doubt, the ideological promises of movements for women's and gay liberation have often (and necessarily) failed us, since no social movement could ever predict in advance the contingent outcomes of its political actions nor adequately heal the magnitude of injury inflicted by a heterosexist society. But their *imaginative* promises, figured in the repository of forms they bequeath to us across time, continue to make good on their commitment to expand what we can think, feel, or conceive of our genders and sexualities, if only we have the "courage to try them out," interpret and reinvent them.[39] Like Juan, who reminds Chiron that Black people are everywhere, that Black masculinity is as wide and deep as the sea, so too, the movements for women's and gay liberation taught us that (we) women and queers of all stripes "are everywhere," that we are legion among and within ourselves, capable of deep feeling and the capacity to change. In this sense, these movements remain steadfast friends to our feminist and queer political aspirations, speaking back to us, offering a hand, providing a symbolic embrace in the countless political tracts, historical accounts, and cultural works they inspired.

The holding of hands and bodies is consistent in all the queer forms I have discussed throughout this book. And indeed, the ability to reach out across bodies, to create meaningful relationships between people with vastly different desires, gender expressions, sexual orientations, ethnic and racial backgrounds, spiritual beliefs, temperaments, abilities, and experiences in the hope of mutual transformation is what projects for gender and sexual freedom have always been about: the fundamental ability to *commune freely*. As Anthony Michael D'Agostino reminds us: "Physical, psychological, and cultural harms are distinct possibilities within the potentials of queer contact and feminist identification across racial [sexual, gender, and embodied] boundaries. . . . [A queer and feminist] touch presents the idea that who we are cannot be wholly determined in advance by the preordained matrix of classification we have come to know as identity."⁴⁰ With this in mind, queer cultural forms suggest what "ethical cross-identification might look like. Specifically . . . it might look like an offered hand."⁴¹ In the spirit of feminist and queer friendship, then, I reach out to my readers, my fellow gender and sexual outlaws, and my beloved, impassioned students—if this book teaches you anything, let it be this: (1) you are not the first generation to imagine gender and sexuality otherwise, or to aspire to a world fit for feminist and queer freedom, and you won't be the last; (2a) far from a retrograde trash heap of political failures, the history of women's and gay liberation is an endlessly rich archive of feminist and queer forms that can aid in your struggle and infuse it with pleasure, elation, resilience, hilarity, and heart; (2b) don't forget that one day you too will be someone else's feminist and queer form, a picture in their mind of what they could be or become—you'll want to leave them shapes rich in hope and possibility, not only the outline of their trauma and pain, or the prison of your moralizing judgments; and (3) for this brief moment that you appear in this dazzling, wonderous, chaotic world, *you have nothing but forms to live by*: keep taking shape, learn to shapeshift with style, clear space for others to do the same, and never stop. Queer forms cannot save us, heal us, or permanently dismantle oppressive regimes, but they can provide equipment for living, and without them we cannot imagine "something else to be."

ACKNOWLEDGMENTS

Queer Forms is a Lebanese American gay man's love letter to feminism. With rare exception, from the time I emigrated to the US at age six until my early thirties, women constituted the core of my emotional universe. As a highly expressive young boy largely shunned by male members of my cohort, it was women of every class, color, spiritual belief, profession, and temperament who befriended and mentored me. My feminist values emerged from a deep love and gratitude to the women and gender outlaws in my life who saw me as inherently valuable, even though we frequently did not share the same gender, objects of desire, ethnic heritage, even age and tastes. These friendships formed my first and most sustained experiences of cross-identification, bonds that organically emerged from proximity, shared dialogue, and trust. This unrestrained affinity led me to feel that the fate of women, men, and queers of all stripes are intimately tied to one another, and that the ability to commune across our differences is possible, desirable, and pleasurable. Accordingly, *Queer Forms* is an extended reckoning with the shared destinies of women and queers everywhere. It puts forward an argument for the necessity of reconceiving what gender and sexuality can be in the imagination, not as fixed identities, social types, or political ideologies, but as endlessly proliferating creative forms we can inhabit together and use to see the world through each another's eyes. The capacity of women and queers to commune freely is not only a historical reality I study, but a bedrock part of my everyday life that infuses every aspect of this book.

During the years I have worked on *Queer Forms*, four friends were my most steadfast advocates and interlocutors. Cindy I-Fen Cheng has been my sister, soulmate, cheerleader, and visionary companion each step of the way. Together, we have articulated every hope, aspiration, and commitment we share about intellectual life, and enhanced one another's potential for growth in all areas of our lives. Cindy and I hold the belief that behind every truly great intellectual endeavor lies a genuine a love of the world. Our bond is written all over this book. Jared Hoffman entered my life at the glorious crescendo of a gay dance party five years ago. We have never stopped shimmying together since. His friendship, based in unconditional mutual compassion, curiosity, and love, has been a healing balm during the most difficult years of writing. My worldly reality has been immeasurably enriched by our "constant sharing of perceptions." Leslie Bow began as my tenure mentor, then became my role model, and finally evolved into a dear friend and kindred spirit. She has followed the evolution of *Queer Forms* since its inception, reading and responding to my developing ideas with keen attention and care. She is a thinker whose rigor, precision, and focus is as exceptional as her intellectual generosity, playfulness, and imagination. Finally, Anthony Michael D'Agostino is my superhero teammate and "telepathic sis" for life, the Jean Grey to my Storm. In the near decade we have been friends, Tony has never minced a single word, held back any idea, feeling, or conviction, or failed to respond to our endless, impassioned dialogue. Anthony's sheer genius, fierce love and investment, and astonishing wit are all superpowers that have contributed to the creation of this book. In the presence of these four extraordinary companions, I keep evolving into my best form.

An inner circle of fellow scholars and friends has sustained me throughout my writing. Darieck Scott is easily one of the most brilliant, creative, bold thinkers I have ever met, with a heart as expansive and all-encompassing as his mind. We have collaborated, commiserated, and cared for one another in more ways than I can count. Damon Young and I have grown up together in academia, following each other's evolution as scholars and teachers, and providing the foundation of trust and honesty required to navigate this bizarre but also enchanting profession. His unwavering belief in me and my work has been one of the great gifts of my adult life. Jennifer Nash is everything I aspire to in life and thought—a bold, unorthodox thinker, an open-hearted friend, a staunch advocate of professional kindness and generosity, and an all-around superhero. David Getsy has been an extraordinary friend, mentor, big brother, and cheerleader to this fellow queer formalist. His vision for all that forms can do to articulate gender and sexual nonconforming life has inspired my own.

I have benefited immeasurably from the support and camaraderie provided by my intellectual community at UW Madison. At various points along the way, my colleagues Monique Allewaert, Leslie Bow, Russ Castronovo, Theresa Kelly, Caroline Levine, Aida Levy-Hussen, Cherene Sherrard-Johnson, Susan Stanford Friedman, Nirvana Tanoukhi, Timothy Yu, and David Zimmerman helped me establish a thriving career while also welcoming me into their lives, homes, and confidences. In my last year of writing, my luminary new colleagues Kristina Huang and James McMaster, and all-around amazing graduate students Elaine Cannell and Adam Schuster, took time to read drafts of every new chapter I developed. The insightfulness of their feedback was unparalleled and helped me ensure that this material would ring true to an emerging generation of young scholars. Finally, a mid-career fellowship from the Department of English gave me the resources to organize a second book forum, which brought together my esteemed peers Leslie Bow, Sara Guyer, Darieck Scott, and Linda Zerilli. Their incredible enthusiasm for this material, exacting eye for detail, and bold queries helped push the final manuscript to its greatest heights. I am infinitely grateful for the time and energy they put into this endeavor.

My research for *Queer Forms* has been underwritten by significant institutional resources. At UW Madison, three years of summer support, a semester-long fellowship at the Institute for Research in the Humanities, and a Vilas Early Career Grant allowed me to consistently produce articles and book chapters, conduct extensive research at the UW Madison Historical Society, and complete three years of interviews in the San Francisco Bay Area. During a semester-long leave in the fall of 2018, I was a visiting fellow at Stanford University's Center for the Comparative Study of Race and Ethnicity. Director Jennifer Devere Brody and Associate Director Rigoberto Marquéz welcomed me with open arms and generously provided me with opportunities to present my work and receive critical feedback. A Stanford Humanities Center Fellowship the following year gave me the final push I needed to complete this project. I am immensely thankful to Director Roland Green, Associate Director Andrea Reese Davies, Kelda Jamison, and the entire SHC staff for their unwavering commitment to supporting my work and maintaining a world-class space for the cultivation of intellectual community. My fellow fellows Heather Hendershot, Brian DeLay, Fiona Griffiths, and Mei Li Inouye brought kindness, levity, and warmth to a turbulent pandemic year. I am indebted to the UW Madison Alumni Association and its Bay

Area chapter for hosting a phenomenally well-attended public event at the San Francisco LGBTQ Historical Society Museum in January 2019, where I was able to debut my research on Armistead Maupin's *Tales of the City* (with the author himself in the crowd!). Lastly, I will forever have heartfelt and boundless gratitude to poet Ron Padgett, artists James Romberger and Marguerite Van Cook, and the twenty-nine original readers of *Tales of the City* for trusting me with their personal histories as dynamic participants in the making of the feminist and queer 1970s and 1980s.

Whatever queer forms I have taken in the course of my life, it has all been possible because of my network of extraordinary friends, all of whom compose a blueprint for the concept of unconditional love. My beloved "Fancy Faggots" crew, Andrew Lopez, Patrick Hanlin, Jared Hoffman, and Matt Wisniewski, have been my queer inner circle for the past four years. In that time, we've laughed, wept, danced, fought, reconciled, adventured, and reinvented ourselves together a million times over. They are my definition of "gay community"—loyal, joyful and infinitely heterogeneous. Countless details in this book, from the structure of certain arguments to my authorial tone and writerly style, have been influenced by the conversations, walks, meals, and long phone calls I've shared with: Michael Burton, Gerald Butters, Monica Canfield-Lenfest, Olivia Clare Friedman, Gannon Curran, Pamela Gill, Lou Groshek, Chris Hanson, Justin Hall, Phil Hammack, Michael Horka, Paul Jermann, Cáel Keegan, Nedda Mehdizadeh, Jerry Miller, Margo Padilla, Gary Patterson, Joseph M. Pierce, Greg Roberts, and Matthew Tinkcom. Ivan Ortiz provided invaluable suggestions for revising my chapter on *Tales of the City*, which helped make this research truly shine. Perhaps the greatest gift to come out of my time at Stanford University was my bond with Ivan Lupić, a visionary intellect who brings equal measures of radical honesty and fierce loyalty to our growing friendship. For the past two years, Antony Tier has been the unwavering voice of compassion, gentleness, and understanding within my inner monologue, which has elevated my intellectual life as much as my interpersonal one. Kathleen Moran and Richard Hutson are my "other" mother and father—my greatest mentors, my chosen kinship, the foundation for my life in academia. No words could capture all they have given me. Finally, near the end of my drafting, Emily Dings joined forces with me as my content editor. Emily copyedited my first published article in the journal *American Literature* nearly a decade ago. Sharing *Queer Forms* with her so many years later, and once more receiving the gift of her enthusiastic and exacting editorial eye, has meant the world to me.

During the period I wrote this book, I had the fortune of reconstituting my relationship with my brother, Samer Fawaz. In this time we have traveled the world, lost ourselves on dance floors, reinvented our fashion stories, given each other endless advice, and helped one another through heartaches and triumphs. We also welcomed a new member of our family, his partner Brian Justin Crum. Brian is the brother I never had, a confidant, friend, and light of joy in a very chaotic world. Finally, in the last eight months of writing *Queer Forms*, I lived with my mama, Roula Fawaz, in our Southern California family home. As I poured my heart out into completing the most ambitious project of my life, my mother gifted me with meals, living room dance parties, TV binges, jalapeño margaritas, countless conversations, moral support, and unconditional love. Every day I have been reminded that my mother is the first person who taught me how to take shape, by modeling a version of self that can withstand and shapeshift in response to this endlessly unpredictable life. Her resilience, ingenuity, generosity, passion, and humor have infused every aspect of my being. Without her, I would be formless, but in her light I know I can take any shape.

NOTES

INTRODUCTION. QUEER FORMS

1   *Thelma & Louise*, directed by Ridley Scott (1991; Beverley Hills, CA: Metro-Goldwyn-Mayer, 2003), DVD.

2   *Thelma & Louise* has inspired voluminous scholarship in feminist film and media studies. The most sustained analysis of the motion picture remains Sturkin's *Thelma & Louise*. Other notable studies include a *Film Quarterly* roundtable, "The Many Faces of 'Thelma & Louise'"; Willis, "Hardware and Hardbodies"; and Griggers, "*Thelma and Louise*."

3   Zerilli, *Abyss of Freedom*, 98. My understanding of "freedom" as an action-oriented collective practice derives from the work of Hannah Arendt and Linda Zerilli. Against the traditional liberal political view, which holds that freedom is located in individual liberty or sovereignty, Arendt and Zerilli conceive of a freedom-centered, democratic politics as fundamentally about people's ability to found new forms of political association and act in concert in response to questions of common concern. As Arendt reminds us in *The Human Condition*: "If it were true that sovereignty and freedom are the same, then indeed no man could be free, because sovereignty, the ideal of uncompromising self-sufficiency and mastership, is contradictory to the very condition of plurality. No man can be sovereign because not one man, but men, inhabit the earth" (234).

4   See Radicalesbians, "Woman-Identified-Woman."

5   This strand of queer theorizing is frequently associated with the anti-identitarian thrust of queer studies, which understands queerness not as a distinct sexual identity, but rather as an open-ended social force, affective energy, or worldly orientation that thwarts the direction of heterosexual life trajectories. While the scholars I have listed here study widely divergent objects and frequently disagree about the ontological nature of queerness—including its material and psychic foundations and inherent qualities—all conceive of queerness in "formless" terms, either as a felt state of being, a "negative" or anti-communal psychic drive, an oblique relationship to time and place, or a complex cultural, political, and embodied "assemblage." See Ahmed, *Queer Phenomenology*; Edelman, *No Future*; Halberstam, *Queer Time and Place*; Muñoz, *Cruising Utopia*; and Puar, *Terrorist Assemblages*.

6   *Queer Forms* contributes to an expanding body of work on feminist and queer formal practices that includes the scholarship of Jennifer Doyle, Jane Gerhard, David Getsy, Phillip Brian Harper, and Eliza Steinbock. These thinkers have

explored the relationship of feminist, queer, and trans* embodiment to avant-garde aesthetic projects, including AIDS activist performance, feminist install-ment art, sculptural and Black abstraction, and experimental film. See Doyle, *Hold It against Me*; Gerhard, *Judy Chicago*; Getsy, *Abstract Bodies*; Harper, *Abstractionist Aesthetics*; and Steinbock, *Shimmering Images*.

7 Mesli, "In Defense of Identity Politics," 5. My thanks to Linda Zerilli for this reference.

8 In a brilliant essay, Cáel Keegan unpacks how, in both queer theory and contem-porary social justice discourse, notions of fluid gender identity are frequently presumed to attach to, and accurately describe all types of transgender embodi-ment and experience. This assumption recruits the category of transgender into theoretical and activist projects aimed at denaturing all gender and sexual categories, which overlooks the fact that many trans* people explicitly wish to be recognized as one or another gender, rather than continually existing in a state of flux between genders. For Keegan, transgender studies is a field characterized by its strategic toggling back and forth between championing flexible or transitive views of gender on the one hand, and honoring the personal and political value of claiming specific gender categories or identities on the other. See "Getting Disciplined."

9 Invisible Committee, *NOW*, 70.

10 Snitow, *Feminism of Uncertainty*, 7.

11 Hesford, *Feeling Women's Liberation*, 14.

12 On the influence of the Civil Rights Movement on women's and gay liberation, see chapters 8–11 in D'Emilio, *Sexual Communities*; Roth, *Separate Roads*; and Breines, *The Trouble between Us*. On the role of lesbian feminism in the women's movement see chapter 14 in Faderman, *Gay Revolution*; Hesford, *Feeling Women's Liberation*; and chapter 5 in Rosen, *World Split Open*. On gay liberation's embrace of the feminist critique of patriarchy, see the essays in Jay and Young, *Out of the Closets*.

13 Young, "Out of the Closets," 30.

14 Combahee River Collective, "Black Feminist Statement," 212.

15 Hesford, *Feeling Women's Liberation*, 19.

16 Zerilli, *Abyss of Freedom*, ix.

17 Muñoz, *Cruising Utopia*, 22.

18 McRuer, "Gay Gatherings," 216.

19 Zerilli, *Abyss of Freedom*, 60.

20 Russ, *Female Man*, 5, 140.

21 Hobson, *Lavender and Red*, 3.

22 See, for example, Hogan, *Feminist Bookstore Movement*; Gaines, *Black Perfor-mance on the Outskirts*; Roth, *Separate Roads*; and Stryker, *Transgender History*. Other notable entries in this project include Mumford, *Not Straight, Not White*; Ramírez, "'That's My Place!'"; Shugar, *Separatism and Women's Community*; and Springer, *Living for the Revolution*.

23 Roth, *Separate Roads*, 8.

24 Ibid.

25 Hesford, *Feeling Women's Liberation*, 8. For trenchant critiques of the feminist supersessionary narrative from within the field of women's studies, see Cooper, "Love No Limit"; Hemmings, *Why Stories Matter*; Lee, "Notes from the (Non) Field"; and chapter 1 in Wiegman, *Object Lessons*.

26 I construct these stories from a combination of canonical histories, popular accounts by contemporary queer and feminist political activists and cultural theorists, and my students' anecdotal perceptions about women's and LGBTQ history, which I have encountered in a variety of pedagogical environments over more than a decade teaching queer and feminist studies courses.

27 Some version of these distinctions are mapped by Firestone in *Dialectic of Sex*, where she draws a rigid dividing line between liberal and radical feminists; Rosen, *World Split Open*; Dicker, *History of US Feminisms*; and MacLean, *American Women's Movement*. In reconstructing primary source documents from the women's movement in the early 1970s, MacLean thoughtfully includes early feminist writing by Black, Chicana, and Asian American women, pushing back against the tendency to see their contributions as subsequent to white feminist analyses of patriarchy. In chapter 1 of *Why Stories Matter*, Hemmings meticulously tracks the construction of the supersessionary narrative as a commonplace of 1980s and 1990s feminist theory. In *The Trouble between Us*, Breines traces how and why interpersonal splits between Black and white women took root in the later years of civil rights organizing, which would create the sense of an irrevocable ideological division between women along racial lines in the 1970s and after. And in the introduction to *Separate Roads to Feminism*, Roth provides a detailed account and critique of the ways that feminist historiography has reproduced the supersessionary narrative, thereby obscuring the mutually informed histories of multiracial US feminisms. Finally, recent works of popular intersectional feminism like Kendall's *Hood Feminism*, Beck's *White Feminism*, and Hamad's *White Tears/Brown Scars* offer bracing critiques of the limits of contemporary mainstream feminism as practiced by white women. Yet they also tend to present "white feminism" as a clearly identifiable, monolithic project, nearly always complicit with white supremacy, and encompassing a vast range of projects undertaken by white women fighting for gender equality throughout US history. These texts frequently sidestep any sustained engagement with the generative ideas or concepts developed by white participants in the women's liberation movement across a range of political writing, focusing primarily on omissions of racial consciousness among white women variously construed.

28 On the historical significance of the Stonewall Rebellion, see Stein, *Stonewall Riots*, and Duberman, *Stonewall*. On the social and political history of transgender identity and activism, see Stryker, *Transgender History*; Hill, "Before Transgender"; and Snorton, *Black on Both Sides*. On the history of pre-Stonewall queer social networks, including the emergence of the homophile movement, see

D'Emilio, *Sexual Communities*; Meeker, *Contacts Desired*; and Ormsbee, *Meaning of Gay*. For social and cultural histories of gay liberation, see Riemer and Brown, *We Are Everywhere*, and Downs, *Stand by Me*. On the role of Black, Latinx, and Asian American participants in LGBTQ social movements, see Ramírez, "'That's My Place!'"; Mumford, *Not Straight, Not White*; and Ordona, *Coming Out Together*.

29   See, for example, the popular *New York Times* YouTube video "The Stonewall You Know Is a Myth: And That's O.K.," which was produced as part of the *Times'* Celebrating Pride campaign on the fiftieth anniversary of the Stonewall Riots: https://www.youtube.com/watch?v=S7jnzOMxb14.

30   Take for instance Kendall's claim in *Hood Feminism* that, in "white feminism," "[t]rans women are often derided or erased, while prominent feminist voices parrot the words of conservative bigots, framing womanhood as biological and determined at birth instead of as a fluid and often arbitrary construct" (2). Without question, transphobic thinking in any feminist and queer political project must be identified, denounced, and held answerable for reproducing dehumanizing forms of gender policing, exclusion, and stigmatization. And yet Kendall's claim overlooks the long history of feminist critiques of biologically essentialist views of the gendered body, including those of prominent white feminists like Shulamith Firestone, Gayle Rubin, Ann Snitow, and Judith Butler to name a few. This view also implies that non-white women and trans* folks *always* necessarily have a "fluid" understanding of gender as an illusory construct because of their distinct subject positions at the intersection of racial and gendered oppression. Even as women-of-color and trans* feminisms offer invaluable political and analytical insights to the broader project for gendered freedom, neither are immune to essentialist thinking. Moreover, it is doubtful that anyone deeply invested in their gender expression—even those who understand it as a socially constructed performance—thinks of it as simply "arbitrary."

31   Radicalesbians, "Woman-Identified-Woman," 172.

32   As Vivian Gornick explained of the transformative power of feminist CR: "Looking at one's history and experience in consciousness-raising sessions is rather like shaking a kaleidoscope and watching all the same pieces rearrange themselves into an altogether other picture, one that suddenly makes the color and shape of each piece appear startlingly new and alive, and full of unexpected meaning." See Gornick, "Consciousness," 288.

33   Gay Revolution Party, "Manifesto," 342.

34   Jay and Young, "Introduction," to *Out of the Closets*, lxi–lxii. The phrase was invented by pioneering gay activist Frank Kameny in 1968 after he heard Black Power leader Stokely Carmichael chant the mantra "Black is Beautiful" that same year.

35   See Campbell, *Gay X Design*.

36   Alphen, *Art in Mind*, xix.

37   Reed, *Art of Protest*, 397.

38 Powell, *Coming Together*, 5.

39 Ibid., 7, 11.

40 See Dinnerstein, *Mermaid and the Minotaur*.

41 See Rossi, "Equality between the Sexes"; Firestone, *Dialectic of Sex*; and Wittman, "A Gay Manifesto." Finn Enke's illuminating essay "Collective Memory and the Trans Feminist 1970s" recovers largely overlooked trans-*affirmative* moments in the history of women's and gay liberation. Enke argues that an overemphasis on transphobic flashpoints in the study of the feminist and queer past—including the shouting down of transgender activist Sylvia Rivera at the 1973 Gay Freedom Day Parade, and the public denouncement of trans-feminist musician Beth Elliot at the 1973 West Coast Lesbian Feminist Conference—has led historians to ignore rich social histories of interpersonal and political alliance between cis and trans* participants in both movements.

42 See Halley, *Split Decisions*.

43 Sedgwick, *Epistemology of the Closet*, 22.

44 Getsy borrows the term "successive states" from minimalist artist Donald Judd, who originally used it to describe the serial formal transformations of abstract sculpture in the 1960s. Getsy links this formal shapeshifting with transgender conceptions of gender expression as an unfolding or evolving process. See *Abstract Bodies*, xvi.

45 Queer formalism remains an inchoate and developing term in literary studies and art history. Art historian William J. Simmons explains that the term "queer formalism" was first used by literary scholars Eric Savoy and Robert Sulcer to describe the relationship of gay sexuality to the practice of art and literary criticism. Both conceive of queer formalism as the distinct interpretative method of the gay critic. In Simmons's essay "Notes on Queer Formalism," he theorizes queer formalism as a characteristic of some contemporary painters' art practice, specifically creators who intentionally try to wed incommensurate forces in their work, including the "singularity" and coherence of artistic medium with the subversive and anti-identitarian energy of queerness. In *Queer Forms*, I flesh out queer formalism as a concrete method for studying cultural production across a range of mediums, materials, and genres. A short genealogy of the term's various uses might include Savoy, "The Jamesian Turn"; Sulcer, "Ten Percent"; Simmons, "Notes on Queer Formalism"; and Doyle and Getsy, "Queer Formalisms." At the time of this writing, Simmons has just released *Queer Formalism: The Return*, in which he further develops his use of the concept in relation to contemporary queer-feminist art and popular culture.

46 Art historians have traditionally understood form as the physical materials used to create a work of art, from the paint applied to canvas to the clay molded into sculptures. Alternatively, literary theorists have tended to see form as describing writerly techniques—like metaphor, enjambment, allegory, or irony—or else poetic and narrative structures that distinguish different genres of writing—like free

verse poetry, sonnets, or novels. Despite placing different kinds of stress on the tactile quality of materials and the structure and deployment of words, both art historical and literary approaches to form are fundamentally about how a creative producer chooses to render or give definition to a set of ideas and affects, characters and representations, objects and scenes. Form is necessarily an expansive term because, technically speaking, everything that exists in the known universe is or can become a form. Consider that even those apparently formless or fluid substances like liquid, gaseous bodies, and theoretical black holes, or seemingly immaterial phenomena like emotions, dreams, or sensory experiences, have some material basis, whether in their chemical composition, their physical inhabitation of space, or their origin in the structure of the human brain, whose neural networks make feeling and sensing possible. Moreover, all of these phenomena can also be aesthetically represented, either drawn, painted, sculpted, performed, or described in countless creative mediums and materials, or imaginatively modeled in the mind.

In *Queer Forms*, I draw on recent cultural studies and art historical uses of the term to describe aesthetic practices of shaping, molding, or rendering human experience in cultural production. A number of recent monographs have revivified the term "form" to better understand, among other things: the link between form and politics, the formal transmission of affect and sensation, and form as a cognitive practice central to the act of interpretation. See, for example, Rooney, "Form and Contentment"; Brinkema, *The Forms of the Affects*; Levine, *Forms*; Kornbluh, *The Order of Forms*; and Alford, *Forms of Poetic Attention.*

47 On the ordering function of forms, see Levine, *Forms*, 3. Levine argues for an expansive view of form as anything that gives order to the world's complex and chaotic social relations, or attempts to organize ideas, beliefs, or emotions into established structures that are capable of being replicated across contexts. She explains, "Form [describes] all shapes and configurations, all ordering principles, all patterns of repetition and difference. . . . [I]t is the work of form to make order. And this means that forms are the stuff of politics" (3). In this book, I take up Levine's call to expand the meaning of forms, to see them in anything and everything that gives shape, pattern, or arrangement to contingent worldly phenomena. But I place less stress on her idea of *ordering* or *organizing*, which tends to invoke the disciplinary character of forms, and more on the ways that form functions as an everyday inventive practice of conceiving something differently or anew in the mind's eye. Consequently, I see the political aspect of forms not simply, or even primarily, in how they structure or arrange people, ideas, and resources, but more so in their capacity to make public and circulate "figures of the newly thinkable" that facilitate innovative thought and collective action.

48 Altman, *Homosexual*, 147; Gornick, "Progress of Feminism," 22.

49 Quoted in Morris, *Eden Built by Eves*, 59.

50 Getsy, *Abstract Bodies*, 34.

51 For excellent reconstructions of these two dominant oppositional polarities within queer studies, see Mesli, "In Defense of Identity Politics," and Wiegman and Wilson, "Queer Conventions."

52 See note 6 above. This includes Halberstam and Elizabeth Freeman's concept of "queer time," which describes the ways that gender and sexual outlaws live in oblique relation to the linear procession of heterosexual life trajectories; and Edelman's theorization of queerness as a "death drive," a relentlessly negative social force that corrodes any and all normative identities and institutional orders. See Halberstam, *In a Queer Time*; Freeman, *Time Binds*; and Edelman, *No Future*.

53 Mesli, "In Defense of Identity Politics," chapter 2.

54 Muñoz, *Cruising Utopia*, 1, 30.

55 Ibid., 1.

56 Ahmed, *Queer Phenomenology*, 172.

57 See Freeman, "Trashing."

58 In her moving study of Black homeless youth in Detroit, Black feminist sociologist Aimee Meredith Cox uses the term "shapeshifting" to "describe how young Black Women living in the United States engage with, confront, challenge, invert, unsettle, and expose the material impact of systemic oppression. Shapeshifting is an act, a theory, and, in this sense, a form of praxis that—although uniquely definitive of and defined by Black girls—reveals our collective vulnerabilities" (*Shapeshifters*, 7). In *Queer Forms*, I conceive of shapeshifting less as strategy or tactic of resistance to hegemonic norms that is "uniquely definitive" of a particular group, and more as a description of the existential fact of human maturation, adaptation, and change. Shapeshifting, then, is a universally shared state of being, yet one that is always experienced in highly particular ways by each person who inhabits a common world and invariably influenced by larger structural realities like social inequality, group affiliation, or geographical location. In this sense, I concur with Cox that shapeshifting "reveals our collective vulnerabilities" because it exposes the human condition. When we recognize shapeshifting as an fundamental phenomenological reality inherent to all life, we can see even the most specific or idiosyncratic expressions of gender and sexual transformation as representative of the fact of human plurality. This view resonates with Lucas Crawford's claim in *Transgender Architectonics* that "the very 'state' of gender is change. If this is true, then transgender is simply a particularly strong and valuable event of gender—not an exception to the rule of otherwise static genders" (4). So too, the very state of *being* is change, and gender and sexual transformation is one "particularly strong and valuable event of" that collective reality, which requires continual figuration or forming in the mind's eye to become apparent to us in meaningful ways. This includes the infinitely variable interpretations that individuals develop toward their own and others' embodied, psychic, and social transformations, as well as cultural representations of our equally varied metamorphoses.

59 Getsy, *Abstract Bodies*, 41.

60 Crawford, *Transgender Architectonics*, 4.
61 Ibid., 32.
62 Anzaldúa, *Borderlands/La Frontera*, 82, 91.
63 Ibid., preface.
64 Lorde, "Poetry Is Not a Luxury," 25.
65 Ibid., 26.
66 Ibid.
67 Rubin, "Of Catamites and Kings," 253.
68 Rooney, "Form and Contentment," 37.
69 Ibid., 38–39.
70 See Smith, "Toward a Black Feminist Criticism."
71 See Butler, *Undoing Gender*, 2–4. Moreover, as Omise'eke Natasha Tinsley presciently reminds us, the image of "liquidity" recalls the literal and figurative liquidation of Black bodies in the history of the Atlantic slave trade. In her haunting essay "Black Atlantic, Queer Atlantic: Queer Imaginings of the Middle Passage," Tinsley explains: "Once loaded onto the slave ships, Africans became fluid bodies under the force of brutality. Tightly or loosely packed in sex-segregated holds . . . surrounded by churning, unseen waters, these brutalized bodies themselves became liquid, oozing." In making this comparison, I am not suggesting that contemporary notions of gender and sexual fluidity are somehow complicit with anti-Black forms of dehumanization. Rather I caution us against so readily embracing a metaphor that recalls horrific forms of bodily liquidation or the pure dissolution of social, psychic, and cultural boundaries. After all, the very practices of *cultural appropriation* social justice projects so vociferously rail against frequently presume a universally fluid sense of self that can effortlessly inhabit, perform, and claim other cultures or ways of life as one's own without the substantive emotional and cultural work required to bridge divides across difference. In putting forward a model of shapeshifting, I ask how we might acknowledge the capacity to engage in mutually transformative exchange across identities, cultures, and worldviews, without wholly dissolving meaningful boundaries that often require thoughtfulness and subtlety to traverse.
72 Arendt, *Human Condition*, 199–207.

CHAPTER 1. STEPFORD WIVES AND FEMALE MEN
1 Joanna Russ, *Female Man*, 157, 160.
2 Ibid., 162.
3 Ibid., 78.
4 Lorde, *Zami*, 226.
5 Ibid.
6 Gerhard, *Debating Women's Equality*, 7.
7 See Scott, "Conundrum of Equality."
8 See Eisenstein, *Female Body and the Law*, 31–41, and Scott, "Conundrum of Equality." The paradigm of "equality versus difference" remains one of the most

enduring and also contested frameworks for understanding women's equality claims in the history of feminist theory. The paradigm has been particularly tenacious in feminist legal theory, because the law's aspiration to universal applicability means that jurisprudence struggles to adequately account for the fine-grained differences between women and men, and among women themselves. A full accounting of feminist debates around equality versus differences is beyond the scope of this chapter, but some key interventions include MacKinnon, "Difference and Dominance"; Rhode, *Theoretical Perspectives*; Grosz, "Conclusion"; and Frye, "Necessity of Differences." For an insightful overview and reconsideration of this paradigm within feminist political thought, see Zerilli, "Feminist Critiques of Liberalism."

9 Scott, "Deconstructing Equality-versus-Difference," 46.

10 *Oxford English Dictionary*, "replicant, n.," https://www-oed-com (accessed May 4, 2020).

11 Firestone, *Dialectic of Sex*, 30–31.

12 Rosen, *World Split Open*, 65–81.

13 See, for example, "Young Lords Party: Position Paper on Women" (1970), reprinted in MacLean, *American Women's Movement*. A number of entries in Toni Cade Bambara's groundbreaking 1970 anthology *The Black Woman* argue for the necessity of Black women's equality with men in the Black liberation struggle, most notably Frances Beale's foundational essay "Double Jeopardy: To Be Black and Female." Benita Roth offers a social and political history of Chicana activism in chapter 4 of *Separate Roads*.

14 Radicalesbians, "Woman-Identified Woman," 175.

15 Zerilli, *Abyss of Freedom*, 110.

16 Levin, *Stepford Wives*, 118.

17 Ibid., 120.

18 As NOW's 1966 Statement of Purpose declared, "We believe that the power of American law, and the protection guaranteed by the US Constitution to the civil rights of all individuals, must be effectively applied and enforced to isolate and remove patterns of sex discrimination" (NOW, "Statement of Purpose," 73–74).

19 NOW's 1968 Bill of Rights, for example, understood women's legal equality to go hand in hand with a public acknowledgement of the value of all aspects of women's experiences, as mothers, professionals, activists, students, and citizens. The organization's eight-point plan detailing the right of women to universal childcare, post-secondary education, and control over reproductive health was liberal in its call for legal reform, but radical in conceiving of institutional transformations that would make half the US population more politically powerful, well-resourced, and capable of participating in democracy. NOW, "Bill of Rights."

20 Levin, *Stepford Wives*, 6, 22, 17.

21 Ibid., 4, 60, 68.

22 Ibid., 2.

23 Ibid., 17–19.

24 Ibid., 22.
25 Ibid., 21.
26 Ibid., 49.
27 Ibid.
28 Ibid., 43.
29 Ibid., 37.
30 Ibid., 25, 49.
31 Ibid., 27.
32 Ibid., 28–30.
33 Ibid., 71.
34 Ibid., 72.
35 Ibid., 73.
36 Ibid., 6.
37 Ibid., 88.
38 Ibid., 108.
39 Ibid., 58.
40 See "NOW Bill of Rights"; Rossi, "Equality between the Sexes," 52–56; and Rosen, *World Split Open*, 90–91. Despite an impressive body of film studies scholarship about the 1975 cinematic adaptation of Levin's novella, there is a dearth of academic writing on the original literary text. A rare exception is Elliot's "Stepford USA," which offers a comparative analysis of the novella and the film; however, Elliot often treats the two texts as identical in content and ideological meaning, and provides a far more sustained analysis of the cinematic adaptation than its literary counterpart. By ignoring the significant differences between these two versions of *The Stepford Wives*, Elliot is able to claim that Levin's novella lacks self-awareness about its own feminist politics and is thus a well-meaning but naïve expression of the most facile aspects of a white liberal feminism. My reading of the original novella rejects this view, arguing instead that Levin provides a strikingly inventive and nuanced critique of white liberal feminism, while drawing from the most radical aspects of the liberal feminist tradition. For a consideration of the 1975 film's engagement with radical feminist politics through its visual form, see Helford, "Stepford Wives and the Gaze." Helford conducts a virtuosic comparative analysis between the film and Laura Mulvey's classic work of feminist film criticism "Visual Pleasure and Narrative Cinema." She illuminates how the movie attempted a critical deconstruction of the traditional male gaze of Hollywood cinema at the very moment that Mulvey was identifying and critiquing it.
41 Russ, *Female Man*, 1.
42 Ibid., 18.
43 Ibid., 29–30.
44 Ibid., 6–7.
45 Ibid., 20, 17–18, 19.
46 Snitow, *Feminism of Uncertainty*, 22.

47 Russ, *Female Man*, 98–99.
48 Ibid., 82.
49 Ibid., 211–212.
50 Ibid., 103.
51 Ibid., 109.
52 Ibid., 95.
53 Ibid., 110.
54 Ibid., 165.
55 Ibid.
56 Ibid., 133, 137–140.
57 Radicalesbians, "Woman-Identified Woman," 172.
58 Combahee River Collective, "Black Feminist Statement," 211.
59 Zerilli, *Abyss of Freedom*, 64.
60 Russ, *Female Man*, 209.
61 It is fitting, then, that Russ dedicates the book "to Anne, to Mary and to the other one and three-quarters billions of us." In this bracing address, Russ simultaneously names the particular women interlocutors who influenced the creation of her book, while reminding us of the sheer numerical volume of women who compose half of the human species. Russ's rhetorical invocation presages Toni Morrison's famous dedication to her Pulitzer Prize–winning novel *Beloved* (1987), "sixty million and more," which referenced the uncountable lives lost to the institution of US slavery.
62 Russ, *Female Man*, 212–213.
63 In Donna Haraway's canonical work of postmodern feminist theory "A Manifesto for Cyborgs," she identifies the four Js as emblematic of a contingent feminist "cyborg politics" that is anti-essentialist and resolutely opposed to the logic of identity (31, 36–37).
64 Arendt, *Human Condition*, 215.
65 Kingston, *Woman Warrior*, 29.
66 Ibid., 166.
67 Ibid., 3, 5.
68 Ibid.
69 Ibid., 5.
70 Ibid., 6, 8.
71 Ibid., 8.
72 Ibid., 5.
73 See, for example, Hunt, "'What Was My Village'"; Jenkins, "Authorizing Female Voice"; Wong, "Necessity and Extravagance"; and Shu, "Chinese-American Female Subjectivity." As Laura Kang documents, because of *The Woman Warrior*'s widespread popularity, and its rapid assimilation into an emergent multiethnic US literary canon, the book has been subject to intense ideological critique by activists and scholars. In the 1970s, Asian American cultural nationalists attacked the book for supposedly circulating negative or stereotypical images of a patriarchal

Chinese culture to white audiences. These critiques were soon followed by the scholarship of Asian American feminists who celebrated the book's aesthetic innovations in representing Chinese and Chinese American women's complex lives across generations. Yet they also questioned Kingston's attachment to Western bourgeois modes of life writing and raised concerns about white readers' potential views of the book as providing an "authentic" portrait of Chinese culture. These approaches tend to overlook the relative insignificance that a so-called dominant white US culture plays in the narrative and fail to acknowledge that the story is often told from the point of view of a developing child, whose perspective is constantly evolving, rather than fully formed. These facts underscore the text's deep ambivalence toward a US culture generally portrayed as racist and sexist, rather than an obvious commitment toward assimilation. For a nuanced reconstruction of *The Woman Warrior*'s critical reception, see chapter 1 of Kang's *Compositional Subjects*.

74 Zerilli, *Democratic Theory*, 237. My framing of *The Woman Warrior* as an exercise in perspective is informed by Zerilli's cogent argument for valuing the quotidian reality of "multiple standpoints" as a basis for democratic thought: "Thinking from the place of the other is best understood . . . not as a practice of identification but as an attempt to see from multiple standpoints in order to form a critical opinion and to make a judgment. It takes for granted that the plural perspectives from which one endeavors to see the world might actually provide a glimpse of the world as it is: perspectives are not irremediably distorting" (181).

75 Kingston, *Woman Warrior*, 19.

76 Ibid., 11.

77 Ibid., 19–20.

78 Ibid., 47, 52–53.

79 Morraga, "La Güera," 26.

80 Yamada, "Asian Pacific American Women," 75, 77.

81 Chuh, *Imagine Otherwise*, 9.

82 Kingston, *Woman Warrior*, 29.

83 Ibid., 67.

84 Ibid., 197–198, 201–204.

85 Ibid., 204–205.

86 Kang, *Compositional Subjects*, 7.

87 Kingston, *Woman Warrior*, 206.

CHAPTER 2. ENTERING THE VORTEX

1 Solanas, *S.C.U.M.*, 217.

2 Ibid., 201, 218.

3 Bunch, "Learning from Lesbian Separatism," 434.

4 For instance, Black lesbian feminist Cheryl Clarke contended that "[l]esbianism is a recognition, an awakening, a reawakening of our passion for each (woman) other (woman) and for the same (woman). This passion will ultimately reverse the

heterosexual imperialism of male culture" ("Lesbianism: An Act of Resistance," 126).

5 Readers familiar with either of these deliciously strange films might recall them as idiosyncratic, even bizarre, cinematic productions more akin to B-films than the commonly celebrated texts of the era's speculative avant-garde, like Stanley Kubrick's *A Clockwork Orange* (1971) or Ridley Scott's *Blade Runner* (1982). My selection of texts is intended to reflect the fact that lesbian separatism, a political philosophy commonly dismissed as a form of irrational utopianism, existed at the ideological margins of women's and gay liberation, consequently finding rich imaginative expression in speculative cinema that similarly sat at the far edge of respectable art film. My thanks to Paul Schwochow for introducing me to *Zardoz* nearly two decades ago.

6 See Young, *Making Sex Public*, introduction.

7 Johnston, *Lesbian Nation*, 190.

8 See, for example, Rensenbrink, "Parthenogenesis"; Davis, *The First Sex*; Gutter Dyke Collective, "Our Hidden Matriarchal Dyke Heritage," *Dykes & Gorgons*, 6–7; and Murray, "Free for All Lesbians."

9 See Meeker, *Contacts Desired*, chapter 6.

10 Describing the heady utopian promises of 1970s feminism in the moment of its ascendancy, Andrea Long Chu states: "The proof of patriarchy's reality was not to be found by sorting through anthropological works about early man or collecting statistics about rates of sexual violence, though feminists did both of these things. Patriarchy existed, quite simply, because *women could feel it.*" See Chu, "Impossibility of Feminism," 72.

11 Hoagland, introduction to *For Lesbians Only*, 35. This chapter extends Julie Enszer's project to recover the political creativity of separatist praxis in her essay "'How to Stop Choking to Death.'" In an excellent article, Alyssa Samek underscores that separatism was only one of a variety of forms of lesbian feminism during and after the second wave. See Samek, "Pivoting Between."

12 Combahee River Collective, "Black Feminist Statement," 212.

13 Bunch, "Perseverance Furthers," 3. This inward-turning vision borrowed and elaborated on the Black Power Movement's notion of "closing ranks," by which they meant "that group solidarity is necessary before a group can operate effectively from a bargaining position of strength in a pluralistic society." See Carmichael and Hamilton, *Black Power*, 44. Echoing this logic, in *Lesbian Nation*, Johnston emphatically stated: "There's no conceivable equality between two species in a relation in which one of the two has been considerably weakened in all aspects of her being over so long a period of historical time. The blacks in America were the first to understand that an oppressed group must withdraw into itself to establish its own identity and rebuild its strength through mutual support and recognition" (167).

14 For instance, Johnston argued that, "with her consciousness that she alone has no vested interests in prevailing cultural forms, [the lesbian] finds that she must

struggle within her sexual peer group to create wholly new nonhierarchical modes of interactive behavior" (*Lesbian Nation*, 182). Similarly, in a 1981 interview on Black feminist organizing, Barbara Smith claimed, "I feel what all of us, and many other Black women who are activists have in common is we looked at things and said, 'This isn't right.' That's a perception that is probably available to any woman of color, given how the system works. But not all of us do the same things with that realization" (Abdulahad et al., "Black/Lesbian Feminist Organizing," 290). While Smith's statement is less categorical than Johnston's, both views stress that the particular social positions of lesbians or women of color make them all uniquely capable of seeing past the ideological ruse of patriarchy and racism.

15 Gutter Dyke Collective, "Over the Walls," 30.

16 Smith and Smith, "Across the Kitchen Table," 121.

17 Combahee River Collective, "Black Feminist Statement," 215.

18 In an essay written for *This Bridge Called My Back*, Black feminist writer and poet doris davenport admitted: "my experiences with white feminists prevent me from seeing dialogue as anything but a naïve beginning. . . . So, Sisters, we might as well give up on them, except in rare and individual cases where the person or group is deliberately and obviously more evolved mentally and spiritually" ("Pathology of Racism," 85).

19 Despite these striking resonances, when in 1981 Adrienne Rich positively compared identity-based cultural and political projects by Black and brown feminists to lesbian separatism, Barbara Smith sharply critiqued her analogy as failing to recognize the structural realities that a priori segregated Black women from mainstream white society. Smith argued that Black women's decisions to band together for their own political uplift was a survival strategy among the disenfranchised born out of a need for personal autonomy, rather than an ideological commitment to separatism. Yet by categorically refusing Rich's more flexible use of the term "separatism" to describe *some* political and creative projects by women of color, Smith reifies the idea that separatism itself can be understood only as a total ideology applicable to, and conceptually owned by, white women. By extension she downplays Black women's agency in choosing to separate, implying that the forms of separation seen among Black feminists are always historically imposed by preexisting forms of racial segregation and exclusion, rather than willfully chosen as a productive strategy for self-empowerment or group cohesion. See Rich, "Notes for a Magazine," and Smith, "Responding to Adrienne Rich." For a Black feminist defense of separatism, see Anderson, "Separatism, Feminism." Anderson argues that separatism remains the most powerful feminist strategy for protecting women from the immediate threat of male violence.

20 Wendy Brown describes this as a left political orientation toward "wounded attachment," which "installs its pain over its unredeemed history in the very foundation of its political claim to recognition as identity." See Brown, "Wounded Attachments," 406.

21 Collective Lesbian International Terrors, "C.L.I.T. Statement #2," 33.

22 Gutter Dyke Collective, multiple items, *Dykes & Gorgons*, 5, 8, 10.

23 Shugar, *Separatism*, 41.

24 Alice, Gordon, Debbie, and Mary, "Separatism," 41.

25 Kinder, "Review: Zardoz by John Boorman," 49. See also Jameson, "History and the Death Wish," 5–8. Jameson interprets *Zardoz* as registering the postmodern loss of universal narratives of proper human progress. Therefore, the story of the Vortex is, in his words, an ideologically "open form" that can be read as either a liberatory fable about the individual's capacity to free themselves from bondage through self-annihilation or a fascist one about the necessity for social control.

26 Johnston, *Lesbian Nation*, 190.

27 Solanas, *S.C.U.M.*, 210.

28 Shugar, quoting Gutter Dyke Collective, 44.

29 Such nonverbal communication gives material expression to the separatist claim that "[w]omen communicate intensely and have an infinite capacity to feel another woman's meaning and intent . . . without speaking" (C.L.I.T., "Statement #2," 30).

30 Redwomon, "Freedom," 77.

31 Radicalesbians, "Woman-Identified-Woman," 177.

32 Solanas, *S.C.U.M.*, 209; Gutter Dyke Collective, "Toward a Female Species," *Dykes & Gorgons*, 10; C.L.I.T., "Statement #2," 27, 31.

33 Solanas, *S.C.U.M.*, 216.

34 Sandilands, "Lesbian Separatist Communities," 141. See also Luis, *Herlands*.

35 Radicalesbians, "Woman-Identified Woman," 177.

36 Alice, Gordon, Debbie, and Mary, "Separatism," 33.

37 Gutter Dyke Collective, "Over the Walls," 29.

38 Shugar, *Separatism*, 45. The Radicalesbians underscored this concern when they stated, "It must be understood that what is crucial is that women begin disengaging from male-defined response patterns. In the privacy of our own psyches, we must cut those cords to the core" ("Woman-Identified Woman," 175).

39 Radicalesbians, "Woman-Identified Woman," 175.

40 Gutter Dyke Collective, "Toward a Female Species," *Dykes & Gorgons*, 10.

41 Lorde discusses, and critiques, the practice of excluding male children from separatist spaces in "Man Child: A Black Lesbian Feminist's Response."

42 Johnston, *Lesbian Nation*, 179–180. This lamentable definition of bisexuality is perfectly captured in Friend's description of the "[i]dle apathetics" as a "melancholy site." When Friend points to one of the apathetics and confesses, "I loved her once," he echoes numerous separatist statements on bisexuality, in which lesbian writers described their betrayal by a bisexual woman they once loved who ultimately, and "obliviously," went on to choose a man as her primary partner.

43 Johnston emphatically argued that "[t]he elimination of butch and femme as we realize our true androgynous nature must inevitably mean the collapse of the heterosexual institution with its role playing dualities" (*Lesbian Nation*, 155).

44 Mulvey, "Visual Pleasure," 835.

45 Ibid.

46 As the Gutter Dyke Collective submitted: "It is known biological and scientific fact that . . . the condition of the human race since the patriarchal revolution has been one of constant catastrophe." See "The Non-Beneficial Mutation," *Dykes & Gorgons*, 8.

47 Ibid.

48 I am repurposing this term from Jameson, "History and the Death Wish."

49 Bunch, "Perseverance," 3–5.

50 Kinder, "Zardoz," 49.

51 Bunch, "Perseverance," 3.

52 Frye, "Some Reflections," 62.

53 According to its own proponents, by the early 1980s, lesbian separatism had become the most embattled and widely denounced expression of second-wave feminism, with separatists "feared, scorned, and misunderstood . . . as a bunch of hard-line weirdos with no feeling and no doubts" (Cowan, "Separatist Symposium," 32).

54 Describing the ideological disintegration of her lesbian feminist community in Durham, North Carolina, around 1983, scholar Kathy Rudy recounted, "Our community was founded on the belief that we—as women—were oppressed, so much so that identification as the oppressor then seemed impossible. . . . The question of race (and later ethnicity) challenged this simple formula and the seamless social world we had built on it" ("Radical Feminism," 201).

55 Reagon, "Coalition Politics," 344.

56 Ibid., 349.

57 See, for instance, Smith and Smith, "Across the Kitchen Table."

58 Consider that nearly every political narrative of feminist consciousness in the late 1960s and early 1970s articulated a disaffection from two forms of oppression and exclusion: first, the realization of having one's identity or way of life violently negated by a larger system of power like patriarchy or white supremacy; which is, second, redoubled in the painful discovery that the people you thought would be natural allies by dint of shared identity or experience, have also rejected you on the basis of some *other* aspect of your selfhood that they denigrate, despise, or simply remain ignorant about. For example, Asian American feminists described feeling inspired by radical feminism, but never fully interpersonally embraced by white women within the movement who were lacking in consciousness about their own racism. Moreover, Asian American *lesbians* in particular wrote about being misunderstood, ostracized, or disowned by their families and ethnic communities for their feminist commitments and sexual orientation, while also having their unique life experiences flattened by other women of color who lumped them into the category "Third World women." Asian American women of all sexual orientations decided that they had to separate, even provisionally, from both white women *and* their immediate ethno-racial communities to forge

a feminist politics grounded in their unique multigenerational, immigrant experience. See Ordona, *Coming Out Together*.

59 Abdulahad et al., "Black/Lesbian Feminist Organizing," 291.

60 Hilderbrand, "Heat of the Moment," 8.

61 Smith and Smith, "Across the Kitchen Table," 118.

62 Conceptually speaking, the initial idea of a Women's Army is itself born out of a primary disaffection with the Socialist Party. Throughout the film, feminists like Adelaide and Wiley frequently express cynicism about and frustration with government claims that, for instance, "[o]urs has been the greatest cultural revolution of all time, through which we have wed democracy . . . with the moral and ethical humanism of American socialism." Like radical feminists of the second wave, they enact an initial affective separation from, or resistance to, dominant left-wing narratives of political freedom such as those espoused by the New Left and the Black Panther Party, which claimed to speak on behalf of all people, but strategically left out women and lesbians of every race and ethnicity.

63 Alice, Gordon, Debbie, and Mary, "Separatism," 32.

64 C.L.I.T., "Statement #1," 6–8.

65 Ibid., 6.

66 Brown, "World on Fire," 588.

67 Cannell, personal communication with the author.

68 See Freeman, *Time Binds*, chapter 2; Hemmings, *Why Stories Matter*, 53, 57; and Nash, *Black Feminism Reimagined*.

69 Wiegman, *Object Lessons*, chapter 1.

70 Bey, "Trans*-Ness of Blackness," 275. See also Edelman, *No Future*, and Wilderson, *Afropessimism*.

71 McMaster, "Revolting Self-Care,"182.

72 Roy Pérez, "Mark Aguhar's Critical Flippancy," Bully Bloggers, August 4, 2012, https://bullybloggers.wordpress.com.

73 Campbell and Manning, *Rise of Victimhood Culture*, 168.

74 Ibid., 23.

75 See chap. 2, n18, above.

76 Wiegman, *Object Lessons*, 125.

77 My commitment to the value of "divergence" is indebted to Robyn Wiegman's and Janet Halley's use of the term to describe feminist theorizing that refuses fixed social and political identities, rigid categories of analysis, or singular methods for the study of gender and sexuality. See Wiegman, *Object Lessons*, and Halley, *Split Decisions*.

78 Anzaldúa, *Borderlands/La Frontera*, 78–79.

CHAPTER 3. "BEWARE THE HOSTILE FAG"

1 Sarachild, "Feminist 'Consciousness Raising,'" 78.

2 Ibid., 79.

3 Gornick, "Consciousness," 288.

4 Michals, "'Consciousness Expansion,'" 41–68.

5 Crowley, *The Boys*, 3. All subsequent citations from the original theatrical production and the film adaptation are respectively from this edition of the play and from *The Boys in the Band*, directed by William Friedkin (1970; Los Angeles: Paramount Studios, 2008), DVD.

6 Sarachild, "Program," 78–79; Jay, *Lavender Menace*, 51; Allen, "Small Group Process," 280–281.

7 Jay, *Lavender Menace*, 94–95; Altman, *Homosexual*, 146–149.

8 A Gay Male Group, "Notes," 293–301.

9 See, for example, Alinder, "My Gay Soul"; Wittman, "A Gay Manifesto"; and Katz, "Smash Phallic Imperialism," all in Jay and Young, *Out of the Closets*; and Dansky, Knoebel, and Pitchford, "Effeminist Manifesto," in Blasius and Phelan, *We Are Everywhere*.

10 Allen, "Group Process," 279. *The Boys in the Band* can be understood as a potent example of what Robert McRuer has called a "gay gathering," a term that describes the diversity of collective or communal forms that gays and lesbians invented in the wake of the Stonewall Riots. In both its theatrical and film versions, *The Boys* depicted a literal social gathering of gay men, but also solicited countless audiences to similarly convene to witness gay men communing with one another. See McRuer, "Gay Gatherings." On gay male communal forms before Stonewall, see Ormsbee, *The Meaning of Gay*.

11 Arendt, *Between Past and Future*, 221. In considering film form as a vehicle for feminist group process, I am extending Hogeland's arguments in *Feminism and Its Fictions* that representations of CR practice in novels of the 1970s encouraged readers to view the act of engaging with and discussing feminist fiction as itself a type of consciousness-raising.

12 Zerilli, "Feminist Theory of Judgment," 18.

13 Jay, *Lavender Menace*, 62.

14 Scroggie, "Producing Identity," 238.

15 Young, "Out of the Closets," 18.

16 Welch, "Homosexuality in America," 66.

17 Sarachild, "Program," 78.

18 A Gay Male Group, "Notes," 293.

19 Altman's groundbreaking study of gay liberation in the early 1970s, *Homosexual: Oppression & Liberation*, stakes an important claim to the rebellious aspect of gay identity, suggesting that "[t]o become a homosexual . . . is to reject the program for marriage, family, and home that our society holds up as normal" (25). Yet while Altman celebrates, redeems, or grapples with the contradictions of numerous works of LGBTQ literature and culture, he repeatedly condemns *The Boys in the Band* as a document of gay male "self-hatred" (76, 36, 38). Altman's approach to the text stands out as a symptomatic blind spot in an otherwise exceptional analysis of the political world-making inherent to a contentious, and anti-assimilationist gay liberationist project.

20 Altman, *Homosexual*, 25.

21 Sarachild, "Program," 79.

22 Allen, "Group Process," 278.

23 Jay, *Lavender Menace*, 52; Knoebel, "Right Direction"; Arnold, "Consciousness-Raising," 285.

24 A Gay Male Group, "Notes," 298–299. Sarachild's original "Program" listed eleven "classic forms of resisting consciousness." The list tended to be general, addressing not specific behaviors but broad habits of thought including "Anti-womanism," "False identification with the oppressor," and "Self-blame!" (79). By contrast, a Gay Male Group's CR program boasts a highly refined twenty-point list calling out specific behaviors and including extensive subentries for four items.

25 Zerilli, "Feminist Theory of Judgment," 14.

26 Knoebel, "Right Direction," 305.

27 Allen, "Group Process," 280–281.

28 Arendt, *Between Past and Future*, 237.

29 Gornick, "Consciousness," 288.

30 Norman, "Consciousness-Raising Document," 43–44.

31 It is telling that the recent Netflix adaptation of *The Boys* (2020), based on the 2018 Broadway revival, casts Puerto Rican actor Robin de Jesús in the role of Emory, thereby explicitly racializing the production's gayest character. Though the script for the recent adaption is nearly identical to the first film, Emory receives new lines apologizing to Bernard for his racial insensitivity. A brief scene is also added at the conclusion, which depicts Bernard and Emory breaking bread at a local diner, presumably providing mutual emotional support in the aftermath of the party.

32 Zerilli, "Feminist Theory of Judgment," 20.

33 Freeman, "Trashing," 49–51, 92–98.

34 Hesford's *Feeling Women's Liberation* remains the most compelling and sustained study of the affective life of second-wave feminism.

35 D'Emilio, forward to *Out of the Closets*, xiv–xv.

36 Ibid., xii.

37 Though the Netflix adaptation of *The Boys* might suggest renewed cultural space for attending to gay male negativity, this version is performed at a perceptibly slower cadence than the original, which dramatically reduces the story's conflictual tension.

CHAPTER 4. QUEER LOVE ON BARBARY LANE

1 The *San Francisco Chronicle* touted itself as having "The Largest Daily Circulation in Northern California." Based on the *Chronicle*'s filings with the US Postal Service Office of Ownership, Management and Circulation, as of October 1, 1976, the paper boasted a total paid circulation of 469,478 (with total circulation at 508,520); in 1977, that increased to 491,132 (and 531,800). These numbers are high considering the total recorded population of San Francisco was 715,674 in

the 1970 census, while the Bay Area more broadly had 4,630,576 residents. This meant that the paper reached roughly 9 percent of the entire Bay Area population, while its circulation figure was more than two-thirds of the city's population. Bay Area Census. "San Francisco City and County Decennial Census Data," http://www.bayareacensus.ca.gov/counties/SanFranciscoCounty70.htm (accessed July 6, 2019).

2 Armistead Maupin, "She's 25, Single And Mad for SF," "Tales of the City," *San Francisco Chronicle*, May 24, 1976. From this point forward, all references to *Tales of the City* will cite installment title and date of publication.

3 "Mary Ann Waits for Lightning to Strike," February 25, 1977.

4 Milk, "Gay Freedom Day Speech," 218.

5 Michael Thorburn (retired concierge), in discussion with author, June 7, 2017.

6 Thanks to Ivan Ortiz for this insight.

7 Mark Giberson (general reader), in discussion with author, June 16, 2017.

8 Filmmakers Andrew Brown and David Weissman explained to me the common distinction made within San Francisco queer activist circles between "sweater queens" and "street queens." Sweater queens were upwardly mobile (usually white) gay men invested in respectability politics, while street queens were radical activists invested in dismantling the establishment. Both explained that Maupin was perceived as a paragon of the "sweater queen" (typified by his political support of Rick Stokes, Harvey Milk's more centrist political rival for supervisor of District 5). Thus many gay liberationists showed disinterest in *Tales* because of its association with white bourgeois gay culture. Despite this, Weissman explained that iconic street queen Harvey Milk followed *Tales* closely to track how often queer life was mentioned in the *Chronicle*. Andrew Brown and David Weissman (filmmakers), in discussion with author, March 3, 2019, and March 17, 2019, respectively.

9 Warhol, "Making 'Gay' and 'Lesbian,'" 381.

10 Ibid., 379–380. While I concur with Warhol's thesis, and take is as the basis of my analysis, I depart from her work both in terms of my archive and method. Despite being a study of *Tales of the City's* serial form, Warhol's essay uses the collected novels to develop her claims. Her analysis also largely sidesteps close reading of the text's formal and rhetorical strategies, focusing instead on broader interpretations of *Tales'* various plots, which Warhol reads as analogous to the logic of contemporaneous television soap operas.

11 Ibid., 379.

12 In 2016, I began my initial solicitation of potential respondents by circulating requests for interviews on Facebook and other social media outlets, and posting fliers in various queer spaces, bars, and community centers in San Francisco's Castro and Mission neighborhoods. In summer 2017, I sought to reach a wider pool of interview subjects by placing a printed request in a daily column of the *San Francisco Chronicle* written by Leah Garchik. This notice garnered more than fifty responses. Ultimately, I conducted nineteen interviews in person or by Skype,

tape-recording and transcribing conversations that lasted from twenty minutes to two hours. I also received seven email responses to an electronic survey I circulated. I completed three more interviews by Skype in the spring of 2019. In both the in-person and electronic interviews, I asked respondents to share information about their everyday lived experiences of San Francisco in the 1970s, their first encounters with *Tales of the City* and the quality of their reading experience, their affective relationship to particular characters and story arcs, and the long-term influence the story has had on their lives.

Most respondents were white, cisgender individuals between the ages of sixty and eighty, though they were collectively a mixture of queer (or LGBTQ) and straight identified. I made many efforts to diversify the ethno-racial makeup of my interview pool, including reaching out to African, Asian, and Latinx American retirement communities, resource centers, and online discussion and reading groups. Unfortunately, I received no responses from these institutions. A Facebook contact did, however, lead to my interview with Andrew Brown, a retired African American filmmaker, and one of the original producers of the queer documentary classic *Word Is Out* (1977). The difficulty of obtaining more interviews with people of color in the Bay Area may be attributed to the changing demographics of the *Chronicle*'s readership, the increasing gentrification of San Francisco, and the legitimate fear that communities of color may have of their histories being misappropriated by academics. Finally, it is important to note that many living Bay Area queer elders of color have already been interviewed by scholars researching queer POC histories in the region and may simply not have wished to engage the process again. See, for example, Johnson, "Influence of Assimilation"; Ramírez, "Communities of Desire"; and Ordona, *Coming Out Together*.

13 My approach is influenced by Richard Dyer's ethnographic work on gay male fans of Judy Garland. See "Judy Garland and Gay Men."

14 Horacio N. Roque Ramírez cites and critiques Maupin's claims of the city's transcendence in his groundbreaking scholarly article "That's My Place!," which documents gay and lesbian Latinx community organizing in 1970s San Francisco. He claims, "The idea of incorporating multiple dimensions of social experience and difference to understand queer history in the San Francisco area challenges that of transcendence. Famed *Tales of the City* white gay author Armistead Maupin has argued that the city's queer history 'transcends the usual boundaries of race, class, and religion'" (225–226). Maupin is quoted in the introduction to Jim Van Buskirk and Susan Stryker, *Gay by the Bay: A History of Queer Culture in the San Francisco Bay Area* (San Francisco: Chronicle Books, 1996).

15 "What Did Mary Ann Find Out?," June 18, 1976.

16 I use the term "transsexual" as it was deployed in this historical moment, and in the context of the original serial, as a synonym for the contemporary category "transgender." The revelation of Madrigal's transness is presented in the installment titled "Tinkerbell Stands Revealed," December 30, 1976.

17 Mary Richardson, email message to author, August 18, 2017.
18 Quoted in Armstrong, *Forging Gay Identities*, 68.
19 Young, "Out of the Closets," 28.
20 Ibid., 135.
21 D'Emilio, "Gay Politics," 85.
22 Rohy, *Lost Causes*, 191.
23 "What's D'or Hiding?," November, 17, 1976.
24 Armistead Maupin (writer), in discussion with author, August 1, 2015.
25 Michael Bluegrass (retired dancer), in discussion with author, June 9, 2017.
26 "The Landlady Confesses," June 10, 1976.
27 Maupin explained to me that this decision was initially imposed upon him by the *Chronicle*'s editors: "I told the editors that Mrs. Madrigal was going to be transsexual, is what we said back then. They were horrified. And said, 'You cannot mention it for at least a year.' It actually annoyed the hell out of me at the time but it was really good advice in a literary sense . . . because everybody got to love her before the secret surfaced and then it didn't matter anymore. There was calculation in all of that." As this anecdote suggests, an editorial imposition based on transphobia unexpectedly provided Maupin with the narrative space to develop Madrigal's character and train his readers in the proper affective orientation to receive the discovery of her transness. Maupin in discussion with author, August 1, 2015.
28 Michael Bluegrass (retired dancer), in discussion with author, June 9, 2017; Randy Alfred (journalist), in discussion with author, July 10, 2017.
29 Tonia Schulberg (retired teacher), in discussion with author, August 21, 2017.
30 Ibid.
31 Paula Lichtenberg (activist), in discussion with author, June 8, 2017.
32 "Preparing for a Big Night on Roller Skates," August 3, 1976. In one juicy anecdote, Maupin relates, "There was a man who was a big butch number that went to Gay Roller Night in South City on a regular basis and his office knew that he went roller-skating on Wednesday nights but it wasn't until *Tales* . . . that they found out [that he was gay]." Maupin in discussion with author, August 1, 2015.
33 Maupin in discussion with author.
34 Beth Grace Silver (artist), email message to author, August 31, 2017.
35 "Mary Ann Exposes Michael," August, 19 1977.
36 "Michael's Chaperoned Halloween," November 1, 1977.
37 Warner, *Publics*, 120.
38 Ibid.
39 Ibid.
40 Paul Quin (retired book publishing production manager), email message to author, July 25, 2017.
41 Beginning in June 1976, little more than a month after *Tales*' debut, the *Chronicle* began publishing an average of one article per month about LGBTQ issues. On August 11, the *Chronicle* printed a front-page story about the coming out of a

transgender high school physical education teacher, Steve Dain, in Union City. This article spurred the publication of a handful of subsequent pieces on the experience of transsexuals in the Bay Area as they acclimated to new gender expressions and the societal pressures they faced. Anita Bryant's "Save Our Children" campaign in February 1977 inaugurated an explosive increase in monthly reporting on LGBTQ issues in the paper and elicited a slew of letters to the editor that largely supported the social and political freedom of LGBTQ people. Simultaneously, Maupin wove Bryant's evangelical movement into one of *Tales'* central storylines, the political coming into consciousness of Michael Tolliver.

42 C. Flowers, Tahoe City, "Stop, Please!," letter to the editor, *San Francisco Chronicle*, June 30, 1977.

43 Judith Anderson, "When Your Child Tells You 'Mom, I'm a Homosexual,'" *San Francisco Chronicle*, September 2, 1977.

44 "Mary Ann's First Adventure On Russian Hill," May 27, 1976.

45 "Michael Writes to His Parents," May 16, 1977.

46 Miller, *Jane Austen*, 59–60.

47 "Michael's Chaperoned Halloween," November 1, 1976.

48 "Brian and . . . Michael?," November 19, 1976.

49 Miller, *Jane Austen*, 66. This quality of intimate knowing has led some scholars to argue that the free indirect style ideologically exerts social control on readers because it claims a God-like "epistemological hegemony" over its subjects. See Finch and Bowen, "Tittle-Tattle of Highbury," 15. Against this claim, literary theorist Dorit Cohn argues that the analogy between omniscient narration and disciplinary power too easily collapses an author's imaginative control over character development and real-world forms of social control (like the prison or the police), which rarely produce the same material or cognitive effects. See Cohn, "Optics and Power."

50 "Mary Ann Bombs at Pick-Up City," May 28, 1976.

51 "A Lonely Evening of . . . Unfinished Business," July 27, 1976.

52 "A Hot Date With THE Man," June 4, 1976.

53 "Mary Ann Remembers the Threat," September 23, 1976.

54 "Tinkerbell Stands Revealed," December 30, 1976.

55 "The Night Mary Ann Heard the News," May 24, 1977.

56 "Looking for Mr. Right," July 16, 1976.

57 "Young, Single, and Male," October 7, 1976.

58 "The Eye Settles on the Horned One," September 15, 1976.

59 "Michael's Search for . . . The Key To the Crimes," December 27, 1976.

60 "Mary Ann Waits for Lightning to Strike," February 25, 1977.

61 Wittman, "Gay Manifesto," 334–335.

62 "Michael's Bittersweet Version of Miami," June 10, 1977.

63 "Anna's Fatherly Concern And Horrid Premonition," March 1, 1977.

64 Daniel Goldstein (artist), in discussion with author, September 17, 2017.

65 Rohy, *Lost Causes*, 190.

66 "The Truth About Anna Madrigal," June 24, 1976.

67 "Mary Ann Is Forced to Spill the Beans," June 29, 1976.

68 "A Terrible Shock for Mary Ann," August 12, 1976.

69 "Barbary Lane Bummer," September 21, 1977.

70 "Some Pillow Talk At Barbary Lane," October 25, 1976.

71 "Edgar's Date at the Beach," July 5, 1976.

72 Gay Revolution Party, "Manifesto," 344.

73 Ordona, "An Ethnohistory," 159.

74 Ramírez, "'That's My Place!'" 238.

75 Ibid.; Ordona, "An Ethnohistory," 121–155.

76 "A Journey of Love," October 18, 1976.

77 "Do'r's Not-So-Dark Past," December 10, 1976.

78 See "Special Features" in *The Untold Tales of Armistead Maupin*, directed by Jennifer Kroot (Glasgow: Tigerlily Pictures, 2017), DVD.

79 Robinson, "It Takes One to Know One," 720.

80 Armstrong, *Forging Gay Identities*, 3.

81 Ibid., 4.

82 Bey and Sakellarides, "When We Enter," 40.

83 David Goldman (retired math teacher), in discussion with author, June 13, 2017.

84 Rima Kittner (former law student), email message to the author, August 8, 2017.

CHAPTER 5. STRIPPED TO THE BONE

1 Wojnarowicz, Romberger, and Van Cook, *7 Miles a Second*, 60–61. From this point forward referred to as *7 Miles*.

2 Ibid., 51.

3 Queer film scholar Damon Young argues that this politicized view of sex and sexuality was exemplified by the emergence of a new category of political being in the 1960s, which he names "the liberal sexual subject." This was a person for whom sexual freedom and political freedom were understood as mutually constitutive aspirations and achievements. See Young, *Making Sex Public*. On the social and political effects of the Kinsey Reports, see Reumann, *American Sexual Character*. On the cultural history of the sexual revolution, including the societal impact of the Masters and Johnson study, see Allyn, *Make Love Not War*, and Gerhard, *Desiring Revolution*.

4 An abridged genealogy of queer comics theory might include: Harrison, "The Queer Spaces"; Cremins, "Bodies, Transfigurations"; Howard, "Politically Incorrect"; Scott, "Big Black Beauty"; Scott and Fawaz, "Queer about Comics," special issue, *American Literature*; Galvan, "Making Space"; and Peppard, *Supersex*.

5 Brainard stopped producing and exhibiting his art in the mid-1980s before dying of AIDS in 1994 at the age of fifty-two. Wojnarowicz produced a flurry of mixed media works up until his own death from AIDS in 1993 at thirty-eight. Despite their early deaths, both were prolific artists during their active years, producing hundreds of works in myriad styles, materials, and genres.

6 McCormick, "Fables," 14. On the centrality of "niceness" or "friendliness" to Brainard's aesthetic style see Glavey, "Friending Joe Brainard."

7 Williams and Brainard, *gAy BC's.*

8 See Weinberg, *Pier Groups*, for a study of the intersection of art and gay sexual cultures at the New York City piers in the 1970s and 1980s.

9 See Kitchen and Danky, *Underground Classics*; Rozenkranz, *Rebel Visions*; Hall, *No Straight Lines*; and Chute, *Why Comics?*

10 My understanding of seriality as a potential vehicle for the articulation of unpredictable queer desires places greater attention on the contingent possibilities of new installments than on the hierarchical order of any given sequence (as Annamarie Jagose does in *Inconsequence*). For Jagose, what she calls "the logic of sexual sequence" is a commonsense norm, which installs heterosexuality as the inaugural entry in a rigidly hierarchized sequence: i.e., heterosexuality is sequentially *before*, and hence presumed to be socially *above*, homosexuality. What happens, however, when a sequence simply begins with an inaugural image or concept understood in nonhierarchical terms as just one of a number of possible starting points, not more or less important than any subsequent entry? This generous use of sequence—one common to comic strip form—embraces multiplicity rather than hierarchy. It deploys a loose order or visual assemblage merely to display a range of identities, desires, performances, or icons instead of marking any given image as more legitimate or primary than any other. When we account for this distinct formal feature of the comics medium, visual sequence surprisingly dovetails with a variety of conceptions of queerness, or nonnormative expressions of sexuality, gender, and erotic desire in queer theory, as a kind of swerving away from the order of heterosexuality.

On sequence, seriality, and repetition in art history, see Foster, *The Return of the Real*, chapter 2; Bateman, "Narrative and Seriality"; Yanhua, "Rethinking Seriality." In literary and media studies, see O'Sullivan, "Broken on Purpose"; Mayer, "Machinic Fu Manchu"; Hughes and Lund, *The Victorian Serial*; and Fitch, *Pop Poetics.*

11 The Nancy series is an exemplary model for Brainard's queer engagement with comics because it embodies his most conceptually daring extension of the formal logic of sequential comics into other mediums and materials, including collage, painting, and found-object art. Brainard understood comics not simply as a medium limited to the technique of drawing or to a distinct narrative genre, but as a formal logic of sequential pictorial unfolding that could be translated across mediums. The infiltration of traditionally high art styles and materials by the logic of comics strikes me as an especially queer deployment of a so-called "low" cultural form. Key readings in Brainard's serial poetics and art include Deming, "Everyday Devotions"; Fitch, *Pop Poetics*; Kernan, "Joe Brainard: All Possible Colors"; Stark, "Nancy and the Queer Adorable"; and Worden, "Joe Brainard's Grid." With the exception of Fitch, nearly all of these writers sidestep Brainard's sexuality as a defining influence on his oeuvre.

12 The original series was issued in 1996 by DC Comics' independent imprint
Vertigo (three years after the initial project was completed). It was revised and
enlarged in graphic novel form for the 2012 reprinting by Fantagraphics Comics. Throughout this essay, I use the reprint edition as the basis for my analysis;
though new images and scenes were added to expand the original text, these were
conceived or drawn in the original planning stages of the 1988–1993 collaboration.

13 This is a direct formal corollary to Eve Sedgwick's classic description of the normative logics of "homosexual definition," which she identified as being structured
by contradictory "minoritizing" and "universalizing" sexual discourses: on the
one hand, a minoritizing view that presumes the existence of "a distinct population of persons who 'really are' gay"; on the other, a "universalizing view" in
which sexual desire is imagined to circulate throughout the social field, even in
"apparently heterosexual persons [who could be] strongly marked by same-sex
influences." The scalar logic of comics, which simultaneously presents individual
frames (minoritizing) as existing within and alongside larger visual assemblages
of panels (universalizing), provides a creative resolution to the original "incoherence" of this dual logic, allowing the specific and general aspects of sexuality to
exist co-equally. Sedgwick, *Epistemology of the Closet*, 85.

14 Dlugos, "Joe Brainard Interview."

15 See Allyn, *Make Love Not War*. On the centrality of clitoral pleasure to radical
feminist ideals of sexual freedom, see Gerhard, *Desiring Revolution*.

16 Lorde, "Uses of the Erotic," 57.

17 A curated selection of these works is collected in Brainard's *The Nancy Book*,
edited by Ron Padgett and Lisa Pearson. All references to works in the series "If
Nancy Was . . ." are from this volume. In 2008, twenty of these works were exhibited as an open-ended sequence at the Colby College Museum of Art.

18 In their canonical comics essay "How to Read Nancy," cartoonists Mark Newgarden and Paul Karasik identified the iconic spareness of Nancy's visual form, as
well as well the basic three- or four-panel sequence in which her storylines took
place, as the defining features that made her available for so many comedic narrative and visual permutations. See Newgarden and Karasik, "How to Read Nancy."

19 In this sense, all of Brainard's appropriations of Nancy can be understood as queer
"misuses" of the comic strip character. As art historian David Getsy argues, "to
prompt us to see a material or an object in a different way—against or to the side
of its intended use—is a queer tactic . . . for allegorizing normativity's disavowal of
its own partiality" (Doyle and Getsy, "Queer Formalisms," 63).

20 In an interview I conducted with poet and Brainard biographer Ron Padgett,
Padgett stressed Brainard's attachment to Nancy, and her medium of origin, as
an expression of the artist's desire to imbue adulthood with the whimsical and
joyful qualities of his youth. Consequently, in Nancy, Brainard seems to have
found a figure through which to express the specificity of his own gayness as a
more expansively understood state of permanent queer childhood. Ron Padgett,
interview conducted by the author, digital recording, May 27, 2016. For a brilliant

explication of Brainard's affective and aesthetic investment in *Nancy*, see Lauter-bach, "Joe Brainard & Nancy," 7–26.

21 Brainard, *Nancy Book*, 30.

22 According to Ron Padgett, Brainard's sexuality was widely known and embraced by his artistic coterie in the New York School of poets and artists. In one interview, however, Brainard stated, "The only thing that ever bothered me about being queer was that I thought maybe people wouldn't like me if they knew." By diffusing queer desires across serialized panels in "If Nancy Was . . . ," Brainard dispels the potential negative connotations that might accrue to the specificity of his own gayness; one effect of this strategy is to blur the distinctions between his individual erotic interests and the potential libidinal attachments of any given viewer of the series. This might be understood as a queer tactic of simultaneous camouflage and collective "coming out of the closet" that elicits joyful attachment to queerness (in other words, an aesthetic technique for warding off being "not liked"). On queer aesthetic strategies of camouflage, see Katz, "Committing the Perfect Crime."

23 Brainard, *Nancy Book*, 59.

24 Ibid., 40.

25 Ahmed, *Queer Phenomenology*, 179.

26 Brainard, *Nancy Book*, 55.

27 Ibid., 57.

28 Ibid., 47.

29 Crimp, "How to Have Promiscuity," 253.

30 See Delany, *Times Square Red*.

31 Gould, *Moving Politics*, 192–196.

32 Wojnarowicz, Romberger, and Van Cook, *7 Miles*, 5.

33 Despite Wojnarowicz's extensive input and influence on all sections of *7 Miles a Second*, this final segment of the narrative was completed after his death on July 22, 1992, by his collaborator James Romberger. Romberger used Wojnarowicz's notes and published writing, alongside his own aesthetic sensibilities as an avant-garde comics artist, to finish the project they had begun in 1988. In my discussion, I will attribute the content of *7 Miles a Second* to both artists, while acknowledging the throughline of Wojnarowicz's aesthetic vision (as executed and influenced by Romberger).

34 Wojnarowicz, Romberger, and Van Cook, *7 Miles*, 40–41.

35 Ibid., 28–32.

36 Ibid., 48–49.

37 Row, "Queer Time," 60–61.

38 This action is documented in Crimp and Rolston, *AIDS Demo Graphics*.

39 Wojnarowicz, Romberger, and Van Cook, *7 Miles*, 58–59.

40 See Benjamin, "Philosophy of History."

41 Marguerite Van Cook, interview conducted by author via email, May 24, 2016.

42 Wojnarowicz, Romberger, and Van Cook, *7 Miles*, 20, 67, 27.

43 Ibid., 53.

44 James Romberger, interview conducted by the author via email, May 24, 2016.

45 Sedgwick, *Tendencies*, 8.

46 Wojnarowicz, *Tongues of Flame*, 53.

47 I am influenced in this endeavor by Hillary Chute's commitment to pursue "*how comics texts model a feminist methodology in their form*, in the complex visual dimension of an author narrating herself on the page as a multiple subject." See Chute, "Space of Graphic Narrative," 200.

48 Here, I build on W. J. T. Mitchell's insight in "Comics as Media" that "comics is transmediatic because it is translatable and transitional, mutating before our eyes into unexpected new forms" (259).

CHAPTER 6. "I CHERISH MY BILE DUCT AS MUCH AS ANY OTHER ORGAN"

1 Kushner, *Angels*, 74. This and subsequent references, with page numbers parenthesized in the main text, are to the Theatre Communications Group 2003 revised edition of *Angels in America: A Gay Fantasia on National Themes Parts I and II* (*Millennium Approaches* and *Perestroika*, respectively). This chapter is dedicated to Samir Hachem, my late uncle, who has always been the gut feeling that guides me. Before he died of AIDS in 1991, Samir's extraordinary essays on queer film for the *Hollywood Reporter* and *Advocate* in the 1980s helped identify what would later be called the New Queer Cinema years before it received the name from B. Ruby Rich. His passion for queer culture and his beautiful writings on what he called "the new sensuality" in independent and Hollywood filmmaking infuse my own writing; he could not have known then that his young nephew would discover this same world of queer film and video, and fall in love with its sexy, rebellious spirit. I only wish I had been able to watch and read the texts I discuss here with him.

2 Borrowing from William Ian Miller and Sara Ahmed, I understand disgust as a socially cultivated response of recoiling from bodies and objects perceived as invading one's physical or psychic integrity; the visceral enactment of this emotional state is often accompanied by "somatic reactions like retching, gagging, vomiting, spitting out" (Miller, "Upward Contempt," 478). See Ahmed, *Cultural Politics of Emotion*, and Miller, "Upward Contempt."

3 Gregg and Seigworth, "Inventory of Shimmers," 1.

4 Cultural theories of affect frequently distinguish affect from emotion by identifying affect as the prelinguistic, nonconscious, visceral intensities registered by the body in everyday encounters with the world. Alternatively, emotion references the entire network of linguistic, cultural, or symbolic signs that come to attach to inchoate and unformed affective experiences, rendering them legible while also narrowing the potentially varied directions visceral sensations could take to a single feeling state. This distinction has had the benefit of acknowledging the body's phenomenological experience of the world without collapsing all material or physiological registers of existence to discourse and social construction; yet it

has also made it difficult to theorize those moments in which discourse functions *as* an intensity that can activate or elicit affective responses. In its most extreme versions, the split between affect and emotion has the potential to reproduce the very conceptual division between the embodied and the representational that cultural analysts of AIDS vehemently and convincingly theorized against. The theoretical partitioning of affect from emotion along prediscursive and discursive lines is frequently attributed to Massumi in *Parables of the Virtual*. For compelling revisions, critiques, and reconsiderations of the affect/emotion split, see Gould, *Moving Politics*; Doyle, *Hold It against Me*; and Gregg and Seigworth, "Inventory of Shimmers."

5 Gould, *Moving Politics*, 23, 28.

6 Thanks to playwright Bonnie Metzgar for this insight. In *Acts of Intervention*, David Román highlights the broader material stakes of *Angels in America* when he states, "The body of the spectator enduring the length of the performance and the physical demands of theatergoing—reaching the theater, walking to our seats . . . needing to stretch, feeling hunger—Identifies metaphorically with the bodies of the actors onstage performing the roles. . . . So while we register the effects of AIDS on Prior Walter's body, we also register the effects of the labor of this presentation on the actor who plays him" (220).

7 Reprinted in Crimp, *Melancholia and Moralism*, 28, 32.

8 See, for example, the essays collected in Crimp, "AIDS: Cultural Activism, Cultural Analysis." Two other foundational texts in the study of AIDS representational politics are Patton, *Inventing* and Simon Watney, *Policing Desire*. Finally, the locus classicus on the uses of AIDS as metaphor is Susan Sontag's *AIDS and Its Metaphors*.

9 Treichler, "Epidemic of Signification," 37–38.

10 Ibid., 32.

11 Gould, *Moving Politics*, 121–214.

12 Crimp, *Melancholia and Moralism*, 145.

13 Ibid.

14 King, "Local and Global," 80. The literature on AIDS art activism is vast. Some notable entries include Bost, *Evidence of Being*; Crimp, *Melancholia and Moralism*; Crimp and Rolston, *AIDS Demo Graphics*; Finkelstein, *After Silence*; Hernández, *Archiving an Epidemic*; and Speretta, *Rebels Rebel*.

15 See Ahmed, *Cultural Politics of Emotion*; Berlant, *Cruel Optimism*; and Ngai, *Ugly Feelings*.

16 It must be noted that the horrific lived realities of AIDS—including facing social and familial homophobia, mourning the loss of countless friends and loved ones, and dealing with the physical and emotional effects of long-term HIV treatment—are far from over for those who lived through the height of the epidemic, as well as those who deal with the disease in the present day. In their recent writings, Sarah Schulman, Gregg Bordowitz, and Douglas Crimp capture the ongoing consequences of having to mourn both the initial event of the AIDS

epidemic in the 1980s as well as the negligent erasure of the history of AIDS activism in contemporary queer culture and politics (not to mention the impact of late-in-life HIV diagnosis). See Schulman, *Gentrification of the Mind*; the introduction to Crimp's *Melancholia and Moralism*; and Bordowitz's discussion of the fears and anxieties that attend long-term HIV management in *General Idea*, 4–5.

17 Wojnarowicz, *Close to the Knives*, 108.

18 Nanney, "I Sing the Body Electric" (interview).

19 Wojnarowicz, *Close to the Knives*, 10.

20 Arguably the most foundational analysis and critique of this logic is offered by Bersani in his field-defining essay "Is the Rectum a Grave?"

21 Wojnarowicz, *Close to the Knives*, 114.

22 Román, *Acts of Intervention*, 213.

23 On the play's staging of conflicts between the mind and the body, and the body and spirit, see Savran, "Ambivalence, Utopia," and Miller, "Heavenquake."

24 It is fitting, then, that the stage instructions indicate the hustler should be played by the same actor who performs the role of Prior.

25 Belize's use of the word "peculiar" to describe Louis's tirade invokes the historical description of slavery as America's "peculiar institution," as well as historian Kenneth Stampp's classic study of slavery, *The Peculiar Institution* (1956). Stampp's book sought to divest historians of the fantasy that slavery served the interests of both white and Black Americans by promoting racial harmony; similarly, Belize attempts to disabuse Louis of his own fantasy that race is a benign ideological fallacy in the US.

26 "FDA Action Handbook," Jim Eigo, Mark Harrington, et al. (September 2, 1988), ACT UP: New York, www.actupny.org/documents/FDAhandbook1.html.

27 Bersani, "Rectum," 201–202.

28 Ibid., Bersani citing Watney, 211.

29 Ibid., 212.

30 Highmore, "Bitter after Taste," 135.

31 McRuer, *Crip Theory*, 31.

32 Highmore, "Bitter after Taste," 135–136.

33 See Cvetkovich, "AIDS Activism," and Gould, *Moving Politics*, 65–71.

34 Schulman, *Gentrification of the Mind*, 51.

35 In *The Queer Renaissance*, Robert McRuer identifies this messiness as central to the play's sexual politics and calls it "queer perestroika: that is, a politics of sexuality emphasizing . . . coming together, mingling, messiness, and disruption" (171).

36 Román similarly asserts that Belize is "the political and ethical center of the plays" in *Acts of Intervention*, 213.

37 See Miller, "Upward Contempt."

38 In a reference so brief that it has gone completely unremarked upon by scholars of *Angels in America*, at the beginning of the play, Cohn reveals that he used the money he laundered to travel to Haiti (where he claims he has legal "clients") (18). The reference implies the possibility that Cohn contracted HIV having sex

with Haitian men, one of the original four high-risk groups identified by the CDC in early AIDS epidemiology. In this way, Cohn is further associated with downwardly mobile racial and class affiliations in the expression of his sexual proclivities.

39 Framji Minwalla conducts an allegorical reading of these lines in "When Girls Collide," 112–113.

40 The switch points between US slavery, national racisms, and HIV/AIDS are numerous: we might consider the literal and symbolic liquidity of Black bodies in the Atlantic slave trade—the comingling of blood, bile, pus, and urine in the cargo hold of slave ships—as a historical antecedent to images of HIV transmitted through exchanges of bodily fluid; mid-twentieth-century fears that race could be transmitted by blood leading to the segregation of wartime blood banks, which discouraged African Americans from donating blood in much the same way that fears of HIV transmission have historically disqualified gay men from blood donation since HIV/AIDS; finally, conspiracy theories that HIV was a creation of the CIA targeted at African Americans, which gained traction in the late 1980s, recalling historical examples of biological assaults on Black bodies including the Tuskegee Syphilis Experiment. On bodily fluidity in the Atlantic slave trade, see Tinsley, "Black Atlantic, Queer Atlantic."

41 Gregg and Seigworth, "Inventory of Shimmers," 14.

42 Fisher, *Gary in Your Pocket*, 239.

43 Ibid., 257–258.

44 Anthony Paul Farley discusses Fisher's depiction of submission as resistance in "The Black Body as Fetish Object," 517.

45 See *Space Oddity (lesson in survival)*, the Chuck Nanney exhibition catalog. Many thanks to David Getsy for introducing me to this fascinating artist.

46 Treichler, "Epidemic of Signification," 68.

CONCLUSION. "SOMETHING ELSE TO BE"

1 Arendt, *Human Condition*, 244.

2 Zerilli, *Abyss of Freedom*, 9.

3 Nixon, *Hannah Arendt*, 7.

4 Ibid., 4.

5 Snitow, *Feminism of Uncertainty*, 2.

6 In order, I am referring to: lesbian separatist Liza Cowan's description of her unexpected friendship with a straight woman neighbor who resided near her farm in upstate New York ("Separatist Symposium," 35–36); Cherríe Moraga's description of a feminist dialogue she shared with a gay male friend ("La Güera," 29); Nellie Y. McKay's career-long friendship with Susan Stanford Friedman, which was related to me through personal correspondence with Friedman; and gay activist Randy Wicker's decades long friendship with transgender activist and community organizer Marsha P. Johnson, as chronicled in the documentary *The Death and Life of Marsha P. Johnson* (dir. David France, 2017).

7 Mitchell and Asta, *Faggots and Their Friends*.

8 Ibid., 7.

9 Lorde, "Uses of the Erotic," 56.

10 Ibid., 57. Extending this logic, in a 1981 interview for the anthology *This Bridge Called My Back*, Black feminist Beverly Smith responded to a question about the impediments to friendships between Black and white women with the following answer: "Sometimes it's as simple as who you can laugh with, who you can cry with and who you can share meals with and whose face you can touch" (121).

11 See Rich, "Heterosexuality and Lesbian Existence."

12 Ibid., 657.

13 Foucault, "Friendship as a Way of Life," 138.

14 Roach, *Friendship*, 15.

15 Consequently, one might venture to say that the rigorous cultivation of polyamorous, open, or ethically nonmonogamous relationships in queer sexual cultures is, at its best, an attempt to infuse the realm of romance and eroticism with the spirit of friendship, which is fundamentally about reciprocal, back-and-forth exchange, rather than emotional or erotic union or possession.

16 See Faludi, "Death of a Revolutionary."

17 See Breines, *The Trouble between Us*.

18 Bunch, "Learning from Lesbian Separatism," 442.

19 On the overstatement of interpersonal harm in left-wing political discourse, see Schulman, *Conflict Is Not Abuse*; on Black feminist "defensiveness" and proprietary claims to the concept of intersectionality, see Nash, *Black Feminism Reimagined*; and on the "punitive" tendency in abolitionist movements, see Brown, *We Will Not Cancel Us*. Foundational studies in left-wing discourses of woundedness and resentment include Brown, "Wounded Attachments," and Nussbaum, *Anger and Forgiveness*. What Adrienne Maree Brown has described as the "punitive tendency" in contemporary social justice movements has produced its own subgenre of popular self-help writing by women-of-color activists who seek to counter the deleterious effects of internecine conflict between movement members. While this work is invaluable, in a perverse twist, the very abolitionist movements that call out and attempt to alleviate the overwhelming emotional labor commonly expected of women of color in a racist and sexist society end up requiring those same women to engage in the additional affective labor of tending to, nurturing, and theorizing ways out of destructive interpersonal social movement dynamics. In addition to Brown, texts in this genre include Haga, *Healing Resistance*; Birdsong, *How We Show Up*; and Piepzna-Samarasinha, Lakshmi, and Dixon, *Beyond Survival*.

20 See Miller, "Upward Contempt"; a precise sociological definition of cancel culture is offered by Campbell and Manning, *Rise of Victimhood Culture*.

21 Brown, *We Will Not Cancel Us*, 11, 42–47.

22 Care Collective, *Care Manifesto*, 1–20.

23 Spade, *Mutual Aid*, 9. See also Malatino's *Trans Care* for a distinctly transgender theory of mutual aid.

24 Zerilli, *Abyss of Freedom*, 8, 10. In *Worldly Ethics*, political theorist Ella Myers draws on Arendt to argue for a world-centered model of "care." This model is based neither on an ethical cultivation of the self, nor on a benevolent orientation toward the other, but instead centralizes the value of strengthening or maximizing collective investment in "'worldly things,' which are the common and contentious objects of concern around which democratic actors mobilize." Cover copy.

25 Zerilli, *Abyss of Freedom*, 8–9.

26 Ibid., 9. We may argue, alongside theorists of care, that people who do not have their basic needs met cannot adequately participate in democratic life (a point Arendt would agree with). And indeed, from this perspective one might reasonably assume that care work is in fact part and parcel of ensuring people access to the ability to act in concert, and hence can itself be seen as a form of collective action. But it would be a grave mistake to presume that meeting needs itself is the ultimate purpose of politics, which reifies bare biological and psychological survival (even at it claims to be about solidarity, mobilization, and conflict resolution) as an ultimate good.

27 Roach, *Friendship*, 9.

28 Undoubtedly, in this process, friends come to provide a form of mutual aid, supporting one another through life's challenges and learning to navigate the intricacies of shared needs. But rather than being the ontological purpose of friendship, this kind of "care work" emerges organically as an aftereffect of the perpetual constitution of a "space of appearance" between interlocutors who radically rearrange one another's view of the world.

29 Snitow, *Feminism of Uncertainty*, 286.

30 This may account for why the word "friend" finds its etymological origin as the noun form of the term "free," an apt description for a social relation based on free (and freely given) discourse but also modeling a type of publicly practiced freedom based not on sovereignty, or individual agency, but on the capacity to act in concert with others (*OED*).

31 Kathie Sarachild and Amy Coenen interviewed by Doug Henwood, "Two Redstockings Interviewed," *Left Business Observer*, WBAI, New York City, January 24, 2002.

32 Johnson, "Nothing Fails Like Success," 332.

33 See Morrison, *Sula*.

34 Ibid., 95.

35 Ibid., 145.

36 Ibid., 146.

37 Ibid., 174.

38 Lorde, "Poetry Is Not a Luxury," 36.

39 Ibid., 38.

40 D'Agostino, "Flesh-to-Flesh Contact," 277.

41 Ibid.

BIBLIOGRAPHY

Abdulahad, Tania, Gwendolyn Rogers, Barbara Smith, and Jameelah Waheed. "Black/
Lesbian Feminist Organizing: A Conversation." In Barbara Smith, ed., *Home Girls:
A Black Feminist Anthology*. New Brunswick, NJ: Rutgers University Press, 2000
[1983], 285–311.

Ahmed, Sara. *The Cultural Politics of Emotion*. London: Routledge, 2004.

———. *Queer Phenomenology: Orientations, Objects, Others*. Durham, NC: Duke University Press, 2006.

Alford, Lucy. *Forms of Poetic Attention*. New York: Columbia University Press, 2020.

Alice, Gordon, Debbie, and Mary. "Separatism" [1973]. In Sarah Lucia Hoagland and
Julia Penelope, eds., *For Lesbians Only: A Separatist Anthology*. London: Onlywomen, 1988, 31–39.

Alinder, Gary. "My Gay Soul." In Karla Jay and Allen Young, eds., *Out of the Closets:
Voices of Gay Liberation*. New York: NYU Press, 1992 [1972], 282–283.

Allen, Pamela. "The Small Group Process." In Barbara Crow, ed., *Radical Feminism:
A Documentary Reader*. New York: NYU Press, 2000, 277–281.

Allyn, David. *Make Love Not War: The Sexual Revolution, an Unfettered History*. New
York: Little Brown & Co., 2000.

Alphen, Ernst van. *Art in Mind: How Contemporary Images Shape Thought*. Chicago:
University of Chicago Press, 2005.

Altman, Dennis. *Homosexual: Oppression and Liberation*. St. Lucia: University of
Queensland Press, 2012 [1972].

Anderson, Jackie. "Separatism, Feminism, and the Betrayal of Reform." *Signs* 19.2
(Winter 1994): 437–448.

Anzaldúa, Gloria. *Borderlands/La Frontera: The New Mestiza*. San Francisco: Aunt Lute
Books, 1987.

Arendt, Hannah. *Between Past and Future*. New York: Penguin, 2006 [1954].

———. *The Human Condition*. Chicago: University of Chicago Press, 2018 [1958].

Armstrong, Elizabeth. *Forging Gay Identities: Organizing Sexuality in San Francisco,
1950–1994*. Chicago: University of Chicago Press, 2002.

Arnold, June. "Consciousness-Raising." In Barbara Crow, ed., *Radical Feminism:
A Documentary Reader*. New York: NYU Press, 2000, 282–286.

Bambara, Toni Cade, ed. *The Black Woman*. New York: Washington Square Press, 2005
[1970].

Bateman, Anita. "Narrative and Seriality in Elizabeth Catlett's Prints." *Journal of Black
Studies* 47.3 (January 2016): 258–272.

Beck, Koa. *White Feminism: From the Suffragettes to the Influencers and Who They Leave Behind*. New York: Atria Books, 2021.

Benjamin, Walter. "Theses on the Philosophy of History." In *Illuminations: Essays and Reflections*. New York: Mariner, 2019 [1955], 196–209.

Berlant, Lauren. *Cruel Optimism*. Durham, NC: Duke University Press, 2011.

Bersani, Leo. "Is the Rectum a Grave?" *October* 43.1 (Winter 1987): 197–222.

Bey, Marquis. "The Trans*-Ness of Blackness, the Blackness of Trans*-Ness." *TSQ* 4.2 (2017): 275–295.

Bey, Marquis, and Theodora Sakellarides. "When We Enter: The Blackness of Rachel Dolezal." *Black Scholar* 46.4 (December 2016): 33–48.

Birdsong, Mia. *How We Show Up: Reclaiming Family, Friendship, and Community*. New York: Hachette, 2020.

Blasius, Mark, and Shane Phelan, ed. *We Are Everywhere: A Historical Sourcecook of Gay and Lesbian Politics*. New York: Routledge, 1997.

Bordowitz, Gregg. *General Idea: Image Virus*. New York: Afterall Books, 2010.

Bost, Darius. *Evidence of Being: The Black Gay Cultural Renaissance and the Politics of Violence*. Chicago: University of Chicago Press, 2018.

Brainard, Joe. *The Nancy Book*, ed. Ron Padgett and Lisa Pearson. Los Angeles: Siglio Press, 2008.

Breines, Winifried. *The Trouble between Us: An Uneasy History of Black and White Women in the Feminist Movement*. Oxford: Oxford University Press, 2007.

Brinkema, Eugenie. *The Forms of the Affects*. Durham, NC: Duke University Press, 2014.

Brown, Adrienne Maree. *We Will Not Cancel Us: And Other Dreams of Transformative Justice*. Oakland, CA: AK Press, 2020.

Brown, Jayna. "World on Fire: Radical Black Feminism in a Dystopian Age." *South Atlantic Quarterly* 117.3 (2017): 581–597.

Brown, Wendy. "Wounded Attachments." *Political Theory* 21.3 (August 1993): 390–410.

Bunch, Charlotte. "Perseverance Furthers: Separatism and Our Future." *Furies: Lesbian/Feminist Monthly* 1.7 (Fall 1972), 3–5.

———. "Learning from Lesbian Separatism." In Karla Jay and Allen Young, eds., *Lavender Culture*. New York: NYU Press, 1994 [1978], 433–444.

Butler, Judith. *Undoing Gender*. New York: Routledge, 2004.

Campbell, Andy. *Queer X Design: 50 Years of Signs, Symbols, Banners, Logos, and Graphic Art of LGBTQ*. Seattle: Black Dog & Leventhal, 2019.

Campbell, Bradley, and Jason Manning. *The Rise of Victimhood Culture: Microaggressions, Safe Spaces, and the New Culture Wars*. London: Palgrave MacMillan, 2000.

Care Collective. *The Care Manifesto: The Politics of Interdependence*. London: Verso, 2020.

Carmichael, Stokely, and Charles Hamilton. *Black Power: The Politics of Liberation*. New York: Random House, 1967.

Chu, Andrea Long. "The Impossibility of Feminism." *differences* 30.1 (2019): 63–81.

Chuh, Kandice. *Imagine Otherwise: On Asian Americanist Critique*. Durham, NC: Duke University Press, 2003.

Chute, Hillary. "The Space of Graphic Narrative: Mapping Bodies, Feminism, and Form." In Robyn Warhol and Susan S. Lanser, eds., *Narrative Theory Unbound: Queer and Feminist Interventions*. Columbus: Ohio State University Press, 2015, 194–209.

———. *Why Comics? From Underground to Everywhere*. New York: HarperCollins, 2019.

Clarke, Cheryl. "Lesbianism: An Act of Resistance." In Cherríe Moraga and Gloria Anzaldúa, eds., *This Bridge Called My Back: Writing by Radical Women of Color*. Albany: SUNY Press, 2015 [1981], 126–135.

Cohn, Dorit. "Optics and Power in the Novel." *New Literary History* 26.1 (1995): 3–20.

Collective Lesbian International Terrors. "C.L.I.T. Statement #1–2." *Dyke: A Quarterly* 1.1 (January 1976): 6–9, 26–34.

Combahee River Collective. "A Black Feminist Statement." In Cherríe Moraga and Gloria Anzaldúa, eds., *This Bridge Called My Back: Writing by Radical Women of Color*. Albany: SUNY Press, 2015 [1981], 210–218.

Cooper, Brittney. "Love No Limit: Towards a Black Feminist Future (in Theory)." *Black Scholar* 45.4 (2015): 7–21.

Cowan, Liza. "Separatist Symposium: Response by Liza Cowen." *Dyke: A Quarterly* 1.6 (1978): 32–38.

Cox, Aimee Meredith. *Shapeshifters: Black Girls and the Choreography of Citizenship*. Durham, NC: Duke University Press, 2015.

Crawford, Lucas. *Transgender Architectonics: The Shape of Change in Modernist Space*. London: Routledge, 2015.

Cremins, Brian. "Bodies, Transfigurations, and Bloodlust in Edie Fake's Graphic Novel *Gaylord Phoenix*." *Journal of Medical Humanities* 34 (2013): 301–313.

Crimp, Douglas, ed. "AIDS: Cultural Activism, Cultural Analysis," special issue, *October* 43.1 (Winter 1987).

———. "How to Have Promiscuity in an Epidemic." *October* 43 (1987): 237–271.

———. *Melancholia and Moralism: Essays on AIDS and Queer Politics*. Cambridge, MA: MIT Press, 2002.

Crimp, Douglas, and Adam Rolston, eds. *AIDS Demo Graphics*. New York: Bay Press, 1990.

Crowley, Mart. *The Boys in the Band*, 40th anniversary ed. New York: Alyson Books, 2008.

Cvetkovich, Ann. *An Archive of Feeling: Trauma, Sexuality, and Lesbian Public Cultures*. Durham, NC: Duke University Press, 2003.

D'Agostino, Anthony Michael. ""Flesh-to-Flesh Contact": Marvel Comics' Rogue and the Queer Feminist Imagination." In Darieck Scott and Ramzi Fawaz, eds., "Queer about Comics," special issue, *American Literature* 90.2 (2018): 251–281.

Dansky, Steven, John Knoebel, and Kenneth Pitchford. "The Effeminist Manifesto." In Mark Blasius and Shane Phelan, eds., *We Are Everywhere: A Historical Sourcebook in Gay and Lesbian Politics*. New York: Routledge, 1997.

davenport, doris. "The Pathology of Racism: A Conversation with Third World Wimmin." In Cherríe Moraga and Gloria Anzaldúa, eds., *This Bridge Called My Back: Writing by Radical Women of Color.* Albany: SUNY Press, 2015 [1981], 81–86.

Davis, Elizabeth Gould. *The First Sex.* New York: Penguin, 1971.

Delany, Samuel. *Times Square Red, Times Square Blue.* New York: NYU Press, 1999.

D'Emilio, John. "Forward, to the Twentieth Anniversary Edition." In Karla Jay and Allen Young, eds., *Out of the Closets: Voices of Gay Liberation.* New York: NYU Press, 1992 [1972]), xi–xxx.

———. "Gay Politics, Gay Community: San Francisco's Experience." Chapter 4 in *Making Trouble: Essays on Gay History, Politics, and the University.* New York: Routledge, 1992.

———. *Sexual Politics, Sexual Communities: The Making of a Homosexual Minority in the United States, 1940–1970.* Chicago: University of Chicago Press, 1998 [1983].

Deming, Richard. "Everyday Devotions: The Art of Joe Brainard." *Yale University Art Gallery Bulletin* (2008): 75–87.

Dicker, Rory C. *A History of US Feminisms.* New York: Seal Press, 2016.

Dinnerstein, Dorothy. *The Mermaid and the Minotaur: Sexual Arrangement and Human Malaise.* New York: Harper & Row, 1976.

Dlugos, Tim. "The Joe Brainard Interview." *Little Caesar,* September 26, 1977.

Downs, Jim. *Stand by Me: The Forgotten History of Gay Liberation.* New York: Basic Books, 2016.

Doyle, Jennifer. *Hold It against Me: Difficulty and Emotion in American Art.* Durham, NC: Duke University Press, 2013.

Doyle, Jennifer, and David Getsy. "Queer Formalisms: Jennifer Doyle and David Getsy in Conversation." *Art Journal* 72.4 (2013): 58–71.

Duberman, Martin. *Stonewall: The Definitive Story of the LGBTQ Rights Uprising That Changed America.* New York: Plume, 2019.

Dyer, Richard. "Judy Garland and Gay Men." Chapter 3 in *Heavenly Bodies: Film Stars and Society.* London: Routledge, 1986.

Edelman, Lee. *No Future: Queer Theory and the Death Drive.* Durham, NC: Duke University Press, 2004.

Eisenstein, Zillah. *The Female Body and the Law.* Berkeley: University of California Press, 1988.

Elliot, Jane. "Stepford USA: Second-Wave Feminism, Domestic Labor, and the Representation of National Time." *Cultural Critique* 70 (Fall 2008): 32–62.

Enke, Finn. "Collective Memory and the Trans Feminist 1970s: Toward a Less Plausible History." *Transgender Studies Quarterly* 5.1 (2018): 9–29.

Enszer, Julie. "'How to Stop Choking to Death': Rethinking Lesbian Separatism as a Vibrant Political Theory and Feminist Practice." *Journal of Lesbian Studies* 20.2 (2016): 180–196.

Faderman, Lillian. *The Gay Revolution: The Story of the Struggle.* New York: Simon & Schuster, 2015.

Faludi, Susan. "Death of a Revolutionary." *New Yorker*, April 8, 2013, www.newyorker
.com.

Farley, Anthony Paul. "The Black Body as Fetish Object." *Oregon Law Review* 76. 3
(1997): 457–535.

Film Quarterly. "The Many Faces of 'Thelma & Louise'" (roundtable). *Film Quarterly*
45.2 (Winter 1991–1992): 20–31.

Finch, Casey, and Peter Bowen. "The Tittle-Tattle of Highbury: Gossip and the Free
Indirect Style in *Emma*." *Representations* 31 (Summer 1990): 1–18.

Finkelstein, Avram. *After Silence: A History of AIDS through Its Images*. Berkeley:
University of California Press, 2017.

Firestone, Shulamith. *The Dialectic of Sex: The Case for Feminist Revolution*. New York:
Farrar, Straus and Giroux, 2003 [1971].

Fisher, Gary. *Gary in Your Pocket: Stories and Notebooks of Gary Fisher*, ed. Eve Kosofsky Sedgwick. Durham, NC: Duke University Press, 1996.

Fitch, Andy. *Pop Poetics: Reframing Joe Brainard*. New York: Dalkey Archive Press,
2012.

Foster, Hal. "The Crux of Minimalism." Chapter 2 in *The Return of the Real: The Avant-
Garde at the End of the Century*. Cambridge, MA: MIT Press, 1996.

Foucault, Michel. "Sex, Power and the Politics of Identity" [1984]. Chapter 1 in *Ethics:
Subjectivity and Truth*. New York: New Press, 1997.

Freeman, Elizabeth. *Time Binds: Queer Temporalities, Queer Histories*. Durham, NC:
Duke University Press, 2010.

Freeman, Jo. "Trashing: The Dark Side of Sisterhood." *Ms.*, April 1976: 49–51, 92–98.

Frye, Marilyn. "Some Reflections on Separatism and Power" [1977]. In Sarah Lucia
Hoagland and Julia Penelope, eds., *For Lesbians Only: A Separatist Anthology*.
London: Onlywomen, 1988, 62–71.

———. "The Necessity of Differences: Constructing a Positive Category of Women."
Signs 21.3 (1996): 991–1010.

Gaines, Malik. *Black Performance on the Outskirts of the Left: A History of the Impossible*. New York: NYU Press, 2017.

Galvan, Margaret. "Making Space: Jennifer Camper, LGBTQ Anthologies, and Queer
Comics Communities." *Journal of Lesbian Studies* 22.4 (2018): 373–389.

A Gay Male Group. "Notes on Gay Male Consciousness Raising." In Karla Jay and Allen Young, eds., *Out of the Closets: Voices of Gay Liberation*. New York: NYU Press,
1992 [1972], 293–300.

Gay Revolution Party. "Gay Revolution Party Manifesto." In Karla Jay and Allen Young,
eds., *Out of the Closets: Voices of Gay Liberation*. New York: NYU Press, 1992 [1972],
342–345.

Gerhard, Jane. *Desiring Revolution: Second-Wave Feminism and the Rewriting of
Twentieth-Century American Sexual Thought, 1920–1980*. New York: Columbia
University Press, 2001.

———. *Judy Chicago and the Power of Popular Feminism, 1970–2007*. Athens: University
of Georgia Press, 2013.

Gerhard, Ute. *Debating Women's Equality: Toward a Feminist Theory of Law from a European Perspective*. New Brunswick, NJ: Rutgers University Press, 2001 [1990].

Glavey, Brian. "Friending Joe Brainard." *Criticism* 60.3 (2018): 315–340.

Gornick, Vivian. "On the Progress of Feminism: The Light of Liberation Can Be Blinding." *Village Voice*, December 10, 1970: 5, 21–22, 31–32.

———. "Consciousness" [1971]. In Barbara Crow, ed., *Radical Feminism: A Documentary Reader*. New York: NYU Press, 2000, 287–300.

Gould, Deborah. *Moving Politics: Emotion and ACT UP's Fight against AIDS*. Chicago: University of Chicago Press, 2009.

Gregg, Melissa, and Gregory Seigworth. "An Inventory of Shimmers." Introduction to Gregg and Seigworth, eds., *The Affect Studies Reader*. Durham, NC: Duke University Press, 2011, 1–25.

Griggers, Cathy. "*Thelma and Louise* and the Cultural Generation of the New Butch-Femme." In Jim Collins, Hilary Radner, and Ava Preacher Collins, eds., *Film Theory Goes to the Movies*. New York: Routledge, 1993, 129–141.

Grosz, Elizabeth. "Conclusion: A Note on Essentialism and Difference." In Sneja Gunew, ed., *Feminist Knowledge: Critique and Construction*. New York: Routledge, 1992, 322–344.

Gutter Dyke Collective. *Dykes & Gorgons* 1.1 (May–June 1973).

———. "Over the Walls, Separatism" [1973]. In Sarah Lucia Hoagland and Julia Penelope, eds., *For Lesbians Only: A Separatist Anthology*. London: Onlywomen, 1988, 27–30.

Haga, Kazu. *Healing Resistance: A Radically Different Response to Harm*. New York: Parallax Press, 2020.

Halberstam, Jack. *In a Queer Time and Place: Transgender Bodies, Subcultural Lives*. New York: NYU Press, 2005.

Hall, Justin, ed. *No Straight Lines: Four Decades of Queer Comics*. Seattle: Fantagraphics Books, 2013.

Halley, Janet. *Split Decisions: How and Why to Take a Break from Feminism*. Princeton, NJ: Princeton University Press, 2006.

Hamad, Ruby. *White Tears/Brown Scars: How White Feminism Betrays Women of Color*. New York: Catapult Press, 2020.

Haraway, Donna. "A Manifesto for Cyborgs: Science, Technology and Socialist Feminism in the 1980s" [1985]. Chapter 1 in *The Haraway Reader*. New York: Routledge, 2004.

Harper, Phillip Brian. *Abstractionist Aesthetics: Artistic Form and Social Critique in African American Culture*. New York: NYU Press, 2015.

Harrison, Michael. "The Queer Spaces and Fluid Bodies of Nazario's Anarcoma." *Postmodern Culture* 19.3 (2009), http://pmc.iath.virginia.edu.

Hemmings, Clare. *Why Stories Matter: The Political Grammar of Feminist Theory*. Durham, NC: Duke University Press, 2011.

Hernández, Robb. *Archiving an Epidemic: Art, AIDS, and the Chicanx Avant-Garde*. New York: NYU Press, 2019.

Hesford, Victoria. *Feeling Women's Liberation*. Durham, NC: Duke University Press, 2013.

Highmore, Ben. "Bitter after Taste: Affect, Food, and Social Aesthetics." In Melissa Gregg and Gregory Seigworth, eds., *The Affect Studies Reader*. Durham, NC: Duke University Press, 2010, 118–137.

Hilderbrand, Lucas. "In the Heat of the Moment: Notes on the Past, Present, and Future of *Born in Flames*." *Woman & Performance* 23.1 (2013): 6–16.

Hill, Robert. "Before Transgender: *Transvestia's* Spectrum of Gender Variance." In Susan Stryker and Stephen Whittle, eds., *The Transgender Studies Reader*. New York: Routledge, 2013, 364–379.

Hobson, Emily. *Lavender and Red: Liberation and Solidarity in the Gay and Lesbian Left* Berkeley: University of California Press, 2016.

Hogan, Kristen. *The Feminist Bookstore Movement: Lesbian Antiracism and Feminist Accountability*. Durham, NC: Duke University Press, 2016.

Hogeland, Lisa Maria. *Feminism and Its Fictions: The Consciousness-Raising Novel and the Women's Liberation Movement*. Philadelphia: University of Pennsylvania Press, 1998.

Howard, Yetta. "Politically Incorrect, Visually Incorrect: *Bitchy Butch's* Unapologetic Discrepancies in Lesbian Identity and Comic Art." *Journal of Popular Culture* 45.1 (2012): 79–98.

Hughes, Linda K., and Michael Lund. *The Victorian Serial*. Richmond: University of Virginia Press, 2015.

Hunt, Linda. "'I Could Not Figure Out What Was My Village': Gender vs. Ethnicity in Maxine Hong Kingston's *The Woman Warrior*." *MELUS* 12.3 (Autumn 1985): 5–12.

Invisible Committee. *NOW*. Boston: MIT Press, 2017.

Jagose, Annamarie. *Inconsequence: Lesbian Representation and the Logic of Sexual Sequence*. Ithaca, NY: Cornell University Press, 2002.

Jameson, Frederic. "History and the Death Wish: *Zardoz* as Open Form." *Jump Cut* 3 (1974): 5–8.

Jay, Karla. *Tales of the Lavender Menace: A Memoir of Liberation*. New York: Basic Books, 2000.

Jenkins, Ruth Y. "Authorizing Female Voice and Experience: Ghosts and Spirits in Kingston's *The Woman Warrior* and Allende's *The House of the Spirits*." *MELUS* 19.3 (Autumn 1994): 61–73.

Johnson, Barbara. "Nothing Fails Like Success" [1980]. In Melissa Feuerstein, Bill Johnson González, Lili Porten, and Keja L. Valens, eds., *The Barbara Johnson Reader: The Surprise of Otherness*. Durham, NC: Duke University Press, 2014, 327–333.

Johnson, Julius Maurice. "Influence of Assimilation on the Psychosocial Adjustment of Black Homosexual Men," PhD diss., California School of Professional Psychology, Berkeley, 1981.

Johnston, Jill. *Lesbian Nation: The Feminist Solution*. New York: Simon & Schuster, 1973.

Kang, Laura. *Compositional Subjects: Enfiguring Asian/American Woman*. Durham, NC: Duke University Press, 2002.

Katz, Jonathan. "'Committing the Perfect Crime': Sexuality, Assemblage, and the Postmodern Turn in American Art." *Art Forum* 67.1 (Spring 2008): 38–53.

Katz. "Smash Phallic Imperialism." In Karla Jay and Allen Young, eds., *Out of the Closets: Voices of Gay Liberation.* New York: NYU Press, 1992 [1972], 259–261.

Keegan, Cáel. "Getting Disciplined: What's Trans* about Queer Studies Now." *Journal of Homosexuality* 67.3 (2020): 384–397.

Kendell, Mikki. *Hood Feminism: Notes from the Women That a Movement Forgot.* New York: Penguin Books, 2020.

Kernan, Nathan. "Joe Brainard: All Possible Colors." *On Paper* 1.4 (March–April 1997): 26–40.

Kinder, Marsha. "Review: *Zardoz* by John Boorman." *Film Quarterly* 27.4 (1974): 49–57.

King, Katie. "Local and Global: AIDS Activism and Feminist Theory." *Camera Obscura* 10.1 (28): 78–99.

Kitchen, Denis, and James Danky. *Underground Classics: The Transformation of Comics into Comix.* Madison, WI: Harry N. Adams and the Chazen Museum of Art, 2009.

Knoebel, John. "Somewhere in the Right Direction: Testimony of My Experience in a Gay Male Living Collective." In Karla Jay and Allen Young, eds., *Out of the Closets: Voices of Gay Liberation.* New York: NYU Press, 1992 [1972], 301–314.

Kornbluh, Anna. *The Order of Forms: Realism, Formalism, and Social Space.* Chicago: University of Chicago Press, 2019.

Kushner, Tony. *Angels in America: A Gay Fantasia on National Themes, Parts One and Two.* New York: Theatre Communications Group, 2013 [1992].

Lauterbach, Anne. "Joe Brainard & Nancy." In Joe Brainard, *The Nancy Book*, ed. Ron Padgett and Lisa Pearson. Los Angeles: Siglio, 2008, 7–26.

Lee, Rachel. "Notes from the (Non) Field: Teaching and Theorizing Women of Color." In Robyn Wiegman, Inderpal Grewal, and Caren Kaplan, eds., *Women's Studies on Its Own: A Next Wave Reader in Institutional Change.* Durham, NC: Duke University Press, 2002, 82–105.

Levin, Ira. *The Stepford Wives.* New York: Perennial, 2002 [1972].

Levine, Caroline. *Forms: Network, Rhythm, Hierarchy, Whole.* Princeton, NJ: Princeton University Press, 2015.

Lorde, Audre. *Zami: A New Spelling of My Name—A Biomythography.* Berkeley, CA: Crossing Press, 1982.

———. "Poetry Is Not a Luxury" [1973]. In *Sister Outsider: Essays and Speeches.* New York: Crossing Press, 2007 [1984], 61–69.

———. "The Uses of the Erotic: The Erotic as Power" [1978]. In *Sister Outsider*, 24–27.

———. "Man Child: A Black Lesbian Feminist's Response" [1979]. In *Sister Outsider*, 41–48.

Luis, Keridwen N. *Herlands: Exploring the Women's Land Movement in the United States.* Minneapolis: University of Minnesota Press, 2018.

MacKinnon, Catharine. "Difference and Dominance: On Sex Discrimination." Chapter 2 in *Feminism Unmodified: Discourses on Life and Law.* Cambridge, MA: Harvard University Press, 1987.

MacLean, Nancy, ed. *The American Women's Movement, 1945–2000: A Brief History with Documents*. New York: Bedford St. Martin, 2008.

Malatino, Hil. *Trans Care*. Minneapolis: University of Minnesota Press, 2020.

Massumi, Brian. *Parables of the Virtual: Movement, Affect, Sensation*. Durham, NC: Duke University Press, 2002.

Mayer, Ruth. "Machinic Fu Manchu, Popular Seriality and the Logic of Spread." *Journal of Narrative Theory* 43.2 (Summer 2013): 186–217.

McCormick, Carlo. "Fables, Facts, Riddles, & Reasons in Wojnarowicz's Mythopoetica." In Barry Blinderman, ed., *Tongues of Flame*. Normal: University Galleries, Illinois State University, 1990, 11–16.

McMaster, James. "Revolting Self-Care: Mark Aguhar's Virtual Separatism." *American Quarterly* 72.1 (2020): 181–205.

McRuer, Robert. *The Queer Renaissance: Contemporary American Literature and the Reinvention of Lesbian and Gay Identities*. New York: NYU Press, 1998.

———. "Gay Gatherings." In Peter Braunstein and Michael William Doyle, eds., *Imagine Nation: The American Counterculture of the 1960s and '70s*. New York: Routledge, 2002, 215–240.

———. *Crip Theory: Cultural Signs of Disability and Queerness*. New York: NYU Press, 2005.

Mesli, Rostom. "In Defense of Identity Politics: A Queer Reclamation of a Radical Concept," PhD diss., University of Michigan, Department of Comparative Literature, 2015.

Meeker, Martin. *Contacts Desired: Gay and Lesbian Communications and Community, 1940s–1970s*. Chicago: University of Chicago Press, 2006.

Michals, Debra. "From 'Consciousness Expansion' to 'Consciousness Raising': Feminism and the Countercultural Politics of the Self." In Peter Braunstein and Michael William Doyle, eds., *Imagine Nation: The American Counterculture of the 1960s and '70s*. New York: Routledge, 2002, 41–68.

Milk, Harvey. "Gay Freedom Day Speech, June 25, 1978." In Jason Edward Black and Charles E. Morris, eds., *Harvey Milk: An Archive of Hope: Harvey Milk's Speeches and Writing*. Berkeley: University of California Press, 2013, 215–220.

Miller, D. A. *Jane Austen, or, The Secret of Style*. Princeton, NJ: Princeton University Press, 2003.

Miller, James. "Heavenquake: Queer Anagogies in Kushner's America." In Deborah R. Geis and Steven F. Kruger, eds., *Approaching the Millennium: Essays on Angels in America*. Ann Arbor: University of Michigan Press, 1997, 56–77.

Miller, William Ian. "Upward Contempt." *Political Theory* 23.3 (August 1995): 476–499.

Minwalla, Framji. "When Girls Collide: Considering Race in Angels in America." In Deborah R. Geis and Steven F. Kruger, eds., *Approaching the Millennium: Essays on Angels in America*. Ann Arbor: University of Michigan Press, 1997, 103–117.

Mitchell, Larry, (writer), and Ned Asta (artist). *The Faggots and Their Friends between Revolutions*. New York: Nightboat Books, 2019 [1977].

Mitchell, W. J. T. "Comics as Media: Afterward." *Critical Inquiry* 40.3 (Spring 2014): 255–265.

Moraga, Cherríe. "La Güera." In Cherríe Moraga and Gloria Anzaldúa, eds., *This Bridge Called My Back: Writing by Radical Women of Color*. Albany: SUNY Press, 2015 [1981], 22–29.

Morris, Bonnie J. *Eden Built by Eves: The Culture of Women's Music Festivals*. Boston: Alyson Books, 1999.

Morrison, Toni. *Sula*. New York: Vintage, 2004 [1973].

Mulvey, Laura. "Visual Pleasure and Narrative Cinema" [1975]. In Leo Braudy and Marshall Cohen, eds., *Film Theory and Criticism: Introductory Readings*. New York: Oxford University Press, 2009.

Mumford, Kevin. *Not Straight, Not White: Black Gay Men from the March on Washington to the AIDS Crisis*. Chapel Hill: University of North Carolina Press, 2019.

Muñoz, José Esteban. *Cruising Utopia: The Then and There of Queer Futurity*. New York: NYU Press, 2009.

Murray, Heather. "Free for All Lesbians: Lesbian Cultural Production and Consumption in the United States in the 1970s." *Journal of the History of Sexuality* 16.2 (May 2007): 251–275.

Myers, Ella. *Worldly Ethics: Democratic Politics and Care for the World*. Durham, NC: Duke University Press, 2013.

Nanney, Chuck. *Space Oddity (lesson in survival)*. New York: Debs & Co., 1999. Exhibition catalog.

———. "I Sing the Body Electric" (interview). *Poz* 52 (October 1999), www.poz.com.

Nash, Jennifer. *Black Feminism Reimagined: After Intersectionality*. Durham, NC: Duke University Press, 2019.

National Organization for Women. "NOW Statement of Purpose" [1966]. In Nancy MacLean, ed., *The American Women's Movement: A Brief History with Documents, 1945–2000*, Boston: Bedford/St. Martin Press, 2009,

———. "NOW Bill of Rights" [1968], https://350fem.blogs.brynmawr.edu (accessed May 4, 2020).

Newgarden, Mark, and Paul Karasik. "How to Read Nancy." In Brian Walker, ed., *The Best of Ernie Bushmiller's Nancy*. New York: Henry Holt, 1988.

Ngai, Sianne. *Ugly Feelings*. Cambridge, MA: Harvard University Press, 2007.

Nixon, Jon. *Hannah Arendt and the Politics of Friendship*. London: Bloomsbury, 2015.

Norman, Brian. "The Consciousness-Raising Document, Feminist Anthologies, and Black Women in *Sisterhood Is Powerful*." *Frontiers: A Journal of Women Studies* 27.23 (2006): 38–64.

Nussbaum, Martha. *Anger and Forgiveness: Resentment, Generosity, Justice*. New York: Oxford University Press, 2018.

Ordona, Trinity A. "An Ethnohistory of the Asian and Pacific Islander Queer Women's and Transgendered People's Movement of San Francisco," PhD diss., University of California, Santa Cruz, 2000.

———. *Coming Out Together: An Ethnohistory of the Asian and Pacific Islander Queer Women's and Transgendered People's Movement of San Francisco*. London: Routledge, 2007.

Ormsbee, J. Todd. *The Meaning of Gay: Interaction, Publicity, and Community among Homosexual Men in 1960s San Francisco*. New York: Lexington Books, 2010.

O'Sullivan, Sean. "Broken on Purpose: Poetry, Serial Television, and the Season." *Storyworlds: A Journal of Narrative Studies* 2 (2010): 59–77.

Patton, Cindy. *Inventing AIDS*. New York: Routledge, 1990.

Peppard, Anna, ed. *Supersex: Sexuality, Fantasy, and the Superhero*. Austin: University of Texas Press, 2020.

Piepzna-Samarasinha, Leah Lakshmi, and Ejeris Dixon, eds. *Beyond Survival: Strategies and Stories from the Transformative Justice Movement*. Vancouver: AK Press, 2020.

Powell, Ryan. *Coming Together: The Cinematic Elaboration of Gay Male Life, 1945–1979*. Chicago: University of Chicago Press, 2019.

Radicalesbians. "The Woman-Identified-Woman" [1970]. In Karla Jay and Allen Young, eds., *Out of the Closets: Voices of Gay Liberation*. New York: NYU Press, 1992 [1972], 172–176.

Ramírez, Horacio N. Roque. "Communities of Desire: Queer Latina/Latino History and Memory, San Francisco Bay Area 1960s–1990s," PhD diss., University of California, Berkeley, Department of Ethnic Studies, 2001.

———. "'That's My Place!': Negotiating Racial, Sexual, and Gender Politics in San Francisco's Gay Latino Alliance, 1975–1983." *Journal of the History of Sexuality* 12.2 (2003): 224–258.

Reagon, Bernice Johnson. "Coalition Politics" [1981]. In Barbara Smith, ed., *Home Girls: A Black Feminist Anthology*. New Brunswick, NJ: Rutgers University Press, 2000 [1983], 343–355.

Reed, T. V. *The Art of Protest: Culture and Activism from the Civil Rights Movement to the Present*. Minneapolis: University of Minnesota Press, 2019.

Redwomon. "Freedom" [1981]. In Sarah Lucia Hoagland and Julia Penelope, eds., *For Lesbians Only: A Separatist Anthology*. London: Onlywomen, 1988, 76–83.

Rensenbrink, Greta. "Parthenogenesis and Lesbian Separatism: Regenerating Women's Community through Virgin Birth in the United States in the 1970s and 1980s." *Journal of the History of Sexuality* 19.2 (May 2012): 288–316.

Reumann, Miriam G. *American Sexual Character: Sex, Gender, and National Identity in the Kinsey Reports*. Berkeley: University of California Press, 2005.

Rhode, Deborah L., ed. *Theoretical Perspectives on Sexual Difference*. New Haven, CT: Yale University Press, 1990.

Rich, Adrienne. "Compulsory Heterosexuality and Lesbian Existence." *Signs* 5.4 (Summer 1980): 631–660.

———. "Notes for a Magazine: What Does Separatism Mean?" *Sinister Wisdom* 18 (1981): 83–91.

Riemer, Matthew, and Leighton Brown. *We Are Everywhere: Protest, Power and Pride in the History of Gay Liberation*. New York: Random House, 2019.

Roach, Tom. *Friendship as a Way of Life: Foucault, AIDS and the Politics of Shared Estrangement*. New York: SUNY Press, 2012.

Robinson, Amy. "It Takes One to Know One: Passing and Communities of Common Interest." *Critical Inquiry* 20.4 (Summer 1994): 715–736.

Rohy, Valerie. *Lost Causes: Narrative, Etiology, and Queer Theory*. New York: Oxford University Press, 2015.

Román, David. *Acts of Intervention: Performance, Gay Culture and AIDS*. Indianapolis: Indiana University Press, 1998.

Rooney, Ellen. "Form and Contentment." *MLQ (Modern Language Quarterly)* 61.1 (2000): 17–40.

Rosen, Ruth. *The World Split Open: How the Modern Women's Movement Changed America*. New York: Penguin, 2006.

Rosenkranz, Patrick. *Rebel Visions: The Underground Comix Revolution*. Seattle: Fantagraphics Books, 2008.

Rossi, Alice. "Equality between the Sexes: An Immodest Proposal." *Daedalus* 93.2 (Summer 1964): 607–652.

Roth, Benita. *Separate Roads to Feminism: Black, Chicana, White Feminist Movements in America's Second Wave*. Cambridge: Cambridge University Press, 2010.

Row, Jennifer. "Queer Time on the Early Modern Stage: France and the Drama of Biopower." *Exemplaria* 29.1 (2017): 58–81.

Rubin, Gayle. "Of Catamites and Kings: Reflection on Butch, Gender, and Boundaries" [1992]. Chapter 10 in *Deviations: A Gayle Rubin Reader*. Durham, NC: Duke University Press, 2012.

Rudy, Kathy. "Radical Feminism, Lesbian Separatism, and Queer Theory." *Feminist Studies* 21.1 (Spring 2001): 190–222.

Russ, Joanna. *The Female Man*. Boston: Beacon Press, 1975.

Samek, Alyssa. "Pivoting between Identity Politics and Coalitional Relationships: Lesbian-Feminist Resistance to the Woman-Identified Woman." *Women's Studies in Communication* 38 (2015): 393–420.

Sandilands, Catriona. "Lesbian Separatist Communities and the Experience of Nature: Toward a Queer Ecology." *Organization & Environment* 15.2 (June 2002): 131–163.

Sarachild, Kathie. "A Program for Feminist 'Consciousness Raising.'" In Shulamith Firestone and Ann Koedt, eds., *Notes from the Second Year: Women's Liberation— Major Writings of the Radical Feminists*. New York: Radical Feminism, 1970, 78–80.

Savoy, Eric. "The Jamesian Turn: A Primer on Queer Formalism." In Kimberly Reed and Peter Beidler, eds., *Approaches to Teaching Henry James's Daisy Miller and The Turn of the Screw*. New York: Modern Language Association of America, 2005.

Savran, David. "Ambivalence, Utopia, and a Queer Sort of Materialism: How *Angels in America* Reconstructs the Nation." In Deborah R. Geis and Steven F. Kruger, eds., *Approaching the Millennium: Essays on* Angels in America. Ann Arbor: University of Michigan Press, 1997, 13–38.

Schulman, Sarah. *The Gentrification of the Mind: Witness to a Lost Imagination*. Berkeley: University of California Press, 2013.

———. *Conflict Is Not Abuse: Overstating Harm, Community Responsibility and the Duty to Repair*. Vancouver: Arsenal Pulp Press, 2016.

Scott, Darieck. "Big Black Beauty Drawing and Naming the Black Male Figure in Superhero and Gay Porn Comics." In Tim Dean, Steven Ruszczycky, and David Squires, eds., *The Porn Archives*. Durham, NC: Duke University Press, 2014: 183–212.

Scott, Darieck, and Ramzi Fawaz, eds. "Queer about Comics," special issue, *American Literature* 90.2 (2018).

Scott, Joan. "Deconstructing Equality-versus-Difference: Or the Use of Poststructuralist Theory for Feminism." *Feminist Studies* 14.1 (1998): 32–50.

———. "The Conundrum of Equality." Chapter 10 in *Gender and the Politics of History*. New York: Columbia University Press, 2018 [1988].

Scroggie, William. "Producing Identity: From *The Boys in the Band* to Gay Liberation." In Patricia Juliana Smith, ed., *The Queer Sixties*. London: Routledge, 1999, 237–254.

Sedgwick, Eve Kosofsky. *Epistemology of the Closet*. Berkeley: University of California Press, 1991.

———. *Tendencies*. Durham, NC: Duke University Press, 1993.

Shu, Yuan. "Cultural Politics and Chinese-American Female Subjectivity: Rethinking Kingston's Woman Warrior." *MELUS* 26.2 (Summer 2001): 199–223.

Shugar, Dana. *Separatism and Women's Community*. Lincoln: University of Nebraska Press, 1995.

Simmons, William J. "Notes on Queer Formalism: Amy Sillman, Nicole Eisenman, Leidy Churchman, and Elise Adibi." *Big Red & Shiny* 2.15 (December 2013), http://bigredandshiny.org.

———. *Queer Formalism: The Return*. Dijon: Floating Opera Press, 2021.

Smith, Barbara. "Toward a Black Feminist Criticism." *Radical Teacher* 7 (March 1978): 20–27.

———. "Responding to Adrienne Rich." *Sinister Wisdom* 20 (February 3, 1982): 100–104.

Smith, Beverly, and Barbara Smith. "Across the Kitchen Table: A Sister-to-Sister Dialogue." In Cherríe Moraga and Gloria Anzaldúa, eds., *This Bridge Called My Back: Writing by Radical Women of Color*. Albany: SUNY Press, 2015 [1981], 111–125.

Snitow, Ann. *The Feminism of Uncertainty: A Gender Diary*. Durham, NC: Duke University Press, 2015.

Snorton, C. Riley. *Black on Both Sides: A Racial History of Trans Identity*. Minneapolis: University of Minnesota Press, 2017.

Solanas, Valerie. *S.C.U.M. Manifesto (Society for Cutting Up Men)* [1968]. In Barbara Crow, ed., *Radical Feminism: A Documentary Reader*. New York: NYU Press, 2000, 201–222.

Sontag, Susan. *AIDS and Its Metaphors*. New York: Farrar, Straus and Giroux, 1988.

Spade, Dean. *Mutual Aid: Building Solidarity during This Crisis (and the Next)*. London: Verso, 2020.

Sperreta, Tomasso. *Rebels Rebel: AIDS, Art and Activism in New York, 1979–1989*. Berlin: AsaMER, 2014.

Springer, Kimberly. *Living for the Revolution: Black Feminist Organizations, 1968–1980*. Durham, NC: Duke University Press, 2005.

Stark, Jessica Quick. "Nancy and the Queer Adorable." In Darieck Scott and Ramzi Fawaz, eds., "Queer about Comics," special issue, *American Literature* 90.2 (2018): 315–345.

Stein, Marc, ed. *The Stonewall Riots: A Documentary Reader*. New York: NYU Press, 2019.

Steinbock, Eliza. *Shimmering Images: Trans Cinema, Embodiment, and the Aesthetics of Change*. Durham, NC: Duke University Press, 2019.

Stryker, Susan. *Transgender History: The Roots of Today's Revolution*. New York: Seal Press, 2017 [2008].

Sturkin, Marita. *Thelma & Louise* (BFI Film Classics). London: British Film Institute, 2000.

Sulcer, Robert. "Ten Percent: Poetry and Pathology." In Richard Dellamora, ed., *Victorian Sexual Dissidence*. Chicago and London: University of Chicago Press, 1999.

Tinsley, Omise'eke Natasha. "Black Atlantic, Queer Atlantic: Queer Imaginings of the Middle Passage." *GLQ: A Journal of Lesbian and Gay Studies*, 14.2–3 (2008): 191–215.

Treichler, Paula. "AIDS, Homophobia, and Biomedical Discourse: An Epidemic of Signification." *October* 43.1 (Winter 1987): 31–70.

Warhol, Robyn. "Making 'Gay' and 'Lesbian' Household Terms: How Serial Form Works in Maupin's *Tales of the City*." *Contemporary Literature* 40.3 (Autumn 1999): 378–402.

Warner, Michael. *Publics and Counterpublics*. New York: Zone Books, 2005.

Watney, Simon. *Policing Desire: Pornography, AIDS, and the Media*. Minneapolis: University of Minnesota Press, 1987.

Weinberg, Jonathan. *Pier Groups: Art and Sex along the New York Water Front*. State College: Pennsylvania State University Press, 2019.

Welch, Paul. "Homosexuality in America." *Life*, June 26, 1964.

Wiegman, Robyn. *Object Lessons*. Durham, NC: Duke University Press, 2012.

Wiegman, Robyn, and Elizabeth A. Wilson. "Introduction: Antinormativity's Queer Conventions." *differences* 26.1 (2015): 1–25.

Wilderson, Frank B., III. *Afropessimism*. New York: Liveright, 2020.

Williams, Jonathan, (writer), and Joe Brainard (artist). *gAy BC's*. Champaign, IL: Finial Press, 1976.

Willis, Sharon. "Hardware and Hardbodies, What Do Women Want?: A Reading of *Thelma and Louise*." In Jim Collins, Hilary Radner, and Ava Preacher Collins, eds., *Film Theory Goes to the Movies*. New York: Routledge, 1993, 120–128.

Wittman, Carl. "A Gay Manifesto." In Karla Jay and Allen Young, eds., *Out of the Closets: Voices of Gay Liberation*. New York: NYU Press, 1992 [1972], 330–341.

Wojnarowicz, David. *Close to the Knives: A Memoir of Disintegration*. New York: Vintage, 1991.

Wojnarowicz, David, (writer), James Romberger (artist), and Marguerite Van Cook (artist). *7 Miles a Second*. Seattle: Fantagraphics Books, 2012 [1996].

Wong, Sau-Ling Cynthia. "Necessity and Extravagance in Maxine Hong Kingston's *The Woman Warrior*: Art and the Ethnic Experience." *MELUS* 15.1 (Spring 1988): 3–26.

Worden, Daniel. "Joe Brainard's Grid, or the Matter of Comics." *Nonsite.org* 15 (January 16, 2015), http://nonsite.org.

Yamada, Mitsuye. "Asian Pacific American Women and Feminism." In Cherríe Moraga and Gloria Anzaldúa, eds., *This Bridge Called My Back: Writing by Radical Women of Color*. Albany: SUNY Press, 2015 [1981], 68–72.

Yanhua, Zhou. "Rethinking Seriality in Minimalist Art Practices." *Canadian Social Science* 11.7 (2015): 148–154.

Young, Allen. "Out of the Closets, into the Streets." In Karla Jay and Allen Young, eds., *Out of the Closets: Voices of Gay Liberation*. New York: NYU Press, 1992 [1972], 6–30.

Young, Damon. *Making Sex Public: And Other Cinematic Fantasies*. Durham, NC: Duke University Press, 2018.

Young Lords Party. "Young Lords Party: Position Paper on Women" [1970]. In Nancy MacLean, ed., *The American Women's Movement: A Brief History with Documents, 1945–2000*. Boston: Bedford/St. Martin's Press, 2009, 91–93.

Zerilli, Linda. *Feminism and the Abyss of Freedom*. Chicago: University of Chicago Press, 2005.

———. "Towards a Feminist Theory of Judgment." *Signs* 34.2 (2009): 295–317.

———. "Feminist Critiques of Liberalism." In Steven Wall, ed., *The Cambridge Companion to Liberalism*. Cambridge: Cambridge University Press, 2015, 355–380.

———. *A Democratic Theory of Judgment*. Chicago: University of Chicago Press, 2016.

INDEX

138–139, 145, 149; in *The Stepford Wives*, 73–75; in *Tales of the City*, 204, 211

Cohn, Dorrit, 395n49

Collective Lesbian International Terrors (CLIT Collective), 119, 146

"Collective Memory and the Trans Feminist 1970s" (Enke), 377n41

Combahee River Collective, 14, 87, 109, 110–112

comic strip, 246, 248–249, 253–256, 262, 278, 279, 289–292. See also *Canal Street Piers: Krazy Kat Comic on Wall* (Wojnarowicz); *gAy BC's*; *Gay Comix*; "If Nancy Was . . . ;" *7 Miles a Second*; *Untitled (One Day This Kid . . .)*; *Wimmen's Comix*

coming out: in *The Boys in the Band*, 183; Harvey Milk and, 15, 23, 198–199; political strategy of, 13, 15, 23, 31–33, 198–200, 206, 208–210, 275, 336, 340–341, 399n22; race and, 23, 238–239; serial experiences of, 51, 199–200, 210, 212–213, 220, 222, 248; in *Tales of the City*, 198–200, 206–208, 211–212, 214, 216, 219–223, 227, 231–232, 237–239, 243–245, 248

Compton's Cafeteria Riot, 20, 336

"Compulsory Heterosexuality and Lesbian Existence" (Rich), 347

consciousness: in *Born in Flames*, 135; feminist, 4, 14, 24, 36, 37, 95, 97; in *The Stepford Wives*, 71, 78, 79, 80, 84, 86, 87; in *Zardoz*, 119, 120–122, 123, 128, 129, 131, 132

consciousness-raising (CR): in *Born in Flames*, 107, 142; in *The Boys in the Band*, 32, 159–163, 168, 169, 170, 173, 179–181, 185, 188; circle, 7, 32, 36, 50–51, 160–161, 162, 163, 179–180, 191; disagreements and, 172–174, 191; feminist, 13, 24, 31, 36, 84, 99, 160–162, 170–172, 175, 191–193 315; in *The Woman Warrior*, 102

counterpublic, 147, 217–218

Cowan, Liza, 403n6

Cox, Aimee Meredith, 379n58

Crawford, Lucas, 44

Crimp, Douglas, 274–275, 289, 298, 300, 320, 401–402n16

critical judgment, 163, 171, 172, 174, 176, 177, 179, 180, 189, 195

cross-examination, 160, 170, 175–176

Crowley, Mart, 32, 160, 161, 164

Cruising Utopia (Muñoz), 15, 41

Cruse, Howard, 291

Cvetkovich, Ann, 315

D'Agostino, Anthony Michael, 365

davenport, doris, 386n18

defensive politics, 117, 156

Delany, Samuel, 275

DeLarverie, Stormé, 22

deluge, 285–287, 289; aesthetics, 286

D'Emilio, John, 192–193, 210

deviant, 165; sexual, 13, 250, 254, 255, 259, 289, 290, 299, 300

Dialectic of Sex, The (Firestone), 34, 375n27

Dick Cavett Show, The (TV show), 208

digestive dysfunction: as constipation, 307–309; as diarrhea, 293–294, 296, 297, 302, 307, 311–312, 313, 315; as vomit, 294, 296, 297, 301–302, 312

digestive politics and poetics of AIDS, 294–295, 296, 297, 298–303, 307, 310, 330–331, 333–334

digestive tract, 8, 308–309, 320, 333

Dinnerstein, Dorothy, 1

disgust: AIDS and, 8, 52, 294–295, 296, 299, 303, 305, 311, 312, 332, 334; racial, 327. See also "upward contempt"

divergence, 36, 44, 122, 127, 157

Dlugos, Tim, 256–257

domesticity, 66, 74, 75

"Don't Ask, Don't Tell," 20, 193

Doyle, Jennifer, 38

Dyer, Richard, 393n13

Dykes to Watch Out For (Bechdel), 355

visceral: language of AIDS, 295–297, 301, 303–306, 310, 320, 328, 330; representation of AIDS, 295–297, 307, 315, 320, 325, 331, 334;
"Visual Pleasure and Narrative Cinema" (Mulvey), 124

Warhol, Robyn, 204, 392n10
Warner, Michael, 204, 217
Watney, Simon, 298
Weissman, David, 392n8
West Coast Lesbian Feminist Conference, 377n41
White, Edmund, 253
white feminism, 18, 19, 62, 102, 109, 150, 152; lesbian, 136, 139, 158; liberal, 67, 68, 75, 77, 79, 101, 382n40; radical, 20
white supremacy, 13, 110, 133, 153, 309
Why Stories Matter (Hemmings), 375n27
Wicker, Randy, 403n6
Wiegman, Robyn, 18, 39, 151, 157, 389n77
Will & Grace (TV show), 355
Williams, Jonathan, 249
Wilson, Elizabeth A., 39
Wimmen's Comix, 253
Wittman, Carl, 34, 231, 232
Wizard of Oz, The (Baum), 128
Wojnarowicz, David, 51, 255–256, 275–276, 289–291, 296, 334, 363; AIDS activism and, 246–247, 249, 253, 255, 273–277, 281, 283, 301–303. See also *Canal Street Piers: Krazy Kat Comic on Wall; Close to the Knives; 7 Miles a Second;* "Stop the Church" campaign; *Untitled (One Day This Kid . . .)*
woman, category of, 74, 144, 151
Woman Warrior: A Memoir of a Girlhood among Ghosts, The (Kingston), 50, 60, 64–65, 89–102; dragon in, 96–97, 101; equality in, 31, 93, 95, 100, 101; female replicant in 90, 91, 99, 101–102; Fa Mu Lan in, 90, 92, 93–94, 96–97; shapeshifting in 60,

90, 97, 101; translation and, 89, 92, 97; women-of-color feminism and, 95, 96, 99–102
women-of-color (WOC) feminism, 33, 62–64, 76, 84, 95, 99, 155, 376n30; lesbian separatism and, 50, 108, 109, 111–112, 134, 136–137, 144, 147, 151, 155
women's and gay liberation: contemporary perceptions of, 34, 39, 346, 349, 358; history of, 7, 12–14, 18–25; as forms of imagination, 15–18, 24, 27, 31, 341, 352–353, 365–366; as social justice movement, 7, 11–14, 24–27, 31, 35, 36–37, 48–49, 52, 336–337; theories on, 14–15, 18–24, 39–40
Women's Health Movement, 315
women's studies, 151–152
"wounded attachments," 151, 157, 351, 386n20

Yamada, Mitsuye, 95, 97
Young, Allen, 14, 161, 164, 193, 209
Young, Damon, 108, 396n3
Young Lords Party, 62–63

Zami: A New Spelling of My Name (Lorde), 57–58, 260
Zardoz (Boorman film), 50, 106, 107, 108, 115; consciousness in 119, 120–122, 123, 128, 129, 131,132; gaze in, 116, 124–127, 131; lesbian feminism in, 113–114, 117, 119, 128, 129, 131–134, 139, 147, 158; lesbian separatism in, 7, 50, 106–107, 113–114, 117–118, 120–124, 125, 128, 131–134, 140, 158; revenge in, 128–129, 155, 157; tabernacle in, 120, 127–128, 130, 140, 155; vortex in, 113–114, 116–118, 120–125, 127–133, 340
Zerilli, Linda: on freedom, 352, 373n3; on imagination, 15, 16, 88; on judgement, 189, 384n74
Zero Patience (Greyson film), 296, 299
"zipless fuck," 260

ABOUT THE AUTHOR

RAMZI FAWAZ is Professor of English at the University of Wisconsin, Madison. He is the author of *The New Mutants: Superheroes and the Radical Imagination of American Comics* (NYU Press, 2016), which won the ASAP Book Prize. With Darieck Scott, he co-edited the *American Literature* special issue "Queer About Comics" (2018), named best special issue of the year by the Council of Editors of Learned Journals. He is also the co-editor of *Keywords for Comics Studies* (NYU Press, 2021), with Deborah E. Whaley and Shelley Streeby.